A BRIEF HISTORY OF STANLEY KAPPEL AND HIS FAMILY

Living and Thriving in Early 20th Century British Columbia's Shuswap Region

Photo of Shuswap Lake taken by Stanley Kappel, 1930s

By Murl E. Leibrecht

The book's cover is taken from this 1905 original oil painting by Janet Kappel, Stanley Kappel's mother.

ISBN: 979-8351947976 (Hard Cover Edition)
Imprint: Independently published

For additional information and/or permission, contact the author at mleibrecht@aol.com

CONTENTS

Stanley Ernest Kappel, Lieutenant, Canadian Army, 1943, Age 24

INTRODUCTION

This book was written by Murl Leibrecht (Stanley's son-in-law, husband of his eldest daughter, Karen), beginning in the latter half of 2020 as COVID-19 raged, and extending into late 2022, with significant help from many sources (especially from Karen, Kristen and Kerry, Stanley's three daughters, and their mother Alice, Stanley's loyal wife, along with many other members of the extended family of Stanley's parents, all of whom will be duly and gratefully credited as this story unfolds)

DEDICATION: To Karen, my beloved, loving and devoted wife who has provided me with so much inspiration over the course of my lifetime that I can never adequately thank her; to Kristen and Kerry, the other two Kappel sisters, who have given me encouragement and inspiration by their examples from the time I first met them; and to Alice, with whom I enjoyed a complex and challenging relationship for 42 years, who encouraged me to succeed more than any other member of my parents' generation, and whom I grew to love and admire more deeply than I could ever have imagined as a result of undertaking this journey of discovery in seeking to uncover and interpret the details of Stanley Kappel's remarkable life.

FORWARD

This is the story of Stanley Ernest Kappel, born Donald Angus Buckingham on October 6, 1918, at Blind Bay, British Columbia, Canada. It is the story of a man with two names, two sets of parents, and two countries. It is the story of Stanley's parents, all of whom emigrated from the British Isles to western Canada in the early 20th century and who became homesteaders in a profoundly courageous effort to improve their lives. And it is a classic, "once-upon-a-time" love story that begins in Stanley's 22nd year and extends far beyond his untimely death only 11 years later at the age of 33. It is the story of a bright young man who became a highly successful mining engineer at a time when the world was undergoing fundamental transformation of such enormous proportions and at such a rapid pace that it must have been dizzying for anyone living in the early 20th century. Finally, this is the story of a life and a love struck down in its prime, leaving behind a legacy of loss and sadness, grief and yearning, hope and inspiration that provided Stanley's survivors and admirers with a special poignancy and richness that changed us all for the better.

But first, a word about the photo of Stanley that appears on the opposite page. It was taken when Stanley entered the Canadian Army, specifically, the Royal Canadian Engineers, in 1943, when he was 24 years old. Take a close look at the image, as I have done. Superficially it portrays a good looking, healthy appearing young white male in his standard issue military dress uniform. But if you look at his eyes, you might notice that they are smiling, they are relaxed, and they are comfortable. It is the same with his smile, which appears very relaxed and authentic, rather than uncomfortable and forced, as you might expect in a photograph of someone who has just become a participant in a massive military organization that is currently involved in the most dangerous war the world has ever experienced.

To me, the most revealing aspect of the photo is the hat. In a typical formal sitting for such an important occasion as the recording of the first image of a newly commissioned military officer, the subject will be uncomfortable, worried about how he looks, fussy about everything, knowing that this photograph may be used by his superiors in the future when they are trying to decide the course of his military career, whether to retain or possibly promote him. Even if the officer isn't fussy, the photographer should be, knowing what is at stake with such an image. But the hat reveals so much about the personality of this young officer.

Please notice, dear reader: this hat appears almost jaunty. It is slightly tilted to the right, and the cap's bill also points a bit to the right side, instead of being perfectly placed, perfectly in line with the face and the rest of the body. Getting the hat in perfect alignment is something that is quite easy to accomplish, so the fact that it isn't suggests that Stanley wasn't concerned about protocol, and was very comfortable in his own skin, and that he wasn't taking either himself or this event too seriously, despite the gravity of the times. This doesn't imply that he was not a good officer, and that he didn't treat the time he spent serving his country in military service with great respect and gravitas, because he did, as we shall see.

After all, here is a young man who grew up in a small village in a semi-wilderness setting, in a highly refined and competent household, someone who has just spent more than two years in the wilds of South America as a fully trained mining engineer, successfully opening up a brand new gold mine with the barest of essentials, far from the main camp, and with only a handful of local miners to accomplish this dangerous, almost herculean task. Here is a young man who has also recently scored a beautiful young wife while immersed in the process of proving himself as a highly capable hard rock miner. It is surprising that Stanley has become so accomplished and self-reliant by the age of 24. And it is equally surprising to this writer, who spent my entire professional career associated with the military, that Stanley appears almost cavalier in this photograph. Would you be feeling so relaxed if you were facing at that moment possible deployment to Europe or the Pacific at a time when the world was in grave peril, with the outcome of World War II at its mid-point still a complete unknown, and with your own future survival at risk? To me, this photograph says so much about our main character, and it recalls the adage: "A picture is worth a thousand words." It is a great image with which to begin our story.

Regrettably, I never met Stanley, yet I have undertaken to write his story late in my life, 70 years after Stanley's unfortunate and untimely death, when the only people remaining with direct memory of Stanley are his 3 daughters, Karen Leibrecht, Kristen Kappel, and Kerry Dearborn. But all three were so young when they lost their father, and so little remains by way of written descriptions of him, that much of this story must be left to the selectivity of the memory, subject to the haziness of time. Whatever comes from this literary enterprise, it is my intent to honor Stanley with as much love, sensitivity, respect, tenderness, and objectivity as possible.

As my research into Stanley's history has unfolded, important characters have emerged that played significant roles in the evolution of this wonderful man. Out of respect and admiration, I eventually felt compelled to develop their individual stories to a greater degree than I had initially planned. This has come about for several reasons. First, their own stories are remarkable tales of courage, determination, resilience, community spirit, personal competence, and kindness, not to mention fascinating character studies in every case. Each of their stories also reveals important details about a pivotal period in Canada's development as a great nation, and it seems to me they each deserve their own separate coverage.

Teachers of creative writing tend to recommend that an aspiring writer "write about what you know about." Aside from Alice, my mother-in-law, who plays a central role in this story, I never met any of the characters I am about to introduce. Yet despite my knowing only one of the subjects of my research, and even though they have all vanished from view, many hints and details are available that point to their respective characters and personalities, and which should enable an imaginative observer to reveal them to the world. Let's hope I am up to the task.

This effort initially stemmed from my desire to record as much of Stanley Kappel's history as I could get my hands on, to reveal and preserve what is known about him for the benefit of his daughters and future generations connected to him. I knew we didn't have an abundance of direct information available regarding Stanley, so I imagined that the story would be relatively short. Then, as each story about the fascinating people directly connected to Stanley slowly emerged, thanks to photographs, documents and stories provided by a host of helpful family members, it became clear that this document would be lengthier and more robust in its scope and depth than I had anticipated.

I am not a professional writer, and I make no pretense about my limited literary talents. But I love research, and I have also in the past few years developed an avid interest in family genealogy. This book should be interpreted, first and foremost, as a reference document that combines both historical and genealogical research. I want to make it clear that I am not trying to write a historical novel about Stanley or his family. In addition to wanting to "flesh out" as many details about Stanley as possible, I hope to make this a source document that may prove useful to others who are more literarily talented than I am. In my writing I have tried to avoid taking unnecessary literary license, although I have been required to do a fair amount of speculating about the nature of the subjects of my research, along with what life must have been like in Canada and elsewhere in the late 19th and early 20th centuries when these stories were unfolding.

As the process evolved and I realized that many specific details about Stanley's unique history were simply unavailable, I began to extend my research beyond hard-copy source documents directly available to me into the realm of the digital universe, and I was delighted at how much is out there, simply waiting to be harvested. For example, while searching the internet I chanced upon a catalog from the Montana School of Mines that was published (and subsequently archived) while Stanley was a student of mining engineering there. It covers the 1936-37 academic year, and as far as I can tell, it is the only such digital document that exists for the School of Mines from the entire first half of the 20th century. It proved to be a rich source of information and insight that explained much about what Stanley experienced as a student hoping to become a mining engineer, but it also provided valuable insight into what constitutes a mining engineer, and even why Stanley might have decided to become one.

ACKNOWLEDGEMENTS

Many of the documents included in this book were provided by family members or were found on the worldwide web. All of them helped me to paint a fairly vivid picture of what life might have been like for Stanley, growing up in a veritable wilderness on the edge of modern civilization at a time when very few written records were being kept by the people going through this process of taming the land and making a life for themselves and their families. Fortunately, records were being kept by a few intrepid journalists, even in far-off corners of the world. And thankfully, in the early 1900s, several local newspapers were being published in the Shuswap area that were subsequently scanned or digitized and found their way into a researchable online venue. These provided me with many newspaper clippings that yielded valuable details about life in the early days of the settlement of the Shuswap region, in addition to revealing important information about the context in which young Stanley came of age. Even Vancouver newspapers attempted to include news from the outlying areas of British Columbia at the time.

Such resources helped me to better understand and explain Stanley, and to imagine his own experiences, his hopes, his dreams, and ambitions. It is sad to me that neither Stanley, his parents, nor his siblings kept diaries. Personal diaries, which often portray the humdrum details of day-to-day life, can be mined to reveal profound truths about the character of an individual and the nature of the environment in which they live. Regrettably, I haven't been able to locate even one such document for any of my characters, aside from Karen's baby book, which Stanley maintained carefully during her early childhood. Who would have guessed that such a document would reveal so much about Stanley's character?

On the other hand, several descendants of Ernie Buckingham and Jeanie Brown, Frank Kappel and Janet Thomson, have taken the time to chronicle details of their conversations with our main characters and to record them for posterity. I am particularly indebted to Jack Brown (aka John Wm Brown), along with Laura Buckingham Goldney and her daughter, Patricia Goldney Millar. Jack sent the American Kappel sisters a series of emails in 2011 that provided me with the inspiration from which grew the idea to write a biography of Stanley Kappel. Jack's contributions included a treasure trove of family documents, in particular, two biographies: one written by Laura for her grandfather, Thomas Brown, and the other written by Patricia for her grandfather, Ernest Buckingham. Both of their stories provide such a watershed of insight into the lives and the characters of their forefathers that I cannot adequately express my admiration and gratitude for their important efforts to catch these stories from the actual characters, in person, before the doors closed and it was too late.

More recently, Donald Dunbar, the son of Stanley Kappel's youngest sister, Marie Buckingham Dunbar, discovered a veritable goldmine in the form of a photo album, as well as several letters and notes that Stanley had written to Marie over a period of years stretching from his early years as a mining engineer until just before his untimely death at age 33. This collection reveals a sample of Stanley's inner thoughts and feelings, and I am forever indebted to Don Dunbar for discovering and sharing these precious documents.

As another late development, Kerry Dearborn, Stanley's youngest daughter who is a highly accomplished professor and community leader, provided me with a box of black and white photographs and negatives that had been hiding in our mother's basement while she lived more than 50 years in the Spokane Valley. Most of the photos and all the negatives had been carefully sorted and filed, presumably by Stanley Kappel, before he passed away in 1952. As I proceeded to scan the photos and negatives, then convert the negatives into positive images with the help of Photoshop, unexpected insights began to emerge into Stanley's early life, from the time that he was adopted at age two, until he left his home in the Shuswap region for the last time at age 21. A picture is truly worth a thousand words, and each image provided a little more insight into the nature of young Stanley, the environment in which he lived as he grew into a young man, and the people with whom he shared his discoveries, his hopes, and his dreams. It is impossible to emphasize what a watershed of discovery those photographic images have given me as I have become more and more submerged in Stanley's life and adventures. In their own way, those images were Stanley's actual diary.

The next unexpected gift came as a 90-minute cassette tape that was recorded by Ernie Buckingham in 1977, very close to the time of his death, recently discovered and shared by his grandsons Geoffrey and Donald Dunbar. *Way With Words* provided a transcription of Ernie's incredible tales so that I could include them in this story.

Shortly after that Jack Brown came back into the picture, providing so much important detail by way of stories, documents, and photographs, that some days I am unable to keep up with the "flood". Jack also recently shared with me a gritty account of life for the early homesteaders of western Canada, written long ago by his father. These stories continue to materialize "out of thin air", and they are invariably mesmerizing. All I can say to Jack and to anyone who reads this biography: thank you, and please keep them coming. This is a work in progress!

Jeanie Dubberley, the daughter of Marie Buckingham Dunbar, and the editor of this book, has also engaged substantially by providing me with family documents and valuable insights into the human dimensions of her grandparents' heartbreaking yet inspiring story. I simply cannot thank her enough for her wisdom, insight, and friendship. She has been very generous with her time and experience in reading and editing this story.

Jean Bosko (Ernie's granddaughter-in-law), Shelley Mujagic (Ernie's granddaughter), and other family members have also made important contributions, sometimes without their specific knowledge, and I hope they won't mind my using them as references.

My beloved wife, Karen, a gifted artist and student of the world who has always been my champion, and my favorite brother, Bruce Leibrecht, a brilliant research scientist, avid genealogist, and a personal mentor throughout my life, have also acted as my "readers" and have given me extremely valuable advice along with enthusiastic encouragement, in bringing this book to fruition. To them I owe so much, and to them I am deeply grateful.

My brother-in-law, Tim Dearborn, a man of inestimable goodness and good will who has published many fine books, offered me valuable insight and guidance that resulted in my choice of a publisher and made the publication process a reality for me. My other brother-in-law, Matt Parry, a successful chemical engineer and mining industry consultant, as well as a consummate jazz guitarist, provided priceless insight into the nature of the mining industry that helped me understand what it means to be a mining engineer. Both men have afforded me deep inspiration over the years.

Karen's cousin, Susanne Setvik, provided inspiration that encouraged me to undertake this biography when she produced a beautiful Leland family heritage book more than 10 years ago. She has also helped me with family trees and timelines, and has helped to identify individuals in Stanley's collection of negatives and photographs from the 1940s and 50s.

My good friends Dr. Richard Stoller (a consummate Southwest artist) and his wife Carol (an avid reader and bookstore manager) encouraged me to write many years ago, and although I ignored them for several decades, their encouragement has stayed with me through the years, and to them I am eternally grateful.

The surviving descendants of this stalwart group of immigrants from the United Kingdom to Canada have added so much depth and breadth to this account of Stanley Kappel's life. Without their contributions I would have been left with a much more limited perspective on what it was like to grow up in the Shuswap in the early 20th century. Instead we have a more vivid impression of the saga of the B.C. interior as it evolved from untamed wilderness to become a lovely example of the best that "civilization" has to offer.

If it weren't for the remarkable Ph.D. thesis written by Andrea Carrión in 2016: *The spatial restructuring of resource regulation. The gold mining enclave of Zaruma and Portovelo, Ecuador, 1860-1980,* my opportunity to gain a basic understanding of the history of the gold mining operations in Ecuador where Stanley and Alice met would have been woefully restricted. When I was struggling to catch the spirit of Stanley's first major foray into the world of hard-rock mining, Andrea Carrión threw me a lifeline. I owe her a deep debt of gratitude for her wonderful research into this topic and for revealing an amazing degree of insight that will enable everyone who reads my book to better appreciate the world of international mining as well as the deep currents that were at play when our two protagonists met and fell in love in this remote corner of the world.

Finally, I wish to thank the following individuals and institutions for their robust contributions to my research that includes documents, newspaper articles and clippings, posters, book covers, stories, family trees, and photographs: *Way With Words; Ancestry.com; Vintage Everyday; Barnardo's Orphanage; Ups and Downs Magazine; Library and Archives of Canada; Essex Record Office Archives; Wikipedia; The Canadian Encyclopedia; Natural Resources of Canada; Saskatchewan Highways and Infrastructure; Wikimedia Commons; Saskatchewan Government Insurance Map of Saskatchewan issued in cooperation with the Department of Transportation and Highways Canada;Ontheworldmap.com; prairie-towns.com; Saskatchewan Archives Board; National Archives of Canada; Flickr; Revelstoke Museum and Archives; Salmon Arm Observer; Kamloops Sentinel; us-canad.com; @angiesliverpool; Canadian Museum of History; Jim Cooperman and shuswappassion.ca; British Home Children Advocacy and Research Association FB group; Neath Port Talbot County Borough Council; The British Museum; bygonely.com; Salmon Arm Museum; BC Archives and the Kamloops Art Gallery; North Shuswap First Responders; Sicamous and District Museum and Historical Society; British Columbia Magazine; Enderby and District Museum and Archives Historical Photograph Collection; Daily Colonist; Dumfries Museum, Robert Burns Project; Scotland's Brick and Tile Manufacturing Industry website; "The Collector", a Canadian website devoted to arts and ideas; Wikimedia Commons; Joseph Thomson Group; Toronto Public Library Archives; mymodernmet.com; Settling the Canadian-American West, 1890-1915, by John William Bennett and Seena B. Kohl, University of Nebraska Press, 1995; Royal British Columbia Museum Archives; Salmon Arm Museum at R.J. Haney Heritage Village; Legion Magazine – Canada's Military History; Canada's History website: "Ties That Bind: the History of Canada's Railway System", written by Nelle Oosterom, November 6, 2014; Northern BC Archives & Special Collections; Sicamous Museum.ca; historian Gordon Mackie, writing in the Revelstoke Review in 2019; Fernie Museum; Internet Archive; Shuswap's Montebello Museum Curator Deborah Chapman; Eagle Valley News; Britannica; Wells Historical Society Museum; The Montana School of Mines Archives (now the Montana Technical University): The Thirty-Seventh Annual Catalogue of the Montana School of Mines, 1936-37; The Montana Standard; Stan Sudol at republicofmining.com; Elizabeth Tweedy Sykes Archive; Andrea Carrión: The spatial restructuring of resource regulation. The gold mining enclave of Zaruma and Portovelo, Ecuador, 1860-1980 (a thesis submitted to the Faculty of Graduate and Postdoctoral Affairs in partial fulfillment of the requirements for the degree of Doctor of Philosophy in Geography with Specialization in Political Economy, Carleton University, Ottawa, Ontario, 2016); Nelson Star; backroadmapbooks.com; the Canadian Broadcasting Corporation; the Canadian Pacific Railway; researchgate.net; The Library of Congress; Karen's Baby Book.*

APOLOGY AND CLARIFICATION

All human thought, and therefore all human history, is highly subjective and obviously dependent on the background, circumstances, and abilities of each participant. Although there is an objective component to all reality and all experience, each of us modifies the objective details to help us to make sense of the world in which we live. It is not my intent to report objective reality in this biographical sketch, but rather to report the details, words, opinions, and images that I have been able to obtain through extensive investigation and simple good luck.

I previously stated that I had decided to develop this biography as a source document, rather than as a literary enterprise replete with imaginary characters, dialogues, fantasies, and achievements. As a result, this story will be filled with lengthy passages that have been written by others who were either more proximate to the central characters, or who have researched and written about the period when these characters were alive in a way that is useful for understanding and explaining the natural, social, and cultural context in which they evolved. I have in most cases identified passages that are direct quotes by placing them within quotation marks and indenting them, so that it is clear when someone other than myself has written the material. In other cases where I have edited or paraphrased from other documents, I have attempted to remain as faithful to the original document as possible.

When someone such as I, a rank amateur in both genealogical research as well as non-fiction historical writing, and when two entirely separate national identities and cultures are involved in the telling of the story, mistakes will inevitably be made, toes will be stepped on, and sensitivities may become inflamed. As an American in my mid-70s, my feelings, attitudes, opinions, and prejudices are pretty well baked into the cake. There have been many surprises as I delved more and more deeply into the nature of Canadian culture, about which I knew surprisingly little, much to my chagrin. For example, I was naïve about the fact that Canada, as a member of the British Commonwealth, is not simply an extension of the former British Empire, but its own government is a constitutional monarchy and a parliamentary democracy, like England's (the two nations are equals, sharing a common monarch); that the King of England is also the King of Canada and Canada's Head of State; the Governor General of Canada is the official representative of the King in Canada; and that many Canadians seem content to bow to their King, even though no law requires them to do so. I was equally unaware that "The Crown" (meaning the "Canadian Crown") owns either all or at least most of Canada's public lands, although the comprehensive meaning of ownership seems to be difficult to define in this case.

I wish to apologize up front to every reader for my clumsiness and naïveté, and for any careless comment that may come across as disrespectful or insensitive. It goes without saying that I do not wish to offend anyone generous enough to spend their precious time reading and digesting my amateur literary efforts, such as they are!

Everyone has their own story to tell or be told. And everyone hopes that the details of their lives will not be lost to the ages. Somehow, when you get it down in writing, it seems to assume a greater sense of permanence. Yet we know that the memory of any one individual will disappear into the mists of time within a hundred years following their death…at least, any normal individual who does not ascend to the heights of such historical importance that may result in many wags and scalawags trying to exploit their stories, one way or the other. It is my heartfelt wish to tell Stanley Kappel's story in as vivid and faithful a manner as I can, hoping that it will enlighten and inspire others to appreciate this man, who sadly died so young, the husband of a uniquely talented and profoundly devoted woman, the father of three wonderful daughters, the son of two remarkable sets of parents, and the brother of so many siblings with so many relatives it makes my head spin. If this story can give Stanley a few extra years of exposure before he disappears entirely from the collective memory, then I will consider this a bonus.

These are the stories of a few genuinely remarkable individuals, every single one of them impressively adventurous, highly intelligent, uniquely talented, and unquestionably competent. They all possessed authentic fortitude, along with a deep sense of independence and self-reliance. Most of them had left their home countries behind and emigrated to North America, specifically to the relative wilds of northwestern North America. Each sought a "better life" far away from the place of their birth, and each was willing to take great risks to fulfill their dreams. Sadly, each of them left so much behind when they made the plunge into an unknown future:

many of them never saw their parents or family or friends again after leaving their homeland. Such is the reality for nearly every person who has ever migrated a great distance from their home, often to another continent, in search of their destiny.

Finally, there is this: most of our heroes and heroines made a conscious decision to leave their homes for reasons that included the opportunity to become landowners instead of tenants, to join their families or to follow a paramour, to seek adventure, to improve their prospects. But most surprising to me was the gradual realization that nearly every one of them reacted at some level, conscious or subconscious, to an aggressive advertising campaign aimed directly at them by the British and Canadian governments, using every possible tool at their disposal to influence good people to join the crusade to settle and civilize their new nation with a citizenry of intelligent, upstanding, hard-working people who would be most likely to succeed in this grand and difficult undertaking.

I have been delighted by the ancillary discoveries that came from my extensive research on the Shuswap in its "early days", the migration of a small group of fascinating individuals who made their way to the region and established themselves in such a wondrous assortment of ways, and the back story that set the stage for the successes and failures of these characters. For example, the story of the Canadian Pacific Railroad and its influence on all of Canada is so colorful and so striking to the little boy in me who has always been fascinated with trains. When I discovered a few details of how vital the CPR was to Sicamous and all of the Shuswap, in fact, all of British Columbia, I was immediately seduced and felt I had to include a separate chapter on the subject.

If you will kindly indulge the little boy inside the body of an old man, trying to convey the joy and allure and amazement that I have felt in pursuing this adventure of discovery that has lasted more than two years by now, I would be most grateful. I am hoping there will be something for everyone who reads these words. If there is something that delights you, something which sparks a forgotten memory that tugs at your heart strings, something that informs you about your own personal family history, or something which adds to your appreciation of a beautiful nation's struggle to come into its own as an equal partner in the grand human drama that we call civilization, then I will feel content.

Above all else, I wish to express my heartfelt gratitude to the wonderful characters whose lives I have attempted to understand and reveal, especially Stanley Kappel, Alice Leland Kappel Peterson, Ernie Buckingham, Jeanie Brown Buckingham, Frank Kappel, Janet Thomson Kappel, and Betty Kappel Ingram. Each of them has become my friend and confidant over the past two years, and I have grown to love and cherish them in ways that have enriched my life immeasurably.

- Camano Island, Washington State, October 2022

KAREN, KRISTEN, AND KERRY KAPPEL'S FAMILY TREE

Below: these are two different family trees for Stanley Kappel, who had two sets of parents due to his adoption: the first is the actual blood line, revealing Stanley's birth parents, Ernest Buckingham and Jeanie Brown; the one below that depicts Stanley's "adoptive" family tree, with Frank Kappel and Janet Thomson in parental roles (Ancestry.com)

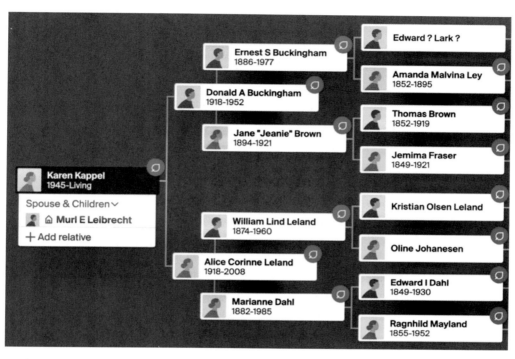

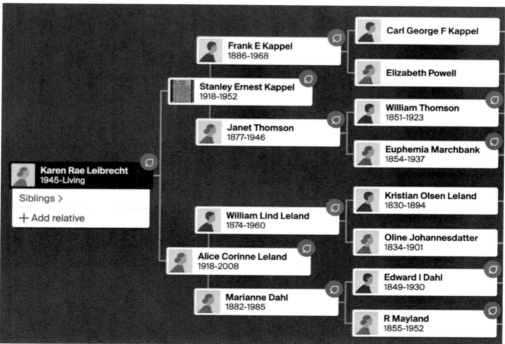

BOOK ONE:

TWO SETS OF PARENTS

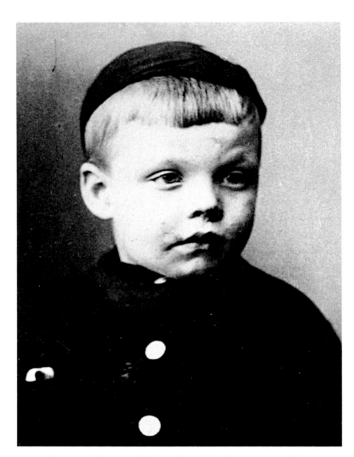

Above: Ernest Silas Buckingham, age 5

CHAPTER 1 – Ernie Buckingham, from Orphan to Emigrant

Excerpt from "The Darkling Thrush"
- by Thomas Hardy

"...At once a voice arose among
    The bleak twigs overhead
In a full-hearted evensong
    Of joy illimited;
An aged thrush, frail, gaunt, and small,
    In blast-beruffled plume,
Had chosen thus to fling his soul
    Upon the growing gloom."

"So little cause for carolings
    Of such ecstatic sound
Was written on terrestrial things
    Afar or nigh around,
That I could think there trembled through
    His happy good-night air
Some blessed Hope, whereof he knew
    And I was unaware."

- 31 December 1900 (at the dawn of a new century)

In the beginning, Donald (Stanley) was the fourth of five children born to Ernest Silas Buckingham and Jean Elizabeth Brown, aka Jeanie Brown. Both of Stanley's birth parents (and both of his adoptive parents) were immigrants to Canada from the British Isles. Ernest emigrated from England in 1898 and Jean left Scotland with her family around 1904.

Perhaps the most remarkable story of all is Ernie's, a Dickensian tale that deserves an entire chapter all its own. Fate was not kind to the family into which Ernie was born. His mother, Amanda Ley, born on 28 April 1852, was originally married to Joseph Buckingham (on 21 January 1872), a chimney sweep who died an untimely death in Plymouth, England, at age 34, nearly five years before Ernie was born on September 19, 1886, in Plymouth, Devon, England. There is no official documentation that Amanda ever remarried after Joseph's death, although she had three additional children, including Ernie.

Ernie spent his very early life at home in Plymouth with his mother and siblings. For all intents and purposes, he became an orphan in 1892 at the age of five, when his sick mother went into a workhouse and he was placed in foster care. His mother died when he was only eight. Ernie became one of thousands of "British Home Children" with no competent parents and no means of supporting themselves.

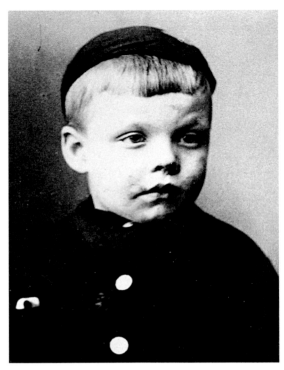

Left: Photo of young Ernie Buckingham, age five, taken at Barnardo's Orphanage, London, England, in 1892 (provided by Donald Dunbar)

Had it not been for Barnardo's Orphanage, a charity that took in homeless children and found for them a means of surviving, Ernie might have been left to his own devices, probably on the mean streets of Plymouth. Instead, Barnardo's found Ernie a foster home with the Willis family in Broxted, England, in Essex County, not far from London. This was an important step up from homelessness for thousands of British children in Ernie's circumstances. A large workhouse was located in Broxted at the time, so Ernie may have been initially sent there until a suitable foster family could be found for him. Available documents suggest it was more likely that he entered Barnardo's immediately after he was taken from his mother and was placed into foster care very quickly. If no foster family had been found to take him on, he would have been taken into a workhouse, along with his mother and siblings, and become a "commodity" available for day labor or seasonal labor such as farming to provide income that would help support the workhouse and his family.

Above left: Young street urchins in Victorian England, most of them either orphaned or neglected, left to their own devices in order to survive, unable to receive even the most basic necessities of life, since there was no social safety net for children in their circumstances; Above right: A young English family cast into poverty by circumstances in Victorian England, late 1800s, when Ernie was part of a one-parent family without a legal father. (Vintage Everyday)

Children such as Ernie had to fend for themselves with little or no assistance from society; children were often required to beg or steal to help with family needs, and single mothers were often forced into domestic service or prostitution; but the inevitable fate of such families was almost always the workhouse, which at least provided a place to live and regular meals, usually in exchange for work, service, and a modicum of "abstinence". As is often the case today, these impoverished folk were considered social liabilities.

The initial admissions document recording Ernie's entry into Barnardo's, recently obtained by one of Ernie's granddaughters, Shelley Mujagic, reveals how desperate the circumstances were for Amanda Ley and her children, and they also suggest a possible father for Ernie:

"The younger of these brothers is illegitimate. They are eight and five years old respectively, and come to us from our Receiving House at Plymouth, the following being the facts of their case:

"The father of the eldest boy, Joseph Buckingham, a chimneysweep, died from cancer on 19th November 1882. *[Ed. note – Barnardo's is off by one full year to the day: Joseph Buckingham's official death certificate lists Joseph's date of death as 19th November 1881, more than two years before Archibald was born on 14th April 1884, meaning that he could not have been Archibald's father]* For three years afterwards the mother worked at sack-making, at which she earned about 9s. per week. At the end of that time, she became engaged to a man named Edward Lark, by whom she was seduced, under promise of marriage, and after the banns had actually been published. Finding then that he did not intend marrying her, she forbade his coming to her house, when he attacked her fiercely, and kicked her with such severity that she was compelled to enter the Workhouse Infirmary shortly afterwards. It was then found that she was pregnant, the subsequent birth of Ernest being the result of her intimacy with Lark, whom she has not seen for five years.

"The mother is now dangerously ill from internal hemorrhoids, owing to which she has undergone four operations, and it is not thought likely that she can possibly live much longer. Her only income is 1 pound monthly allowed her by her eldest son, and such slight assistance as may be afforded by charitable neighbors and others. Apart from the fall above named, she appears to bear good character. She is not in receipt of parish relief.

"Archibald has been living with his maternal aunt Mrs. Packett for some time past, but she is described as a drunken, foul-mouthed woman, and appears to have frequently ill-treated the boy, who is somewhat dull in consequence. Ernest has been living with his mother, but she was unable to give him sufficient food, and informed our officer that if the boy was not admitted here, she would have to send him to the Workhouse, to obviate his being continually half-starved."

This admissions document from Barnardo's answers several important questions about Ernie's early childhood, and it also suggests the reason why Ernie later in his life stated that he remembered nothing of his life prior to age five, and that he never knew his parents. Amanda spent her final years in the Plymouth Workhouse with several of her children. Her life was so challenging, so bereft of the most basic necessities of life, it leaves this writer almost speechless to contemplate. It is also important to note that the health issue leaving her "dangerously ill", stated as "internal hemorrhoids", suggests that she was very likely suffering from chronic blood loss resulting from this condition, something that is easily treated today. But in 1891 we had very little understanding of severe iron deficiency anemia, nor how to treat it, since blood transfusions and iron infusions were unknown back then, and surgical methods were inadequate, at best.

Amanda's death certificate states the cause of her death (on 21 April 1895) was heart disease and anasarca (a build-up of fluid in the body due to congestive heart failure). Amanda was living at 19 Francis Street in Plymouth at the time of her death. This information, extracted from official documents, suggests that Amanda's health was much more serious than would have resulted from internal hemorrhoids and iron deficiency anemia.

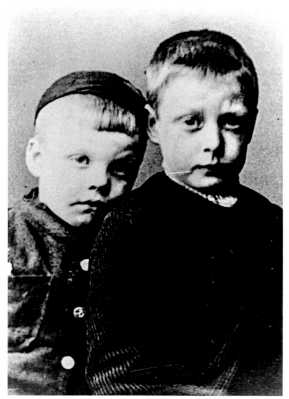

Left: Ernie and his brother, Archibald (aka Prosper), who was three years older than Ernie, when they entered Barnardo's Orphanage in February of 1892. The sadness on the faces of these young brothers is hard to miss. They had spent the first part of their lives with their mother, Amanda Ley, in dire poverty, both penniless and fatherless. Prosper's story has been difficult to uncover, but it seems that he was living with his maternal aunt during the 1891 census in Britain and was listed as her son. He was subsequently sent to Canada as a British Home Child (with the Buckingham surname) in 1899 and eventually arrived in Saskatchewan, where he was reported in the census in 1906. At some point he moved to the United States (North Dakota) and married an American woman, served in the US military in the First World War, and later moved to Oregon, where he died in 1942. It is unclear if Ernie and "Prosper" ever saw one another again after they sailed to Canada. (furnished by Donald Dunbar)

Children were often required to work in gardens belonging to the workhouse that provided

produce for general consumption by the "students" and staff members. However difficult his time in Broxted may have been, Ernie appears to have survived six years in foster care intact.

Left: Group of farm boys working in a field at the Philanthropic Society Farm School, 1989-1910, Redhill, Surrey, England (Library and Archives of Canada, C-086484)

Then, like so many other British Home Children, young Ernie, age

11, was transported to Canada on a ship (the S.S. Labrador, which departed from Liverpool on July 14, 1898, and landed in Montreal, Quebec Province, on July 30th) laden with British orphans who were a burden and therefore unwanted by their own country. Imagine the stress on a young boy, never having set foot off solid ground, enduring the long voyage filled with many other frightened children, many of them seasick, crying, terrified of what was to come, and not knowing why they had suddenly been torn from whatever living circumstances they may have become accustomed to, however difficult, and thrown literally into an abyss of chaos and uncertainty.

Right: Group of school-age boys in Essex, near Broxted, tending the garden they managed to provide food for themselves and their "school", late Victorian period (Essex Record Office Archives)

An informative article on the website "Who Do You Think You Are?" appeared in June 2021, and included the following passages describing the reality of being a British Home Child who was deported to Canada in the late 1800s and early 1900s; whether or not any of these descriptions apply to Ernie Buckingham, age 11, is unknown, but they are helpful in understanding what Ernie may have experienced:

"The children were taken by train to Liverpool where they left for Canada on mail ships. They were taken out by tender and boarded onto the ship, where each of them had a medical examination and were returned to shore if they did not pass. The children were unprepared for the sea voyage and seasickness worsened their first experiences.

Right: British Home Children, onboard the S.S. Numidian, bound for Canada, on their way to an unknown future (Library and Archives of Canada)

"A boy travelling in 1910 describes the accommodation aboard the *Mongolian*: "My cabin was in steerage… The cabin was over the works of the ship and the clank of the steering gear together with the whine of the propeller shaft, the smell of hot oil and steam, and no ventilation, drove me out. I spent my nights hidden in a corner on deck against a ventilator shaft for warmth.

"The abrupt change from their life in England, much of it in urban settings, to isolated farms in rural Canada was difficult for all the children. The climate was harsh, the work extremely hard and there was no one around to care much how they fared. Some experienced terrible cruelty, others simply neglect, and the lucky ones found a happy home. One of the worst consequences of child emigration was to take children from their families. Children were separated from friends they had known in the Homes and from their relatives, especially their brothers and sisters.

Left: Political map of Canada in 1898, when Ernie arrived; His ultimate destination was in the lower right corner of the North-West Territories. (Wikipedia)

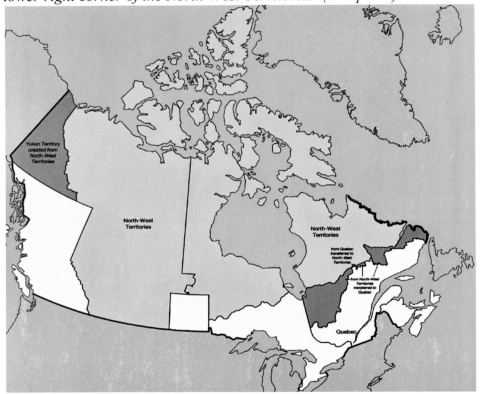

"From their point of disembarkation, the children journeyed by train – often for three days – before arriving tired, hungry, and bewildered at the receiving Home…then taken away to the farms and their new lives in Canada. The work was very hard. This description from a nine-year-old boy was not uncommon: I walked one mile to school daily and did the chores night and morning. I had to gather eggs, feed the chickens, carry in wood and water…(and) milked cows… I got plenty of horse whip from George who was a bit of a sadist." Another man, looking back to his time on a farm in the early 1900s said: "Those seven years were hell. I was beat up with pieces of harness, anything that came in handy… I herded cattle for five years – no horse, no dog – nothing to tell the time by. I had to have the cattle home by 5.30 in the afternoon. If I was late, I got beat up. My dinner was dry as old toast… I never had a coat when it was raining. Just a grain sack over my shoulders and no shoes."

Right: Group of immigrant boys on route to Stratford, Ontario, 1908 (Library and Archives of Canada/PA-020909)

Susan Brazeau, a retired Canadian college professor whose grandmother was a British Home Child, wrote about the plight of these children in her Master's Thesis submitted in 2012 to the Athabasca University Department of Integrated Studies:

"Some of these children were homeless and found on the streets. Most, however, were typically from broken or single parent homes or from families who were poverty stricken. The intention was to take the children, from what was believed to be unhealthy and socially and morally unacceptable living conditions in England, and place them in Canadian homes, farms, and families. Here, it was expected the children would learn skills and become productive members of the working class, training as helpers of some sort: house servants, child companions, and farm labourers were the most common.

"Controversy, doubts, and suspicions eventually grew around the benevolent societies and religious organizations that developed and carried out child migration schemes, and also extended to the children, many of whom came to be looked upon as having criminal tendencies or low intellect and moral standards or being without feelings. Further, recent research carried out with some Home Children, as they were called, points out the devastating effect such views had on the children. Perceptions of shame and unworthiness and believing they were not as good as other people persisted throughout their adult lives."

From the Canadian Encyclopedia:

"The children (most of whom were age 8 to 16 though there were many who came at 4 and 5 years of age) were almost always taken first to Ontario receiving homes in Belleville, Stratford, Niagara-on-the-Lake, and Toronto. Advertisements were usually placed in local papers announcing the arrival of another shipment of children and inviting farmers to visit the home for a prospective "home boy" or "home girl.

"The child was only rarely adopted but was indentured, the farmer in return providing lodging, a modest allowance (to be placed in a bank account ostensibly in trust until the child reached maturity) and schooling. Very often, few of these obligations were met. There were, as might be expected, a great many cases of abuse of all kinds, physical, emotional, and mental. Children were often returned to the home as being unsuitable - too small, too slow, too difficult.

"Some youngsters fared reasonably well. These were in most cases, very young children who, being too young to work, were taken into families simply as children, not as workers. But quite apart from the numerous youngsters who suffered great physical or emotional abuse - isolated on farms with virtually no supervision and where adult farm labourers were often undesirable wanderers - the very practice of child emigration must be viewed with deep scepticism. It uprooted children at the most crucial period of their lives, shipped them like commodities, placed them in a foreign environment and set them to work; they were robbed of childhood."

Left: Contemporary political map of Canada and its provinces, which was current as of December 6, 2001; Yukon Territory became known as Yukon on April 1, 2003. (Wikipedia)

Ernie apparently never spoke much about this period in his life, presumably because it was so painful for him, and he left no written record of his feelings or thoughts at the time. However, shortly before his death in 1977, Ernie made a 90-minute audio cassette tape of his early life that has been digitized and transcribed. The details that Ernie shares in this tape are important in establishing what he went through as a young orphan and British Home Child who had been exported to Canada from his home country. Passages from this tape will be incorporated into the rest of Ernie's story, identified periodically with "ET" (for Ernie's Tape). The script of the tape has also been changed to Arial 10.5 in order to set it apart from the main text.

ET: "Hello, everyone. This is "to whom it may concern", possibly a long, drawn-out story of my life. I've been requested to do this on cassette tape, and I hope I can make it. I do remember most of what happened to me after I was about five years old. Up to that time, I don't know what happened.

"All I do know is I was an orphan. And a couple of men came along there. I was playing around the house, and they said, do you live here? And I said, yes. My mummy is upstairs, and there was a lady there who looked after us. He says, okay, come on with us upstairs.

"So, eventually, all I do know is they took me away to a great, big house. From there, I was in there about two or three days, when I was what they call… I don't know what you call it, farmed out, as it were. I and another little boy about my age, too. I think he was older, a couple of years older.

"And we went to a party with the name of Willis, Mr. and Mrs. Willis. And they had just had a little baby boy when we were there, and that's where we stayed. I thought they was our parents, really, at that time. I know now, of course, they weren't. But nevertheless, I started to school there. Five years old. And they treated us awfully nice.

"I expect they got paid to keep us, I don't know, like they do in this country, you see. And we were back and forth at school. I was quite sharp at some lessons at school, and quite dull in others. But anyway, I passed through every class, as they called it there. And up until I was 14 years old *[Ed. Note - we know he was actually 11]*, we stayed with them same people.

"Then a lady came one day at school, and she talked to the principal a little while, and then he called me, and she says, I'm going to take you home. So, away home we goes, to Mrs. Willis's place, and, I don't know, I think some money changed hands there. This other boy, he stayed in school, and I didn't know what was going on. So, away we went on a train, for gosh sakes.

"On a train anyway. They took me on a train and landed me at this big house. Enormous place. Big playground and lots of kids and one thing and another. And I can remember quite well that the overhead railway ran right across our yard, right across the top of us. We could see it every day, dozens of trains. Not too much noise either up there. It was way up high.

"From what I can really remember, I was there about two weeks, and I wondered where this other little boy went to, what happened to him and all this stuff. After all, you know, we was together there at that place for ten years anyway, you see, but I never saw him after. *[Ed. note – the duration of Ernie's time with the Willis family could not have exceeded six years]*

"There were a bunch of boys, all got together, and my name was called, of course. B starts right off A, and then B, and I didn't know what we were doing there. We all had to go in and have a big bath and everything. New clothes, and we got a parcel with kind of a brown grip, with handles on it, like your air bags here now. And the first thing I knew, there was a man and a woman come and said, you're coming with us.

"Now, this was all frustrating for a little fellow, you know, I didn't know where the heck to get off and what they were going to do with me or anything. And the first thing I knew, we were on a train. We went to their house. That's it. We went to their house, and we stayed there a couple of days. I expect we had to get tickets and screened and all that stuff.

"Anyway, away we went on the boat. Oh, was I ever sick in that boat. I think we were ten or 11 days going across: rough sea, let me see now what time of the year it was. It would be in the summer, about June or July, I think, because I know that the little town of Oxbow, where we ended up finally in Saskatchewan, the town road there was very, very dusty. It was deep in clay dust, and I used to like to play in that."

Ed. note – Please see the next page to examine the composite document accompanying this caption; the document is part of the British Home Children Advocacy and Research Association's efforts to document every British Home Child who left the British Isles from the late 1860s until 1948; the next page provides their documentation of Ernie Buckingham's emigration from England to Canada in 1898 on the SS Labrador, arriving in Toronto; the document states that Ernie had been placed with the Gregson household. [Ed. note – the middle and lower thirds of the document are identical, except that an image of the SS Labrador is overlaid onto the Emigration/Placement section in the middle third; when the ship's image is removed, as it is in the lower third, the Placement section includes the heading "Placed With/Indentured To", a telling statement suggesting the true status of a British Home Child as interpreted by the people who paid for the child's passage, i.e., INDENTURED.

BHCARA
British Home Children Registry

British Home Child Information Sheet

Name & Birth

BHC Registry ID #: 59.
Claimed: No ⓘ

Surname: BUCKINGHAM
Given Names: Ernest S

Born: 1886
Gender: Male

Born at: England

ⓘ **Surname Adopted:**
ⓘ **A.K.A. Surnames:**
ⓘ **Given Names Adopted:**
ⓘ **A.K.A. Given Names:**

Emigration

Sending or Escorting Organization: Barnardo's
Canadian Distribution Home Name/Address: Toronto, Ontario
Age at Emigration: 11
Ship Sailed: Labrador 📷
Departure Date: 14 July 189
Arrival Date: 23 July 189
UK Boys/Girls Home Name/Address:
UK Workhouse/Union Name/Address:

Placements

Start Date	End Date	Surname	Placed V
		GREGSON	

Census

Year	Country	Prov/State	Address, City	Head of Household	tionsh to Head

Emigration

Sending or Escorting Organization: Barnardo's
Canadian Distribution Home Name/Address: Toronto, Ontario
Age at Emigration: 11
Ship Sailed: Labrador 📷
Departure Date: 14 July 1898
Port of Departure: Liverpool
Arrival Date: 23 July 1898
Port of Arrival: Quebec
UK Boys/Girls Home Name/Address:
UK Workhouse/Union Name/Address:

Placements

		Placed With / Indentured To		
Start Date	End Date	Surname	Given Name	Placement Location
		GREGSON		Oxbow, Northwest Territories, Canada

CHAPTER 2 – A New Beginning on the Canadian Prairies

After arriving in Canada, Ernie became a ward of the government and was sent to Winnipeg, Manitoba, then placed on a farm in Saskatchewan near Oxbow (again as a child laborer) under the care of "legal guardians", the Gregson family. Oxbow is a farming community that is situated in the southeast corner of the province, less than 20 miles from the US border with North Dakota. The closest big town is Estevan (see maps below). A 1901 Canadian census lists Ernie as a member of the Gregson household. Aside from the record of his arrival in Canada on the S.S. Labrador in 1898, this is the first official documentation of Ernie's presence in Canada.

Right: British Home Children: boy ploughing at Doctor Barnardo's Industrial Farm, circa 1900, Russell, Manitoba (Library and Archives of Canada, PA-117285)

Ernie's tape continues, ET: "I had to wait there until something happened, and the folks went home, and they left me in the hotel. I didn't mind it. I was in the hotel a couple of days, and then he come in with a team and a load of wood and delivered it. I got up on the seat beside him. He was quite an elderly man. Young men didn't wear whiskers those days, and he had quite a bushy, well-trimmed whisker-beard.

"You might wonder how he knew where he was going, you know, but he had a cousin with a farm, a big farm there, at Oxbow, and he had been out a year before that, with a big land rush that was there, around Oxbow. The CPR were selling the land they had got for putting the railroad through. They were selling their land at 50 cents an acre. Remember that, 50 cents an acre. Beautiful land it was, and he had come, Mr. Gregson, that was the name of the people that brought me over.

"He had already got a homestead, and you could get another one there, what they called a pre-emption. That was a half section, two quarters. And you could buy this CPR land, and there was one quarter right next to him, angle ways with him. As level as a table. 50 cents an acre. And that's what he came out to buy that time and straighten up with his cousin for looking after his farm. He had a beautiful place there. Oats, wheat, and all. You might wonder how they knew where they were coming, but that clears that up.

"Nevertheless, everything went pretty smooth. That was the time of July because the wild berries had started. Blackberries and saskatoons and all that. There was abundance of them all over the place because the Souris River run right through his place, from end to end, a mile. And there was brush… not brush, but timber, wood, elm, ash, maple, and stuff like that, on each side of the river. And the river, his land ran half a mile across there. So, the river divided him a quarter of a mile each side, you see.

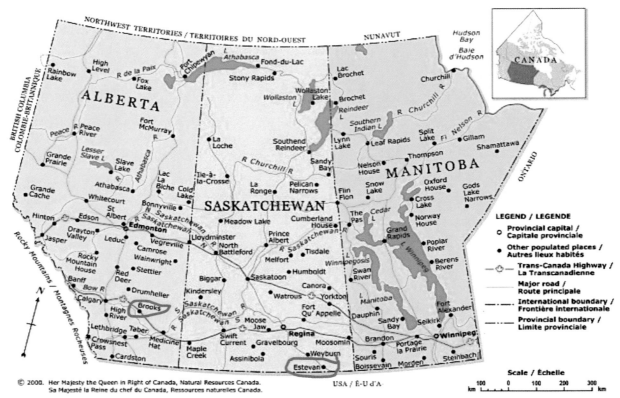

Above: Natural Resources Canada map includes Saskatchewan (formerly Assiniboine Province). Oxbow is near Estevan, below Regina and Weyburn (extreme southeastern corner of the province – see map below). Brooks is in Alberta, northwest of Medicine Hat, southeast of Edmonton. [Ed. note - The intended Bragg homestead, where Ernie also intended to find a homestead in 1909 – see p. 45 - was located somewhere between these two towns. Bassano was in the vicinity of Brooks.]

Left: Map of southeastern Saskatchewan, with Oxbow in the lower right corner circled in red (Saskatchewan Highways and Infrastructure)

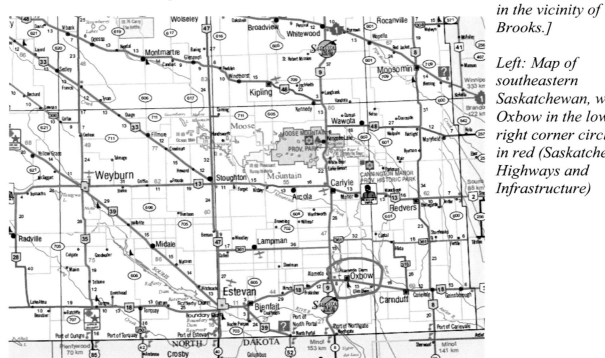

Right: Oxbow Park in 1910, with the Souris River on the left; The Gregson farm, as it was described by Ernie in his tape, was probably similar to this landscape, with trees and brush lining the slopes along the river. (prairie-towns.com)

Ernie's tape continues, ET: "And I started right in on the gardens and all because the cousin had kept his garden up. What we call a garden here and what they called a garden was two different things. They had two gardens. One was the house garden. They had strawberries there, gooseberries, redcurrants, blackcurrants, rhubarb, all in this little house garden, and a few rows of carrots and stuff like that, beets, to pull when they were young.

"Now, they also had a field garden. Carrots, turnips, mangels, beets and all that kind of stuff for cattle and also for the house. And that was my job pretty well, to keep that… to thin it out. Keep the weeds out of it. And oh my god, it looked to me to be about an acre of that field garden. It must have been because they used horses and everything in it. Every once in a while, they put the horse in it, with a cultivator, and really dug her up a bit in between the rows.

"That was my job anyway, all summer long. In the fall, I helped take them out. I remember quite well, them gol' darn Swede turnips they called them. Them lovely turnips you buy here, about 50 cents apiece here now. And they grew to enormous size there because they had their garden in the lowland, what they call the lowland, down below the house. And in a big flood, one flood was there while I was there, that all was underwater. The Souris River overflowed and come right over the banks and down onto that garden. So, everything grew prolific there.

"And the way we done it, I went ahead, and I had a hoe, a sharp hoe. The turnips, as you know, they grow, stand right up in the garden, right out of the ground, practically speaking. And I went along with a hoe, and I cut these tops right off at the turnip top. Right at the turnip. Walked up the row and cut each side off, and I had them all topped like that. Then I went along with a fork and gathered all the tops up and put them in a pile. Then the man would come along. We had a hired man, and the hired man would come along with two horses, and a long beam. The horses were on each end of it. We called it a sweep, and the hired man stood on that. He got me to help him, too. I stood on it, too, as much as I could. He had the lines to balance them and put that in the garden, started at the end of the row of the turnips and just started off, and that took every turnip out of the ground without injuring them. After we passed over them, they were laying on the ground, just all up and nice. Of course, we put them in what they call the big root cellars they had there, and they never froze. No. It was all well-built and all this stuff.

"They had quite a number of cattle, too, you know. Not little cows, but beef animals. He would sell one every once in a while. Gregson was known for his fat stock, well looked after and well fed. So, any time of the year, a butcher could come in there and buy a couple of animals ready for the market, which stayed with me all my life. I figured it was far more thrifty to feed those cattle well than having a whole bunch half fed, and that's the way that worked.

"Then he had a binder there. I remember there were three horses on this binder. Four-foot binder. I'd go around there to beat hell. No, I think the binder was five-foot. Three horses on it, not four. And then I stooked the grain. I learnt how to stook.

"No, my gosh, it wasn't a binder. It was a reaper. And it cut so long, and then it swept. He would touch something, and it would sweep it off the canvas like a sheaf and left it on the ground. And I'd come by, and I learned how to turn it, make that twisted straw for a binder, to the twine. I got pretty fast at that. I wasn't very old yet.

"And I done a lot of things that way. Helped the neighbours. He sent me over to the neighbours and all this stuff. I never was idle one minute, one waking moment. I was always working at something."

Not only is Ernie's personal description of his first impressions and experiences in Saskatchewan remarkable in their richness of detail, but they also reveal the Gregsons to be cruel and demanding of an 11-year-old boy. It appears that Ernie was expected to work like a man, and for extremely long hours every day of the week, with little or no time for rest. In addition, Ernie received no pay for his efforts, as we shall see later in his narrative, and he wasn't even provided with adequate clothing to accommodate to the severity of his environment, which ranged from extreme heat in the summer to extreme cold in the winter.

Below is a letter shared by Jeanie Dubberley, Ernie's admiring granddaughter and Karen's first cousin. It appeared in the April 1901 edition of "Ups and Downs Magazine", the quarterly magazine published by Dr. Barnardo's Homes in Toronto between 1895 and 1949. The letter was written by young Ernie Buckingham, three years after he arrived in Canada in 1898, when he was just 14 years old.

February 4th, 1901

"Dear Mr. Owen, -- In answer to your letter, I now take the pleasure in writing you a few lines. I am getting on first-rate, all but breaking a few articles. Dear sir, I came out here in 1898. I came across the ocean on the good old ship, *Labrador,* and we landed at Quebec, where we took the C.P.R. to Winnipeg, which was a three days' trip. When we got to our landing place, we were all glad to stand on solid ground again. We stayed in Winnipeg three days, and then I was sent to my destination, which was Mr. Gregson. When I was going home – for that is what I call it – I did a lot of talking and asking questions about those little Gophers, which are quite strange to me. When I arrived it was dinnertime, and I done justice to everything that was on the table. After dinner I went out to explore the farm. It was haying time, so I went out to help them draw in. It was so hot that I could hardly work. They – the man and Mr. Gregson – kept telling me about the mosquitos; but I could not make out where they were; but they told me to wait and see, so I waited patiently, for I wanted to see. They were very bad that night. Mr. Gregson began laughing, and all at once the mosquitoes began to bite so wicked it kept me slapping my face and hands; but after a while I quit slapping myself, but I was just covered with lumps. Then the harvest began and then the Winter. We had to cut a lot of wood, and we cut 300 cords of wood. I like the country fine, all but the Winter; but it is healthy, and that is the best part of it. We have two men this winter, and we are cutting a lot of wood. I must now bring my letter to a close with best wishes to Dr. Barnardo and all the girls and boys of the home. I think this is all this time. Yours truly, Ernest S. Buckingham"

It is possible that Ernie's letter was "dictated" to or even written by someone else. It is also possible that Barnardo's paraphrased Ernie's words to make them cast a more positive light on the institution's influence on their young orphans and foster children. It is even possible that the staff at Barnardo's wanted to "tastefully edit" these letters from children who had been transported to Canada to remove or at least soften negative comments that might have thrown a less than positive light on the efforts of Barnardo's, dependent as it was on the good will of so many, including private benefactors and the British and Canadian government sponsors. Regardless, Barnardo's was a powerful force for good in a very difficult world, and most of their orphans derived more benefits than liabilities from their association with the institution.

Ernie's letter is probably the real deal, at least as far as it goes: it is a charming letter written in all sincerity by a young teenager who was gaining some sense of himself in a world that had heretofore seemed unkind and unforgiving, and yet that world had thrown a lifeline, albeit threadbare, to someone who was, through no fault of his own, in the direst of circumstances. Despite whatever roadblocks the Gregson family may have presented to Ernie in his quest to become himself, it was a reasonable start, given our knowledge of how difficult life was for so many British Home Children who were deported from England and delivered to all corners of the Empire.

To me, there are several layers of meaning contained in this letter: most important is that Ernie was thoughtful, well-spoken, and literate beyond his years; that he had quite obviously been attending school more-or-less regularly while he was a foster child in England; since the letter was written in the winter, Ernie was probably still 14 at the time of the writing; that Ernie liked his new "home country"; that he probably liked the Gregson family, at least initially; that the Gregson family were able to provide the basic necessities of life, including shelter and nourishment, in addition to safety and security, giving Ernie sufficient reason to consider the Gregson farm his home; that Ernie was still living on the Gregson farm in 1901; that the Gregsons had a lot of trees available on their land to be converted into cord-wood, presumably on their own homestead; that this wood lot was able to provide enough income to the Gregson family to support two additional "men"; that Ernie was doing a man's work at age 14, of that there can be little doubt (he states "we have two men this winter, and we are cutting a lot of wood", but it isn't clear if one of the men is Ernie, or if Ernie is a third worker); in spite of his hard work, Ernie was proud of what he had learned and accomplished during his two and one half years with the Gregsons; that he possessed a sense of gratitude to Dr. Barnardo for "rescuing" him when he was very young; and that he also possessed compassion for the other children who found themselves at Dr. Barnardo's in circumstances at least as dire as his own.

This letter points to a very bright young Ernie, very bright, indeed. He was also curious about his environment, "doing a lot of talking and asking questions about 'those little Gophers, they are quite strange to me.'" This (and everything else about the letter) reveals an awareness of the world that I find remarkable in a 14-year-old child. No wonder Ernie's descendants were and are all highly intelligent and competent!

Be that as it may, the 1901 census document is puzzling. Ernie's granddaughter and principal biographer, Patricia Goldney Millar, stated that he worked on various farms throughout Saskatchewan, including a Mr. J. Wood at Oxbow in January 1900. This may simply reflect a comment in Ernie's tape that he was "sent over to help the neighbors" when his work was finished at the Gregsons. In addition, Geoffrey Dunbar, Ernie's grandson, who discussed the subject of Ernie's time in Saskatchewan with Ernie himself, wrote: "Ernie 'escaped' his first sponsor and was taken in by another farmer nearby." Ernie's letter to Barnardo's suggests that he was still with the Gregsons in February of 1901. It seems fair to assume that the Gregsons were less than forthright with the census taker, who suggested that Ernie was "unavailable" at the time of the interview, casting doubt on the reliability of this important document. The census also records that Ernie had been adopted by the Gregsons, and that he was married. Neither of these seems likely. If he had been adopted, why would Ernie have been listed in the census as Ernest Buckingham, and not Ernest Gregson? And why wouldn't his wife, if she really existed, have been listed in the census with Ernie? We know that Ernie was given the surname of Buckingham at the time of his birth, and it remained his surname until he died. This would suggest that he was never adopted by the Gregsons or any other family, since he would almost surely have taken his adopting family's surname. In addition, Ernie's tape also suggests that his presence in the Gregson household may have enabled them to qualify for an additional quarter-section of land that they wanted to add to their holdings.

Whatever the case, life in the middle of the Canadian Prairie Provinces in the earliest part of the 20th century wouldn't have been easy, not for Ernie, and not for anyone trying to eke out a living from the soil without any of the modern mechanical agricultural methods we take for granted today. This was extremely remote country, far removed from what might have passed as modern urban amenities in those days. Roads were primitive and pavement was non-existent. The main source of transport in Oxbow in 1900 was the horse-drawn wagon or buggy. Although the Canadian Pacific Railroad ran through Regina to the north, and the Soo Line ran from the United States through Estevan and Weyburn, there were apparently no railway spurs to Oxbow.

Left: Oxbow, Saskatchewan, in 1909 (prairie-towns.com)

The photo above depicts Oxbow as looking well settled by 1909, sporting churches, schools, and commercial buildings. We don't know how close to Oxbow Ernie lived during his time on the prairies, but he undoubtedly "went to town" on a regular basis. Oxbow was the principal center of culture for a large rural area that included farmers and their families as well as resident villagers. Ernie would almost certainly have interacted with both sets of folks on a regular, if infrequent, basis. This locale was the center of social life for Ernie Buckingham from 1898 for at least a few years. But Ernie's cultural opportunities seem to have excluded attending school.

According to the timetoast.com website, in an article about life on the Canadian prairie provinces at the turn of the last century: "At the end of the 19th century, and beginning of the 20th century, Europeans began to come to Saskatchewan. Even though they had been in the country (Canada) for quite a while, it was difficult to travel to the West Coast, for lack of a railway. The Europeans brought more of the 'traditional' grain (grain we grow today), such as wheat, growing only what was needed. Also, many of the European families created homesteads, allowing them to raise livestock (rather than following wild animals)."

Ernie's tape lends significant insight into the way he was treated by the Gregsons, his attitude toward them, and the repercussions for mistakes he made, as well as how he eventually seized control of his situation.

ET: "The other things were, forgetfulness mostly on my part, like if I forgot to fill the wood box in the morning, I'd go without sugar for a week in my porridge. That was the penalty there. Forget it a second time, which I did, I'd go without the porridge altogether for another week. That's two weeks. Oi! And there were other little things that I used to do, and that was always my penalty: go without this, go without that. It all irritated me to beat the band, because a kid will forget, sure. You had no chance. They never did beat me for anything I did, but they had other things that they used on me.

"Anyway, the third year I was there, I'm starting off now pretty well on my own, on this story. The third year I was there, in the fall of the year, November, the herd law was lifted for the winter. And of course, then he could let the cattle out to that big pasture where he had a half section that the cattle could roam in, with that Souris River running through it. That was my job. I ended up working all day, doing something, and then I'd have to go and get the cattle at night.

"Now they were free to run all over the hills there, the hills and dells, as they call them. Up and down and on. Sometimes they wouldn't let me go early enough, the sun would be going down in the fall like that, and sometimes I couldn't find them.

"But they'd always be awake. They'd be in bed when I'd get home, ten or 11 o'clock. I'd stay out like…I couldn't find them because they had this one old cow, he wasn't a milker, but she was the leader, and she had a bell on her. But after the cows were feeding all day long and dusk came, they'd all lay down, and that bell wouldn't move, you see. Unless it just happened to be just right when she was chewing the cud, then the bell would ding-dong, ding-dong, not very loud. Not as loud as it would be if it were up and feeding on the plain.

"I was always afraid if I couldn't get them they would make me get up in the morning early, five o'clock. Go and get them, bring them home. I didn't know what they wanted. Of course, they wanted them home. That was it, every night, that was the dribble.

"Well, I got fed up with that kind of thing. I looked and looked and looked, and I got home that night, I know it was 11 o'clock. Of course, I didn't start until nine. It got dark then at nine o'clock, at that time of year, November. And he called out from his bedroom: did you find the cows? I said no. Of course, they knew I didn't because they couldn't hear no bell. They were in bed. So he said: listen, you get up in the morning now, first thing. I'll ring that bell, and you get up and go and get them. Bring them home, put them in the corral, and count them.

"I didn't know what all this was about, but anyway, I said, okay. Now all I had to wear in them days was a pair of shorts, what they call knickers, a pair of low stockings, running shoes, and a little shirt. No coat yet.

"So, I went out in the morning. There was white frost all over everything, I can remember that. It was pretty cold, and I didn't know where my little jacket was. I didn't care anyway because I was fat as a pig. And away I went, up on the mountain. The sun was coming up. Of course, the cattle were up, too. They were about half a mile from the house. We were built down in the valley, and right behind the house you'd find a little what they call a hillside, with the prairie up there at the top, flat prairie for miles.

"Of course, I heard the bell right away. God, I was fuming inside. I said, I'm not going to put up with this kind of stuff. So, I started 'em all home, and they were all obedient, so they all went along, then they'd eat a bit, then go on home. Finally, I guess they landed at home. I don't know. I never went back. I just kept walking on what they call the Boscurvis [Ed. note – Boscurvis is Latin for oxbow] highway, from Oxbow to…what was the name of that place in the States? [Ed. Note - Probably Northgate]) It was 12 miles to the border, the United States border. I had never been, in my three years there, across the border. So, I headed that way.

"There used to be a lot of men coming there for loads of wood, cut wood. *[Ed. Note - To the Gregson farm]* They'd just take a cord of it and take it home for their fireplaces and whatnot, furnaces. I was walking along the highway and I was about a mile from the Boscurvis. There was a little lake there. I was hungry, getting hungry, you know, I was a kid. There was a house right alongside, and I saw a man there in the yard, and I went in the yard. By now, I was about 18, 17 anyway, 17 *[Ed. Note - 14, in all probability]*. And the guy, lo and behold, he was one of the men that used to come for wood once in a while.

"And he says, what the hell, he says, are you doing out here, he says, way out from your place, this early in the morning? And so I told him my story, and why and wherefores, all the little, funny, pernickety things they used to do to me. They never beat me up or anything. But they had other ways of making me remember things.

"Well, he says, you better come in and have some breakfast. He says, I'm batchin', and my wife is down in Ontario for the winter, and I'm going to have breakfast, tea, and stuff like that. You want to come in and have some breakfast and tell me all about it? So, I did that, and I was hungry. I ate, I guess, like a horse.

"And he says, what are you going to do? I said, I don't know. I may have to go back, I guess. I don't know. I don't want to go back. I've had enough. They're just using me like a hired man. Every moment I was awake, I had to be doing something. I couldn't just sit and relax like a boy should be able to.

"So, he says, well, how would you like to stay here a while? Oh, I said, I'd like that. I said, I can look after your stock, your horses and everything. I'm used to that. I know what to feed them and everything. He says, we'll see about that. And so, he says, you make up your mind. You're going to stay for a day or two, or a week. I got some grain to haul to town, and it'd be very nice to have somebody here to feed the stock in the daytime and look after the place anyway when I'm gone. We were about, let me see, five miles from where I left, from Oxbow. I walked about eight miles… No. I walked about six miles from there. I walked about six miles to his place. So, he says, you stick around. I'll feed you. I can't give you any money, though. I said, that's all right, I never have any money anyway.

"He must have told the people, phoned them, you see, because the main road didn't go by his place. The road went straight through from his place to Oxbow, the Boscurvis highway. That was easily five miles away. But he must have saw somebody in town to tell him that I was there, you see. Every time I saw one of them redcoats *[Ed. Note – A Royal Canadian Mounted Policeman]* riding his horse up the trail, up the road, I'd go and hide. A lot of good that did me, I know, but they never bothered me. Gregson never sent anybody after me or anything.

"And finally, the fellow came home one day, and he says, I saw Gregson. I told him you were here, and that you were happy here, and that you were feeding my stock and one thing and another, and if he wanted you home, I'd take you home. No, he says, if he's happy there and not happy here, just leave him there. Just let him stay there and look after him. I didn't need looking after. God I was a full-grown, knowledgeable man. *[Ed. note – At least Ernie thought of himself that way, even if he was still only 14 or 15]*, I could do all the work there was to do on the prairie. How much of a bushel to put in the ground and everything.

"Soon he drew half a dozen loads of wheat to the elevator. I guess he wanted the money, you see. Now, he says to me one morning, I'm going to Ontario, where my wife's folks is. And he says, I'll be there all winter. I'll be back here at about the middle of March. And do you think you'd like to stay here and look after my stock?

"There was a bunch of nice horses, work horses, and some cattle. There was one cow. Yes, one cow, milk cow. Do you think you can do that? Heck yes, I said, I'd like to do that. Anybody can do that. And the responsibility never entered my head at all, you know.

"Away he went, and that's where I put in the longest winter I ever put in. It blew, and it snowed, and it drifted. Fortunately, the barn wasn't too far from the house, and I had some neighbours came there. One of the neighbour men came, and he said, you want to be very careful now about going out on this here prairie. He says, in the winter, when you go from the barn to the house and back to the barn, you let it be so you can see the barn. Don't you go out if you can't see it, unless you have a big rope and tie it on the house, and then take the rope and walk to the barn and tie it there securely, and then you follow that rope back and forth during the storm. Okay, I said, I think I know now what you mean.

"So, I put in the winter anyway, and he came back, him and his wife, very happy. And I saved his mail for him and sent him any letters and stuff like that. I tied them in a bundle and sent them to his address down there.

"Well, when he came back, everything was so nice in the house. I kept the house clean and all. It was quite a big home, upstairs and all, but I just used the downstairs. He gave me about $50 and said he was sorry that he couldn't use me for the summer. And he said he could handle all he had there by himself. He was just a new man there, practically speaking. In fact, everything new up on that flat plateau. Yes, it was all new. New people there and everything. Further down in the Souris River Valley, where Gregsons was, that had been settled a few years. "

This is such a wealth of information to process. We now know how cruelly the Gregsons treated Ernie and how much they took him for granted. It is also unmistakable how Ernie really felt about his treatment and his deprivations, despite his obviously trying to warm to his "captors". Someone had paid Ernie's passage from England, probably the Gregsons, and they apparently considered it reasonable to expect a return on their investment. Judging from the way Ernie describes his treatment by them, they probably didn't consider him a full-fledged member of the family. They may have intended to formally adopt him, but there is no record that it ever happened. This may have been a simple matter of inconvenience: any administrative action invariably required time, money, and trouble, even in those days. It is hard to find fault with the Gregsons on that account, yet it is difficult to embrace the falsification of Ernie's status in their household in the 1901 census. Poor young Ernie was stuck in the middle and was eventually forced to flee this unfortunate and unforgiving environment.

The location where Ernie fled is obscure, but it was five or six miles south of Oxbow near the Boscurvis Highway. This brings us to try to imagine Ernie's difficulty with time and his age during this passage in his life. He says he remained with the Willis family in Broxted for eight years, but we know it was six; he says he was 14 when he reached Oxbow, but we know he was 11. We shall see as we thread our way through his taped autobiography, which is spellbinding, that he gives us little by way of actual dates in which we can find anchors in his personal timeline. Children are unlikely to remember dates, especially when they are no longer attending school and when they aren't involved in a world that requires them to know the day of the week, let alone the year, and when there are few if any references to time such as we now take for granted in our highly connected world. We are thus left to guess about these things as Ernie proceeds through the next few years, up until the time when he reaches British Columbia in early 1910. Be that as it may, I will try to make sense of Ernie's timeline as we proceed with our journey. *[Ed. note – I have actually compiled Ernie's personal timeline, which is included as an appendix at the end of this book.]*

Even though Ernie's sense of time makes it seem that he remained for less than a year at the first farm he came to after fleeing the Gregsons, that seems unlikely to me. Ernie gives the impression in his tape that he left the Gregsons in November of 1901. However mature and competent he may have been at age 15, it seems highly unlikely that the farmer who took him in would have been willing to leave his large farm, complete with horses and cows, in Ernie's care within a month or two of Ernie's arriving on the scene. I would guess that the farmer left the farm under Ernie's care during the following winter, which means that Ernie may have spent more than a year and a half on that farm, rather than little more than half a year, and would have turned 16 by then. And all of a sudden he becomes homeless, cast adrift in the wide world without anyone to look after him. And he remains a rolling stone for the next 8 ½ years.

ET continues: "So, I went back into Oxbow, in the town, and I knew a lot of people there. That is, in a way, I knew them. They knew me anyway. They knew where I came from, what I'd done. Ran away from Gregson's and all.

"I got to talking to the harness maker there. Amos, his name was. That's his last name, Amos. And he says, what are you going to do, kid, for the winter? He says things are pretty tough around here in the winter. He says, there's no cattle to feed. There's no nothing. Nobody wants to have anybody around to try to earn their keep. I said, I don't know. He says, how would you like to learn harness making? I said, I don't know. Of course, harness making was the whole thing them days. There was no cars or anything. I thought it might be all right, too.

"He says, I got a brother, a harness maker over in Arcola. I think he could use a young fellow like you. I'll drop him a phone call and see. If so, it was only 20 miles across. I'll drive you over because I'm going over there anyway. I want to see him on business.

"So, there he goes. The brothers talked a while. And he says, I've got a young fellow over here from Oxbow. He says he thinks he'd like to learn the harness making trade, and I know that you could maybe use him. You were talking about that once, having a young lad. Yes, he says, I can use him. So that's where I got on. I could sleep in his place. Eat, board, and room in his place, you see?

"Well, he was a funny little fellow, but he had a big trade there. Harness maker. Good name, all them big tugs and everything else that was connected with harness, the breeching and all, all handsewn. And I learnt the hard way how to sew all that leather, join them up and sew them. And my fingers, my little fingers, both little fingers were just about cut off yanking that thread because I yanked it hard, and it was necessary, you know. And I had to learn to make that thread. Thread the needle. But it was an enjoyable time.

"He wasn't making any money then. It was winter time, everyone had already brought in their harnesses to be sewn up and ready for spring, with all the breakages and one thing another, and we got that caught up. The extra hand like mine, I did all the little work, and the men that he had hired, they done the heavy work. So, we got all caught up pretty well. But there was enough work for the three of us.

"I used to put in my spare time around the hockey rink there, you know. The skating rink and the curling rink and all. It was one of the biggest in the territory there. It was the biggest west of Winnipeg. And I used to go over there and talk to the fellow that was looking after that rink. It was just one man. He had a big deal to do there for one man, but the town paid him miserable wages, you know. And he was a married man with one child. Lived just on the outskirts, 100 yards or so from the town, in a tar-roofed shanty. Two bedrooms in it, and a kitchen-sitting room. That was all. A couple of windows and a door.

"And I want to tell you this now. The outside door opened inside. Most of them opened to the outside, like a barn door. And there was a reason for that.

"But anyway, there come along quite a heavy snowstorm. It really snowed, and it snowed for three or four days and nights, and it banked up some snow there, not any wind, but big flakes of snow. Dry, frozen snow. It banked it up there about two feet. And no farmers came in, no nothing.

"So, little Tommy Amos, that was the brother that I was working for, he said, hey kid, I don't know, I can't afford to keep you any longer. He says, I hate like hell to turn you out in this kind of weather. He says, I don't know where you'd go. But I had already, as I said, made acquaintances with Mr. Cooney, who looked after the skating rink, and I went over there, after I slept that night at Tommy Amos's place.

"I went over to his place then, at the skating rink. He was working there to beat hell. And he had a lot to do because he was snowed in practically, you know, the approaches. People had to come there at night to skate, regardless.

"So, I was a pretty husky lad then. I was then 18 *[Ed. note - More likely 15]* years old. So, without any asking or anything, I got one of the big snow shovels, and I went at it, and I dug out the walkway into the skating rink. You didn't shovel any more than you had to, I mean, out any further than you had to. You shoveled the approach from the sleigh road outside into the skating rink. You shoveled outside of the windows, too, because we had to open them in order to throw the ice out when we cleared the rink.

"He says, why aren't you working? I said, god I got laid off. I got nothing there to do. There are no teams coming in, no harnesses coming in, so I don't know what I'll do now. He says, how would you like to come over and stay with me and help me with the skating rink? He says, I don't feel very good. He says, I feel tough as hell. And he says, your hands would be very handy here, but I can't pay you one nickel. They are not paying me enough, really.

"I said, I don't care. I'm not using any money anyway. My clothes was getting pretty well threadbare, though, just the same. My underwear was getting worn out. That's the main thing. I had short underwear on in that bitter cold weather, and I wanted long johns, you see. So, his wife, I don't know where she got 'em or anything about these things, Salvation Army. She got me two sets somewhere, free, and I felt pretty good then. Boy oh boy, I could brave most anything.

"But the wind came up. The snow quit. The sky cleared just as blue as your eyes, you know, and the wind started. And Cooney, he says to me, he says, do you know about the weather around here? And I said, I know that we're going to get a big windstorm. That means a three-day blizzard. Yes, he says, and more than that. He says, there was five stars inside the ring of the moon last night, and that's five days of storm, and he was right. There was more than five days. It blew, and it blew, and it blew. It just drifted all that soft 18 inches of snow like it was salt.

"Covered up the low houses, his included. And that's the reason they had their doors opening on the inside, never outside, because they had the screen doors, the storm doors and all. The storm doors opened on the inside also. Otherwise, you could be frozen in. You couldn't get out.

"So, it blew and it covered up everything. Covered up our big skating rink. We used to walk over through that snow and dig it out. It was less than a quarter of a mile…300 yards. For some reason or other, with the storms it never seemed to get very cold.

"But anyway, one morning I went over, and there was no skating rink. The thing had just drifted in so full and it drifted over the top. I don't know how many feet was on it when I saw it last in the daytime. And that night, nobody knows when, it collapsed. The whole roof fell in, and it was not long after the skating rink had been plum full of people. That's the only place that the town people had to go. There were no movies, nothing like that. So, the skating rink was the place to go.

"A nickel was the charge for grown-ups, and kids were free. Anybody under 14 was free. My job was to clean that whole skating rink before they came and after they left at 12 o'clock. Clean that up before it froze. Throw it out those windows. And you would get a tonne of snow on the ice from the skating, you see. I had a huge scraper you run by hand.

"Well, now then, what to do? Holy lightnin'! Mr. Cooney, what I was saying a while back, I just went over myself there a little bit. I told you he was feeling very tough. Well, he got the flu, and he couldn't move out of the house. So I took care of the whole thing. Now, after the roof fell, there was no wages for Cooney. No skaters. So, how was he going to keep me? He couldn't afford to feed me."

Once again young Ernie, age 16, was left homeless and on his own. But not for long. Fortunately he was resilient, adaptable, and opportunistic. And he was also willing to try anything if it would give him some sense of stability and safety. Ernie's story continues:

ET continues: "So, I had saved this money, and I was a better saver in them days than I am now. I'd saved this money that that fellow *[Ed. note – The farmer south of Oxbow on the Boscurvis highway, where Ernie first lived after leaving the Gregsons]* gave me, $50, because I knew I couldn't get any more until I got proper wages. And I used some of that money, and I went from Arcola…I went up to Kisbey. It was the next town, Kisbey.

"Now, what time of the year that was, I don't know, but it was somewheres about March. We always got mud in March. And I met a fellow there, a farmer. He'd just come in to town. The storm, well, away from buildings, it just drifted, went on to somebody else's place, you see, and it wasn't that bad. It was passable. People had to come to town to get groceries and stuff. There were three big stores in Kisbey, and five grain elevators. That's all there was. There was no real population in there at all.

"I met a fellow there, in the hotel. That was the place you went if you wanted to find out anything. Either that or the barber shop. I went to the hotel first. They knew I was a stranger, and they said, where did you come from? I said, Arcola. I came up on the train. I said, that's the first train that's come through since the storm, and I came up on it. It didn't cost me anything either. I just got on it.

"Well then I remember I went to the store. The storekeeper, he noticed that I was a stranger in town. He said, how did you get here, after all that storm? I came up from Arcola. It snowed in. I came up on the snowplow train.

"He says, what are you going to do here? I said, I don't know. I'll find something, won't I? Then this man come in, a farmer. He was lame. He noticed I was a stranger, and he said, you're a stranger here, aren't you? Yes, I said, I am. He says, what are you doing? Nothin', I said, I'll have to find something pretty soon.

"How would you like to come out, he said, and work for me a little while? I said, that'd be fine. At least I'd have a place to sleep, wouldn't I? Yes, a good, warm house and everything. He says, I won't be able to pay you any money, though, until the first of April. Regardless, he says, first of April.

"I was getting to look like a man by this time, 18. I was husky, 19 I guess I was then. *[Ed. note – Probably 16 or 17]*. And he says you could help me around my place with chores and one thing another. I have a bunch of stock there to feed and snow to shovel and one thing another. You won't be working very hard, mainly because we've got to clean all of the seed grain. That's all got to be done. And then we've got to formaldehyde it and bluestone it and everything for smut. So, I could use you quite handy if you'd like to come out. Oh god, yes, I said, let me come out!

"So, he had a cutter. A damn good team of trotters and a cutter. Two-seater, you know. *[Ed. note – A cutter is a lightweight, open, horse-drawn sleigh.]* We got in that cutter, put the buffalo robe over us, pulled down our hoods over our heads, and away we went. Well, that turned out to be pretty good. I worked all through the summer. And it was sand, grain and one thing another, until seeding time come, and then he started to pay me.

"In the fall, I said, well, I want to go threshing. I said, I got to make more money than this for the winter, $26, $1 a day. That's all I got for working steady. Five o'clock in the morning, nine, ten o'clock at night. Well, he said that I could go threshing. He said, I don't know what you want to go threshing for. That's a hell of a job. No good place to sleep or anything. I said, it's good money. Threshing went up to $4 a day. Mind you, it was about 12 hours."

Ed. note –In the settlement and early post settlement era threshing and harvesting the fall wheat crop was usually too large a task for farmers to accomplish themselves. Up until the late 1930s it was common to engage custom threshing crews with the manpower and equipment needed for the task. It took a crew of 10-12 men an average of one week to thresh the average farm. Men and boys traveled to the Canadian west from the USA and Eastern Canada to work on such crews.

Right: David Willet's threshing outfit operating ca. 1900, with at least 17 men employed in this crew, equipped with an early steam tractor and separator (Saskatchewan Archives Board)

ET continues: "So, I went threshing, and I got quite a bit of money. We got 60 days threshing there, $4 a day made quite a sum of money, and you didn't spend any. What the hell, there's nothing much to buy…you might buy a pair of gloves or something. Sweater or something. But it was all cheap. Everything was cheap.

"So, when the threshing was over, I couldn't see staying in that country anymore. So, I headed up for Regina. Well, there was nothing to do in Regina. That was a farming country, too. The wind used to sweep across the plains. Qu'Appelle was the coldest damn place around there. Regina was supposed to be, but Qu'Appelle was just 40 miles away. It was the coldest spot on that part of prairie.

"So, I went back down the line. It didn't cost me very much. Three cents a mile on the railroad. If you could get a boxcar and jump into it, they had to stop at every station. So, I went down to what they called Stoughton. Lo and behold, the brother-in-law of the place I had just left lived in Stoughton. And he says to me, darn it, he says, there are lots of little chores around town here. He says, I think I can get you on for the winter. Oh god, I said, that's fine!

"He says, you can stay with me if you want. I won't charge you much for board and room. And he says, you'll get paid for the work you do cleaning out the barn, and working the livery barn, and I don't know, there are a lot of different things. Hauling coal from the livery barn. Take the team and haul. Empty a car of coal and all this stuff, you see. I made out all right. I got paid a little bit for that. $1 a day."

The 1906 Canadian census of the Northwest Provinces lists Ernie as living as a hired man in the household of George Hall, Jr., in Assiniboia East, which was the name of the political district in Saskatchewan where Oxbow is located. Four other members of the household were listed, including George's wife, Jessie, two young sons, and Ethel Regh, an immigrant from England who was listed as a "boarder". This would seem to confirm that Ernie did not spend all his 12 years on the prairies in Oxbow, living with the Gregsons.

Jean Bosko, Ernie's granddaughter-in-law, remembers many of Ernie's stories, and related one that is both interesting and revealing: "Then he had another story to tell about when he rode the rails in his younger days. He told us they used to have a board that he would throw between the wheels and jump on and ride on that board. Under the train. He would have to jump off while the train was still moving but slowing down for a town. He said they had to hide from the railway police who would walk along and check underneath

for those trying to get a free ride. Then as the train started up again, he would throw the board and jump on again if he wanted to go further."

Left: Young "hobo" riding the rods in the early 1900s, somewhere in North America (Wikimedia Commons)

From Wikipedia: "In the 1900 to 1920 days of wood frame freight car construction, steel truss rods were used to support the underside of the car in order to provide it with the strength to carry heavy loads. There could be four or more of these truss rods under the car floor running the length of the car, and hobos would "ride the rods." Some would carry a board to place across the rods to lie on. Others would lie on just one rod and hold on tightly. Riding the rods was very dangerous. When a train moved at high speed, the cars could bounce and rock violently if the track was rough, and rock ballast might be tossed up which could strike a rider."

Suffice it to say that Ernie led many lives during his time in Saskatchewan, some of them risky, some of them exciting, a few of them boring, but all of them added to his metamorphosis into the remarkable person he was becoming.

Ernie would most likely have "aged out" of any formal dependency on either Barnardo's orphanage sponsorship or the wardship of the Canadian government and become a full-fledged Canadian citizen at age 18, in 1904, but he remained in his "adopted province" of Saskatchewan long after he was free to leave. It was, after all, the only home in Canada he had ever known.

ET continues: "Springtime came and I headed back to Regina. One day I was sitting in a park there, along with a fellow by the name of Mr. Morrison. He was a retired farmer from Stoughton, and that's where I just had come from, and that's how I'd come to talk to him. We're sitting there, talking away, where I'd been, what I'd done, all that stuff.

"Then a little fellow, Mr. Jenkins, came and stood right in front of us. It was a very, very pleasant day: not warm, but warm as far as the prairie goes. Above zero. And he asked, do either one of you fellows want a job for the summer? Well, Morrison says, I really don't need any job. He says, I'm retired. But he says, this young fellow here is looking for work, and he says, I can recommend him. I've known him for quite a while, and he says, he knows all about farming.

"Well, he says, would you like to go out to my farm with me? I said, I don't know, I don't know. What wages are you paying? What are you paying now for starting. When do you want to start? He says, as soon as you say you're going to go out with me, your wages start right there. No monkeying around. He was a Yankee from the States, up in Canada there for his health. He'd been a dentist in Omaha.

"Oi, says Morrison, now, there's a chance for you. Well, I said, I'm taking it, too. When do we start? Jenkins says, I'm on my way home right now, and 17 miles we drove. It was cold, and it soon got colder and colder. I didn't have any good clothes for riding out there, in the bare prairie, so we got out and run behind. He did, too. He got cold. The horses went anyway.

"I stayed there all summer, $1 a day and board. That was high wages. This was the highest any man could get, no matter how good he was. There was no one who knew any more about that kind of farming than me. I'd grown up to it.

"In the fall, Mr. Jenkins says, I don't think I'd like to put in the winter here, from what I've heard. He had bought this place, half a section, from a farmer. And he says, my wife and I want to go back to Omaha for the winter. He says, we'll be playing in the orchestra there again, like when I left. Could you stay here for the winter?

"Yes, I said, but I won't stay for nothing. No, he says, you'll get $1 a day for the winter, because I'm going to have to ask you to draw the flax…there was no wheat there. It was all flax. I'm going to ask you to draw a carload of flax as soon as it's the right time, and then another carload later on. Well, I said, that's fine. I said, sure, I'll look after your stock, too.

"Anyway, Mr. Jenkins was a great solo violinist. He was the leader, a violin leader, in a big orchestra in Omaha, and his wife was one of many good pianists that was in the country at that time. *[Ed. note – Mr. Jenkins was probably the orchestra's concertmaster.]* So, they had lots of music. They would get music from Omaha in a roll. And it didn't matter if hell froze over, he would go right in the house after the mailman came, and he'd unroll that music, and if I was around, they'd holler for me to come in.

"By the way, we only got our mail once a week then. Remember that? Once a week. And so, he'd get his violin out, and his wife would sit down at the piano, and they would play that off of the roll, just like they both were reading the newspaper. Never saw it before. It was wonderful the way they could play.

"And in order to induce me to stay, in addition to a little higher wages and all, he said he would get me a good violin. I was playing the violin. I had already learned to play the violin. I bought it when I was working for Mr. Finn. If you remember, I mentioned Finn before. He had two nice daughters. That's the one I mean. *[Ed. note – We actually do not know anything about Mr. Finn or his two nice daughters, where they lived, and when Ernie worked for them.]*

"And I went to town, and I saw a fellow there getting a violin for his kid, just before Christmas. Believe it or not, it was in a drugstore. Drugstores carried everything in them days, in them little towns. But believe it or not, that violin case, bow, rosin, all of it was $5. Well, I needed a violin. I liked the violin all right.

"So, I couldn't wait 'til that guy got out of the store. I watched him and marched up to the counter, and I said, I would like one of those violins. Well, being the age I was, that man knew it was no good for me. So, he just simply said, I wouldn't sell you one of those kids' violins. But I have a nice violin here, with a bow, rosin, and some extra strings. By the way, there was no steel strings in them days. They were all gut, plain gut. And there was a nice case for it, too. A canvas case, of course.

"The man said everything together would cost $10. Well, that's all the money I had. That's all I had with me, $10. So, I said, that just takes away all my money, my $10, and I wanted to get a couple of other things for Mr. Finn, the man I was working for. He asked me, what did you want? So, I told him. He went and got them, and he says, there you are. You have the violin and the two items that you wanted. $10.

"My god, I couldn't wait until I got home. I had bought the old gent (Mr. Finn) a couple of bottles, one bottle of gin for the missus, and a bottle of Irish whiskey for him. And I learned to play that violin just the same.

"So, when I bought that little, cheap violin, little did I know right then how much a violin would mean to me for the rest of my lifetime. But I surely have profited from buying that little violin.

"Here I was, all alone in that house again (the Jenkins' farm), alone on the prairie. I don't know how I ever made out, but I wasn't daunted at nothing. When I saw my way clear, I took it. And then I got word. I'd been there about a month, and I got word from Jenkins to start drawing 1,000 bushels of flax. They go by bushels there. Here, they go by tonnes. 1,000 bushels of flax. He wrote the people at the elevator can start right in with it as soon as you get this letter.

ET continues: "So, I did that, and that's where I first met Bragg. He also was hauling flax off his father's place. His father had a rented place down below, about a mile straight as a string from my place. The road ran right by the house where I was staying.

"I always started out on my own, never thought about Bragg. But one time I was a little slow getting started. Snow had drifted and drifted all night long, and the wind was coming across the big yard Jenkins had there, making drifts, and I had quite a big job getting started. I always got my load ready to go the day before. So, I hitched the four horses on the sled right away and got the big hammer, a big sledge, and I hit each one of the four runners, so as to break off the ice from them. Away we went out on the road. I got in there to the elevator, got my load off and weighed. It took me from nine to ten trips to fill that elevator, then the elevator would put the flax in a railroad car. Before starting for home I went to the local restaurant to eat.

"On one occasion, on the way back from the elevator, Bragg followed me about half a mile back. I think my horses were faster than his. And I got quite a bit ahead of Bragg and had the horses unloaded and in the livery barn before Bragg went by.

"A few days after that, I think it was my fourth or fifth trip, I saw Bragg coming up the road again just as I was getting ready to leave the farm. And I said, Jesus, I'm not gonna break that goddamn trail from here to hereafter for him. The road was rutted, about six or eight inches deep, and it was lovely sledding if the wind wasn't blowing. But the wind would blow crossways across that road and fill those ruts full, and so we had to break that trail. So, I said to myself, hang on, when Bragg goes by, I'll slip my four horses out of the barn, and hitch 'em up, and I'll follow him. But that didn't make any difference. Bragg hadn't gone 100 yards when the ruts were blown full of snow just the same. That wind just would cut the eyes right out of you, you know.

"But anyway, I caught up to him. He stopped, and I caught up to him, and we talked. I think he was a couple of years younger than me. And he asked me where I was going, and I told him. Well, he says, we'll start off the horses and we'll walk. So, he started his team, and we walked behind his team, and mine followed us, you see. All them horses knew what they had to do. Big, lovely, handsome horses. No Cayuses. So, I got talking to him, and he says, what do you do anyway? I said I read a lot, and I said, the farmer I'm working for, Jenkins, sent a bunch of apples up from somewhere."

The previous passage, quite lengthy, is very important, but once again it is vague about the passage of time in Ernie's life from age 17 to 23, or where the Jenkins farm was located. Most importantly, however, Ernie has told us how he acquired his first violin, even if he doesn't identify where the drugstore was when he acquired it or who sold it to him. Nor does he identify the year, though it sounds like it was during the winter. In addition, his story line suggests that he was living in the Jenkins household when he acquired it, but even this is unclear. The Jenkins couple, apparently professional musicians in Omaha, with the suggestion that Mr. Jenkins was the concertmaster of the symphony orchestra in Omaha, had an important and fortunate influence on Ernie's interest in music.

Ernie doesn't say if he acquired his first violin while he was living in the Jenkins household, or if the acquisition occurred prior to his arrival there. But his story suggests to me that he received significant musical encouragement, and possibly instruction, from the Jenkins. It also hints at the possibility that Mr. Jenkins gifted him with a better violin than he initially possessed, possibly to encourage and reward him for extending his stay with them.

I can only guess that Ernie spent several years at the Jenkins' farm, even if Ernie's taped story makes it seem as if he may have spent less than a year with them, and that he acquired much more than musical instruction from the couple. In the meantime, while the Jenkins were spending the winter season in Omaha, leaving Ernie to tend to the farm, Ernie met Noble Bragg, a young man who had a profound influence on Ernie's destiny, perhaps more than any other single character in Ernie's beguiling story, as we shall soon see. Once again, Ernie neglected to give us an anchor in his timeline, so we are left to speculate about what happened. The lack of a specific timeline, with reliable dates, doesn't detract much from the wonderful story that Ernie is telling, nor does it detract from the most important details. At age 90, when Ernie made the tape recording, his ability to remember salient details about his life that stretch back 85 years is extraordinary. But then, Ernie Buckingham was an extraordinary man who led a truly extraordinary life.

Taken all by itself, you can't help feeling deep compassion for young Ernie, who was separated from his mother at age five, possibly earlier, with no indication that he ever knew his father or that he ever saw any of his siblings again. Add to this the fact that he was very likely never adopted by anyone; rather, he was initially placed in foster care and was eventually sent to a distant country because he was too much of a burden on his own homeland. All these facts taken together wouldn't predict a hopeful outcome for Ernie. By the time he reached the age of 23, one might be hard pressed to predict that Ernie had the potential to blossom into a successful homesteader, husband, father, musician, poet, entertainer, carpenter, and full-fledged Canadian citizen who made many important contributions to the development of British Columbia. Yet that is exactly what transpired, as we shall see.

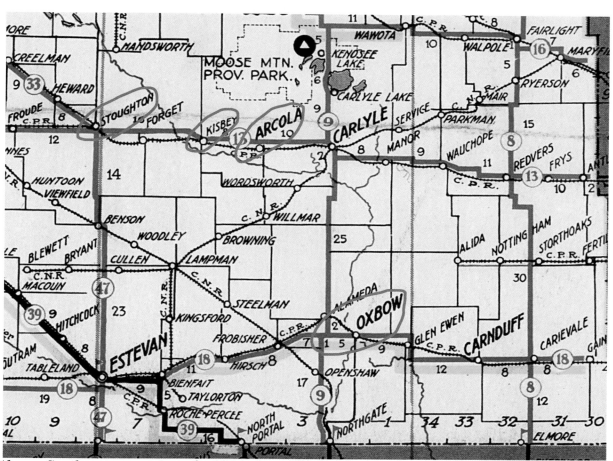

Above: Southeastern section of a 1954 map of Saskatchewan showing the main towns where Ernie Buckingham lived during his years on the prairies, including Oxbow, Arcola, Kisbey, and Stoughton; All are circled in red; The CPR and CNR railroad routes that Ernie used for transportation are also shown. (Saskatchewan Government Insurance Map of Saskatchewan issued in cooperation with the Department of Transportation and Highways Canada)

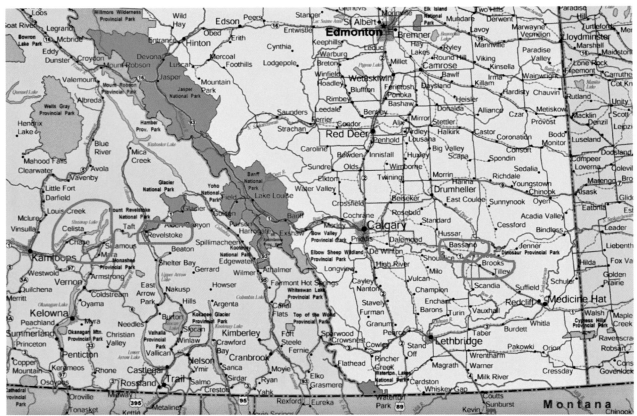

Above: Map of southern Alberta and southeastern British Columbia that enables us to see the route Ernie Buckingham and Noble Bragg took on their epic journey from Saskatchewan to the Shuswap Lake; They took the train with all their worldly belongings through Medicine Hat to Brooks and Bassano, then struck north to find their homestead; they returned to Bassano and hopped a freight to Revelstoke, then on to Notch Hill on Shuswap Lake via Sicamous, Tappen

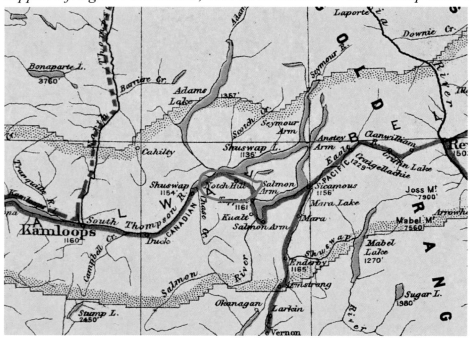

and Salmon Arm. (ontheworldmap.com); Left:1912 map showing the CPR the route in purple that ran from Revelstoke at the right edge of the map, through Sicamous, Salmon Arm, Tappen, and Notch Hill, the last being the town where both Ernie Buckingham and Frank Kappel got off the train and began their adventures in the Shuswap.

CHAPTER 3 – Into the Unknown: a New Life in British Columbia

"It should not be denied... that being footloose has always exhilarated us. It is associated in our minds with escape from history and oppression and law and irksome obligations, with absolute freedom, and the road has always led West."
- Wallace Stegner

Ernie's tape recording continues, ET: "I could say a lot more about that kind of thing, but I don't think it'd be very attractive reading, really. So, figured all around, I guess I better start right now on what I call living. So, we'll go right on now, carry on to Bragg's father and him and all. I followed Bragg. So, we'll carry on, 'eh?

"Well, away we all went on the railroad, up to Regina. We loaded all what they call settlers' effects on the train. We had a pig that was expecting. We had a cow, harrow, binder, mower, everything else that was demanded. Four wagons and four teams. There was four of us. It was Mr. Bragg, Noble Bragg, who was my friend, and his brother, which I had never met before then, and myself.

"So, we each drove a wagon, and we loaded them all up on the train. My wagon was full of lumber, full to the top, about 2,000 feet of lumber. I think Braggs had lumber, too, and a lot of other stuff. And we found out at the Regina land office that there was land available, homesteads available, about 60 to 80 miles northwest of Bassano. That meant it was about straight north from Brooks, Alberta. This is Alberta we're talking about now."

Right: Two young men trekking west from Moose Jaw, Saskatchewan, 1909, in an uncovered "prairie schooner" pulled by 2 oxen, similar to the wagon Ernie Buckingham would have driven for the Bragg family when they moved from Oxbow to Brooks, Alberta (Library and Archives of Canada/C-4988)

Right: A "prairie schooner" wagon, pulled by 6 oxen, on the Cariboo Road in the vicinity of Rogers Pass, Selkirk Mountains, British Columbia, by Edward Roper (1833-1909); More oxen than the usual 2 or 4 would have been required to pull a heavy wagon over the high mountain passes. (Wikipedia)

Against all odds, this young orphan boy from England who had been passed around and overlooked for most of his life, having received encouragement from very few of the people he knew, was seized by his hopes, dreams, and ambitions. Those mysterious forces that drive us all to embrace our destinies had entered Ernie's heart. Canada in the early 20th century was a land of boundless opportunity, and young Ernie was ready to charge headlong into his future.

At some point in the later period of his residence in Saskatchewan, according to Patricia Goldney Millar: "Ernie, aka "Buck", met Noble Bragg in Regina, they became fast friends, shared a love of music, and began to make plans. Noble's parents were going to Brooks, Alberta to homestead. Ernie went along with them and drove one of their three wagons. They arrived to find their quarter section had just been crossed by a prairie fire. There was no water on the land and with no feed for their stock, the Braggs decided to return to Bassano, Alberta. Instead of taking everything back with them they sold their livestock, a load of lumber, and two wagons to a man on the next homestead."

Left: Cover of Canada West magazine in 1909, promoting the attractiveness of moving to the Western Provinces (National Archives of Canada, C-30620)

An intriguing article that appeared in print in *Canada West: The Last Best West* magazine, a periodical that was widely read by Canadians at the time, may have been read by Ernie and even played a role in his deciding to travel west to seek his fortune. From the website Canada's History, Graham Chandler posted an article in September 2016:

"Living is cheap; climate is good; education and land are free."

"So proclaimed *Canada West: The Last Best West* magazine in 1910. More promotional brochure for immigration than magazine, it was part of the Canadian government's drive to attract skilled farmers–British and American immigrants were primarily targeted–to settle and till the soils of Manitoba, Saskatchewan, Alberta, and British Columbia, and turn the land into a cornucopia to feed industrialized eastern Canada and Europe.

"Sir John A. Macdonald thought the best way to encourage eastern industrial growth was to establish reliable food production for its growing population on Canadian soil. The ideal agricultural society envisioned by government officials was modern, highly developed, and based on family values; this agenda was articulated in their magazine, considered by immigration agents to be the most useful publication for promoting the West.

"With artistic covers portraying an idyllic prairie life of blue skies, golden crops, happy families, friendly neighbours, sunshine, and independence, Canada West was packed with advice for the prospective pioneer. Unlike our modern world of empty advertising spin, and though Canada West had purely promotional ambitions, its success hinged on providing practical information.

"Canada West contained everything the Canadian government thought the prospective farm owner needed to know. Issues repackaged the same message, often running the same kinds of articles every year: statistics on farm yields; information on railways, telephones, immigration, homesteading, schools, building materials, climate, cattle, and hog prices; river and lake access; land and customs regulations; different church denominations; freight rates; and much more.

"Issues always included a string of success stories and testimonials, such as one provided by an American newcomer who enthused, "I make five times per acre what I made in Iowa.

Right: This poster advertising for immigrants to Western Canada appeared in 1909. It had a cowboy-farmer flair and may have been seen by Ernie in Saskatchewan. (National Archives of Canada, C-126299)

"In the late decades of the nineteenth century, Canada's population was heavily weighted in the five eastern provinces: Quebec, Ontario, Nova Scotia, Prince Edward Island, and New Brunswick. Eastern Canada boasted some large urban centres, but the future of the country depended on attracting farmers to settle the West.

"Not only did Ottawa want agriculture to flourish, but it also wanted to populate the West to bolster a political stronghold. Concerned about the population imbalance, the government began a fervent campaign to promote western settlement.

"Hints abounded, from "For the Man Who Has Less than $300" (this man had better work for wages the first year) to "The Man Who Has $600" (get hold of your 160 homestead acres at once and build your shack) to "What $1,200 Will Buy" (this would provide decent equipment and include one stubble plough at $20).

"For the land-hungry homesteader, it offered detailed colour maps of each of the four provinces, growing in later editions to four-page foldouts, which included the checkerboards of surveyed township borders showing where new farmland was available and its proximity to rivers, towns, roads, and railways."

Ernie's tape continues, ET: "At Brooks they couldn't help us with the business of locating a homestead. So, they said, you need to go to Bassano, unload there, get the land office to give you a list of what homesteads is available, and then you have to go out and you find that section of land. Each one of you wants a quarter, I understand. You find that section of land, come back again and file on it, and then nobody else can get it.

"In the meantime, you don't really have to live on it the first month or so. Well, we said, that's what we want. We're going out there to stay. He said, you do what I tell you and you'll be all right. So, way up there we went on the train.

"And the folks at the land office at Bassano were very sharp. They got right in there, and they told us they were looking for settlers for sure, and they told us where to go, and where it was marked on the map, where this section was, and that section. God, we went away happy. Everything was loaded up and all and ready to go. There was lots of grass on the prairie for the horses and the cow. We had lots of feed for the pig. By god, we had some chickens, too. They laid eggs. All this time, they were laying eggs.

"So we started out across the prairie. Now, anyone that's done it will tell you this is the truth. We had no idea where we were going except it was northwest of Bassano. Mr. Bragg had a bit of knowledge of…I don't know what you call it…hunting land or something. So he carried the map, and we went from stake to stake. We found these stakes without any trouble. He just led us right to them. We had quite a nice time. It was about 80 miles, and it took us about three days to get there.

"The weather was lovely and warm. Remember that. Keep that in your mind, will you? It was lovely and warm. We slept under the wagon. There were no sleeping bags in them days, really, but we had lots of blankets. I had lots of blankets and tarpaulins. And we slept under the wagons. In the morning, when we would get up, the antelope was right across there out on the prairie. They couldn't understand these funny things on the prairie, wagons and horses and stuff. Every once in a while our cow would give a big moo, and boy would they ever go. Those antelope can really run. I guess they're the fastest thing on foot almost, in the deer line. But soon they'd come back again and feed and everything else.

"We never shot at them. We didn't need to. We had nice little rifles, and we had big rifles, too. We used to shoot gophers, though, and one thing and another. They were popping up through holes in the prairie. It was really lots of fun.

"Near the end of, I think it was, the third day, we were told by a fellow that was coming toward us that the prairie was burnt black in front of us, about five miles further on. He said, where do you want to go? We told him, we showed him the map. By god, he says, I believe that part is burnt also. Where I come from, it missed me.

"Anyway, we had nothing else to do but to go on. There we were, out there on the lone prairie, as the fellow says, and we had this lumber. So, we went on. Sure enough, five miles on then, the prairie was burnt black. It had just been burned about two days before.

"That made the stakes easier to find, since there was no prairie wool, as they called it, growing up to cover them. But there was no pasture for the horses or cow. We had a bit of hay with us, so we got to our destination anyway. One stake had four numbers on it. It had one of our numbers, so that was good enough.

"We set the shack up in no time. We got to our destination about half past one in the daytime. And we just went to work, the four of us, and we put that shack up, and we had the roof on before dark: not shingles, but just the roof by that time, for the night. So, we all slept in our blankets and one thing another in that shack. It was 18 by 24 feet.

"When we arrived we had to tie the horses up to the wagon spokes and one thing and another. There wasn't a thing to eat. And a little bit of wind came up, and it blew the ashes off that grass, upon my word, everything was covered with soot. And we had to take the horses over a mile down to some river. I forget the name of that river now. Could be Bassano River or something like that.

"Anyway, we took 'em down there, and we had made up a kind of stone-boat, out of the extra timber stuff, the two by sixes, and braced it up good. We put a barrel on that we had brought with us that had a lot of miscellaneous stuff we needed. We just dumped the stuff out of the barrel, wired the barrel on the stone boat, and we took it with us. The prairie was fairly smooth, but not that smooth, so the barrel upset twice on the trip to the river.

"But anyway, we got back from the river with a barrel of water for the stock left behind because they couldn't be led, like the pigs and the chickens and what-nots. We led the cow, and everybody went. I'd like to have a picture of that.

"But nevertheless, we talked about the whole mess, and we wondered what we should do. There was only one thing to do. Go back to Bassano and go to the land office and abandon these homesteads. Just simply tell them, we don't want them. We'll write a script. And that's exactly what we did. At the land office they gave us a piece of paper, and we wrote on that, and they gave us a duplicate of that, and that meant that now we didn't have a homestead. It meant a lot to me later the next year. You had to have abandonment papers, you see. *[Ed. note – In order to be able to get another homestead somewhere else, since each settler was allowed only one homestead in Canada]*

"Well, what to do now? Old Man Bragg says, I'm going to go back where I came from, Regina and out there, where we were, and I'll re-rent that same farm if it's available. Nobody would know it was for rent anyway, so it should be available, since it was only a couple of weeks since we left it."

Whether or not Ernie was directly influenced by articles advertising the far west of Canada, he obviously had enough of the prairies. After more than twelve years of living in the middle provinces of Canada, Ernie made his way with his friend Noble to British Columbia.

Patricia Goldney Millar wrote: "Ernie and Noble decided to move on to B.C. Ernie took his fiddle, Noble took his banjo, and they hopped a freight. It was the end of March 1910, and the snow was gone on the prairies - but they arrived in Revelstoke to find twelve feet of snow.

"Staying at the Oriental Hotel they were to have a job in two weeks at the Big Eddy Mill, but before their job started - the Columbia River flooded, and the mill closed down. Word came, a survey party needed two young men in Sicamous, and they left immediately. At Mobley Bay they lived in tents. The first campsite was the present site of Twin Cedars, at Anglemont. The survey party had to move camps several times to avoid high water.

Ernie's tape continues: "Well, Noble said, I'm not going to go back there, no, sir. And I said, "Well I'm staying with you". But Kerry, the other brother, said "Well, I'm going with the old man". So they went east, and we went west. And we dealed ourselves for Revelstoke, British Columbia, the land of the apples and all the peaches and plums. Boy oh boy, would we ever have a bunch of them. Now, we had perfect weather. The sun came up out of the ground since it was so flat, and the sun went down into the ground just the same. No hills, no nothing. We didn't want that anymore.

"The train came back to Bassano that night. It came by there about nine o'clock. We got on with our fiddle and our blankets and a trunk we had. We loaded that on, since it was included with our passage money. I had my fiddle, of course, and away we went. We got to Revelstoke at

midnight or thereabouts. I don't know just when it was. It may have been that day or the next day.

Left: Old postcard of Revelstoke, B.C., ca 1910, Lower Town & Columbia River, where Ernie and Buck stayed

Below left: Photo of Upper Revelstoke, taken between 1908 and 1910; This is not how McKenzie Avenue it would have appeared when Ernie and Noble Bragg arrived in March, because Ernie said in his tape that there were 12' of snow piled along the streets then. (Revelstoke Museum and Archives)

"We didn't know what to do when we got to

Revelstoke. There was two towns, they told us. Upper town, lower town. If you go to lower town, all the expenses were way lower than upper town. In upper town was where the railroad station was, and all the big shots lived in upper town. Lower town was not so good. It was for loggers, really, for loggers, and pole makers and everyone else, like river drivers.

"There were three hotels there, the Lakewood, and the Oriental, and I forget the other name. Rosewood or something like that. They were all built on the banks of the Columbia. We were told the best place for us two, in our condition, not knowing anybody, would be the Oriental, because the man that owned it, ran it, Mr. Stone, Albert Stone his name was, he was a very good to fellows that were down and out. We said, we're really not down and out, but we will be if we don't get some work.

Right: The Oriental Hotel in Lower Revelstoke, ca. 1910, on Front Street, where Ernie and Noble Bragg stayed and played their music for room and board (Revelstoke Museum and Archives)

"Now, I missed a little bit of stuff there. When we got off the train, we couldn't believe our eyes. You couldn't see over the station platform for snow that was 12 feet high. The snowplow had come along there just a day or two before and just threw that right out of the street, threw it every place. We went down to lower town, believe it or not, in a horseless buggy. It was a buggy with a big motor in it and a chain on the back wheel. It was the first of the horseless carriages. We went down in that. That was the taxi.

"He landed us at Albert Stone's and we got a room there. The price was $5 a week, bed, board, bath, and everything that went with it, everything in a good hotel, $5 a week. So, we gave him $10 each. We thought we'd make sure we'd have it for two weeks anyway. And we said, where could we put the trunk? He said, I'll have it put up in the attic. I got a lot of them up there.

"And he says, what are you going to do? We heard about the Big Eddy sawmill was going to open up soon. Oh well, he said, that won't be soon now because we had this terrific snowstorm here. It snowed four to five feet of snow nearly overnight, one day and a night. That's why you see so much snow just lately. Well, we figured we'd be all right anyway.

"So we went up the bedroom. Well, we were music crazy, Bragg and I. He loved that banjo, and I loved the fiddle. So, we must have both gotten along pretty well together. We were in the room the next day, and I said, what do you suppose, should we get out our instruments and practice a little? Oh, yeah, Bragg says. So we got them out and all tuned up, and we were just going to town there, Arkansas Traveler, Soldier's Joy and all that stuff.

"I believed I could play the fiddle pretty well in them days. And it wasn't long until Albert Stone came up, and he knocked at the door, and I opened it. I said, it's you. I guess we've been a nuisance. We shouldn't be playing here. Far from that, he says. Far from that, my boy. We were really boys yet, you see. He says, you come right down. Bring them instruments down to the big sitting room and play down there. You don't need to play in your bedroom. So, he says, come down after lunch, after you've had your lunch.

"So, we went and had dinner, what we call dinner. About two o'clock, he come, he says, how about giving us a little music there now on them two instruments? So, we rattled away there for a couple of hours. A lot of people congregated, and they bought a lot of drinks. Albert Stone had a wonderful, big place there, a regular lumberjacks' hotel. Lots of room, sitting room was a huge place.

"And they began to dance. They came in after supper, cork shoes and half boozed up, and we quit playing, you see, Bragg and I. They all stopped dancing and looked at us. Stone was tending the bar, and he came over, and he says, what's the trouble? You want a drink or something? I said, no, I said, look at that floor. If we keep playing, there won't be any more floor left. Don't you worry about that floor, he says. You just keep playing as long as you want to play, and I'll worry about the floor.

"He didn't know who he was talking to because we could play a long, long time. And we played, and they came from the Lakewood Hotel, and they came from that other hotel, and they all was in there, in our hotel.

"God damn, stag dancing, mind you. No women, just men, just rarin' to beat hell, whoopin' and hollerin'. Mostly Swedish, Scandinavian. And I could play an awful lot of Scandinavian waltzes and polkas at that time. I think I can yet. They just never heard anything like that at Albert Stone's. Where did you boys come from? What do you do for a living? We says, we did come here to work at the Big Eddy. That's all. So, that's the way it was.

"At that time, what I should have mentioned about this whole thing was that we were absolute strangers. We were prairie chickens, they called us. We had no idea about logging or the huge mountains that we saw when we woke up in the morning. Revelstoke is just at the foot of them all, with the raging river, the Columbia River below us. The snow had started to melt up high, and holy smoke, we were really stunned, in a way.

"But like I said, little did I know, when I'd bought that little old fiddle, how much that fiddle was going to mean to me, and it sure was paying off now. Because when the snow melted more, the Columbia raised up, and the Big Eddy was just what it was supposed to be. The mill was on the top, and the Eddy was like the thumb in your hand. The river was your hand, and the thumb was the Eddy.

"You could put a couple of million feet of logs in there, and even more in the cove. And they weren't toothpicks, these logs, we found out. They were anywhere from six to eight feet wide at the butt and 40 feet long, 20 feet long and all that stuff.

"And we went down every day to see how things was, find out when the mill was going to start up. They'd say, oh, we're just about ready, just about ready, and that was fine. We'd go back and tell Stone that, well, she's just about ready. That night, the flood came down that river, and it went by the Big Eddy so fast that the suction of that river drawed the logs out into that Eddy.

"And it drawed them all out. Once they started moving they whirled and whirled and whirled. When we went down the next morning, there was a dozen experienced dynamite men riding those big logs, boring holes in them, and putting dynamite in it to blow them up so that they would stop the whirl. They were just whirling like mad, round and round and round. I suppose there was about 20 acres of eddy there, and it full of them big logs.

"But by night, there wasn't one log left. They all went down the river. Where and to whom we don't know. So that ended our Big Eddy prospects. We went back to the hotel, and of course the news had gotten all around that the Big Eddy had gone out.

"And when we went in, I guess we didn't look very pleased, because we'd figured on starting the next day or so at the Big Eddy mill. We were running short on money. Bragg had more money than I did, because he was given more money, you see, and he didn't spend unless he had to, but I would. And we said to Albert Stone, well, we're getting kind of short on money, and we don't know what to do. We don't want to stick around here until we can pay. He said, I tell you what, as long as you two boys play them two instruments here, you can stay for free.

"Now, that wasn't much what they call recompense for fiddling. $5 a week was all we had to pay for board. But we played the fiddle and banjo there, we'd play every night, since that was the best we could do. We got no money for the playing.

"What I forgot to mention a while ago was that neither Bragg or I drank whiskey or anything like that, at that time. That was pretty unusual for young fellows. But we smoked. And we didn't smoke cigars much, and cigarettes wasn't… I don't know. You never saw anybody smoke cigarettes in those days. *[Ed. note - Everyone rolled their own using loose tobacco and cigarette papers.]*

"We were used to smoking pipes. And Noble Bragg could smoke a pipe when he was playing the banjo. I couldn't smoke when I was playing the fiddle because the pipe went on the top of the fiddle and made a funny noise. So, I had to let off smoking until we had a kind of recess, and then I'd smoke the pipe. But we never smoked cigarettes or cigars.

"So we didn't drink, and the lumberjacks were astonished that two grown-up men didn't drink whiskey, what was the matter with them? But they still made up for it. They gave us cigarettes and cigars to the tune of everything, all we wanted. So, that's how it happened, you see. We could get everything we wanted for free. Fiddle and banjo together were something worth listening to. It must have been. Well anyway, I'm going to stop this and make coffee right now. So, toodle-oo."

From Patricia Goldney Millar's biography, Ernie Buckingham remembered the year 1910: "About my arrival on the Shuswap Lake. I came there with Chief Doug Stewarts Survey gang May 10th, 1910.

"As far as any accomplishments I guess I wasn't one of that kind. I fell through the ice the year I was married skating from Celista to Cliffords' place when I was helping MacKay build the place. It's still there too, I saw it the last time I was up there. I got frozen in the lake in Mr. John Reedman's' boat and we all walked out on the ice in a few hours, that's about the extent of my adventures. You might say I never started to live until I hit that lake.

Above: Thunderstorm on Shuswap Lake, British Columbia, oil painting by Grafton Tyler Brown, 1882 (Salmon Arm Observer)

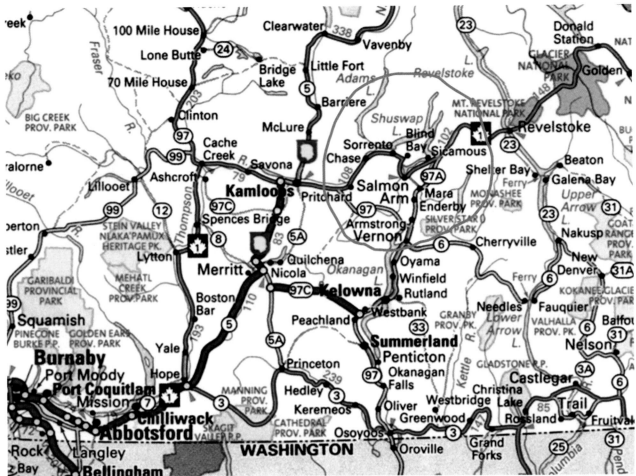

Above: Map of southern British Columbia, including Kamloops, Shuswap Lake, and Salmon Arm (us-canad.com) [Ed. note – The area where our story takes place is circled in red.]

"Coming from that hot dry Prairie it sure was a big change all I can say is that I enjoyed every day I was in the district, getting into the root cellar, and tapping the cider barrels and pouring water on the floor below it to make the Senior Reedman think that the tap had leaked. We used to come back from the White Lake dances to get a couple more jugs of the stuff, it must have been 10 over proof, sure was strong. It seemed everyone was happy them days, all had something to keep them busy no one seemed to complain. Dancing, skating, and sleigh riding were the things we enjoyed in those days."

Now begins what was to be the most important chapter in Ernie Buckingham's life. According to Wikipedia:

"Shuswap Lake consists of four arms, forming a shape reminiscent of the letter H. The four arms are called Salmon Arm (southwest), Shuswap Arm (west), Anstey Arm (northeast), and Seymour Arm (north). Shuswap Lake connects to Little Shuswap Lake via the Little River, which flows from the end of Shuswap Lake.

"The central interior plateau of British Columbia drained by the Fraser and Okanagan rivers is part of the Shuswap terrain in British Columbia and northern Washington state. It is dissected by numerous elongated, glacially-<u>over-deepened</u> lake basins which are formed by the same mechanisms as coastal <u>fjords</u> (i.e., glaciers during the last ice age).

"To the north-west it is fed by the <u>Adams River</u>, which drains <u>Adams Lake</u>. The Salmon Arm of Shuswap Lake connects to <u>Mara Lake</u> at the Sicamous Channel. The <u>Shuswap River</u> connects via <u>Mara Lake</u>. In the south-west the Salmon River flows into the lake at <u>Salmon Arm</u>. The <u>Eagle River</u> runs down from the <u>Eagle Pass</u> in the <u>Monashees</u> to enter the lake at <u>Sicamous,</u> in the east. The <u>Seymour River</u> empties into the northern end of the Seymour Arm. In addition to these rivers, numerous creeks feed the lake, including Scotch Creek, which runs south to the north shore of the main arm, near the community of the same name."

From the Salmon Arm Lodge of the Freemasons website:

"In the interior of British Columbia lies Shuswap Lake, a comparatively narrow body of water winding its way for many miles among the mountains. Ever since the coming of the white man the long southern branch of this lake has been known as Salmon Arm. The Salmon River, an important river, flowing from the south, flows into the southern end of this area of the lake.

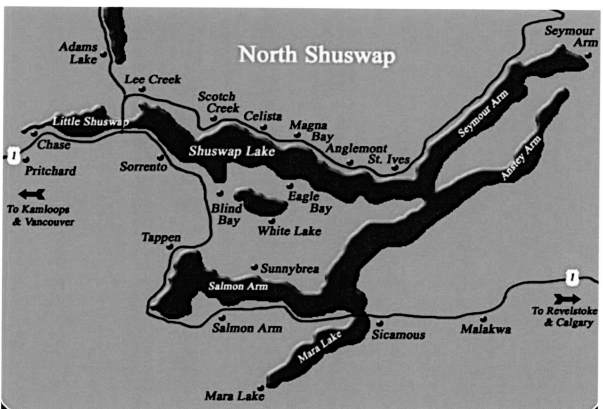

Above: Map of the Shuswap region, including all 4 arms (Salmon, Seymour, Shuswap, and Anstey), along with Chase, Sorrento, Scotch Creek, Celista, Magna Bay (where Frank and Janet Kappel first lived), Blind Bay (where Ernie and Jeanie had their homestead), Sicamous (where the Kappels later lived), Eagle Bay, Malakwa, Adams Lake, and Salmon Arm (North Shuswap First Responders)

"Before the coming of the Canadian Pacific Railway in 1886, the stretch of fertile land along the Salmon River was unknown, except to a few hunters and trappers, but as soon as the means of transportation was provided, settlement followed the rails. Land surveys, dividing the district into sections and quarter sections, were commenced in 1887, and soon homesteaders were busy taking up homes for themselves and their families. The land in the valley, fertile as it was, was heavily timbered and it took time and hard work to bring it into cultivation. Eventually, not only the land in the river valley, outside of the Indian Reserve at the mouth of the Salmon River, passed into private ownership, but also all the arable bench lands to the east and west of the river.

"It was soon discovered that these bench lands were particularly suitable for fruit growing as well as for mixed farming. It, therefore, followed that as soon as Crown Grants were issued for the homesteads, they were subdivided into smaller blocks, and disposed of, and more intensified farming and fruit growing resulted. The first school building was erected in 1890; the first church, in 1895, although religious services had been held before that time. The growth of the settlement is shown by the fact that the district was sufficiently settled to warrant its incorporation as a municipality, under the name of the Municipality of Salmon Arm, in May 1905. In this district there grew up a town and business centre, which was incorporated as the city of Salmon Arm, in March 1912."

Left: Canadian survey team known as Dominion Land Surveyors that surveyed much of the Northwest Territories in the early days of the 20th century, much like what Ernie Buckingham was doing when he first arrived in the Shuswap area in 1910 (The Canadian Encyclopedia)

According to author Derek Hayes: "British Columbia was among the last temperate places on Earth to appear on the map of the world, a function of its position: remote from Europe. When gold was finally discovered in quantity in 1858, leading to the gold rush that created British Columbia as a new colony, the interior was mostly unknown except for the routes blazed by the fur traders seeking the "soft gold" that characterized the exploration of much of Canada. The efforts of the explorers, the fur traders, the gold seekers, and the railway builders all involved the production of maps that showed what they had found, the routes and the settlements, the plans and the strategies that developed the province into what we know today."

Buck and Brag Orchestra 1910- 1912

Ernest Buckingham and Nobel Bragg

Right: Buck and Bragg Orchestra, ca. 1911 (provided by Jack Brown)

Patricia Goldney Millar's biography of Ernie continues: "Ernie and Noble quickly started a band and became well-known as "Buck and Bragg" that became famous throughout the region. At a community dance, to celebrate the opening of the new school at Celista, the survey crew found the musicians hadn't shown up. The boss 'volunteered' Ernie and Noble's services, and the 'Buck and Bragg' orchestra got their start in the Shuswap area. Ernie said, "From then on we were paid well to play anywhere we could get to." Their two-man band took them to many areas.

"Noble Bragg homesteaded at Celista and quit the band. Ernie found a new musical partner in his neighbour, Ole Widmark, and together they performed at many country dances. He helped to build the Sorrento Hall, and the log church in 1912.

"Ernie remembers the winter of 1912 /1913; there was no snow, and the ice on the Shuswap Lake was two feet thick. He said, "I skated from Celista to Seymour Arm.""

And as fate would have it, Ernie met a Scottish girl from nearby Celista, Jean Brown. They apparently fell madly in love and Jean became pregnant. They were married December 26, 1912, at Chase Ranch by Rev. Watkins, and their wedding reception was held in the new Celista school. One of the many gifts to the young couple was a boat from 'boat builder' Harry Fowler. Theirs was a happy and productive marriage, by all accounts (more on this later).

Right: Ernie and Noble, "Buck and Bragg", at Seymore Arm on Shuswap Lake, ca. 1910 (provided by Jack Brown)

Fortunately, several independent newspapers were actively publishing in the Shuswap area around the time

Ernie Buckingham and Noble Bragg Leaving Seymour Arm for parts unknown

our heroes arrived, chronicling several notable events that reveal the compelling drama of our story, while adding valuable insight into what life was like for the local citizens.

The following article appeared in the Chase Tribune (a local Shuswap newspaper), August 2, 1912:

Blind Bay. "As was to be expected, the production of "Box and Cox" by the Blind Bay Amateur Dramatic Club, on Friday evening was a success. The Crombie brought over a bunch from the Driving Camp. H.L. McLean's boat brought up a party from Chase, and there was a large attendance from nearer points. The actors were Mrs. Dunne, Stanley Reedman, and Ernest Buckingham.

"Miss Jean Brown gave an exhibition of her ever-popular sword dance. There was a piano solo by Miss Maggie Smith, also a duet by the Misses Smith.

"The dance that finished off the program lasted till 4 o'clock. The oral report given us of the good supper they had made us sorry we didn't go."

The Agassiz Record and The Chase Tribune (local Shuswap newspapers) ran the following story on December 20, 1912:

Wharf Finished at Sicamous: Completion of the Work Was Celebrated by a Big Ball in the Bellevue Hotel.

"The new government wharf at Sicamous was completed last week. The structure is 160 feet long with a 70-foot ell, the approach being 17 feet wide. At low water there is a depth of nine feet at the end of the wharf. This much needed improvement will be a distinct addition to the shipping facilities of what is expected to become an important lake port.

"The work was in charge of C.W. Cameron, of Chase, who took most of his men from here and in Celista. Most of them from here, including Mr. and Mrs. Cameron, Mr. and Mrs. Will Bradley, and John Westburg, returned on Tuesday. Those from Celista, Mr. and Mrs. Parsons, Mr. and Mrs. Bragg, Ernest Buckingham, W.J. Reddy, and W. Gray, returned on the "Maud Annis".

"The dance that wound up the operations was a complete success. The spacious dining room of the Bellevue hotel was well filled with about forty couples. The music was furnished by the well-known Buck and Bragg orchestra. The wharf boys wish to thank Mrs. Congreve for the trouble she took to make the evening such a pleasant one. Proceeds of the ball were given to the Solsqua public school."

From the Chase Tribune this article appeared on August 15, 1913:

"The Blind Bay folks were at home to their neighbors from Celista, Notch Hill and Chase last Friday evening. The most of them were literally at home, perhaps to leave that much more room for the visitors. But there were enough there to give the outsiders a hearty welcome and see that they had a good time. Mrs. Dunne and Mrs. Baines presided in the corner from which the refreshments issued.

"They were ably seconded by the other Blind Bay guests who were present in making their visitors feel thoroughly welcome.

"All that need to be said about the music is that Tom Brown and Ernest Buckingham were there with their violins. There was no official pianist, so that instrument had to take its chances, which turned out to be all right, there being plenty of available talent among the guests. Harry Fowler was floor manager. Harry ought to name a successor to that office, so that in case of a gasoline explosion or some other accident putting him out of business there would be someone to take his place. He kept things lively on Friday night, putting in plenty of variety – too much for some who didn't know the dances.

"There were several boats over from Celista, bringing, among others, Mr. and Mrs. Frank Kappel, Alfred and Thomas Thomson, Mr. and Mrs. Tom Brown, Billy, Joe and John Brown, H.A. Fowler and Misses Charlotte and Beatrice Fowler, and some of the accompanied by his two sisters, the Misses Salt, who are visiting on his homestead.

"Those who took the long boat trip from Chase had perhaps the best time of all. new settlers whom the reporter did not know. Roland P. Salt *[Ed. note - Frank Kappel's friend from Germany]* was down from Eagle Bay, they arrived home in the morning in good time to begin the day's work. The band did not find the excursion a financial success, but this we hope will not deter them from putting on at least one more before the season is out."

Right: Photo of young Ernie Buckingham (to our right), sitting with Noble Bragg, in front of their tent; They both continued working on survey crews for several years after their arrival. (provided by Donald Dunbar and Jack Brown)

From the Chase Tribune, August 15, 1913:

Two Members of the Survey Crew in Magna Bay, Shuswap Lake, British Columbia, Canada - circa 1910

Noble Searle Bragg playing the violin and Ernest Silas Buckingham playing the guitar.

Sorrento: "The dance held in the Blind Bay Hall on Friday Aug. 8th under the auspices of the Chase band which chartered the steamer Andover and brought in a number of people from Chase was a success in every way and has greatly reduced the debt on the piano and left a nice balance in the bank towards the Blind Bay Hall. About a hundred people from Chase, Celista, Notch Hill and Blind Bay danced until four o'clock next morning to the music rendered by the following artists: Violinists, Messrs. Brown and Buckingham, pianists, Mr. Ferguson of Seattle, Mrs. McAlpine of Chase, and Mrs. Graham, also of Chase. Refreshments were served all through the evening by Mrs. Dunne who was assisted by Mrs. Baines and at the close of the dance a substantial supper was served by these ladies a la buffet. The next dance notified is that to be held in Chase for the Knights of Pythias on Friday August 15th.

"Raspberries are nearly over but shipments of blackcaps and dewberries are in full swing from Sorrento and Blind Bay fruit farms. And cultivated blackberries are nearly ready for shipment."

And from the Chase Tribune on August 22, 1913:

K.P. Ball Was Most Largely Attended for Many Months:

"The K.P. ball on Friday night was all that had been expected, and then some. Visitors came in by boat and by train and the town came out en masse. There were seventeen passengers by the Andover from Celista. Some came by launch from Blind Bay. By rail they came from as far east as Sicamous. By nine o'clock the hall was filled with the largest crowd that has gathered there for a dance for a good many months.

"All arrangements had been carefully made and everything went through without a hitch. Music of both the dreamy and lively kind was furnished by a four-piece orchestra, two violins played by Ernest Buckingham and Tom Brown, and Noble Bragg's banjo, accompanied by Miss Stewart on the piano. For a time, there were five pieces, Mrs. Buckingham joined in with the mandolin. Harry Fowler gave the usual satisfaction as floor manager.

"The reception committee were right on their job. They refused to listen to advice of one member "Let's introduce the strangers to all the old womans that we don't want ourselves."

"Both natives and strangers must have enjoyed themselves or they would not have stayed so long. The home waltz was called about 4:30 a.m.""

It is clear from these fascinating newspaper articles that the residents of the Shuswap area enjoyed quite an active social life, in spite of their relative isolation, and that both Ernie and Jeanie were very talented entertainers.

Left: Ruggedly handsome young Ernie Buckingham, 30 years old, sitting with his two eldest daughters, Laura Margaret and May Catherine, on their homestead, ca. 1916; He is holding a hunting rifle, and the dead animal is probably a wolf that Ernie had shot. He would either have used the pelt for clothing or to sell or barter for something the family needed but was unable to produce on their own. (provided by Donald Dunbar)

CHAPTER 4 – Jeanie Brown and the Famous Browns of Scotland

There Went a Fair Maid Forth to Walk

- Ancient Scottish song, author unknown

There went a fair maid forth to walk
  In the sweet twilight of July,
Bonnie she was and frank and young;
  But she met wi' a lad unruly.
The flowers smelled rich aneath their feet,
  The birds o'erhead sang hoolie,
Till the bright moon came glancing down
  Through the balmy air of July.

There were oft pausings in their walk –
  Words breathed out meek and lowly,
And smother'd sighs, and oft vowed vows,
  And looks so warm and holy!
He took her by the lily white hand,
  And swore he loved her truly –
The lad forgot, but the maid thought on;
  It was in the month of July.

Jean (or Jeanie) Brown was born on February 11, 1894, in Glasgow, Scotland the eleventh and youngest child of Thomas and Jemima (Fraser) Brown. The 1901 Scotland Census lists Jean's parents, Thomas and Jemima Brown, as living in Glasgow St. George, Lanarkshire, Scotland. St. George is a suburb of Glasgow on the northwest outskirts of the city.

Jean Brown 1894 - 1921

Right: Photo inscribed "Jean Brown 1902" (provided by Jack Brown) [Ed. note - Jeanie appears to be 4 or 5 years old, so the date should probably read 1898 or 1899.]

According to a biography of Thomas Brown written by his granddaughter, Laura Goldney:

"My grandparents, Thomas and Jemima Brown, lived in Glasgow with their large family. In 1904, when Canada was advertising for new settlers, saying that free land and golden opportunities awaited, the Browns answered the call. Some wag said that when Canada needed settlers they sent for the Browns. Hugh *[Ed. note – Second son)* has written about the trip over the Atlantic and their landing at Halifax, as well as the train ride to their destination in Saskatchewan. Tom (Jr.) and family got a homestead in Saskatchewan, but Grampa (Tom) and the others went to Moose Jaw, Saskatchewan."

THE BROOMIELAW, GLASGOW — LOOKING WEST

Left: Glasgow on the River Clyde, Scotland, 1889 (original antique print published by T. Nelson and Sons)

Left: Thomas and Jemima (Fraser) Brown with their large family and possibly some of the Fraser relatives, standing in front of their residence at 22 Grove

St., Glasgow, in August of 1895; The group totals 26, with the Brown family clustered in the left third of the photograph. Jeanie is at our left front in the photo, age 18 months (two of the Brown children do not appear in the photo). Apparently only the Brown children have their shoes on. (provided by Jack Brown)

The 1881 Scottish census lists Thomas Brown as a railway clerk living in Barony Parish (the formal name given to the Glasgow Parish). The 1891 Scottish census lists Thomas Brown as a bookkeeper living in the Glasgow St. George Parish at 22 Grove Street with 9 children ranging from 1 to 17 years of age.

The 1901 Scottish Census lists Thomas as a bakery clerk, living at the address: 61 Grove St. in the Glasgow St. George Parish. Jane (aka Jeanie) is listed as living in the household and was seven at the time of the census, with seven children listed in that census. Charles Dickens' well-known short story, "A Christmas Carol", in which Bob Cratchit is an underpaid clerk barely eking out a meager living for his large family, comes to mind, but a photo provided by Thomas Brown's great-grandson, shows five of the Brown children enjoying time at the seashore. That photo appears to have been made into a postcard, with T. Brown, Glasgow, inscribed on the right side in elegant script, suggesting that the Brown family was not impoverished.

Below: Photo card, with T. Brown, Glasgow, inscribed on the side, shows five of the Brown children enjoying time by the seashore; A handwritten inscription reads "Younger members of the Thomas Brown I family at the seashore circa. 1898; left to right: Joseph (15), Jemima (13), Jean (4), Margaret (8), and William (11). (provided by Jack Brown)

Younger members of the Thomas Brown I Family at the Seashore circa 1898

Left to right: Joseph Brown (15), Jemima Brown (13), Jean Brown (4), Margaret Brown (8), and William Brown (11).

Another photo (*on the next page)* shows Thomas Brown I around 1900, dressed in a tweed suit with pipe in hand, appearing quite prosperous.

There are other reasons why the Brown family may have decided to emigrate to Canada. Another Hugh Brown *[Ed. note – A grandson]* wrote a remarkable story late in his life about coming to Canada from Scotland with his parents in 1901 that sheds light on this subject: "My Father and Mother, Thomas Brown II and Jane Coats McGowan, decided to come out to Canada, the land of the golden opportunities, free land etc. according to the headlines in the papers over there. Conditions were very bad in Scotland at that time, so many unemployed."

Left: Thomas Brown I, ca. 1900, pipe in hand (provided by Jack Brown)

Thomas Brown I circa 1900

In the latter part of the 19th century, both the British and Canadian governments were advertising heavily to encourage both British and European citizens to emigrate to the prairies of Canada. According to the Canadian Museum of History website:

"Encouraging British and European immigrants to settle on the prairies was part of Prime Minister Sir John A. Macdonald's plan to establish Canadian sovereignty over the newly-acquired North-West Territories.

"Stretching from Ontario's border to British Columbia, (still a British colony), the Territories were transferred to Canada by the Hudson's Bay Company in 1869. Settlement was an urgent matter, and so was a railway to carry settlers west. There was already talk in the mid-western United States of expanding north of the border. Sir John's promise of a trans-Canada railway persuaded British Columbia to enter Confederation in 1871.

"The government offered a cash bonus of $10 to every farmer who settled on a free 160-acre homestead within six months of leaving Britain. Additional bonuses of $5 were offered to wives and family members over the age of 12 if they accompanied the homesteader. (Settlers had to farm and live on a homestead for six months a year over three years before they could claim title to their land).

"Several Official Handbooks for immigrants were published annually by the Department of the Interior in the mid-1890s. The cameo harvest scene on the cover set the pattern for advertising the Canadian west for the next 30 years: farmers harvesting their golden grain under a sunny blue sky. The message on the back cover, that there were bustling cities in Canada as well as millions of acres of arable land, was also repeated.

"Sir Wilfrid Laurier, Prime Minister of Canada, 1896 - 1911. Sir Wilfrid coined the phrase "As the nineteenth century was that of the United States, so I think we can claim that Canada shall build the twentieth". The phrase was quickly simplified to: "The twentieth century belongs to Canada."

"Suddenly a number of key factors came together to make possible large-scale settlement of the Canadian west. New technology was one of these factors. Fast new steamships could bring farm workers from Britain and Europe to Canada in a few days. The Canadian Pacific Railway, and other lines, made western Canada easily accessible. New agricultural machinery made "breaking the prairie sod" much easier than before, and specially developed new strains of wheat were producing bumper crops. American farmers, seeing that the wide-open spaces on their "frontier" were fast filling up, were buying land in The Last Best West, and bringing valuable expertise, equipment and capital with them.

Right: Official Handbook of Information Relating to The Dominion of Canada, published in January 1896 (National Library of Canada)

"The kind of hardy agricultural workers likely to succeed in the Canadian west were only to be found in Scotland, the north of England and, to a lesser degree, the western counties, and Wales. But advertising in the over-populated "mother country" was a political necessity. The British government wanted to relieve population pressures at home.

"In 1904 a remarkable horse-drawn wagon, brightly painted in vermilion red, toured through northern Scotland, where farmers had to be tough and persevering to survive - just the kind of hardy people authorities wanted to settle the Canadian prairies."

J. Bruce Walker, Canadian Government Agent in Glasgow, June 1904, wrote: "This Wagon is just now concluding a road trip of nearly 400 miles - away from the Railway, and through scores of villages and hamlets never reached by lecturers, and only indifferently touched by newspapers. It is returning from a trip up the entire North-East coast of Scotland

Left: J. Bruce Walker's "brainchild" that toured northern Scotland in 1904 to drum up interest among Scottish farmers in emigrating to Canada (National Archives of Canada)

It would be impossible to know if any members of the large Thomas Brown family saw the vermillion wagon, but it is certain that the wagon's tour of northern Scotland caught the interest of newspapers in Glasgow. Many factors were at play in Scotland and elsewhere in the British Isles in the early 1900s that may have influenced Thomas Brown to pack up four of his children, along with his wife, Jemima, and depart from Glasgow on a ship to a remote and unknown continent. Given the information from grandson Hugh Brown on page 52, i.e., "Canada, the land of the golden opportunities, free land etc. according to the headlines in the papers over there", it is very likely that the influence of the government advertising campaign was very strong. At the very least, it enabled the citizens of the UK and Europe to think about the opportunities that were available to them, to store this concept in the back of their minds, and to bring it forward into their list of options when necessity or ambition dictated.

Left: Moose Jaw, NWT, 1910, where the Thomas Brown family initially settled after arriving in Canada (prairie-towns.com)

A passenger list contained in the Canadian Immigration and Emigration Archives reveals that Thomas and Jemima Brown sailed from Glasgow on the 9th of April 1905, on the S.S. Pretoria, arriving in Quebec on 8 May 1905, and were accompanied by four of their children, including Jemima (age 19), William (17), Margaret (15) and Jeanie (11). Thomas Brown's occupation is listed in the document as a bookkeeper and farmer, and Moose Jaw, North West Territories, is listed as the family's destination. The document also states that Thomas was able to read and write. The 1906 Canada Census lists Jean's parents, along with six children, including Jeanie, aka Jennie, as living in Moose Jaw, Saskatchewan.

Laura Goldney's biography of her grandfather, Thomas Brown, continues: "In 1907 Joe (the sixth Brown child), who was a surveyor and civil servant, went on to B.C. by train *[Ed. note – Canadian Pacific Railroad, or C.P.R.]),* to Notch Hill, a destination that seemed to be the "jumping off" place for settlers who were bound for Eagle Bay, Blind Bay, Balmoral, Sorrento, and the north side of Shuswap Lake. There were few roads anywhere then. Joe preempted a homestead up Meadow Creek. The C.P.R. was the only link to the outside world. Joe coaxed his father to bring the family (including Jean) to Shuswap as it was much nicer than the prairies, so in 1908 they all packed up and came to quite a wilderness. Joe met the train, and they went by horse and buggy in Sorrento, then on a launch to what is now Celista. They must have wondered what was coming next.

"There was a two-room cabin on Joe's place, so that is where they all had to live until their new big house was built. Grampa filed for his homestead where Meadow Creek Estates is now. Land was cleared and the house made of logs was started. Harry Fowler, a man with many trades and talents, the first pioneer in the area, worked on the house, too, so with other help it was ready to live in by fall of 1910."

Right: The Thomas Brown Sr. house ca. 1909; Thomas and Jemima Fraser Brown are leaning against the tree to the right of the stairs. (provided by Jack Brown)

Laura Goldney continues: "Granny's new house must have seemed like a palace with so many rooms and upstairs, too. They all kept busy with gardens, planting fruit trees and some lilac bushes, etc., as well as building fences. The first cow was always wandering off, and someone had to find her, which took time. Clearing land was an ongoing job to make fields for hay.

"They were a fun-loving family as well as hard workers, and the Scottish dances and songs made life brighter. Tom Jr. played violin, Jeanie played the mandolin, and they knew all the dances.

"Communication was a problem. Only trails existed until 1913 or 14, when the first roads were built; no phones until 1915; and of course, no radios. Travel was by stern-wheeler or other boats. Then the ferry (at Scotch Creek) started, but the only way to get between neighbors was by horse and buggy, sleigh, or walking. Building the roads meant summer jobs for most of the men. It was hard work: no bull dozers or trucks then.

House warming picnic at Thomson beach - circa 1910

Back L to R: Billy ?, Harry A Fowler, Jimmy Thomson, Jack Josephson, Thomas McGowan, Billy Sims, Billy Gray, Billy Walker, John Brown, William Brown, Joseph Brown, Robert Thomson, Arthur H Chambers, Ted Jones.
Middle: Charlotte Fowler, Jeannie Brown, William Thomson, Euphemia Marchbank-Thomson, Thomas Brown II (holding Thomas Brown III), Jane Coats McGowan-Brown, Margaret (Maggie) Brown, Catherine Thomson, Jessie Fowler
Standing (in front of Thomas Brown II and Jane Coats McGowan): Jean McGowan Brown, James McGowan Brown and Hugh Brown.
Front Sitting: John Lee Fowler, Ken Josephson, Ben Josephson.

Above: Thomas Brown and William Thomson families attending the housewarming of the new Thomson family home, at Thomson Beach near Celista, on the Shuswap, ca. 1910; Jeanie is in the middle row, second from our left. (photo provided by Jack Brown) [Ed. note - Jack also wrote in a 2009 email: "The Thomson property was about 1 mile West of our Great Grandfather, Thomas Brown's homestead in Celista. In the picture, your grandmother Jeannie Brown is sitting next to William Thomson and Euphemia Marchbank, the parents of your adoptive grandmother Janet Thomson."]

"In 1910 the surveyors came to Shuswap, they camped in various places on the beaches. My father, Ernie "Buck" Buckingham and friend Nobel Bragg were with them. Buck played the fiddle and Nobel the banjo or guitar, and "Buck and Bragg" became quite well known when it came to dances and parties. Buck got a homestead, 160 acres where Shuswap Estates is now, and Nobel got one in North Shuswap. In 1912, Buck married Jeanie Brown. Jeanie and Maggie loved dancing and were favorites whenever they attended the dances in Chase or Sorrento or anywhere."

Grandson Hugh Brown, in his richly detailed memoir about moving from Scotland with his parents to a homestead in Saskatchewan, and eventually ending up in the Shuswap, adds to the story of the Brown family's migration:

"We left Nokomas on November 23 according to brother James (I say it was December 23). We went to Saskatoon, had to stay over a day there to catch the mainline to B.C. We arrived at the Shuswap Lake November 28, 1909, according to brother James, (I say it was December 28). We were held up by a train wreck at Tappen for a day as a pusher engine had run away from Notch Hill while the crew were in the hotel café. We had a very unpleasant trip all the way, there always was delays of some sort. Smith's store boat made a special trip across the lake for us after spending a cold night on the beach at Sorrento crouched around a bonfire. When we arrived at Fowler's beach as it was called then (Celista later years), Thomas Brown Senior and all their family were there to meet us in about two feet of snow. We stayed in tents on Joe's place that winter. The rest of the story is B.C. history."

Right: Jeanie Brown Buckingham ca. 1919, sitting in a chair on the family homestead with a wolf skin behind her [Ed. note – Possibly from the same wolf Ernie is shown with in an earlier photo] (provided by Don Dunbar)

Laura Goldney continues: "Buck and Jeanie's family grew quickly. I was born in 1913, their first child. In 1917 Grampa had a stroke, which left him in a wheelchair until his death in 1919. By now, Buck and Jeanie had four more children, including May, Jean Ellen, Donald, and Marie. Aunt Maggie contracted that terrible flu that swept the country and died in 1918. My mother, Jeanie, died in January 1921, near her 26th birthday, in Kamloops Hospital. In the fall of 1921 Granny was laid to rest, some said she died of a broken heart. In 1922 Tom Jr., father of 7, was killed in a logging accident."

Another remarkable account of the Thomas Brown family's journey from Scotland to the Shuswap was written by James McGowan Brown, son of Thomas Brown Jr. *[Ed. note – Stanley Kappel's uncle]* and Jane Coats McGowan-Brown, to commemorate his own family's adventures *[Ed. note – In James' own words: "the trials, events, happiness and sorrows")]* starting prior to their arrival at Celista:

"The family came to Celista after five years of isolation and hardship on the prairie; poor water, mosquitoes, horseflies, blizzards in the winter, sometimes 40 below for weeks at a time, and home was a sod house. Fuel was hard to come by. British Columbia seemed so much better.

"In the year 1909, Mr. & Mrs. Thomas Brown Jr. sold their farm in Saskatchewan and moved to B. C. with their four children, Hugh, James, Jean, and Thomas. They arrived at

Notch Hill on December 3, 1909, too late to get across the lake that day to Celista. W. T. Smith of Smith and Son General Store hauled them to the beach at Sorrento where they spent the night. Thomas McGowan, brother of Mrs. Brown, was with the family.

"It was a bitter, cold night. The first snow of winter had already fallen and there was a cold wind blowing eastward on the lake. With some ingenuity, the men arranged some rowboats that were on the beach in a half circle, standing them on their sides and filling in the open spaces with snow. This made a fair windbreak. Collecting drift on the beach, they made a good fire in the half circle and kept it going all night. Next morning, December 4th, W. T. Smith arrived and took them to Celista in his freight launch.

"They were met there by other members of the Thomas Brown Sr. family who had preceded them to Celista. They were father and mother, Thomas Sr., and Jemima; brothers John, Joseph, and William; sisters Margaret and Jean. Also, there to meet them was Harry Fowler, who truly was a friend in need. With his team and sleigh, he hauled them up to the Meadow Creek valley to the homestead of Joe Brown, where they spent the winter in a one room log cabin. It was crowded to say the least and had bed bugs which some loggers had left behind.

"In the spring of 1910, Tom Brown Jr. moved the family to the lakeshore on the homestead of Thomas Brown Sr. where he had erected a lumber floor with side walls and over this a large tent. This was fairly comfortable during the summer months, but when a strong wind blew across the lake, they were never quite sure the whole thing would not blow away. The tent was situated near the lake, so there was only a short distance to carry water.

"That summer, the log house of Tom Brown Sr. was being built. Harry Fowler hewed the logs and supervised the building bee. Tom Brown Sr. also purchased a cow that year. Hugh and Jim got the chore of finding the cow where she might be grazing anywhere within a radius of three miles. Hugh milked the cow morning and night, for which he received one quart of milk. If she kicked the bucket over and spilled the milk, he got nothing.

"There were plenty of fish in the lake in the early days, and by keeping a flock of hens and a couple of pigs, food wasn't too much of a problem in the summer, but winter was a different story. There was no such thing as fresh vegetables, fruit, or meat except deer meat, which passed around in season or out; people had to survive.

"One source of food was salmon. The government was operating a fish hatchery at Tappen and they had fish traps at the mouth of Scotch Creek. Some of the settlers raided the traps, picking out the best-looking fish, and after cleaning and cutting to size, they were stored in a barrel of salt brine and would keep over the winter.

"Brown beans were the order of the day and just about everybody had a large pot simmering on the stove with a slab of salt pork. The only fruits available were dried apples and prunes ("C.P.R. strawberries"). Sourdough pancakes were popular at that period, and Harry Fowler estimated that the Browns ate about seven acres of pancakes during the winter. This may have been a slight overestimate, but nobody contradicted him.

"In 1910 the only roads in the settlement were rough logging roads from the back country down to the lake. The only way to get to the railroad was by boat or over the ice when the lake was frozen over. The lake froze over every winter in those days - twenty-nine inches of ice was recorded one winter.

"Before travel to the outside came to a halt for the winter, people would stock up on necessities. The Thomas Brown supply would consist of four hundred pounds of flour, two hundred pounds of sugar, two hundred pounds of rolled oats, and fairly large quantities of lard, salt, butter, yeast, soap, etc.

"In the late fall, Tom Brown Jr. moved the family up Meadow Creek valley to an abandoned cabin formally owned by Billy Gray, who had found a better homestead. This was a rough winter for the family. Insulation was unknown in those days, and on a clear night stars could be seen through the shake roof, although it never leaked. Water had to be carried quite a distance from the creek. One good point - wood was plentiful, not like the prairie, where it took three days to get a load of wood.

"All through 1910 and on into 1911, Tom Brown (Thomas Jr.) had not received the money for the farm, and Mrs. Brown (who had endured five years in a sod shack on the prairie) wanted a house built of lumber. Without that money, they were unable to get a house started. In 1911 they again lived in the tent on the beach. On August 19th, William John Brown was born in the tent. Harry Fowler called him Billy Jack, and the name stayed with him.

"In the late fall, the family was again moved up to the old Billy Gray cabin. The school had been built during the summer, so Hugh, Jim and Jean had to travel about three miles to get to school. During the winter there was over five feet of snow in the valley, so travel was very difficult. They got home sometimes long after dark.

"That winter the money came through for the sale of the farm, and in the spring of 1912 building material was purchased from the Adams River Lumber Co. and the new house got under way with the help of all the brothers and good neighbors. Thomas McGowan drafted the plans for the house and supervised the building. The house was finished before the cold weather started; a barn was also built, a cow was bought, and things became a lot better for the Brown family.

"During the preceding years, Tom Brown Jr. worked wherever he could get work. One year he worked at Sorrento clearing land, and the only way for him to get there and back was by rowboat. He would row over on Sunday night and back on Saturday after work. He also cut cord wood in the winter, which had to be hauled to the lakeshore and stacked in piles for the sternwheelers that were on the lake at that time.

"In 1913 the provincial road building program got underway. Harry Fowler was put in charge of the work, and quite a number of the local residents found steady work for at least six months of the year, including Tom Brown, who drove team. Harry Fowler, who could do almost anything he put his mind to, surveyed by eye the route the road would take. He went ahead of the crew with an axe and blazed trees in the line the road would take, and it says a lot for his ability, as the route he laid out has hardly been changed to this day.

"By the time the road was completed to the lakeshore opposite Sorrento, landing slips had been built and a free ferry began operating to Sorrento skippered by Captain Ivens. The people of the north shore could now travel by team and wagon or horse and buggy to Notch Hill. The road building program went on for a number of years east and west along the lake and up into the back country. When the road building program was finished on the north side of the lake, Harry Fowler took his crew to Chase and built the road from Chase to Turtle Valley.

"Harry Fowler had a large workshop on his farm on Meadow Creek and this is where dances were held until the school was built on the lakeshore. The school then became the meeting place for all social activities. The Christmas concert was one of the highlights of the year, with all the school children doing their bit. After this was over, Santa Claus would arrive, and he would hand out presents to all the children. Then the benches would be pushed to the wall, the floor swept, and the dance would begin. It wouldn't stop until four or five in the morning. Ernie Buckingham and Noble Bragg, who came in with the survey crew and stayed in the district, were popular dance musicians of that era and when they were not available, Tom Brown Jr., Hugh and Jim supplied the music for a number of years. Although the quality of their music was a far cry from the orchestras of later years, it did fill a need at the time and since it was the only music available, it was not criticized too severely.

"It is of interest to note that many of the pioneers could add something to the entertainment of social gatherings of that time. Harry Fowler was very good at calling quadrilles and square dances and could get on stage and recite Robert Service poems of the north from start to finish without a note of writing. Charlie Riley was also good at calling the dances. Tommy McGowan would do the cake walk; Jean Brown would do the sword dance. Mrs. Bragg and Billy Gray would sing a duet, maybe "Danny Boy". Mrs. Bragg would get so emotional before the end of the song that tears would start, then most of the women in the audience would be in tears as well.

"Joe Brown and John Brown would contribute their singing ability. Tom Brown Jr. with his fiddle and Harold Noakes with his flute would supply the background music. Then there were other contributions as well such as the odd tap dance. Nobody but nobody ever missed these social events unless they had a broken leg or something. These shindigs were the only times a lot of people got to see each other because they lived quite a distance apart and travel was difficult.

"In 1915 a telephone line was strung along the new road, and people could communicate with the outside. 1916 was the year the first students graduated from the North Shuswap School. In the fourth reader class were Hugh and Jim Brown. In 1917, Thomas Brown Sr. suffered a severe stroke and was paralyzed. In 1919 a second stroke proved fatal. Mrs. Thomas Brown Sr. passed away in 1921."

The story of the many tragedies suffered by the Thomas Brown family reflects the fragility of life on the frontier in the early 20th century, where one careless step or stroke of bad luck could cause an injury that would prove fatal in the absence of readily available medical care at a hospital. Even if a hospital was available, and the patient was able to reach the hospital before becoming terminally ill, aggressive treatments such as emergency surgery, fluid resuscitation, blood transfusions, or even antibiotics simply weren't available. Pneumonia was a leading cause of death at the time, as was septicemia, diarrhea, shock, diphtheria, and tuberculosis. Prior to the advent of modern medicine in the early 1900s, 5% of all women died during childbirth, and 10% of infants didn't live to see their first birthday.

So many stories, so much history, so much tragedy. Life was unimaginably challenging in the early days of the Shuswap, as it was nearly everywhere else in the world, especially when you compare it to the lives we live now, in the 21st century, in a new millennium.

The details of life in the early days of the Shuswap that are recalled by James McCowan Brown provide us with a deeper understanding of the daily routines and admirable efforts of those courageous pioneers, struggling to make a safe and comfortable life for themselves and their families at a time when safety and comfort were scarce commodities. But safety and comfort were elusive, while danger and hardship were the norm for our heroes and heroines, as we shall see as we continue the rest of Ernie Buckingham and Jeanie Brown's adventure together. *[Ed. note – The complete memoir of James McGowan Brown is included as an appendix at the end of this book.]*

CHAPTER 5 – Buck and Jeanie, a Love Story

The following article appeared in the Agassiz Record (a local Shuswap newspaper), January 3, 1913:

"Celista: "Mr. and Mrs. Thos. Brown Sr. gave a wedding dance on the 27th in honor of their daughter Jeannie, who was married at Chase on Christmas day, to Ernest Buckingham. Never in the history of Celista has there been such a crowd at a dance. The schoolhouse could accommodate only about half of the dancers. Oliver Freeman came from Blind Bay with his launch, and when he had disgorged his cargo, it was found he had brought over 25 people. Judging from the numerous presents, both useful and costly, received by the young couple it was evident that both of them were very popular in the district."

Left: An early photo of Jeanie Brown, probably taken on her wedding day, 26 Dec 1912, that sits on the mantle of her granddaughter, Jeanie Dubberley, in Winnipeg (provided by Jack Brown)

Jean Brown 1894 - 1921
Wedding 26 Dec 1912

Right: The young Ernie Buckingham family, with Jeanie playing the mandolin and Ernie playing his violin, along with their first child, Laura, born in July of 1913 (provided by Jack Brown)

Ernie Buckingham was eight years older than Jeanie Brown. The young couple took over a homestead of 160 acres on a hill at Blind Bay on the southwest end of Shuswap Lake, and built a log house, consisting of one large room with an attic and a lean-to, with the help of local family members and neighbors. Ernie and Jeanie, both of whom were intelligent and highly competent, had a very busy life filled with hard work to ensure their survival, but they also found ways to have fun with their family. Ernie played the fiddle, Jean played the mandolin, and they entertained often in the Notch Hill settlement. Ernie, a happy and fun-loving man with a great sense of humor, was also known for his oral recitations, among them, "The Face on the Barroom Floor", a long,

Jean Brown and Ernie Buckingham

(The toddler is Laura - jwb)

tragicomic ballad about a drunken artist ruined by love that was made into a short film starring Charlie Chaplin in 1914.

Here is yet another mystery: Ernie was an outgoing, happy-go-lucky, ambitious, and hard-working man by now. Life was moving in a good direction for him, finally. And it appears that he considered himself an entertainer, possibly above all else. He played the fiddle, he became well-known around the area for his music, he gave oral recitations of lengthy famous poems. So, where and when did Ernie launch this alternative career? There is no indication in his tape that it began prior to his arrival in Revelstoke. However, everything points to the likelihood that he and Noble Bragg had been playing together for some time prior to that moment.

Celista, Shuswap Lake, British Columbia, Canada
Winter 1912 - 1913

L to R: Margaret (Gertrude) Ormond Hill Bragg (1892 - 1981)
Noble Searle Bragg (1890 - 1957)
Jane (Jeanie) Brown Buckingham (1894 - 1921) and
Ernest Silas Buckingham (1886 - 1977)

Left: Good friends, the Braggs and the Buckinghams, posing in front of the Buckingham home for an unknown photographer, with two dogs in the mix; Since Jeanie was in short sleeves, it is easy to assume that she had just slipped out of the warmth of their home for a moment. She would have been fairly early in her first pregnancy at the time. She delivered her first child in July of 1913. The details of the log cabin that was built by Ernie and his fellow homesteaders are worth noting, not to mention the two dogs patiently waiting in the snow. (provided by Jack Brown)

Below right: Ernie sitting in front of the house he and Jeanie built at Blind Bay to accommodate their growing family, date unknown (provided by Donald Dunbar)

Ernie sent a tape to Karen in the 1970s that includes examples of his fiddle playing

and singing. Included with the tape is a note that Ernie had hand-written: "The Arkansas Traveler is just an imaginary thought I had, and I kept adding on a bit here and there to make it more descriptive like. When I was around 18 *[Ed. note - i.e., still living in Saskatchewan]* I was in a little group that put on plays, in school concerts. It was just a short show piece, till the other actors got ready. I enlarged on it to a great extent, with the results you hear now. I had lots of fun making it, you may be sure. I hope you can get the trip idea. I had difficulties making the change of voices and kicking over the table…These are recitations I did in those old days also at concerts."

Right: Ernie Buckingham, Vancouver, 1940s (when he was in his late 50s)

The penmanship and grammar are both high quality, especially for a man in his 80s. We know that Ernie spent at least six years in classrooms, learning to read and write, absorbing the basics. The tape he recorded shortly before he died suggests that he was able to attend school while he was a foster child in England, living with the Willis family, but he never mentions receiving any formal schooling after he arrived in Canada. If he was acting and making music at school performances when he was 18, it even suggests he might have attended high school, at least erratically, although he doesn't mention this in either tape. However, it certainly confirms that he was highly intelligent.

One thing can be certain: Ernie had his fiddle, and it was a major part of his life from quite an early age. Regardless of where the road led Ernie, his fiddle was his constant, faithful companion who never let him down. Late into his life he was making music and even producing recordings that included his fiddle music. This writer suspects that, in the end, Ernie's fiddle was his best friend.

Below right: Early photo of the four oldest children of Ernie and Jeanie Buckingham, taken at the "Buck" Buckingham homestead on Blind Bay, ca. 1919, provided by Jeanie Dubberley. Laura Margaret (left), Jean Ellen(middle) and May Catherine are standing; Donald Angus (Stanley) is the infant sitting in the foreground. Note the rustic appearance of the fence in the background, emblematic of most homesteads.

Left: A happy, waving baby Stanley with his older sister, Jean Ellen, 1919; The two appear to be sitting in the same chair their mother, Jeanie, was using in the previous chapter. (provided by Jack Brown)

Jeanie and Ernie began their family quickly and produced five children: Laura Margaret was born in 1913; May Catherine arrived in 1915, Jean Ellen in 1916, Donald Angus in 1918, and Mina Marie was born in 1919. All indicators suggest that the young couple had developed a deep and abiding love for one another, and that their children were born of their passion for one another and for establishing a happy, thriving family on their homestead at Blind Bay. After a tumultuous and utterly deprived youth, Ernie had finally been able to find a modicum of stability and contentment in his life. It is easy to imagine that he could hardly believe his good fortune.

Jean Bosko, one of Ernie's granddaughters-in-law, wrote about him with great fondness: "He had homesteaded a piece of land where he and the family lived, next door to the Widmarks. They lived near a pond, Widmarks lived across the pond from them. When one of the children was being born, he would go out and holler across the pond and Mrs. Widmark would come running to help."

Left: Marie, youngest of the Buckingham children, in the chicken coop at the "Buck" Buckingham homestead on Blind Bay, ca. 1920 (provided by Donald Dunbar)

Despite the incredibly hard work required by every member of the growing family, this was a period in history when otherwise disadvantaged but ambitious members of society could become landowners in a spectacular New World, simply by applying their wit and will and muscle power to clear the land and establish a farm that could potentially grow into a prosperous, self-sustaining enterprise. Everyone in the neighborhood was undertaking the same journey, and everyone in the community worked together to help one another through their respective challenges and setbacks. The land was richly endowed with the necessary resources, the climate was moderate, the woods and waters teemed with food, and the surrounding forests seemed endless. Rivers flowed to supply power, and along with the many lakes in the region provided avenues of transport, both winter and summer, since roads were primitive, and railroads were scarce.

Right: Ernie and two of his daughters [Ed. note – probably Laura and May] feeding chickens at their homestead, early 1920s (provided by Donald Dunbar)

Right: Blind Bay Hall Costume New Year's Party, 1920. It is impossible to know if the Ernie Buckingham family are included in this photo, but it is equally impossible to imagine that they aren't. (Shuswappassion.ca)

An important edition of "The Story Behind the Photo", a contemporary blog by Jim Cooperman, a local Shuswap journalist, provides valuable insight into a fascinating aspect of the lives of early Blind Bay citizens, including Jeanie and Ernie. Jim's articles are posted on the *shuswappassion.ca* website.

Jim was preparing an educational guide to the book for use in the schools and stated: "For every page there will be suggestions for further research, study questions, links to more information and ideas for projects. Each of the hundreds of photos in the book can inspire the reader to ponder about the image, its significance, its history, and its backstory, as well as to compare it with other locations or situations.

"In the history of settlement chapter there is a box about how the pioneers celebrated the holiday season. One of the photos shows more than 75 Blind Bay residents and friends gathered in their hall posing in the costumes they wore for their annual New Year's Eve party held in 1920. This photo first appeared in Ann Chidwick's book *Voices of Settlers, Stories from the South Shore of Shuswap Lake.*

"The photo evokes many themes, including community social life, cohesiveness, and holiday joyfulness. One might wonder what occurred prior to the photo being taken, as there was likely much preparation needed prior to the event. And since there were no phones then, neighbours actually had to visit each other in person to spread the news of upcoming events, share costume ideas and materials and make plans.

"There are children in the group photo, which meant that, unlike today, these parties were for all ages and there was little concern for any problems resulting from over consumption of alcohol. Some of the costumes are old-fashioned formal wear, along with clowns, maids, butlers, and three people in blackface. Just two coal-oil lamps light the log hall, so the photographer likely used a hot flash in order to capture the image.

"Despite an evening of much gaiety, there is not one smile on any of the faces. In 1920, cameras were few and far between. Having one's photo taken was more of a solemn affair that involved holding still and looking serious. No doubt, once the photographer was finished, the crowd returned to party mode again with dancing, drinking, laughing, and flirting.

"Early Shuswap pioneer life was not just all work and no play, as one of the first structures built by most communities was a hall where they could get together for meals, dances, meetings, and holidays. In the case of Blind Bay, the first step was raising the funds to build the hall on donated land. Friends came to help from the north side of the lake, logs were hauled in with oxen and the women assisted by preparing pots of stew and cleaning up the site.

"The work lasted for only a week until the roof, built with pole rafters and shakes, was up. The grand opening on March 17, 1907, was well attended by 150 people dancing to a band playing square dance tunes, Nordic songs, and polkas. Over the following decades, the hall was well used for dances, drama productions, church services and sports, including badminton. People from communities around the lake would come by boat and if there was a storm, they would spend the night in the hall.

"Nearly every Shuswap pioneer community built a hall like the one pictured in Blind Bay and some of these continue to be well used today, including those in: Celista, Mara, Notch Hill, Cambie, and Silver Creek."

Ernest Silas Buckingham Homestead
Blind Bay, Shuswap Lake, British Columbia, Canada - circa 1919

L to R: Laura Margaret, Donald Angus, Jean Ellen and May Catherine Buckingham
(Donald Angus aka Stanley Ernest Kappel, Jean Ellen aka Fern Evelyn Morrison)

(provided by Jack Brown)

Above: Ernie, Jeanie, and three of their children, enjoying a "snow day" at their homestead in Blind Bay, ca.1917 (provided by Donald Dunbar)

Above: View of Shuswap Lake from the Buck and Jeanie's homestead, most likely taken in the early 1920s; Below, left and right: 1912 legal survey of Blind Bay that includes the 160-acre homestead of Ernie Buckingham, parcels 1, 2, 7 and 8 (both provided by Donald Dunbar)

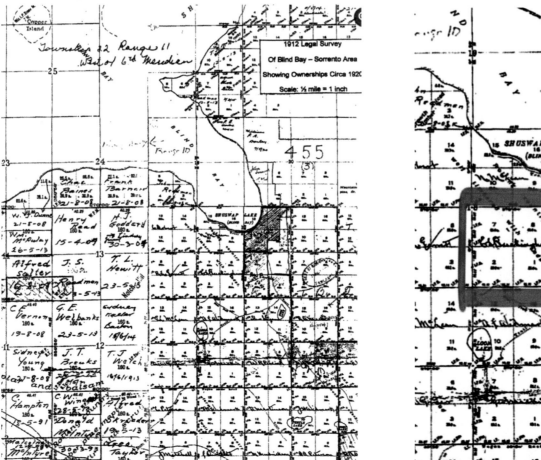

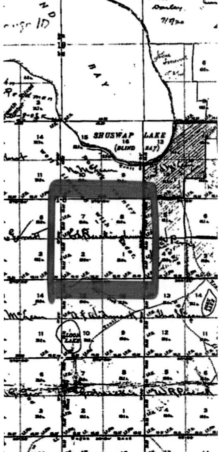

CHAPTER 6 – Tragedy Strikes Again

Jeanie became pregnant with a sixth child, then suddenly, on January 27, 1921, she passed away from complications of a ruptured ectopic pregnancy, a medical aberration that carried a high mortality rate at the time, especially in a remote area such as Blind Bay, where no hospital existed. This event was a bolt from the blue, and it was undoubtedly catastrophic for Ernie and his family. He struggled to cope with the grief and loss of his beloved life partner while facing the daunting task of raising five young children on his own, at least one of whom was still in diapers. Ernie soon realized he couldn't provide the care needed by five children ranging in age from one to seven.

In that time, in that remote district of British Columbia, it was difficult to find temporary foster homes for young children. That might have helped Ernie get through this difficult period until he could get back on his feet and take them all back into his own home. Few details are available regarding Jean's family, although we know that her parents lived in Celista, not far from Blind Bay. Jean's father, Thomas Brown, had died in 1919, and her mother died in November of 1921, 10 months after Jean's passing.

An article written by the youngest Buckingham, Marie, in 1977, adds important information to help us understand what happened immediately after Jeanie's death. It is accompanied by a photograph of Marie, who became Dora Immel, and appeared in the Kamloops Sentinel's Shoppers Guide on June 14th, page 26:

"Left to right: Florence, Bill and Gladys Immel (now Mrs. Albert Massey, Kamloops). Front: Dora Immel, an adopted daughter, who is the youngest child of Ernie Buckingham and his first wife Jeanie. Now D. Marie Dunbar, of 7776 Osler St., Vancouver, B.C. V6P 4C7, she writes:

BLIND BAY — 1924-25 WINTER

"Your article about the Rev. Grice Hutchison was of interest to me as he and his wife were very anxious to adopt me - however, Mrs. Immel decided to keep me. I believe that she probably regretted her decision occasionally later on, as whenever I was mischievous, she would say one of two things to me (sometimes both!) "I'll skin you alive" or "I wish I'd let Reverend Grice-Hutchison have you - he'd fix you". As everything around the homestead that needed "fixing" was repaired with bailing wire, binder twine, soldering, or whatever, I spent, in my childish innocence some rather anxious moments wondering just which of these methods the Rev. would have applied to me.

"In retrospect I have the greatest admiration for Mrs. Immel. Left a widow, (her husband had been tragically killed early in 1919 at the 8th Ave. railway crossing in Kamloops when his team of horses bolted) she had to manage the homestead with only the help of her three remaining children (a 13-year-old daughter Laura had died of diabetes) and the management of the Immel homestead - a large clearing on the north side of Blind Bay which is so visible in photographs of that era - must have been a monumental task for her. Not only did she have her own family, but for a while she had, along with me, my brother (later adopted by Frank Kappel of Sicamous and known as Stanley) and my three sisters. She raised chickens, rabbits, had horses and a cow, plus acres of raspberries and strawberries and the usual large vegetable garden. Children's diseases such as whooping-cough, scarlet fever and measles were not so well controlled then as now and most of us had them all. Along with the anxiety, there must have been mountains of extra laundry -all to be done by hand, of course.

"Though I am unsure about the actual date I can vividly remember "The year of the caterpillars". They were so numerous that they even impeded the normal progress of the trains at Notch Hill, as the tracks were covered with them. I was two or three at the time and was given a most important job -that of toddling along the rows of raspberries, and picking off the caterpillars which I dropped into a lard pail containing kerosene, that handle of which was looped through the belt of my rompers. Another of my tasks -a favourite - was to lead the very accommodating and affable old "Dobbin", who was pulling a stone-boat on which there was positioned a large barrel, down to the lake and again using a lard pail (though presumably not the same one!) I preceded to fill the barrel with water and then lead the horse back up to the house. I truly feel sorry for some of the children today. I had no toys geared to "ages 1-3" or "3-5" but I spent wonderfully pleasant hours playing with, and feeding the chickens and rabbits, the magpie which Mrs. Immel had taught to talk, picking wild strawberries, searching for lovely violets and other flowers which grew in profusion throughout the wooded areas, rolling about in Mrs. Immel's beautiful beds of tulips because of the very satisfying and fascinating "squeaks" this activity produced – (plus an inevitable "I'll skin you alive"!), going to the "crick" to get some butter out of a large crock that was kept cool there. And once encountering a fairly large bear who had removed the lid of the crock and was sitting there - placidly dipping one large paw into the crock while holding it with the other and favouring me with, as I thought at the time, a large buttery smile."

It is clear from Marie's well-written, charming, and evocative article that all five of Ernie's children went to live with Gladys Immel very soon after Jeanie's death. Others have written that, despite the crisis that had arrived so suddenly, Ernie needed to continue working to support his young family, which required him to be away from home for lengthy periods. In the absence of someone who could move into the household and take care of his children, Ernie had no choice but to farm them out to whomever was available to care for them.

No fewer than eight of Thomas Brown's 11 children had moved to Canada with their parents, and at least six of them lived in British Columbia, some close to where Jean and Ernie resided. It appears, however, that none of Jean's siblings were able to provide Ernie with much assistance after Jean's sudden and untimely death. This may have been due to physical separation alone: without automobiles, even a mile or two would have provided a daunting challenge for someone wanting to provide regular assistance to Ernie's suffering family.

Ernie's granddaughter, Jeanie Dubberley, daughter of Marie (aka Dora Immel, see above), has also proposed another reason why Jeanie's family may have been less than gracious in offering Ernie at least temporary help with his young family: "I have wondered too why Jeanie's many brothers and sisters didn't take the younger children. I wonder if there were any hard feelings left for Ernie, who got her 'into trouble', leading to a hurried marriage. They may have blamed him too for her early death, or he may have felt some bitterness towards them."

Fortunately, there were other options available to Ernie in addition to Mrs. Immel. Many of Ernie's neighbors, unable to have as many children as they wanted on their own, expressed a wish to adopt a child. Ernie, feeling he had no better choice, decided to adopt out his three youngest children, including Donald Angus. He was able to keep the two eldest daughters with him to help run the household. Having grown up fatherless and motherless (remember: his mother spent her last years in a workhouse and died when Ernie was only eight), there can be little doubt that Ernie's decision to give three of his children to other parents permanently was among the most difficult decisions he would ever have to make (even if he was also thinking how lucky it would have been for him if he had been adopted by a loving and supportive family when he was a young orphan in England).

Right: Stanley's birth certificate; Note mother's maiden name, <u>Jeanie</u> Brown

One possible added dimension of Ernie's suffering comes to mind: of the five children from his first marriage, only one was male. Donald Angus was Ernie's only son. With all possible respect for the four daughters in the family, one can readily appreciate how desperate Ernie was after Jeanie died, so desperate, in fact, that he gave up his only son, just as he had been given up by his own mother. At two years and three months, well into his "terrible twos", Donald was not only far too young to pull his own weight in the struggling family, but he would also have required so much supportive care in order to thrive that Ernie and his two eldest daughters (aged five and seven) decided it was impossible for them to take on such a gargantuan task as

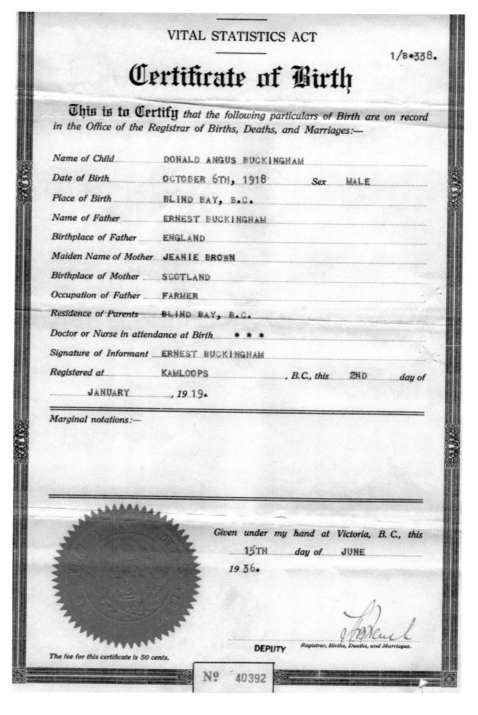

VITAL STATISTICS ACT

Certificate of Birth

1/B•338.

This is to Certify that the following particulars of Birth are on record in the Office of the Registrar of Births, Deaths, and Marriages:—

Name of Child .... DONALD ANGUS BUCKINGHAM

Date of Birth .... OCTOBER 6TH, 1918   Sex   MALE

Place of Birth .... BLIND BAY, B.C.

Name of Father .... ERNEST BUCKINGHAM

Birthplace of Father .... ENGLAND

Maiden Name of Mother .... JEANIE BROWN

Birthplace of Mother .... SCOTLAND

Occupation of Father .... FARMER

Residence of Parents .... BLIND BAY, B.C.

Doctor or Nurse in attendance at Birth .... * * *

Signature of Informant .... ERNEST BUCKINGHAM

Registered at .... KAMLOOPS .... , B.C., this   2ND   day of .... JANUARY .... , 19 19.

Marginal notations:—

Given under my hand at Victoria, B. C., this .... 15TH .... day of .... JUNE .... 19 36.

DEPUTY   Registrar, Births, Deaths, and Marriages.

The fee for this certificate is 50 cents.

Nº 40392

managing three younger siblings (aged four, two and one), in addition to themselves, while simultaneously trying to keep a demanding homestead from descending into ruin. To this writer it is little wonder that Ernie tried to reconnect with his only son years later, after Stanley Kappel had become a successful man and one that Ernie could be justifiably proud of.

Patricia Goldney Millar's biography of Ernie continues: "Ernie worked many places, including Chase where he worked for the mill.

"Two years later October 1923, Ernie married Constance Harrison of Pritchard. They lived in his old homestead, and several other places to accommodate Ernie's work. In 1927 they moved to the coast. They had two children; Elmer Ernest, born in Blind Bay; and Herbert Oliver, born in Vancouver.

"Ernie's first job in Vancouver was working for B. C. Electric on the streetcar tracks. The 1929 depression made jobs hard to get, but he always had his music. He formed an old-time orchestra, called the 'Joy Makers'; they played regularly on radio station CKMO and for dances; he also renovated houses. After the depression Ernie got a job in a furniture factory, where he learned the skills for his hobby, making doll furniture for his grandchildren, mechanical wood Ferris-wheels, houses, people etc.

"Ernie and Connie, and their family, continued to live and work in Vancouver. Connie worked in a gift and China shop in Vancouver; it was a job she really enjoyed. Constance died of cancer May 9, 1960.

"Ernie had a zest for life; he bought a two-pant suit for his 80th Birthday party and did the same for his 90th. He even checked with the hall committee in Burnaby to make sure the hall would be available in another ten years' time.

"During the summer, Ernie was a frequent visitor at the home of his daughter, Laura, and his son-in-law Bill, at Magna Bay, where he would entertain the young people with his fiddle and his recitations. He taught his great-grandchildren how to play crib.

"Failing eyesight and hearing, emphysema, and some heart trouble, didn't keep Ernie down. He would say "There's lots worse than me". He was visiting friends in Balmoral, Sorrento, playing his fiddle, when he had a fatal heart attack, July 23, 1977."

Ernie Buckingham: a fatherless boy who spent his earliest days in a workhouse, became an orphan at age eight, a British Home Child, then an emigrant, immigrant, farmer, pioneer, homesteader, builder, musician, storyteller, poet, husband, father, and grandfather, stands tall in the eyes of this humble writer. But he was, first and foremost, an entertainer, and for him, it was "all about the show", to borrow a few choice and memorable words from Terry Pratchett. Where Ernie found his muse, and where he found his voice, is impossible to divine from this distance. But wherever Ernie found himself from early in his remarkable life, he provided joy, laughter, merriment, and humor to the many fellow immigrants who journeyed with him to British Columbia and built a new community in a veritable wilderness. Ernie was an unabashed extrovert and was able to rise above the most unimaginably dire of circumstances.

Jean Bosko recently wrote that when she and her husband (Fair) would take Ernie from Vancouver to stay with them on the farm they had purchased near Shuswap Lake:

"He would stand on our property and look towards the lake (we couldn't see it at all). He told us where he lived in his early days in the area. I don't remember when his wife Jeanie died, but I think they lived there at that time. There was no water and he moved with the children down to a piece of land near the Shuswap Lake. I don't remember if that was before he had to give up some of the girls.

"He was always telling stories. His memory was amazing, he remembered people and where they lived (he hadn't seen them or talked to them in many years.) He would direct Fair where to go to see them and we would just drive up and Grampa would tell them who he was, and they would invite us in for tea. I was in awe how they remembered each other after no contact for so many years. We took several trips off in a strange direction to find someone he remembered and to my surprise they were still there. He loved visiting us on the farm."

Jeanie Dubberley also wrote a wonderful tribute to her grandfather, Ernie:

"This is a biography I wrote about him for the British Home Children Advocacy and Research Association FB group:

"My grandfather Ernie "Buck" Buckingham was one of them. The youngest of eight children whose widowed mother was in poor health, at the age of 11 he was sent to Canada from the Barnardo Home where he had been placed when he was 5. He was sent to Saskatchewan to live on a farm, where he was expected to work to earn his keep. He left the farm and went to B.C. where he homesteaded at Shuswap Lake. He married a young Scottish girl, and they had five children (my mother being the youngest). Two years after my grandmother died (just 27 years old) he married again and had two more children.

"Grandpa lived a long and happy life, dying just before his 91st birthday. He was a musician, playing the fiddle, banjo, mandolin and harmonica, and a talented woodworker, creating whimsical folk-art pieces.

"His descendants were his seven children, nineteen grandchildren, and many great-grandchildren.

"Although the lives of the children sent to Canada were often very difficult, with exploitation and abuse being common, many were able to transcend this difficult start to their lives. My heart goes out to the families of the many "home children" whose lives were scarred by the circumstances of their lives after being sent to Canada, and who never reconnected with their families.

"I do believe that my grandfather's life in England would have been far more difficult, and I suspect that his life would have been much shorter. When I look at the achievements of his children, grandchildren, great-grandchildren, and now many of the "great-greats", I can't help but be grateful that he ended up in Canada."

Ernie's obituary was published in Dr. Barnardo's Orphanage Christmas 1977 magazine:

"Ernest Buckingham left his country for Canada in July 1898 and in February this year his daughter, Mrs. Dunbar, wrote from Vancouver telling us that at the age of 90 he was in good health and spirits. Then in September when writing again Mrs. Dunbar said: "My father died on 23rd July during a cribbage game with an old friend whom he was visiting in the Shuswap Area he loved so much. It was exactly the way he had always wanted to go, so we were happy about that. We miss him very much." It has given us much pleasure to hear from Mrs. Dunbar and to receive a telephone call from her brother while he was over here on holiday, and we are sure that they have many happy memories of a very wonderful father.

We are glad, too, that we were able to renew contact with him through his family, if only for a few months."

This is such a beautiful, fitting tribute, written by Marie Dunbar, who was Ernie's youngest daughter. In 1977, Ernie's life story had come full circle, stretching almost all the way back to where it had begun in such profoundly challenging circumstances so many years earlier in Plymouth, England.

Ernie's son, by his second wife, finished "dictating" Ernie's marvelous tape recording of his early life story, since Ernie apparently never got back to finishing the tape after he stopped to make coffee. So, we will let Elmer fill in a few more details of Ernie's remarkable life:

ET: "The story was told by Ernest Silas Buckingham a few months before his death on July 24 (sic), 1977. The recording was found amongst his belongings, but unfortunately, we cannot find the ending to the story. So, we can only presume that he never did get around to completing the history.

"I am his son Elmer and will briefly describe the next 60 years of his life. Ernie and his buddy got the job with the survey party and worked the Shuswap Lake area for many years, and as he told you, played for many dances and parties throughout his lifetime. Some of the dates in his part of the story are out a few years. For instance, he was 12 years old when he arrived in Canada in 1898.

"Ernie married Jean Brown of Celista and had five children, Laura, May, Fern, Stanley, and Marie. All are living today, with exception of Stanley, who passed away at around 30 years of age.

"Ernie's wife Jean passed away, leaving him with the five children, living in a small homestead at Blind Bay, on the Shuswap Lake. He was unable to work and care for all of them, the youngest being only two or three years of age (sic). The three youngest were adopted out, leaving Laura and May to stay with Dad as they were older, about seven and eight, and could look after themselves with the help of the neighbours.

"Ernie married Connie Harrison of Pritchard and had two sons, Elmer, and Herbert. He tried the homestead again, but the lack of water made it impossible to farm. So, he went to Chase to work in the sawmill. He also held down various and sundry other jobs until 1926, when he moved to Vancouver. He worked for BC Electric for a few years, but with the... As with others, the Depression took its toll, and he was laid off.

"Ernie then fell back on his carpentry trade, which he had learned during the two or three-year period between survey jobs. He went into the renovation business and worked for many years around Vancouver.

"During the Second World War, he got a factory job, which he stayed with until he retired at about age 70. To augment his wages, he formed an orchestra and played for two to four dances a week for many years. This was an old-time dance band. In listening to his recorded music of late, we can only wish that recordings had been made when he was in his heyday. If there is time left on this tape, I will record a portion of his fiddle music as he played it in the last years.

"There are many things that could be told about Ernie, but this tape is almost over. If other histories are located, we will augment this tape with them. Thank you for listening."

Patricia Goldney Millar wrote: "Ernie was always a clean-shaven pioneer, when most men had full beards; it made him look younger...he was very good-looking. This was very evident in his early photographs. Learning photography and dark-room developing was a hobby he taught himself - so there was a legacy of photographs of his early life and his family."

Above: A portrait of Ernest Silas Buckingham painted in 1974; Ernie Buckingham's happy-go-lucky and cheerful disposition that is so well chronicled throughout his adult life by those who knew him suggests to this author that Ernie was not poorly treated in his childhood, in spite of the tragedy of his circumstances. It also suggests that Amanda, his mother, was a loving, caring mother who passed on to Ernie a sense of gratitude and hopefulness, coupled with enthusiasm and independence that seems to underscore his basic character and disposition. (provided by Donald Dunbar)

Above: Portrait of Ernie Buckingham painted by his son, Herb, in 1965

Here's an interesting tidbit: Jemima Brown, Jeanie's mother, was listed as a French polisher prior to her marriage to Thomas, according to the 1871 Scottish Census. This is a skilled profession, both interesting and tedious, that involves applying multiple coats of shellac to the surface of wood, resulting in a highly polished surface. The process is used in both the manufacture and the restoration of fine furniture and is still considered a skilled profession in high demand today. Jemima apparently stopped working outside the home after she and Thomas were married, although it is unclear whether she took in pieces of furniture to polish at home.

The question of how the families in our story were able to save enough money in order to move themselves and their often large families all the way to British Columbia, then establish themselves in a household before they could begin to start supporting themselves from their efforts on their homesteads and around the Shuswap District, is a mystery to this writer. But the possibility that Jemima may have been able to take in work at home while she was producing and raising a large family is interesting, and it may lend insight as to why a simple clerk with a large family was able to make it all the way to southern Canada by steamship and railway.

CHAPTER 7 – Frank Kappel, A Man for All Seasons

Three stanzas from "The Call of the Wild"
  -   By Robert W. Service

"Have you gazed on naked grandeur where there's nothing else to gaze on,
Set pieces and drop-curtain scenes galore,
Big mountains heaved to heaven, which the blinding sunsets blazon,
Black canyons where the rapids rip and roar?
Have you swept the visioned valley with the green stream streaking through it,
Searched the Vastness for a something you have lost?
Have you strung your soul to silence? Then for God's sake go and do it;
Hear the challenge, learn the lesson, pay the cost...

"Have you suffered, starved and triumphed, groveled down, yet grasped at glory,
Grown bigger in the bigness of the whole?
"Done things" just for the doing, letting babblers tell the story,
Seeing through the nice veneer the naked soul?
Have you seen God in His splendors, heard the text that nature renders?
(You'll never hear it in the family pew.)
The simple things, the true things, the silent men who do things—
Then listen to the Wild—it's calling you.

"They have cradled you in custom, they have primed you with their preaching,
They have soaked you in convention through and through;
They have put you in a showcase; you're a credit to their teaching—
But can't you hear the Wild?—it's calling you.
Let us probe the silent places, let us seek what luck betide us;
Let us journey to a lonely land I know.
There's a whisper on the night-wind, there's a star agleam to guide us,
And the Wild is calling, calling . . . let us go."

Happily, Donald Angus, the main character in our story, was adopted by a well-established and loving couple who lived in Sicamous on Shuswap Lake at a junction point for the North Okanogan and Canadian Pacific Railroads, not far from the Buckingham homestead at Blind Bay. Frank and Janet (Thomson) Kappel already had a daughter of their own but were unable to have any more children. They became Donald's proud parents and immediately changed his name to Stanley Ernest Kappel, honoring Ernie, along with Frank's brother, Stanley, in the process.

Frank Engelhardt Kappel was born in Neath, Glamorganshire, South Wales, on May 4th, 1886, the second of 4 children. His father, Carl Georg Ferdinand Kappel, was born in London of German ancestry but moved to Wales and married Elizabeth Powell, a local girl from Neath, in

1883. The 1901 Wales Census lists Carl Kappel as a retired wine merchant. Neath is located near Swansea and was the site of the Neath Abbey Ironworks, which operated between 1792 and 1886, the year Frank was born. Neath incorporated nearby Port Talbot on Swansea Bay, which served as a major copper ore importing conduit as well as a major coal exporting facility throughout the 19th and early 20th centuries.

Left: Painting of Neath bridge and town from the early 18th century by Charles Dean (Neath Port Talbot County Borough Council)

According to Britannica: "Coal, which underlies almost the whole surface of the Glamorgan uplands, began to be worked on a large scale toward the mid-18th century. Also during the 18th century copper and lead smelting had begun in the lower valleys of the Neath and the Tawe, using the local timber and ores brought by sea from Cornwall and North Wales. The prosperity of much of Glamorgan quickly came to depend on coal mining, and Cardiff grew from a small coastal town into the world's largest coal port by 1913."

Left: Etching of Neath, Glamorganshire, South Wales, ca. 1880, the place where Frank Kappel was born in 1886; The inscription reads: "View of Neath from the distance, with a steam train going to the left, mountain in the background with smoke coming out from a building at the top, rocks in foreground. (The British Museum)

Right: Portrait of the Carl Georg Ferdinand Kappel family taken in Wales, ca. 1902; Back row, from left: Charles, Carl, Frank; Front row: Ernest Stanley, Elizabeth (Powell), and Gertrude (provided by Lynne and Roger Beeson)

Frank wrote his memoirs to his five granddaughters in 1961 *[Ed. note – Throughout the rest of this book, Frank's memoirs will refer to the original document he sent to his granddaughters, along with other stories of his life that he provided through letters, personal interaction, newspaper articles, etc.]*: "These memoirs from "Grandpa" Frank Kappel, Eagle Bay, B.C. (Shuswap Lake) in 1961, were written to his grandchildren: Dale and Lynne Ingram of Victoria and Karen, Kristen & Kerry Kappel (the 3 KK's) of Spokane, WA., USA:

"My Dears:

"First let me say how proud I am to have such a wonderful bunch of granddaughters. I wish sometimes that one or two of you could have been boys, to carry on the name, but that was not to be, and I am well pleased the way it is, for you are all lovely girls.

"From time to time I have told you about incidents that happened in my young days, and you showed so much interest in them that you asked me on several occasions to sit down and write the story of my life, so that you and your children will have a better knowledge of what kind of a chap Grandpa Kappel was and what he did with his life. Unfortunately I never knew any of my grandparents – they all passed away either before I was born or I was too young to know them, so that actually I know nothing about them. But I have come to realize that grandparents are nice people to have around, to tell stories, to listen to one's little troubles, and they are usually a soft touch for a bottle of pop, a hamburger or the odd dollar for spending money. If at times I have appeared to be impatient with you, it is not because I loved you less, but because as one gets older one does not have the patience one had in one's younger days – and don't forget that you kids can be a little bit aggravating at times!

"This is the summer of 1961 and I am out in my cottage at Eagle Bay on the shore of the beautiful Shuswap Lake. I am now over three quarters of a century old, so I have had good long innings, but now the shadows are lengthening, evening falls for me, the busy world is hushed, the fever of life is over and my work is done. So before the light fails I had better get busy and write this story for you.

"My father was born in London, England, of German ancestry, my mother in Neath of pure Welsh stock. My father, a fine man, was in the Wine and Spirit business at Neath, and apparently was very successful, for he retired at a comparatively early age, though he later lost a lot of money in some unfortunate coal-mining ventures. He was inclined to be a somewhat strict disciplinarian – he carefully supervised our studies and while he would reprimand us for our failures at times to come up to his standard, he was most generous in rewarding us for work well done. He died in 1910.

"Mother was a wonderful woman. In those days domestic help was plentiful and cheap, and we always had maids in the house so that Mother was able to devote a lot of time and care to her family. We had a lovely home at Neath and did a lot of entertaining. Both Father and Mother came of genteel families, and were away above in social and educational background. One of Mother's brothers was a celebrated lawyer, became a Member of the British House of Commons, and ended up as Senior Judge of the British Exchequer Court. He was knighted by Queen Victoria. A nephew of mine by marriage, Sir Ian MacLennan, is in the British Diplomatic Corps, and at the present time is British Ambassador to the Republic of Ireland. He was knighted a few years ago by Queen Elizabeth.

"When I was four years old, my brother Charlie and I went to an "Infants School" at Neath – something like the present-day kindergartens except that we delved right into the three "R"s – Reading, Writing and Arithmetic, so that when we were old enough to enter public school, we did not have to start in the baby class. At nine years of age I started in the Neath County School, which would be the equivalent of today's high school. There again, thanks to the tutoring we received at home and during the holidays, which we spent at our Summer home at Porthcawl, we started in a higher class, and right away we had such subjects as Grammar, Algebra, Euclid, Chemistry, French, Latin and other subjects – and of course, lots of homework.

Left: Namur, Belgium, ca. 1900, where Frank Kappel spent his first two years at a Catholic boarding school after leaving his home in Wales, learning French; Below left: Trier, Germany, ca. 1900, around the time when Frank Kappel was there to study the German language; It is a city on the banks of the Moselle River, founded by the Celts in the late 4th century BC and conquered 300 years later by the Romans. Trier is considered Germany's oldest city, and is also the oldest seat of a bishop north of the Alps.

"Both Charlie and I matriculated in 1901, and we were then given the choice of entering a profession or going abroad to study foreign languages. Charlie chose the law, but to me travelling abroad appeared more interesting, so I chose the latter. The next two years I spent at a large boarding school in Namur, Belgium, where I studied French. It was a Catholic school, run by the Christian Brothers, and I was one of the very few protestants there. In spite of my French studies at school, I found, when I was dumped amongst French boys who could not speak any English, that I could not express myself in French, so if I wanted to mix with them, I would just have to dig in and learn to speak French, and it was surprising how quickly I achieved this objective, and at the end of the two years I had acquired a pretty good knowledge of the French language.

"The following year I went to Germany; Dad came over with me, and before he settled me down at Trier, on the Moselle River, at the home of a German schoolteacher who had been recommended to him, we took a trip down the Rhine River to Frankfurt which was most interesting. At the teacher's home in Trier there were two French boys who were there for the same purpose as myself, to learn German – we attended the teacher's classes where language was taken, and in the evenings we had private tutoring from the teacher at his home, so at the end of the year we had acquired a good knowledge of this language also, as we had all received German lessons before going to Trier.

Right: Kassel, Germany, main square and train station, ca. 1905. Also known as Cassel, this is the city where Frank Kappel lived from 1905 for one year

"It seemed to me then that I had been long enough at school and that I should start out on my own. So, without saying anything to Dad, I hunted me a job and got the position of foreign correspondent at a little place called Ludenscheid in a factory where they made fine copper and bronze wire, most of which was exported. Here I gained office experience and this helped me to get a much better job at Kassel in a similar capacity; I stayed there nearly a year, and Kassel was an interesting place to live, but I wanted to get to a large city, so I applied for a job with Germany's largest steamship company, the Hamburg-American Line, at Hamburg. They asked me to come up for an interview, and I got a good job there right away. I stayed with them for five years. In 1908 they sent me to Spain for eight months to get acquainted with their agencies in that country, and I spent some time at all the ports in Northern Spain and in Portugal, and when I returned to Hamburg I was given another promotion. During my stay in Spain I managed to get the odd week in Madrid and saw many Spanish bull-fights, which were gory but thrilling.

"Hamburg was a very fine city. It was the custom in those days for merchants in other countries to send their sons to Hamburg to learn German business methods, so I associated there with young men my own age from all parts of the world, and we really had a gay time. Amongst other activities I was a member of a rowing club and took part in many regattas in four and eight-oared boat races. I still have some of the trophies we won at these events. One year, after the training was over, five of us took a boat and made a two-weeks trip through the rivers, canals and lakes of Northern Germany, camping out and enjoying ourselves. At the end of the trip, still having a week's holidays in hand, we went to Berlin and spent a few

days there. My contacts with these chaps from practically every country in the world were most interesting, and I gained insight into the life in those countries which I could not have got from books. I mixed with all colours and creeds amongst them. They were a nice bunch of boys.

Above left: Frank Kappel, third from our left, crewing in the Summer Regatta at Schwerin, Germany, 1908, when Frank was living and working in Hamburg (SPC); Below left: Hamburg, Germany, ca. 1900, where Frank lived from 1906 until 1910

"One day in 1910 my friend Roland Salt and I were sitting in the Club feeling pretty fed up with Germany and everything German. Up to about that time the British were very popular in Germany, and the natives liked to associate with them and copy their manners, their clothes, etc., and of course they loved to ventilate what knowledge they had of English. But gradually the feeling was changing. The old Kaiser had for years been building up a great and powerful military machine, and to justify the huge expenditure of the taxpayers' money he had to do something with these millions of trained soldiers who were all dressed up and had no place to go. Besides, the population was getting too large for the available room, and more "Lebensraum" – room to expand – was needed. The British Empire at that time was at its peak of power, and owned most of the world's desirable real estate – the Empire on which the sun never set. The Germans cast covetous eyes on all these overseas colonies, which they of course could only acquire by means of a successful war against Britain. So an anti-British complex was being fostered and this led eventually to World War I."

Other factors may also have influenced young Frank Kappel's decision to emigrate to Canada. The British government waged an aggressive campaign to encourage emigration for many decades, starting in 1870. "Westward the Star of Empire Takes Its Way" is the Imperial message at the bottom of the second poster below. Another important message says, "There's Nothing to Fear" when immigrants arrive and settlers are "Protected By the Government", which implies the Royal Canadian Northwest Mounted Police. But what might British settlers fear? American-style lawlessness on the Canadian "frontier"? Contact with native people, perhaps? Canadian First Nation people were hardly ever mentioned in immigration material except to reassure readers they had "nothing to fear".

Multiple editions of pamphlets advertising the attractiveness of emigrating from Britain to Canada were printed, including the one below, printed in 1910 by the Immigration Branch, that is entirely Welsh. Other editions were printed in Gaelic for potential emigrants from rural Scotland.

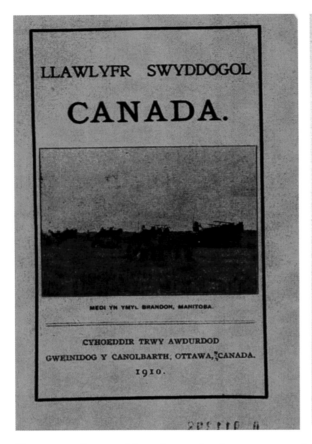

Poster and pamphlet above, both courtesy of the National Library of Canada [Ed. note – The red cover is printed in the Welsh language; Frank didn't speak Welsh, but his mother did.]

The prospect of being able to obtain the right to 160 acres of free land through one's own hard work and determination was given special emphasis and was advertised widely throughout the British Isles. Both the British and Canadian governments also advertised as heavily as the law would permit in many countries across Europe, using as many venues as possible to publicize their message. This included cooperating with steamship owners who were eager to book passages to North America, Western Europe, Scandinavia and Eastern Europe on their growing fleet of passenger liners as part of their campaign. Having lost the United States from the Empire during the Revolutionary War, Britain was not about to lose its hold on Canada as one of the premier jewels in its crown.

According to the Canadian Museum of History: "Encouraging British and European immigrants to settle on the prairies was part of Prime Minister Sir John A. Macdonald's plan to establish Canadian sovereignty over the newly acquired North-West Territories. Stretching from Ontario's border to British Columbia, (still a British colony), the Territories were transferred to Canada by the Hudson's Bay Company in 1869. Settlement was an urgent matter, and so was a railway to carry settlers west. There was already talk in the mid-western United States of expanding north of the border. Sir John's promise of a trans-Canada railway persuaded British Columbia to enter Confederation in 1871.

"The Canadian Pacific Railway, so necessary to opening up the Territories to large-scale settlement, was a massive project that took many years to finance. Surveying prairie land for railway-building and white settlement signalled displacement to Native people and the Métis, and an end to their traditional way of life. 1885, the year the CPR was completed, was also the year of the second Metis uprising, and the execution of its leader, Louis Riel.

"When Laurier became Prime Minister in 1896, he appointed Clifford Sifton to the key portfolio of the Interior, with responsibility for the twin fields of immigration and land settlement.

"Sifton was a successful Manitoba businessman, lawyer, land speculator and former Cabinet member in the Manitoba government. He was also a dynamic western booster, and as publisher of the influential *Manitoba Free Press*, he well understood the power of advertising.

Right: "The Wonderful Canadian Arch in Whitehall", erected near Buckingham Palace in London, 1902 (Look and Learn, Illustration of Charles Edwin Flower for The Coronation Book of Edward VII by WJ Loftie, Cassell 1902); 56 feet high, and 60 feet wide, the whole structure being capped by an open lantern with a roof of crown formation; It is "thatched" with wheat sheaves from Manitoba, and Canada's national emblem, the maple leaf. (Canadian Museum of History website)

Suffice it to say that Sifton's campaign was a multi-faceted and multi-media blitzkrieg. "The Wonderful Canadian Arch in Whitehall", as the *London Sphere* described it, was erected on the ceremonial route from Buckingham Palace to Westminster Abbey for the coronation of King Edward VII in July 1902.

"Sifton immediately hired energetic, experienced communicators and promoters to spread the word those vast areas of good prairie land were open for settlement, and 160 acres of that land were available free to every agricultural settler. The advertising campaign focussed on three major sources of agricultural immigrants: the United States, central and eastern Europe, and Britain, the over-populated "mother country" and hub of the British Empire. Sifton's timing was perfect.

"Clifford Sifton's staff seized the opportunity to combine Imperial sentiments with a magnificent advertising opportunity. Photographs of the arch *[Ed. note – "The Wonderful Canadian Arch in Whitehall"; see caption next to the photograph on the previous page]* appeared in newspapers throughout Britain. Brilliantly lit with electric lights, messages on both sides of the arch were visible night and day. "Canada. Britain's Granary. God Bless Our King and Queen" appeared on the side facing Buckingham Palace. The message on the other side read "Canada. Free Homes for Millions. God Bless the Royal Family."

Below: The poster on the left, from 1893, shows Canada's five new Experimental Farms, where crops best suited to each region of Canada were developed and tested. A Canadian Pacific Railway advertisement appears at the bottom of this poster, which was produced by the Department of the Interior. (National Archives of Canada, Government Archives TR 76/12)

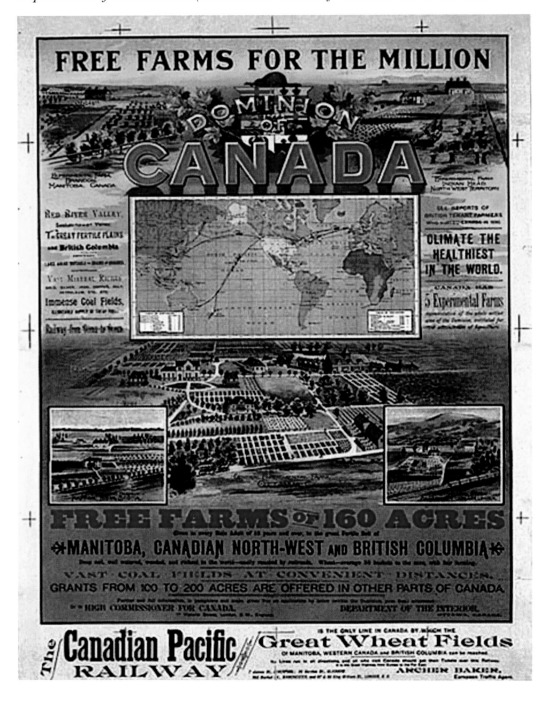

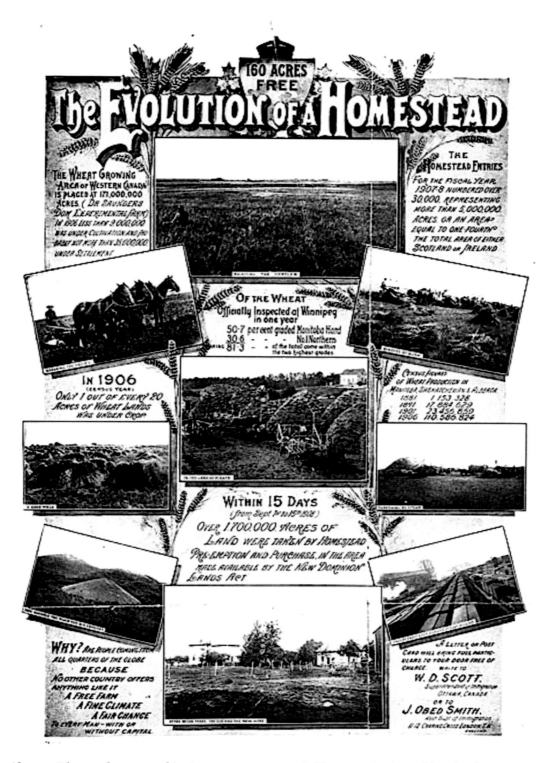

Above: These photographic images were specially commissioned by the Immigration Branch, incorporated into a poster, and probably used again in other formats as suited illustrations for pamphlets, and as hand-coloured lantern slides to accompany lectures by Canadian agents. (National Archives of Canada C-126300)

This advertising extravaganza surely did not escape young Frank Kappel's attention. A German-language pamphlet was published and circulated throughout the country during the time Frank was living in Germany.

Canada

Arbeit
Löhne
Land

Die Eisenbahn-Route nach einer freien Farm

Leute gesucht, die dazu passen und energisch sind

Herausgegeben auf Verordnung des Ministers des Innern, Ottawa, Canada
1908

The 1908 German-language pamphlet to the left reads:

"Canada. Work, Wages, Land. The Railway Route to a Free Farm" is the title of this pamphlet, which also appeared in Scandinavian languages. Inside the pamphlet reads:

WANTED

*14,000 men to build Railways in Canada.
100,000 men to take, cultivate and own farms in Canada.
Highest wages in Railway work.
160 acres of the best land in the world free.
The industrious poor man's chance....
(National Library of Canada)*

CHAPTER 8 – Time for a Change: Frank Emigrates to the Shuswap

Getting back to Frank Kappel's memoirs: "Roland and I decided we had had enough of it. So there and then we made up our minds to give up our jobs and move to pastures new. That brought the question of where to go. I had friends in the Argentine to whom I could go any time, in Mexico, in Guatemala, in the U.S.A. and in Canada. We discussed the merits and disadvantages of all these possibilities and finally decided on Canada. Two factors made us come to this decision – first, we would be among British people who spoke our language and whose way of life were the same as ours, and secondly, I was engaged to be married to a very charming Scottish lady, whom I met in Germany where she was studying art, whose family *[Ed. note - The William Thomson family, for whom Thomson Hill in Celista was named]* had moved to Canada a couple of years earlier and had settled in British Columbia. Their new home was on a beautiful lake called the Shuswap Lake, and we thought we would go there first and make that our headquarters while looking around for some place to settle and find employment. So next day we told our respective employers in Hamburg of our intention, and in spite of the glowing picture they painted to me of my future prospects with the company, they could not change my mind.

"So in due course I left Hamburg and went back to Wales for a three months holiday, the first long holiday I'd had at my parents' home since I was a boy. The company asked me to let them know about when I was going to leave England, and I did this and received a reply advising me that they had booked passage for me on one of their big liners to New York, luxury accommodation etc., with the company's compliments. When I arrived at New York I was met at the boat by one of the company's officials who informed me that he had been instructed to look after me, show me the sights of New York, take me anywhere I wanted to go, all at the company's expense. This was very unexpected, and I spent a very pleasant and interesting two weeks there. Then to Montreal and after that the next step was across Canada to Notch Hill, British Columbia, where I arrived late in the evening of April 2nd, 1911. *[Ed. note – Frank and Roland sailed on the S.S. President Lincoln, owned by the Hamburg-Amerika Line, from Southampton on March 13th, 1911, arriving at Ellis Island on March 24th, occupation listed as merchant, status listed as "in transit to Notch Hill."]*

Right: Detailed map of Sicamous and environs, including Magna Bay at the center on the north shore of Shuswap Lake, where Frank and Janet set up their first household in 1912, and Blind Bay, where Ernie and Jeanie Buckingham set up their homestead in 1912 (North Shuswap First Responders)

They were supposed to have been met by a

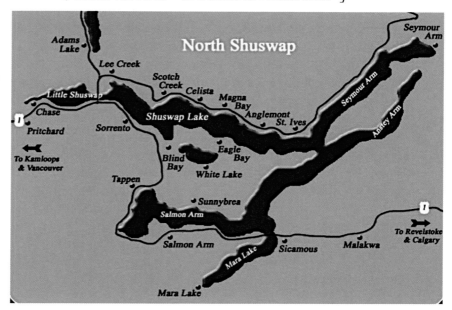

member of the Thomson family on their arrival at Notch Hill, which lies on the south side of the main body of Shuswap Lake: "I had been told to stay at the Royal Hotel at Notch Hill if there was no one at the station to meet me. As a matter of fact there was no one at the station to meet me, as ice conditions on the lake were such that it was not safe to walk over on the ice, but it was impossible to push a boat through the slush, so I had to wait three days before communication with the North Shore could be established. For two or three days on the train I had been looking forward to a nice hot bath on arrival at Notch Hill, but to my dismay I was informed that the "Royal" Hotel did not boast a bathroom nor any inside plumbing!

Instead of the delay posing an inconvenience to Frank and his friend, spending a few nights at proved its advantage. The newcomers were treated like royalty by the barman and the mostly male hotel lodgers, since the arrival of anyone from England was apparently always a cause for celebration. The barman opened a couple of bottles of champagne, much to Frank's surprise, and a good time was had by all. Next day he and Roland walked down to the shore of the lake.

Left: 1912 photo of the Royal Hotel at Notch Hill; The caption reads: "The Royal Hotel must have been the place to stay in Notch Hill. Built on Davies Road, it fronted the C.P. Railway tracks. Gertrude Hill and Noble Bragg [Ed. note – Ernie Buckingham's "Buck and Bragg" sidekick] were married there on March 9, 1912. (Salmon Arm Museum)

Frank's memoirs continue: "Finally, I saw the Shuswap Lake and it was a case of love at first sight. In all my travels I had never seen a more beautiful lake, and I decided right then that I had no need to look any further for a place to settle down.

"Within a few days the icy conditions improved and I was able to get a boat across the lake to Celista, where most of Janet Thomson's family had their homesteads. I quickly found employment and was able to accrue the means to build a suitable home for a family. The Thomsons made me feel very welcome. When I told them how impressed I was by what I had seen of the area, and how much I desired to establish a home there, they immediately showed me a few areas they had picked out for a potential homestead.

"In those days a Homestead Law was in effect whereby a prospective settler could file on a quarter section of land, 160 acres, and when he had complied with certain regulations regarding residence and putting an area of land under cultivation, he was granted clear title. There were very few settlers around the lake at that time so one had plenty of choice. I quickly found a partial homestead at Magna Bay that was available because the man who had built a sturdy log cabin and also done some of the clearing required to pre-empt a homestead had recently been found dead on the shore of the lake near his home. So I went down to Kamloops to see the Dominion Land Agent about purchasing the homestead. It was about 87 acres, right on the lake shore, and when the agent asked me how much I thought the improvements were worth, I told him "about $200". He sent a communication to the man's family in England, and pretty soon I was the happy owner of my new home.

"My homestead was on the lakeshore at Magna Bay, almost straight across the lake from Eagle Bay where I now am. Then I went to work, and I soon got acquainted with a double-bitted axe, a cross-cut saw and a mattock and started cutting down trees and making a clearing. After the trees were down, they had to be burned and the stumps had to be pulled; for this latter job we had to get the help of a team of horses or of oxen – sometimes horse and ox were hitched up together, and the big stumps were blasted out with dynamite.

Right: Early 1900s homestead, or "stump ranch", overlooking Shuswap Lake, similar to what Frank Kappel's homestead on Magna Bay may have looked like (SPC)

"The community spirit on the north shore of Shuswap Lake was wonderful, and the "old-timers" were very helpful to us newcomers. They would take us under their wings and show us how to do the things we needed to learn to succeed. And we would help them in exchange, doing unskilled work or whatever they might need. Clearing land was the biggest job. We had to cut the trees down and burn them and pull the stumps out. For this latter job it was necessary to get the help of a team of horses or oxen using a special stump-puller. Sometimes horse and oxen were hitched up together, but if that didn't work the big stumps had to be blasted out with dynamite.

"My next job was to build a house, something I knew nothing about. The cabin built by the previous owner wasn't suitable for a family, so I soon learned about double-bladed axes, cross-cut saws, and mattocks. I arranged for two young men in the area to help me cut cord wood on the property in order to get some cash in hand, and we shared the profits. Any logs that were suitable for a log house were put aside and the rest we cut for cord wood.

"There was no land-clearing machinery available, so the work was slow and hard. Long, straight trees were peeled and hauled into a pile on the site where I intended to build my house. In the fall, with the assistance of neighbours, we had a "bee" and got the walls up and the roof on before winter set in. The skilled axe men came and worked the corners, notched them and so on to make certain they were solid and secure. And the ladies would come and bring lunch.

"We would have dances in the schoolhouse in the evening if there was a reason to celebrate. The women would bring their kids with them, we would pile the desks against the wall, and the babies were tucked in there and covered up. There was always lots of volunteer music, a guitar and a fiddle and a banjo, but no piano. As I said, the members of the community were very sociable. It was a rough life for most people in those early days, no one had much money, but everyone pitched in to make our lives as enjoyable as possible. We also attended dances in Notch Hill on occasion. We'd go out on Blind Bay in a rowboat, pull it up on the beach, and walk over the hill about five miles to Notch Hill and dance all night, returning to our homes after the sun came up and it was safe to be out on the lake.

"Winter came early that year, and practically all the lumber I used in the house had to be hauled across the ice from Sorrento on sleighs drawn by horses. Good progress was made during the ensuing months, and by spring the house was almost ready for the finishing work inside, and I had become fairly proficient as a carpenter.

"In the spring of 1912, my house was pretty well completed, my fiancée came out from Europe, and we got married in Kamloops on June 24, 1912. In due time we would become parents, but in the fall of 1912 the weather was bad, and it looked like an early winter. I thought it was just not right to expose my new wife, in her first winter in Canada, to the rigours of six months or more in the bush, with no amenities and few neighbours.

"So we went to Vancouver where I discovered there was no demand for a man who spoke several languages. Instead I got a job right away in a Chartered Accountants office, making $100 a month. We rented a nice little furnished house in North Vancouver where Betty was born the following year. During the winter I was sent to Kamloops to audit the city books for the year 1912, and then on to Salmon Arm to do the audit of the municipality. It was my first independent audit, and everything went fine. By summer Jenny and I were back on our homestead."

"When we first moved to our new home at Magna Bay, there were no real roads, only primitive access roads for individual homesteads. In order to cross the lake, we had to go down to Scotch Creek and cross on a ferry. The man who operated the ferry was paid by the government to take people across because there was no school on the south side. Since the nearest school was located at Sorrento, across the lake from Scotch Creek, the kids had to cross on that ferry to get to school.

"As I said, back in those very early days, transportation wasn't easy, and using horses to get around was popular. So in the fall of 1912 I went down to Chase and bought a team of horses from the natives down there, a team of Cayuses. You could get a nice little horse there for $25 in those days. I took a friend down with me, and I bought the two horses and they lent us a couple of saddles to get back to Magna Bay.

"Since there were very few roads, we had to follow the lake shore in most places until we came to some game trails that had been slashed out. It was in the fall of the year and the salmon were running in the lake. In fact, Adams River and Scotch Creek were some of the greatest salmon spawning locations anywhere in BC. When we came to the river you couldn't see its bed, it was just covered with the fish. The fish apparently don't eat anything from the time they leave salt water until they get up to their spawning place.

"Once they arrive at their destination and finish with their spawning the fish would lie on the beaches around the lake and die. I would take advantage of this in the fall, especially the year I was planting an orchard. I dug the holes for the trees first, and there were so many dead salmon that I put two or three big fish in each hole. They made wonderful fertiliser, even though they smelled pretty bad.

"Money was not the all-important factor it is today, our wants were few, we were frugal in our way of life, but still we had to eat, and many of the settlers spent three or four months of each year working out in the harvest fields or in the mines, and the proceeds of their labour would keep them in groceries for the rest of the year. In the process of clearing the land, many of the settlers would cut logs for the sawmills and cordwood for the stern-wheel boats which towed booms of logs to the mills at Chase and Kamloops. All this was hard work, and the country is indebted to the old pioneers for opening up districts which otherwise would still be uninhabited. Some people say these pioneers were crazy to try to make farms out of the bush, miles away from transportation, but it was this spirit of craziness which helped to make Canada the great country it is today, and built a railway line from the Atlantic to the Pacific. The old pioneering spirit is not much in evidence today, and the young people who remained on the farms are reaping the advantage of the work their fathers did to make these farms out of the virgin bush."

Right: Road building crew at near Sicamous, ca. 1910, [Ed. note – Frank Kappel and Ernie Buckingham worked on them to earn cash when they first arrived in the Shuswap]; Frank is 3rd from the left in the middle row. (provided by Lynne and Roger Beeson)

"Like the other settlers, I did various jobs to earn some money to finish and furnish my house and carry on with the land clearing. I worked on the Government road as an axeman and also as a teamster. I remember one time the foreman on the road, Harry Fowler, the oldest of the old-timers, told me to go to the barn and bring out the team there to hitch on to the grader. I found two big horses in the barn and a miscellaneous collection of harness hanging up on the wall. Now, I did not know the difference between a hame-strap and a bellyband, and my efforts to get the harness on the horses were not very successful. However, a friend of mine passed by and saw I was in difficulties, so he came in and showed me how to harness the team, and I marched out behind the team, hitched it on to the grader, shouted Gee and Haw and everything was lovely. I stayed on as teamster for a couple of weeks until the regular teamster came back on the job.

"Another job I tackled was carpenter on the Government Wharf that was then being built at Magna Bay. I had lots of nerve calling myself a carpenter, but managed to get away with it, and hung on to it until the job was completed. Then, in the spring of 1914 my brother and I went to the coast and got work at the Britannia Mine on Howe Sound, working underground. This really was a new experience for us, but we learned quickly and came away with some money in our pockets. After all, swinging a shovel did not call for many brains. When a person takes a job of any kind, he must give the best he has to do the work properly, as well he can. Heaven helps those who help themselves.

"When I got back to Magna Bay I found that the position of Fire Warden was about to become vacant; I applied for it and got it. Fortunately that first year there were no fires in my district, and I made good use of my time going over all my territory, learning the theory of firefighting, and making friends with the people. All my travelling was on horseback, as there were no cars and few roads and trails; I also did much of my ranging by boat, from the center of the lake where I could pretty well see the whole district. The following year there were lots of fires and I really had a busy time. The Chief Ranger at that time was Jim Evans of Salmon Arm, and he was wise enough to leave all the responsibility to the individual ranger.

"One day I was really worried – the weather was hot and dry, and I had a dozen fires burning. Someone told me that old Jim had just passed in his car and as I wanted to see him badly and report on the fire situation, I just camped in the middle of the road awaiting his return. He greeted me with, "Well Frank, what's all the excitement about?" – I told him my sad story of all the fires burning, and his reply was, "Well, well. Have you got crews fighting the fires?" Yes. "Have you got a good foreman on each of them?" Yes. "Are they getting plenty of grub?" Yes. "Well, what more can you do except pray for rain. Remember that next Winter we will be having snow again, and the fires will all be out!" And he jumped in his car and left. That was a fine lesson for me, and it taught me to always keep calm and collected in an emergency – worrying and getting excited never helps.

"A special character I remember was the old postmaster, Riley, a Cockney man who ran a hotel and store at Notch Hill. When I bought my two horses at Chase in 1912, one of them was a mare, pretty heavy in foal, and I was worried because I'd never been present at a birth. So I went to this old postman and asked if he would look after the mare for me when it came time for the birth. He said, sure, you let me know. And everything turned out fine.

"Now a word about your grandmother, my wife *[Ed. note – Janet "Jenny" Thomson]*. She was a truly wonderful wife and mother, and we were happy together for thirty-four years. She was a great help to me in every way, as she was to all who came to her for help and advice, and they were many. She was kind, generous, a talented artist, gifted with a sharp mind, always a gracious hostess, and a real homemaker. Our home at Sicamous, as with the one at Magna Bay, was the center of the social life of the community. We were blessed with two children, Betty and Stanley, and they and their friends helped to liven things up and make "Kappel's place" a wonderful place to have fun and parties. Mother's death in 1946 was a sad blow not only to the children and me but also to the whole community.

"Going back to 1914. On August 4th of that year war was declared. After I got my affairs straightened out, I went to Kamloops with Uncle Tom *[Ed. note – Tommie Thomson]* and some of the other local boys and we all enlisted in the 54th *[Ed. note – Canadian Battalion]*. Many of these boys unfortunately never came back. In a short time our battalion, which was stationed at Vernon, entrained for overseas and went into camp at Bramshott in Southern England. The weather was terrible and the camp was a sea of mud, so when the sergeant major on parade one day called for men experienced in auditing, I thought here's a chance to get out of the mud, and I stepped forward. Next day I was on my way to London, where Mother and Betty were staying. I got into the Audit Office of the Canadian Corps and was quickly promoted to Staff Sergeant. But when the Spring came I wanted to get to France and applied for and obtained a transfer to the Canadian Artillery and was posted to a battery using 8" Howitzers. We took an intensive course in guns at Cooden Camp, on the South coast, and were soon in France and a few days afterwards, we were in action. It was heavy work – our shells weighed 200 pounds each – but it was interesting.

54ᵗʰ Ky. Batt. C.E.F. (Vernon B.C. 1915)

Above: The entire 54ᵗʰ Kootenay Canadian Infantry Battalion, consisting of 1,111 men and 36 officers, included a brass band and the battalion mascot "Koots", a black bear cub who can be seen just above the word "C.E.F." (Sicamous and District Museum and Historical Society)

Right: Photo of the "Shuswap Lake Boys" taken at Vernon, B.C. in 1915 (provided by Jack Brown)

"Shuswap Lake Boys" (with) 54ᵗʰ Ky. Batt. C.E.F. (Vernon B.C. 1915)

Top row.–L to R. John Brown, Tommy Thompson, Nigel Cowley, Frank Kappel, Bill Vernon.
Bottom row, Four Sorrento Men, Roland Salt, of Eagle Bay.
Front " Billy Smith, (Leo's Brother).

"In the spring of 1918 I was called out and told to report to Canadian Corps H.Q. – there they said I was wanted up at British First Army H.Q., what for nobody seemed to know. However, when I reached there one of the first men I met was Roland Salt, who came out to Canada with me, and he told me I was being posted to Army Intelligence, thanks to my knowledge of French and German. That was good news to me, because once you'd worked in intelligence you couldn't go back to the front lines again, for fear that if you were taken prisoner you would know too much.

"This work was intensely interesting as we were in touch with things we knew nothing about when we were up the line. And of course, up at H.Q. we were far away from those nasty German shells. Most of my intelligence work consisted of decoding German messages. There'd be a series of letters or figures intercepted, then we had to decode them. I caught onto it pretty well and stayed with it until the armistice.

"Then came the Armistice on November 11th, 1918, and I went on two weeks leave to Blighty. I arrived in London on Armistice night and everybody was wild, and no sleep that night. On the 14th, I went to Netley Hospital, up the Thames River, to visit Stanley who had been a patient there since he was evacuated from France *[Ed. note – to recount from Frank's earlier comments: In the big push at Amiens in August 1918, just three months before the Armistice, he was badly wounded and his leg had to be amputated.]*. But I found that he had been transferred a couple of days before to a hospital in Liverpool, so I headed for Mother's home in Cardiff and spent a lovely restful holiday there. When the time came for me to return to France, the Chief of Medical Service in Cardiff, a friend of the family, hinted that it might be possible to get an extension of my leave! So he gave me a certificate to the effect that I was medically unfit to travel, and that way I was able to wangle an extra two weeks' leave.

"I visited Stanley in Liverpool and finally got back to the outfit in France. There I was posted in a liaison capacity to the 2nd Canadian Engineers and with them marched into Germany. My job at first was to go ahead with the quartermaster and a couple of other chaps in a nice car and arrange for billets at the Engineers' next stopping place. As soon as they arrived and were found accommodation, we stocked up our car with supplies and moved on to the next stop-over, and so we went on and finally arrived at our destination at Troisdorf, in Germany, a few miles East of Bonn. There I resumed Intelligence work and also acted as interpreter for the town commandant. Being able to speak German, my contacts with the natives were most interesting.

"At the end of February I was transferred to Le Havre in France, where even at the time communistic propaganda was being spread amongst the troops, and our job was to find out the source of the trouble. We were moderately successful in this and made a number of arrests. Finally in April I was moved to England, first to Fountain Abbey in Yorkshire, then to the embarkation camp at Rhyl in North Wales. From there I took a ship at Liverpool and

arrived in Halifax on May 24th, 1919. A week later I was back at Magna Bay with Mother and Betty and it was wonderful to be back here again.

Left: Frank Kappel, Sergeant, Royal Canadian Army, WWI, ca. 1915 (Stanley's collection)

"Well, as I said, I came back home when the war was over – we came back covered with glory, and with an empty purse, as is the fate of many heroes! Fortunately I got my fire warden job back right away, and as that paid me $5.00 a day, seven days a week, which at that time was big money, we managed to keep the wolf from the door. It didn't take me long to find out that I was never meant to be a farmer. That Winter Uncle Sandy (Thomson) and I took on a logging contract at Celista – we took out a lot of logs, the hard way, but when we came to count up our take-home pay at the end of the job we were not much richer than when we started. So I was glad to get back on the fire job again, and was agreeably surprised to find that I was being promoted to be deputy fire chief for the whole district, which gave me work not only during the fire season, but also for a few weeks in Kamloops compiling statistics of the fires and mapping out the areas burned over. The following year a headquarters office was built in Sicamous, with myself in charge.

Right: cutting and removing timber by hand, with 3 horses, in the Shuswap in winter, as Frank and "Uncle Sandy Thomson", his brother-in-law did in 1919 (Sicamous and District Museum and Historical Society)

"Then came fall again. At that time there was a big sawmill at Chase, the Adams River Lumber Company, and I went down there to see if I could get a job in one of their logging camps as time-keeper or store-keeper. Luckily for me there was an opening for a timber scaler at their camp up on Adams River, and I got the job. I didn't know too much about scaling, but I soon caught on, and stayed there until the contract was completed. Then I turned in a full report, made some recommendations which were well received and apparently my work was quite satisfactory. Up at the camp the wife of the contractor, Mrs. Fusee, a great horse-woman, had two racehorses that were just eating their heads off. I asked some of the old-timers what they thought my chances would be to borrow one of the horses once in a while to visit my family at Magna Bay on week-ends. They told me I was crazy to think of it, that Mrs. Fusee would not let the horses out of her sight. But one day, when I was feeling very brave, I did approach her, and to my great surprise she was delighted with the idea, said the horses needed exercise, and I could take one of them each week, turn and turnabout, so I had lots of fun galloping to Eagle Bay and back every week-end.

Right: photo of a timber processing operation, including peeling and scaling by hand, preparing logs for the sawmill, early 1900s. Frank Kappel became a timber scaler for the Adams Lumber Company after returning from the Great War in 1919. (Sicamous and District Museum and Historical Society)

"Then back to the fire warden job again for the Summer, this time at Sicamous, where I got better acquainted with Mr. R. Bruhn who had his headquarters there. In the fall a big logging camp was starting up at Eagle Bay, with the Adams River Company taking the logs, while Mr. Bruhn took the poles and ties. They wanted a resident scaler on the job, and this time I did not have to apply for it, they offered it to me, and of course I was glad to accept. It was not far from home and I managed to get home almost every week-end, part of the time by boat, and when the lake froze over I walked on the ice. In the Spring of the year the ice gets kind of tricky and one has to be careful, it gets mushy and wet, and someday a wind comes up and presto – overnight the ice disappears; that spring I walked across the lake on the Saturday and on Monday morning went back to camp in my motor-boat!

"That year Mr. Bruhn suggested that I give up my fire warden job and come to work for him – his business was growing and he needed someone to run the office for him – I accepted and I and my family moved to Sicamous. Once we got established I built a house there, which you have all seen, and there we lived for the next 26 years. In 1924 Mr. Bruhn entered politics, got elected to the British Columbia Legislature *[Ed. note – later he also became Minister of Public Works in the B.C. Cabinet]*, necessitating more and more time away from the business, and the management fell into my hands. We had camps all over the lake and our tugboats brought in large booms of timber products which we loaded on cars and shipped via the Canadian Pacific Railway. Besides the lake business we bought poles, ties and posts at the railway sidings from Kamloops to Revelstoke and as far south as Vernon.

"In the mean time I sat for my scaler examination, and in 1920 obtained my Government certificate as a Provincial Licensed Scaler. In 1925 I was appointed to be a Notary Public. *[Editor's note – According to Wikipedia: "The Log Scaler measures the cut trees to determine the scale (volume) and quality (grade) of the wood to be used for manufacturing. When logs are sold, in order to determine the basis for a sale price in a standard way, the*

logs are "scaled" which means they are measured, identified as to species, and deductions for defects assigned to produce a net volume of merchantable wood. There are several different scales or rules that are used to determine the volume of wood."]

"During this period I built myself a cottage at Eagle Bay, which you girls know very well, and I have spent many happy summers there."

Even though Frank eventually decided he wasn't cut out to be a homesteader, he always asserted his love for the Shuswap area, for the natural beauty that surrounded him, and how glad he was that he had finally found his home in British Columbia with Janet. It was entirely different from anything he had experienced up to that point in his life, and he wished he had discovered it much earlier.

Left: Frank relaxing on the shores of Shuswap Lake (provided by Lynne and Roger Beeson)

Frank Kappel was the subject of a valuable article that he had sent to Alice, The Vernon News, dated May 29, 1947, author unknown. The subject of the article is a talk given to the local Rotary Club by Frank. This article provides valuable detail about "the early history and wonders of the Shuswap Lake area": "The speaker began his address by giving the Rotarians a geographical description of the lake. He told of its area, its main branches, the rivers it connects with, the height above sea level and other topographical features. He also spoke of the huge watershed, amounting to hundreds of square miles, which the lake drains.

Right: First Nation petroglyphs found in the Shuswap area (Sicamous and District Museum and Historical Society)

"Turning to the history of the area, Mr. Kappel stated before the white men knew anything about this lake, Shuswap was the winter home of a great many members of the Shuswap tribe. Fish and game were plentiful and they could get enough game in the summer to last them throughout the winter months. Later the Hudson's Bay Company established a trading post at Kamloops with outposts at Pierre's Point and at Chase. 'All along the north shore of the main lake, and at the Narrows, large numbers of "kigley holes" were found. These holes were 10 to 20 feet in diameter and over them the Indians had erected their teepees.' Many Indian relics were found in this area.

"Indian Battles: "This rich hunting ground also was the centre of attraction for many other Indian tribes such as the Blackfeet and Smokies from Alberta and the Okanagans from this Valley. Many battles were fought, especially around Enderby, Sicamous, Salmon Arm, Squilax and Chase. Mr. Kappel stated that in his talks with old Indians, he found their stories of these battles very interesting.

"Navigation by white men on Shuswap Lake commenced in the year of 1866 at the time of the Big Bend gold rush. The speaker quoted an old poster which had been printed at Victoria in 1866 and which advertised 'the safest, the shortest and the cheapest route to these extraordinary placer mines.' The poster asserted that the government of Vancouver Island and British Columbia had subsidized a number of first-class steamers to carry miners from San Francisco to Victoria and New Westminster direct.

Bubble Burst: "After the stampede was over, there were still steamers on the lake. Settlement of the Kamloops and Okanagan districts provided markets between the two areas and in 1878, the new steamer, 'Lady Dufferin,' made regular trips between Kamloops and Enderby.

"The railway route through Sicamous and Salmon Arm was surveyed by Walter Moberly in 1865. In 1885, the contractors, Sinclair and Tappen, prepared the right of way and steel was laid in the fall of that year. At this time, J.A. Mara was running three steamers on the lake.

Above left: Primitive woodburning "tugs" used to tow large "booms" of logs that had been cut in surrounding forests and floated down the rivers running into Shuswap Lake, early 1900s.
Above right: Tugboat AnnaBee approaching shore in Shuswap Lake, early 1900s (Sicamous & District Museum and Historical Society)

Right: Shuswap Lake during the time of water transportation that included paddle-wheeler steamships, date unknown (photo converted from a negative found in Stanley's collection)

"With the arrival of the railway the district around Salmon Arm began to develop. The farms had to be cleared out of dense virgin bushland, but the pioneers were tough and persistent. Today, there are some 7,000 people in settlements adjacent to Shuswap Lake.

"The Cariboo Trail poster read, 'from Yale to Savona Ferry, a distance of 133 miles, there is a splendid wagon road and comfortable wayside houses every few miles.' Over this road travellers could easily walk or could ride in fast four-horse stages. The first 426 miles of the journey *[Ed. note – From Vancouver to the Big Bend Gold Fields]* took 63 hours and cost $54. The last 35 miles was by an 'excellent' government pack trail and took 18 hours to complete.

Famous Names: "On June 2, 1886, the Sicamous and Okanagan Railway was incorporated by an Act of the Dominion Government. The shareholders in this company were men whose names are famous in the history of the Okanagan Valley. The line was started in 1887 and service was opened in 1892.

"Mr. Kappel then turned to the history of some of the well-developed and prosperous communities around the shores of Shuswap Lake. He began with the biggest centre, Salmon Arm. 'In the early days, Salmon Arm was the neglected centre of a triangle for the three main lines of communication. These were Kamloops to Sicamous on the one side, Sicamous to Okanagan on the east, and Okanagan to Kamloops on the other. It was not until the Canadian Pacific Railway was under construction that the area began to become populated. The manufacture of ties, cutting of cordwood for the locomotives and land clearing provided work for early settlers.

Right: Eagle Pass Landing, 1866, was originally known as a rough and tumble town filled with intoxicated men gambling and fighting. It was located near what would later become Sicamous. (BC Archives and the Kamloops Art Gallery); Below right: Saloon life, drinking and gambling in British Columbia, 1898 (British Columbia Magazine)

Moonshine:

"Sicamous was derived from a native word meaning 'Sunset Waters' or 'Shimmering Waters.' In the early days the steamers landed at Old Town, then known as Eagle Pass Landing, across the bay from Sicamous. At that time, the town had a population of 3,000 and there were 3 or 4 hotels, a Mounted Police barracks, a number of private residences, and even a jail.

"The Mounties were apparently kept very busy, for although officially no liquor was allowed in the construction camps, much bootleg whiskey and moonshine managed to find its way to the ready market.

"The speaker then told of Chase, Sorrento, Tappen, Seymour Arm, Anstey Arm, Main Lake, and Blind Bay. He mentioned briefly the timber industry, dairying, fish and game, the value of the area as a holiday resort and other features.

"In conclusion, Mr. Kappel said, 'So when you hear us Shuswapians talk about our lake, it is easy to understand why we are so proud of it and we do not hesitate to extend a cordial invitation to the world to come and see for themselves its beauty, its charm, and its future possibilities."

Above left and right: Views of the Kappel family home in Sicamous, overlooking Shuswap Lake, in summer and winter, early 1930s; They moved into this home in 1922, after Frank was hired to help run the nearby R.W. Bruhn Company, and lived continuously in the home until Janet's death in 1947. Frank continued with the Bruhn company until his retirement in 1948. (SPC)

Above: Ross Graham's truck loaded with ties in front of Finlayson's Garage in Sicamous, 1941; Established as Finlayson's Store in 1892, this was one of very few commercial establishments serving Sicamous in its early days. A jail was also built in 1892, a post office was added in 1904, and its first school opened around 1908. (Sicamous & District Museum and Historical Society)

A newspaper article from 1947, found in Karen's baby book, reads: **Frank Kappel is Honored at Farewell Event:** *Residents of Sicamous Join in Paying Tribute to Well-Known Resident of Shuswap Territory*

"Sicamous – Described as the "No. 1 Citizen" of Sicamous, Frank Kappel, pioneer resident of the Shuswap Lake country, was the guest of honor at a farewell dinner held in the Sicamous Women's Institute Hall last Friday evening. The enjoyable function was attended by more than 100 residents of the town and Eagle Valley and a number from Salmon Arm who joined in paying tribute to the sterling worth of Mr. Kappel, who has played an active role in all community affairs for many years.

Above: Early photo of the R.W. Bruhn lumber processing mill at Old Town Bay [Ed. note – Formerly Eagle Pass Landing] next to Lake Mara in Sicamous, ca. 1939, one part of the Bruhn timber firm which Frank managed for many years (Sicamous and District Museum and Historical Society); Below right: Photo of Frank in his office at the R. W. Bruhn Company, late in his career; He appears to have the weight of the world on his shoulders. (provided by Lynne and Roger Beeson)

"A resident of Sicamous for more than 25 years, Mr. Kappel has retired from the position of secretary-treasurer of R. W. Bruhn Ltd., a prominent B.C. timber firm, with which he had long been associated. In his retirement he is planning to reside at his lakeshore cottage at Eagle

Bay, for the summer at least.

"S.D. Finlayson, Sicamous merchant, was chairman at the dinner, and in his introductory remarks briefly recounted some of the many community projects in which Mr. Kappel had given assistance. If anyone wanted anything done, Frank Kappel would do it," said Mr. Finlayson, who recalled that the guest of honor was a charter member of the Sicamous branch of the Canadian Legion and had helped organize the branch.

"Striving constantly to make Sicamous a better place in which to live, Mr. Kappel worked untiringly for and was greatly endeared by all of the town's children, said Mrs. N. Jackson, of the Sicamous Women's Institute. He was a central figure in the annual May Day celebration and will be greatly missed, she added.

"As a tangible mark of the high esteem in which he was held, Mr. Kappel was presented with a purse containing a substantial sum of money and was also made the recipient of a life membership in the Canadian Legion. In addition, a carved "key to the city" was given by Mr. Finlayson, with the promise that the "welcome mat" would always be out for Mr. Kappel.

"Replying to the encomiums showered upon him, Mr. Kappel said he considered it a man's duty to help his neighbors. "Sicamous is a good community, and it is only right that we should help each other. Sympathy and kindness cost nothing, but like charity they bless him that gives as well as those who receive."

The date of this article is 1947, appearing after Janet Kappel's death in April 1946.

Left: Photo of Frank and daughter Betty with a large salmon one of them had caught, ca. 1928 (provided by Lynne and Roger Beeson)

Frank's memoirs continue: "Sicamous, where your grandmother and I spent most of our life together, was at one time quite a town. It served as headquarters and supply depot for the railway construction between Sicamous and Revelstoke. The railroad workers had a large number of houses there. There were beer parlours and liquor stores and ladies of easy virtue. The Mounted Police had their headquarters there. Around 1893, when they built the railway from Sicamous to the Okanagan, the CPR built their big hotel.

"Sicamous became the junction point for the Okanagan Valley. The trains arrived in the evening, stopped for the night, and went out to the Okanagan in the morning, so they had to have some place to stay. Since the roads were poor, there wasn't much car traffic in those days, and most of the transportation was by train. There were also a few boat liveries and a couple of little sawmills, but that was it. "

The earliest paragraphs of Frank's memoir to his granddaughters, which were excluded from the first chapter of his remarkable story, seem more appropriate to be added here: "My elder brother, Charlie, became a lawyer and died in 1952. I came next, then my sister Gertrude, and finally the baby of the family, Stanley. Gertrude was a teacher in the Old

Above left: Frank and Janet Kappel in front of their Sicamous home, dressed to the nines, early 1930s. Above right: Frank Kappel, ca. 1940, rifle in hand, ready for a day of hunting in appropriate attire [Ed. note – In addition to hunting game and waterfowl, Frank played golf, attended to his flower garden, and fished; he was by all accounts an avid outdoorsman.]

Country. After the First World War she came out to visit me at Magna Bay, and got married at my home there to Jim Armstrong, who had served through the war in the same outfit as Stanley. Gertrude is a clever girl - she lives now at Langford, is a widow, and spends much of her time writing stories and articles for the papers and magazines.

"Uncle Stanley served through World War I in the 72nd Battalion, the Seaforth Highlanders of Canada. In the big push at Amiens in August 1918, just three months before the Armistice, he was badly wounded and his leg had to be amputated. The stump was too short for him to use an artificial leg, so he has to use crutches. He is still in Vancouver where he has lived ever since he left the hospital. He is senior partner in an old, established Real Estate and Insurance firm, but expects to retire from business at the end of this year. He has led an active life and is well-known and respected in the social and business life of British Columbia.

The final paragraphs of Frank's memoir fill in a few more important details of his family history as well as his remarkable life and the pride he felt in both his family and his lifetime of accomplishment: "During this time I built myself a cottage at Eagle Bay. 1942 was a black year for me as far as the business was concerned. Our management consisted of four men: R. Bruhn, his son Ted, Mardie McKay, our field man, and myself. The first three all died within a period of six months, and I was left holding the bag. Your grandmother's health was beginning to fail about that time, and this combined with the business worries, began to get me down and my old stomach ulcer became active again. I kept on going, but when your grandmother died in 1946, I had had enough. I sold out my interest in the business to Mr. Bruhn's son-in-law, Max Patterson.

"In 1947 I moved to Salmon Arm *[Ed. note – where Betty lived]*. When World War II broke out I tried to get back in the Army. They would have taken me for Home Service, which I did not want, but told me flatly that I was too old for overseas service. So I stayed in Sicamous and became Chief Air Raid Warden, President of the Red Cross, and a member of the Pacific Coast Militia Rangers.

"In 1952 *[Ed. note – the year Stanley died]* the old stomach ulcer got me down and I had to undergo surgery first in Kamloops and afterwards in Victoria. In all I was 82 days in hospital and came out with only one third of my original stomach left. However the ultimate results were eminently satisfactory and I have enjoyed pretty good health ever since.

"Now I have retired again, and this time I think it is for keeps, and I spend my time between Eagle Bay, Salmon Arm, Victoria, Spokane and Laguna Beach, California. I have lived a long life and have many happy memories to support me in my old age. What the future holds in store I do not know. In my lifetime I have seen many changes and life today is very different from what it was 75 years ago. I can well remember the horse-drawn street cars, the naked yellow gas lamps to light our homes, the penny-in-the-slot hot water heaters, the outside privies except where the new invention, the flush toilet, was being installed in the better class homes, the old wax cylinder gramophones, and so forth.

"Many of the conveniences which we now take for granted were unheard of. The steam automobile was just coming on the roads – these had built in steam engines, and when they got into action they shot out streams of steam which scared all the horses on the streets. Telephones and typewriters were new inventions, as was electric light. There were no radios or T.V. sets, no airplanes, refrigerators, washing machines, submarines, wonder drugs, vitamin pills, radar, motor boats, picture shows, supermarkets, luxury trains and ships, and so forth. Life was very much simpler than it is today. I do not doubt but that the next fifty years will bring forth new inventions that will make people think that we who lived in the 1960s were pretty simple and old-fashioned. You girls will live to see many of these changes, and I hope they will all be for the best and that they will make you happy.

"Up to the time of the First Great War, Canada was predominantly an agricultural country, its main exports being wheat, lumber and fish. It was during that war that Canada came into manhood and started developing her industrial resources. From then on she has continued to expand in stature and in wealth until today she ranks with the old established countries as one of the great nations of the world. British Columbia has more than kept pace with the other Canadian Provinces, industrially and economically, and we who have, in our small way, helped in this development may well be proud of what has been accomplished. In 1958, the Centennial Year of this province, the Government of British Columbia presented me with an elaborate scroll, signed by the Lieutenant Governor and the Premier, commending me for my part in the prosperity and development of my community, which I felt was a great honour.

"This then, is the story of my life. I certainly did not intend to make it so long, but once I got started, the thoughts and memories kept crowding in on me, and I could not stop. However, after reading this you will perhaps know more about me than you did before, and you will be able to tell your children and grandchildren what sort of a man your old grandpa was. And I hope you will think of me sometimes and remember me as one who loved you very much and who wishes you a long and happy life, and success in whatever you undertake."

"God bless you."

Frank made an important comment in his memoirs about Janet's passing: "Mother's death in 1946 was a sad blow not only to the children and me but also to the whole community." Janet Kappel suffered from Parkinson's disease for 19 years, according to her death certificate. Her gradual downward health spiral eventually left her quite debilitated, and this, along with other important events, caused deep wounds in Frank Kappel, wounds he rarely spoke of with anyone in his family.

Lynne Beeson, Frank's granddaughter and Betty Kappel Ingram's daughter, recently shared a surprising detail about Frank's life that no one in his family was aware of: the certificate below which documents Frank's confirmation into the Catholic church at Grindrod [Ed. note – Grindrod is 12 miles from Sicamous.], dated May 6, 1945. Lynne states that in all the years she knew Frank she was unaware that he had become a Catholic. In fact, Frank's marriage certificate records that he belonged to the Church of England, as did Janet.

It is difficult to process what must have been a profoundly important event in Frank's long life. To this author, it suggests that he may have experienced a crisis of faith as his life unfolded and the impending death of his beloved Janet drew near. His three longstanding business partners had all died within six months of one another in 1940. His daughter was married in June of 1945, a month after Frank's confirmation, and she then moved to Salmon Arm immediately. His son was already married and was moving on, never to return to live in the area of the Shuswap near his parental home and family.

When this is all taken together, it is clear that Frank's world was slowly unraveling. He even states in his memoir that when Janet died in 1946 he "had had enough", and that he was suffering from a stomach ulcer. In other words, he was exhausted, he was demoralized, and he was undoubtedly heartbroken. Still, I have found no obvious connections in my research that would explain why he converted to Catholicism rather than

Diocese of Kootenay, B. C.

In the Name of the Father, and of the Son, and of the Holy Ghost. Amen.

We do certify:

That, after the example of the Holy Apostles and in accordance with the practice of the Holy Catholic Church, by prayer and the laying on of hands, we did administer to

Frank

(Family Name) Kappel

The Sacramental Rite of Confirmation

wherein are covenanted the Sevenfold Gifts of the Holy Spirit; which administration was upon the Sixth day of May in the year of our Lord, one thousand nine hundred and forty five in the Church of St Paul Enderby Grindrod, B.C.

Signed T W Sharman Vicar

Walter Kootenay

simply become more active in his own Church of England. He did have a two-year association with the Catholic religion early in his life, when he was studying French in Belgium at a Catholic boarding school that was run by the Christian Brothers. Perhaps that is the connection.

Frank's association with Freemasonry started many years earlier, yet the longstanding conflict between the Catholic Church and the Masons is well known. Frank never mentioned his deep involvement in Freemasonry in any of his personal memoirs. His boss and mentor, Rolf Bruhn, was a prominent member of the Salmon Arm Masonic Lodge, as well as a prominent businessman and politician who played an important role in building up the economy around the Shuswap. Frank also served in various leadership positions during his long association with the Salmon Arm Masonic Lodge. So why did he end his association with the Freemasons, and when did he take that step? Perhaps we'll never know.

Why did Frank Kappel become a Catholic? Was Frank required to renounce his association with the Masons in order to become a Catholic in 1945? Frank apparently chose not to share the answers to those questions with his descendents, including his son and daughter.

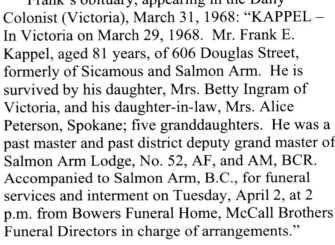

Frank's obituary, appearing in the Daily Colonist (Victoria), March 31, 1968: "KAPPEL – In Victoria on March 29, 1968. Mr. Frank E. Kappel, aged 81 years, of 606 Douglas Street, formerly of Sicamous and Salmon Arm. He is survived by his daughter, Mrs. Betty Ingram of Victoria, and his daughter-in-law, Mrs. Alice Peterson, Spokane; five granddaughters. He was a past master and past district deputy grand master of Salmon Arm Lodge, No. 52, AF, and AM, BCR. Accompanied to Salmon Arm, B.C., for funeral services and interment on Tuesday, April 2, at 2 p.m. from Bowers Funeral Home, McCall Brothers Funeral Directors in charge of arrangements."

Left: Frank Kappel photographed in his Masonic dress clothing, date unknown (photo provided by Lynne and Roger Beeson)

We are already aware that the Frank Kappel household provided a focus of social life for the citizens of Sicamous, but several news clippings from local newspapers of the 1930s and 40s provide additional insight into the richness of the social life enjoyed by the community. An article appearing in The Vernon Herald, a local newspaper, dated March 16th, 1933, reports: "AMATEUR PLAY AT SICAMOUS ENJOYED; On Thursday evening the dramatic club, sponsored by the Sicamous Women's Institute, presented the three-act comedy, Deacon Dubbs, to a capacity audience at the Sicamous Hall. The crowd was kept in a continual roar of laughter throughout the entire play, and the well selected cast showed that they must have spent considerable work and study under the direction of Mrs. W. K. Finlayson and Frank Kappel." Later in the same article:

"Miss Partington and Miss O'Shea, of Vancouver, who participated in the Interior Badminton Championships at Vernon last week, were the guests of Mr. and Mrs. F. Kappel over the weekend."

Frank Kappel's talents and his involvement in his community were seemingly limitless. He was a member of the Eagle Valley Mosquito League devoted to eradicating mosquitos from the Shuswap region. He was a member of the Pacific Coast Militia Rangers, BC's own "Home Guard" consisting of a group of patriotic male citizens. According to the Naval History Museum, the Rangers were "unique to the west coast of Canada and were formed in early 1942 to protect British Columbia (BC) and calm public unease over possible enemy activities."

Right: Photo of the Shuswap branch of the Pacific Coast Militia Rangers, with Frank standing in the second row just left of center (Sicamous and District Museum and Historical Society); Below right: Frank's discharge certificate from the Pacific Coast Militia Rangers, with his dates of service noted as August 10, 1942 to September 30, 1945 (provided by Lynne and Roger Beeson)

From the CFB Esquimalt Naval Military Museum: "After the attack at Pearl Harbour and declaration of war against Japan, patrols of BC's rugged country appeared to be a necessity, one that could not be carried out by local militia forces, who were deemed more suited to populated areas. Experienced men such as loggers, trappers, prospectors, and ranchers were sought for this distinctive role. These men had knowledge of the local topography and terrain. Those who were close to populated centres were trained and employed at a local Ranger Training Camp in intelligence duties and local defence against minor raids. They were also instructed in tactical situations that included observation, especially coast watching against the possible Japanese invasion, anti-sabotage measures and protection of lines of communication and transportation."

Summing up Frank Kappel's remarkable life is daunting to this writer: Pioneer, homesteader, horseman, community leader, politician, philanthropist, businessman, Rotarian, Mason, historian, fire warden, lumberman, scaler, miner, road builder, axe man, teamster, carpenter, cartographer, devoted husband and father, brother, grandfather, soldier, Canadian Legionnaire, linguist (Frank spoke 5 languages), interpreter, public speaker, artist, actor, singer, pianist, humorist, foreign correspondent, oarsman, hunter, avid stamp collector, and proud Canadian…this is such an amazing list of talents and abilities, it makes Frank seem like a polymath. He started out in an upper middle-class household; his advantages enabled him to study languages in Europe and become an accomplished linguist; he also worked in various financial and commercial establishments, adding much to his unique skill set. Then he launched himself into an unknown life of adventure in a remote corner of the Canadian wilds, rising from simple homesteader to community leader. Suffice it to say: Frank was brilliant in his own right, and he left the world a better place than he found it.

Left: Sicamous May Day celebration, ca. 1940; The dogs belonged to a local dogsledder. Frank Kappel, a May Day official in the light suit, walked at the rear of the procession. (Sicamous & District Museum and Historical Society)

One sentence in Frank's personal memoir stands out in the mind of this writer: "It didn't take me long to find out that I was never meant to be a farmer." Frank had grown up in a town in Wales, situated in a rural setting. He moved to Europe at a fairly young age and spent the next 10 years of his life in quite sophisticated cities, working in an office. By the time he left Europe to move to Canada in 1911, he had apparently had enough of cities, and he "returned to his roots" when he chose the Shuswap area, where he spent the rest of his life. Having discovered that he was not a peasant, and that his roots were not in the soil, he moved to town as soon as he could sell his homestead.

Although Sicamous wasn't much more than a village at the time, Frank clearly felt more at home in Sicamous, and he became one of its most prominent citizens, leaving a legacy that included a street being named after him.

Right: Although the newspaper article is self-explanatory, it is worth noting that Frank Kappel remained active in Sicamous up to the moment that he moved to Salmon Arm in 1947.

Frank's granddaughter, Lynne Ingram Beeson, remembered Frank in a recent email: "One of the things that people ALWAYS said about

Heritage Highlights

Street names: Where do they come from?

Kappel Street in Sicamous is named after Frank Kappel, shown here with 1946 May Queen, Dorothy Spelay (nee Kingling.) Mr. Kappel was a bookkeeper for R.W. Bruhn's sawmill operation and lived on CPR Hill.
(Courtesy Sicamous Museum & Historical Society)

Grandpa was that he was such a kind gentleman. And it's true. With all the time we spent with him at the cabin and in Victoria, I never heard him raise his voice, or complain. He was always fairly soft spoken but intelligent and always laughed so easily."

"Thinking of which, I can add a couple of other occupations to Grandpa. At one time he was a cartographer – drew maps. This came up when I was in high school and needed to draw a map for an assignment. I also have a picture of Grandpa at his desk at work doing this. The other thing I discovered when I was trying to clean out the attic at the Blind Bay cabin, was a notary seal with Grandpa's name on it."

"When my own kids were little, I wrote for the newspaper, and for quite a while did articles on old timers in the area. As it turned out, every single person I interviewed knew grandpa and without fail, raved about him, saying what a wonderfully kind gentleman he was, and how good he was at all his jobs."

Paying tribute to his innumerable accomplishments as a leading citizen of Sicamous and the greater Shuswap District, the city of Sicamous bestowed upon Frank and Janet Kappel a fitting affirmation: a street in South Sicamous was named Kappel Street to honor this important family. Few members of this frontier community "rose to the challenge" in more significant ways than they did.

Here is one very personal story about Frank Kappel from Karen, Frank's oldest granddaughter: "In addition to visiting our family in the Spokane Valley after Stanley's death in 1952, Grandfather Kappel invited us to spend time with him in British Columbia. We used to travel to Shuswap Lake in the summer to spend a week with Frank at his cabin on Eagle Bay. He lived very simply there, as the cabin was without electricity or an indoor toilet. He used kerosene lanterns for lighting, and he also had an outhouse. His only source of refrigeration was a special wooden icebox buried in the ground next to his cabin that had to be frequently resupplied with ice blocks obtained from a nearby store. The last time we visited Frank on Shuswap Lake, in 1962, he had electricity and a brand new refrigerator, although he still had that outhouse.

"This was a grand adventure for us three sisters. We would spend our days swimming in the lake or playing with a fun-loving neighbor boy, Stew Brechin, and our cousins, Dale and Lynne Ingram, who had a cabin at Blind Bay. Despite the lack of conveniences, Mother always managed to prepare fabulous meals on Frank's wood-fired range. Frank loved roast beef with Yorkshire pudding, and Mother never failed to produce that feast for him, even without electricity.

"When we weren't swimming or playing in the sunshine, Frank might suggest that we all hop into his car and take a spin around the lake to visit his old friends. Along the way we would invariably meet someone Frank knew, since he knew nearly everyone. Frank would stop the car and get out for a chat, which could go on for hours, or so it seemed to Kristen, Kerry and me. He was a very affable man, and everyone seemed to love him.

"The cabin was right on the lake, but it wasn't winterized, so Frank would travel down to southern California to spend the winter in a small apartment he had rented at Laguna Beach. This went on for many years, and one can easily imagine that Frank had as many friends and as many lengthy conversations with the people he met in Laguna Beach as he had around his beloved Shuswap District.

"Frank was a superb storyteller. I remember we would all sit around an open campfire in the evening on the beach when we were visiting and Frank would tell stories. They were stories about his past, about life around the Shuswap, about his friends, and about his family, including our father, Stanley. He also wrote a memoir for his five granddaughters that I still treasure. I think he wanted to create a family mythology that we could keep in our hearts after he was gone. My most vivid memory of Frank, sitting on that beach, the stars twinkling overhead, was when he would recite "The Cremation of Sam McGee". It was a magical moment for me, for all of us."

The last member of Karen's family to see Frank alive was Karen's sister, Kristen Kappel, who sent us a sensitive and moving tribute to Frank by email recently that discussed her final visit with Frank in 1968: "My loyalties have always been with our Grandfather Kappel, who treated our father like a son. He is the only parental figure I ever truly loved and it is why I will carry his name to my eventual demise. A few days before he died I scraped together every penny (not many, since I was a student at the University of Washington at the time) and flew up to Victoria to sit by his bedside for several days. His description of picking up a 'disheveled little boy with a small bundle of clothing, who called him dad within a few minutes' makes me tear up even after all these years."

As we move inexorably toward the story of Stanley Kappel, our main character, it is little wonder that he became so successful at such an early age. Given the genetic inheritance of Ernie and Jeanie Buckingham, combined with the splendid example and careful nurturing of Frank and Jenny Kappel, one can easily envy young Stanley. Yet, as we shall learn, life is never easy, and it is always unpredictable. Every single member of Stanley's extended family, along with everyone else who finds their way into this compelling story, was a hero in their own right.

Above: Frank Kappel's painting of a forest of birch trees with a stream, rocks, and sunset, that hangs in our home, signed but undated (photo taken by the author)

Photo portrait of Janet Thomson as a young woman

CHAPTER 9 – Janet Kappel, a Woman Ahead of Her Time

"While Europe's eye is fix'd on mighty things,
The fate of empires and the fall of kings;
While quacks of state must each produce his plan,
And even children lisp the Rights of Man;
Amid this mighty fuss just let me mention,
The Rights of Woman merit some attention."

- Robert "Robbie" Burns, from "The Rights of Woman", 1792

Janet Thomson, Stanley's adopted mother, was born in Thornhill, Dumfriesshire, Scotland, on April 27th, 1877. This part of Scotland, tucked into its southwest corner, has a long, colorful history that included Romans, Gaelic clans, and Robert the Bruce, who fought a bloody battle there in 1306 before he became King of the Scots. Bonnie Prince Charlie, the Stuart pretender to the throne of England, lived there in 1745 while plotting against the British Royal Establishment. Robert Burns, Scotland's most famous poet, moved there in 1788 and lived near Greyfriars Church, spending the last few years of his life in residence.

Jenny, her preferred name throughout her life, was a young lass during the time when the voice of Robbie Burns was still echoing over the Highlands and down into the Scottish glens, and she was no doubt affected by such stimulating influences, both historic and contemporary.

Right: Lithograph of Ellisand, the last home of Robert Burns in Dumfriesshire, Scotland, ca. 1800 (Dumfries Museum, Robert Burns Project)

Her parents were William Thomson and Euphemia Marchbank, both from the local area. William's large family operated a stone quarry that apparently provided them all with a good living. They had 15 children *[Ed. note - Or possibly 17, according to Euphemia's obituary in The Vancouver Province newspaper dated 23 November 1937]* including Janet, who was the fourth oldest child. Her uncle, Joseph Thomson, a brother of William's, was the famous Scottish geologist and explorer who participated in the "Scramble for Africa" and for whom the Thomson's gazelle was named.

Left: Watercolor drawing of Goldiela, an estate southwest of Thornhill, Scotland, ca. 1875, near where Janet Thomsen was born in 1877 (Dumfries Museum, Robert Burns Project)

Famous uncle, indeed! According to the Joseph Thomson Group website: "Joseph Thomson was born in Sundial Cottage on February 14th, 1858. He was the 5th and final son of William and Agnes Thomson, who had moved there in 1856 and remained until 1868, when they moved to Gatelawbridge where Joseph's father, a master stonemason, had leased a farm with a freestone (sandstone) quarry."

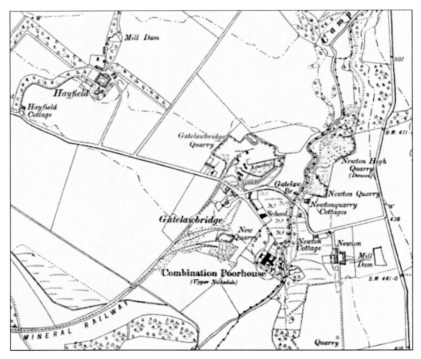

Left: Map from 1898 showing the Gatelawbridge Quarries, operated by William Thomson and his two sons, William, Jr., and Robert, between 1868 and 1899

From an entry in Scotland's Brick and Tile Manufacturing Industry website: "William George Thomson leased a quarry at Gatelawbridge from 1868 to 1899 and records show he was a Master, Quarry Mason. Thomson leased the land from the Duke of Buccleuch."

"Two of his sons – William Thomson 1851-1923 and Robert Thomson 1855-1913 worked with their father William George Thomson. William Jr. started in 1868 and Robert in 1870. William Thomson would purchase land and build or have built houses for his family or to sell on, and it is believed he manufactured bricks for this purpose and for selling on to other local builders. It is believed the brickworks were in operation from 1875 to around the 1890s."

"The Thomson Brothers continued the business after their father died in 1899 and were involved with some other quarries in the area; the Thomson's finished renting in 1903 and various others worked Gatelawbridge until 1912 when the quarry was closed."

More from the Joseph Thomson Group website:

"He who goes gently goes safely; he who goes safely goes far."

"Joseph Thomson led six expeditions into uncharted areas of Africa. He opened up new routes to Lake Nyasa and Victoria Nyanza, was the first white man to enter the Rift Valley, mapped huge expanses of what are now Kenya, Morocco, and Nigeria, made important scientific discoveries about Lake Tanganyika, Mount Kilimanjaro and Mount Kenya and discovered Thomson's Falls (named after his father) as well as new species of plants and animals, including Thomson's Gazelle.

"Gifted with phenomenal stamina and fitness, Thomson is also famous for his reliance on friendly words and persuasion, rather than threats of violence, when faced with difficult situations on his travels. In all his expeditions, none of his travelling companions met a violent end.

"…my fondest boast is, not that I have travelled over hundreds of miles hitherto untrodden by the foot of a white man, but that I have been able to do so as a Christian and a Scotchman, carrying everywhere goodwill and friendship, finding that a gentle word was more potent than gunpowder, and that it was not necessary, even in Central Africa, to sacrifice the lives of men in order to throw light upon its dark corners." - 'Dumfries & Galloway Standard' 15 Sep 1880

"It is tragic that Thomson died – in 1895, at the age of only 37 – from illnesses acquired during his expeditions."

Being related to Joseph Thomson in the 19th century was exceptional since he was well known and widely admired for his many accomplishments in Africa and elsewhere. He is buried in the Thornhill cemetery in Dumphriesshire, and a large sandstone and bronze monument to him was erected there in 1897, long before the William Thomson family emigrated to Canada. His stories were surely discussed by members of his family long after his death, including the Frank Kappel household where Stanley grew up. For young Janet, being a woman meant options were limited, but having a famous uncle and possibly even being able to spend time with him revealed to her what an adventure life could be. Being so personally associated with someone of such international caliber as Joseph Thomson would also have opened many doors almost anywhere that might otherwise have been closed to Jenny.

Among Jenny's "advantages" was the opportunity to study art in Europe, where she met Frank in the early years of the 20th century. While living there she became an accomplished painter, and one of her marvelous oil paintings of the Alps hangs on our dining room wall. She continued to paint well into her later years, with examples of her artistic talents gracing the walls of many homes and institutions in North America up to the present day. The painting in our dining room has a date of 1905 and is a mature example of someone who had been painting for many years.

In 1905 Jenny Thomson was already 28 years old, something quite unusual in its own right. Most women of her generation, her class, and her birth location, would already have been long married by that age, and comfortably ensconced in a middle-class lifestyle in their country of birth, with many children to care for. Yet here was Jenny Thomson, far away from home, living in Europe, a spinster by definition, studying painting with obvious dedication, and being exposed to other artists who undoubtedly made a lasting impression on her, both intellectually and spiritually. She most likely met Frank Kappel while he was working in Kassel for a large shipping firm between 1906 and 1911. We have already discussed why Frank decided to leave Germany when the Germans were beginning to talk of "lebensraum", and it is easy to conclude

that Jenny, too, was troubled by the developing talk of aggression and imperial entitlements among her German acquaintances, many of whom were artists or intellectuals.

Left: Striking portrait of Jenny Thomson taken in Scotland; She appears to be 18-20 years old, so the date of the photo would be ca. 1895-97. (provided by Lynne and Roger Beeson)

I have seen no written documentation covering the time Jenny spent in Europe, or even when she left Scotland to travel to the continent. It is therefore difficult to divine why she decided to spend much of her early life there, or how she was supported financially during all the time she remained there. Did she work, and if yes, what did she do to earn a living? Although few facts are available, the 1901 Scotland Census lists Janet Thomson as living and working as a servant in the household of James Glendinning on the Evertown Farm in Canonbie, Dumfriesshire, and the details given suggest that the "general farm servant" listed is our own Janet Thomson. Evertown Farm was part of the huge holdings of the Duke of Buccleuch at the time *[Ed. note – Janet's father, William Thomson, leased his stone quarry at Gatelawbridge from the Duke of Buccleuch.]* and is located nearly 50 miles from Gatelawbridge. As the fourth child in a family of at least 15 children, regardless of her family's financial circumstances, it appears that Janet needed to earn her own living by 1901, when she was 24 years old. Let's imagine that Janet was also trying to save money to study art in Europe at the time. Perhaps the most important point to be taken is that she was not in Europe in 1901, and it also means that she would have lived in Europe for no more than ten or 11 years prior to moving to Canada in 1912. Her 1905 painting of the Alps suggests she had moved to Europe from Scotland no later than 1904 or 1905.

It seems likely that she had discovered her love of painting while she was a student in Scotland. Perhaps she found genuine encouragement and was possibly mentored by a teacher or fellow artist prior to deciding to take the bold step of studying art in Europe. Even though she was already 23 years old at the turn of the century, she had undoubtedly been exposed to influential female role models while she was growing up who would have inspired her to seek her own personal muse. The most obvious example might have been Queen Victoria, who reigned through the first 24 years of Jenny's life and even spent much of her later life in Scotland. Queen Victoria was a strong, independent woman, even though the Victorian Era was noted for its emphasis on family values, with women playing the central role subservient to their husbands as homemakers, wives and mothers, not as independent women who were out on their own forging their own careers and identities. In Victorian England the nuclear family became both the ideal and the reality, according to Wikipedia, making Jenny's departure from those values all the more remarkable.

Above: Large oil painting done by Jenny Kappel while she was living and studying in Europe in the early 1900. The painting, which appears to have been made in the Alps, hangs on the wall in our dining room and is one of our prized possessions. It is masterly and mature in its execution. The alpine location suggests that Jenny traveled extensively throughout Europe prior to moving to British Columbia to marry Frank Kappel in 1912. It is signed "Jenny Thomson", with a date of 1905 beside her signature, and measures 28" x 42". (photo taken by the author)

Fortunately, the nineteenth century was blessed with an abundance of inspiring female artists in prose, poetry, and the visual arts, and Jenny was probably exposed to at least a few of them. Successful female authors included Jane Austen, the Bronte sisters, and Mary Wollstonecraft, whose book *A Vindication of the Rights of Women* may have caught Jenny's attention. There were also many male artists with romantic inclinations who could also have played a role in shaping her sense of herself as an artist with authentic potential.

According to "The Collector", a Canadian website devoted to arts and ideas: "Although female artists have existed throughout the history of art, the 19th century's social and economic changes allowed for more women to enter and find success within the art scene. Art schools were created specifically for female artists. Featured within exhibitions and the Salons of Paris were many prominent female artists of the 19th century. The democratization of art allowed for many underrepresented demographics to become more successful, including female artists."

Many aspiring women hoping to succeed in the creative arts found their way to Paris throughout the 19th century, but we don't know if Jenny made Paris her first stop after arriving in Europe. What we do know is that she eventually met Frank Kappel, and there is every reason to believe that they first met in northern Germany where Frank was working. While Paris may have been the center of opportunity for artistically gifted women when Jenny was coming of age,

every other European country could boast fine examples of important female artists who were trained in art schools that catered to women.

Left: "The Highland Shepherd", a painting by Rosa Bonheur dated 1859 (Wikimedia Commons)

Rosa Bonheur, who lived from 1822 to 1899, was a brilliant artist who painted a lovely rendition of a Scottish shepherd tending to his flock in the Highlands in 1859. She spent most of her life in France where she lived in a French country chateau, and she never married.

From the website mymodernmet.com: "She wore her hair short, obtained a then-necessary permit to wear men's clothes, and even owned a pet lioness. She was the first female artist awarded the *Légion d'Honneur* after Empress Eugénie visited her studio. The empress famously declared that "Genius has no sex" after viewing Bonheur's paintings. Bonheur became very famous during her lifetime. She met countless heads of state and was appreciated by the artistic likes of Eugène Delacroix and John Ruskin. She found success in the Paris Salon and was received as a celebrity of the art world in London."

One is tempted to imagine that Rosa Bonheur and other prominent female artists of the 18th and 19th centuries may have provided Jenny with the inspiration she needed to pursue her own career in art. Perhaps she was fortunate enough to meet a few of them, and perhaps she even gained their attention and approval.

Jenny's father was a prosperous businessman whom she probably admired. His family had been successful stonemasons for many decades, and Jenny would probably have felt comfortable with a businessman as a husband, even if her own leanings were toward the more creative pursuits. As we have already learned, Frank was in his own right very creative and had already proven his talent in the world of business by the time he and Jenny connected. Whichever forces of nature brought them together, Jenny and Frank became very fond of one another and were soon becoming comfortable with the prospect of spending the rest of their lives as a married couple. This would have been a natural life decision for Frank Kappel, a young man in his early 20s. But for Jenny, who was eight years Frank's senior and had been living "on her own" as an independent woman for many years, such a decision may have been more difficult to make.

A few years earlier Jenny's parents had decided to emigrate from Gatelawbridge to British Columbia. *[Ed. note – Euphemia's 1937 obituary in The Province states the Thomson family settled in the Shuswap area in 1910,while others have said it was in 1909. They were located in the vicinity of Celista, the same community where Jean Brown, Stanley's birth mother, was living when she met Ernie Buckingham around 1911.]* This writer found no clear indication as to why the William Thomson family abandoned their successful stone quarrying business in Scotland and took such a huge gamble on their future in an entirely unknown and far-off land, so one can only imagine the reasons for their bold and risky decision. Frank was of the opinion that his father-in-law thought he'd stand a better chance in a new country like Canada, an opinion that also probably reflects what influenced Frank's decision to emigrate. Frank also liked the idea of getting away from the confines of working in an office to the wide, open spaces of the an untamed land in the far west of North America.

Many place names around the Shuswap bear Scottish names, so it is also possible that the Thomsons already knew at least one other Scottish family in addition to their sons who had blazed a trail to Canada and set the stage for the Thomsons' arrival. In fact, Canada had long attracted Scottish immigrants, starting with Nova Scotia, which means "New Scotland".

From Wikipedia: "Owing to the role that the <u>Hudson's Bay Company</u>, a company dominated by the Scottish managerial class, played in the colonial settlement of <u>British Columbia</u>, many of the leading early colonial officials were Scottish or of Scottish descent."

Frank held that Jenny's father, William Thomson, was already considered "Laird of the Manor" on the north shore of Shuswap Lake by the time he arrived in the spring of 1911. Thomson Hill in Celista, where the Thomsons had their homestead, is named for William Thomson. Many members of the Thomson family had sent glowing reports about the Shuswap to Jenny and were eager for her to rejoin the family. This much seems clear: they felt they had been in Europe long enough and they both wanted something different, something new and adventurous they could share together as a newly married couple. Jenny arrived in Canada in June of 1912, more than a year after Frank and his friend Roland Salt made their long trip through New York City. She had taken the RMS Hesperian from Liverpool, disembarking at Quebec City. As noted in their marriage certificate, the two were wed shortly after Janet arrived in Celista, on June 24th, 1912, at St. Paul's Church in Kamloops.

[Ed. note – The RMS Hesperian was built in Glasgow, Scotland, in 1907 and began service from Liverpool to Quebec and Montreal in April 1908. It continued its service until it was torpedoed and sunk by a German U-boat in September of 1915. The commander of the U-boat was the same one who sank the Lusitania in May of that same year.]

House warming picnic at Thomson beach - circa 1910

Back L to R: Billy ?, Harry A Fowler, Jimmy Thomson, Jack Josephson, Thomas McGowan, Billy Sims, Billy Gray, Billy Walker, John Brown, William Brown, Joseph Brown, Robert Thomson, Arthur H Chambers, Ted Jones.
Middle: Charlotte Fowler, Jeannie Brown, William Thomson, Euphemia Marchbank-Thomson, Thomas Brown II (holding Thomas Brown III), Jane Coats McGowan-Brown, Margaret (Maggie) Brown, Catherine Thomson, Jessie Fowler
Standing (in front of Thomas Brown II and Jane Coats McGowan): Jean McGowan Brown, James McGowan Brown and Hugh Brown.
Front Sitting: John Lee Fowler, Ken Josephson, Ben Josephson.

Above: William Thomson and Thomas Brown families attending the housewarming of the new Thomson family home, at Thomson Beach near Celista, on the Shuswap, ca. 1910, two years prior to Jenny's arrival from Europe. At least 5 members of the Thomson family are present in the photo. (provided by Jack Brown) [Ed. note – Jack also wrote in a 2009 email: "The Thomson property was about 1 mile West of our Great Grandfather, Thomas Brown's homestead in Celista. In the picture, your grandmother Jeannie Brown is sitting next to William Thomson and Euphemia Marchbank, the parents of your adoptive grandmother Janet Thomson."]

An excerpt from the book *Settling the Canadian-American West, 1890-1915,* by John William Bennett and Seena B. Kohl, University of Nebraska Press, 1995, includes an insightful passage from Kate Mills' autobiography, written in 1938. Kate Mills emigrated from Scotland in 1905 to marry her fiancé, who was already in Canada:

"From 1901 to 1905 the West was being advertised everywhere. "Come to Canada where wealth awaits you."…Like many others I had given my promise to come and help build a home in the Great West….The fateful day arrived, and we all seemed afraid to make a noise….The cab arrived which was to take me to the ship, and only then did I realize fully the step I was taking….Down in my cabin I found friends, who like myself were going to join those who had started their home. They were all having a good cry, so I was able to give vent to my feelings. One of them asked how did my mother take it, and when I thought of her sad face, as I clasped her hand in farewell, I said, "If this ship stops at Greenock, I'm going home"; but I felt better by the time we got there, and so I came to Canada."

The insight contained in this paragraph speaks volumes about the myriad feelings experienced by every brave pioneer man and woman who have left their homes to find new lives in distant foreign lands over many centuries. In Jenny Thomson's case, she left Scotland (and Europe) to join her family and her fiancé. In Frank Kappel's case, he left all but two of his family and friends behind in Wales at the age of 24 when he moved to Canada, never to see many of them again. This was the case in so many instances where part of a family emigrated, but most were left behind: broken-hearted mothers, worried sisters, anxious brothers, and concerned grandparents. For those of us who grew up in the age of commercial aviation and robust telecommunications, it is difficult to imagine the chasm that existed between these two groups, thousands of miles apart, with nothing more than irregular mail service to convey the love, the loneliness, the yearnings, and the emptiness felt by so many families that would never meet again.

Right: Early photo of Frank and Jenny Kappel, probably taken shortly after their marriage in 1912 (provided by Lynne and Roger Beeson, LRB)

Inevitably, life goes on, and in Jenny's case, she was able to see her parents and most of her siblings regularly after arriving in Canada. Frank Kappel had his brother and sister living nearby in the Vancouver area. And there was so much to do in their new home.

Still, Jenny Kappel had to learn to manage a homestead and many challenges that confronted families living in a daunting environment. For example, Frank shared with his family that mail service was extremely limited in the early days while he and Janet were on their homestead near Magna Bay, which didn't even have its own post office. Mail service was provided by the hotel and store owner at Notch Hill. Most supplies that were not produced locally by various members of the north shore community had to be ordered in advance. Fortunately, mail order sources had been established by 1912.

The mail order business is an important detail about life in Canada for those living "off the grid" in the early 20th century. According to Wikipedia: "The Eaton's catalogue was a mail-order catalogue published by Eaton's from 1884 to 1976. It was "one of the first to be distributed by a Canadian retail store".

"The first version of the catalogue was a 32-page booklet handed out at the Industrial Exhibition (now the <u>Canadian National Exhibition</u>). Within twelve years, the company's mail-order department was filling over 200,000 orders per year. Eaton's actively sought out new subscribers, particularly in rural areas, by employing such tactics as offering gifts for the contact information of non-subscribers.

"Additions to the earliest versions of the catalogue included illustrations in 1887 (the first catalogues were text-only), colour in 1915, and photographs in 1919. The first mail-order office was in Toronto, but additional offices were opened in <u>Winnipeg</u> in 1905 and <u>Moncton</u> in 1918. Early catalogues sold clothing almost exclusively, though operations gradually expanded to include such products as pharmaceuticals, books, furniture, china, farm tools, and whole pre-fabricated houses.

"The Eaton's catalogue has been featured in multiple works of <u>Canadian literature</u>, including <u>The Hockey Sweater</u> and <u>Anne's House of Dreams</u>. The publication itself was used to teach literacy in some classrooms. In <u>Western Canada</u>, the catalogue was dubbed the "Homesteader's Bible" or the "Family Bible". This "Canadian symbol" was used for such diverse purposes as shin pads, home insulation, and <u>outhouse</u> toilet paper."

Below: Two catalog covers from the early 20th century that would have been available to the families in our story; Both are in the public domain; Although the Eaton's catalogue was more popular, its cover images are owned by Sears Canada Inc. and are subject to copyright. The Christie's catalog below left is dated 1918. P.T. Legaré was based in Montréal and published its first catalog in 1910. The cover below right appeared in 1920. (Library and Archives of Canada)

There can be little doubt that every household featured in our story was not only familiar with the Eaton's catalog, but were very likely to have ordered many items from it while they were living in the relatively remote setting of the Shuswap region in the early 20th century. Other catalogs were also available to families across Canada, the majority of whom lived in rural areas. According to the Library and Archives of Canada: "By the 1920s, Hudson's Bay, Morgan's and Woodward's all had a mail order service.

Further comments from the Library and Archives of Canada: "Mail order catalogues have been available in Canada since the 1880s. For years, they were eagerly awaited and much needed by the people living in our country's isolated regions. So beloved was the Eaton's catalogue, for example, that it became affectionately known by many nicknames: the Bible, the Prairie Bible, the Homesteaders' Bible, the Farmers' Bible, the Wishing Book, the Wish Book, the Want book and simply, the Book. Many other stores also produced catalogues that found their way into people's lives and hearts.

"Each fall and spring, the long-awaited catalogue would finally arrive. It was an event similar to that of a distant relative paying a long-overdue visit. There was something for everyone. In particular, the arrival of the latest catalogue was the moment that many children waited for because they would then be given the old catalogue to amuse themselves with.

"Many winter days and nights were spent poring over the pages of the catalogue, dreaming of the possibilities it offered. But the catalogue was used for many other purposes besides ordering goods from afar. Some of them may be surprising from today's perspective, where entertainment is only as far away as the television, radio, bookshelf, cinema, theatre or local sports centre.

"Besides ordering goods, here are the top ten uses (in random order) for mail order catalogues in times past:

1. Little girls searched the pages for figures to cut to make paper dolls. They then tried to find outfits that would fit the cut-out figures. Sometimes they made entire paper families to play with. Some even cut out pictures of furniture and used the cut-outs to furnish homemade doll houses.
2. Pictures cut from old catalogues would often be used for school projects or to decorate scrapbooks.
3. Boys would strap a catalogue to each shin to make goalie pads when playing hockey.
4. Teachers in many one-room schoolhouses used the catalogues to teach children to read. Sometimes it was the only book they had to read. Catalogues were also cut up to create alphabet books using the illustrations.
5. Some adult immigrants who couldn't speak English used the catalogue to teach themselves words; by studying the picture and description they not only increased their vocabulary, but learned how to spell.
6. Women eagerly awaited the catalogue to learn of the latest fashion styles. Many cut their own patterns from newspapers and sewed their family's clothes, based on illustrations from catalogues.
7. Pictures were cut out of the catalogues and used to decorate homesteaders' walls.
8. Pages could be torn out, crumpled up and used as insulation to fill in drafty cracks in cabin walls.
9. For people living in isolated rural areas, catalogues provided a cultural link with the outside world. They allowed people to keep up with the trends in fashion and home furnishings, provided new avenues for conversation, eased loneliness and created needed stimulation in many homesteaders' lives.

10. And then there was the catalogue's final destination: out to the outhouse, where it was used to decorate the walls, for reading material and finally, as toilet paper.

"Today, old catalogues are valuable research tools. Their contents provide important information to museum curators, historians, sociologists, writers, antiquarians, as well as collectors and dealers in anything from the past. The details they hold allow costume and set designers to be authentic and true to a period in their work. But you don't have to fall into any of these categories to enjoy vintage catalogues. Thumbing through the pages and discovering each era's distinct mood can bring hours of enjoyment -- just as it did when the original owners looked through the same pages for the very first time."

Ed. note – Having browsed numerous websites online while conducting my research for this book, just as the author of the above article recommends in her last paragraph, I would heartily encourage the reader to set aside some time to do the same. Among the best resources available for browsing are: Toronto Public Library Archives; Library and Archives of Canada; Royal British Columbia Museum Archives; the Sicamous & District Museum and Historical Society; to name just a few.

Left: Cover of the Steele, Briggs' Garden Guide for 1928; Below right: Page from the same catalog extolling the virtues of "The Canadian Tomato" (Toronto Public Library)

Tomato—The Canadian

The "Canadian" is earlier than any other sort without exception. In comparative tests with Earliana, seeds sown at the same time and plants set out at the same time, the "Canadian" gave ripe fruit five days sooner. The "Canadian" is surprisingly productive. We have seen clusters containing 20 full-size fruits. This variety is remarkable in this respect.

"Canadian" is perfectly smooth from beginning to end of season. No variety is more uniform in shape, all the tomatoes on a cluster ripen at once and are all about the same size. Its color is a beautiful, deep glossy scarlet, and very attractive. Flesh is thick and solid with comparatively few seeds. The flavor is all that can be desired. A first class variety for the home garden and unquestionably the very best early Tomato for the market. Ready for market in about 60 days from time of setting out the plants. Even under adverse conditions, the "Canadian" will yield a surprisingly good crop. Pkt. 25c.

TOMATO THE CANADIAN

According to a fascinating article appearing on the Toronto Public Library web site June 8, 2020, Pamela, a contributor, wrote: "For many decades, families across Ontario looked forward to getting seed catalogues in the mail so that they could start to plan their gardens. Flower and vegetable gardening were popular, and sometimes even essential over, the course of Toronto's history.

"John S. Steele, Richard Clarke Steele and Sylvester E. Briggs founded the Steele Briggs Seed company in 1873. This Toronto company paid particular attention to developing seeds suitable for the colder, Canadian climate.

"The Steele, Briggs' Garden Guide for 1928 includes a description of "The Canadian Tomato". According to the guide, it is "perfectly smooth from beginning to end of season. No variety is more uniform in shape, all the tomatoes on a cluster ripen at once and are all about the same size. Its color is a beautiful, deep glossy scarlet, and very attractive. Flesh is thick and solid with comparatively few seeds. The flavor is all that can be desired."

One may safely to assume that these popular catalogs would not have escaped the attention of Janet Kappel and her family.

Another serious challenge to remote settlers in the Kappel's situation faced occurred when winter arrived and ice began to choke the nearby lake, rivers and streams. Ice made the lake nearly impassable, unless the lake was completely frozen over with thick ice, in which case the lake became an easy and fairly safe highway the locals could use for their commerce. Most of us today may project our daily needs out for a few weeks, at most. But what if you had to plan for up to half the year in advance? Frank discussed this dilemma repeatedly in his letters and conversations with family members and journalists, stating adamantly how important it was to order everything the entire family might need to survive and thrive well in advance of the ice's arrival. Careful planning was required of everyone. Every family in the area was in the same boat, and most of them probably ordered more than they would need to simply survive. That meant that if someone in the community forgot to order sufficient quantities of an important household staple, they would be able to borrow it from one of the neighbors who had more than they required. This interdependence and willingness to share was an essential element to the welfare of the entire community, and it helped many families to set aside whatever differences they might feel for their neighbors and focus on the needs of everyone around them.

The same concept held true for those things which the community was able to produce, according to Frank. Nearly every family had a large garden and orchard which could be relied upon to provide them with healthy food that nourished them all year long. We have already seen how important seed catalogues were to isolated communities in helping them to plant and harvest healthy produce. Many settlers also kept seeds from their successful crops to use the following year, and shared them with their neighbors, as well.

Food technology had progressed to the point in the early 20th century that most isolated families could put food by to last them through the winter, after the hard frosts had arrived and eating fresh produce was no longer possible. Mankind has been salting, canning, drying, and applying other methods of preservation to the food they have available to them "in season" that enabled groups experiencing climate stress or overpopulation to move from regions that were warm and productive all year long into more northerly areas with shorter growing seasons.

Frank's memoirs discuss the abundance of fish and game in the Shuswap region. It was possible to hunt deer and bear almost any time of year, and even if the rivers and lakes were frozen over, it might still be able to find fish beneath the ice. Most homesteaders also kept milk and meat-producing animals: cattle, sheep, goats, and chickens, which also had the advantage of laying eggs continuously if they were fed properly. He said that local north Shuswap community members would share what they had slaughtered with their neighbors, since animals were usually too large for a family to consume before the meat had spoiled. Fresh meat is usually tastier and healthier than preserved meat, and slaughtering on a rotating basis among community members would be an easier way to manage their daily needs for protein.

Frank thought his wife enjoyed living in the country and struggling to raise her young daughter in relative isolation, often while Frank was away for lengthy periods trying to earn money to finance their homesteading enterprise – not to mention his lengthy absence during the First World War. We have no personal written record from Janet that reveals how she felt about the demands that arose on a frequent basis without the benefit of electricity, indoor plumbing, central heating, or nearby supermarkets. But the Frank Kappel household clearly prospered, and the couple coped with their challenges together to a degree that this writer would have to assess as nothing short of miraculous.

Betty Kappel wrote a brief memoir of her father that included family details I have found nowhere else: "When war broke out my Dad enlisted and my Mother and I also went to England but after two years had to return. This was a very difficult time for my Mother, being far away from a post office and living alone in a partly finished house." We have so few glimpses of what life was like for Jenny on that isolated homestead, but it is easy to imagine that she was relieved when the family moved to Sicamous. Betty also wrote in the same memoir: "Eventually the farm was sold for the princely sum of $2,500.00."

Thinking about Janet and Betty living in that primitive cabin with almost no modern amenities, the two of them without Frank to do the heavy lifting for nearly three years before he returned from the war, leaves this writer feeling awe and respect for Janet Kappel. The strength, courage, and fortitude such an endeavor would have required is undeniable. Janet was a woman well aware of larger forces confronting the world in 1912, even if it would have been difficult for her to imagine what her life would be like as a frontier woman living in western Canada prior to her arrival. Did any of her experiences in Scotland and the Continent prepare her to face the many challenges this new, wild environment thrust upon her and every other newcomer?

Fortunately, Janet's community was made up of men and women who had been surviving and even thriving on the North shore of the Shuswap prior to her arrival. They included her own family members as well as her neighbors, some of whom had grown up on farms and were already familiar with farming methods when they arrived. Being a woman of intelligence she would have consulted them freely from the beginning, even before she and Frank were married. Excellent books had been written on the subject and were readily available by mail order to provide insight and advice to anyone who could read and was willing to listen to the wisdom that had been gleaned from years of personal experience living in similar circumstances.

One of the most famous and practical of these books was written by a woman who emigrated to Canada from England in the mid-19th century and who had translated the lessons of her experiences into a practical compilation of "how-to" instructions with great success. Catherine Parr Traill was truly "a woman ahead of her time" when it came to inventing a life for herself and her family in the "backwoods" wilderness of northern Ontario. Her first book, *The Backwoods of Canada,* according to Wikipedia, "was published in 1836 and was collected from letters she had written home to England during her first three years of pioneering. It was addressed primarily to women of her own class, to the wives of gentlemen or of gentlemen immigrants who might be both entertained and profitably instructed by a simple, factual and optimistic account of the Traills' early days in Upper Canada. Her writing efforts eventually led to the publication of *The Canadian Settlers' Guide,* which she announced when it was first published in 1854, 22 years after her arrival in Upper Canada, as (more particularly for the wives and daughters of small farmers, and part of it is also addressed to the wives of labourers and mechanics)."

Right: Cover of "The Canadian Settlers' Guide", Fifth Edition, written by Catherine Parr Traill

THE

Canadian Settler's Guide:

BY

MRS. C. P. TRAILL,

AUTHORESS OF

THE "BACKWOODS OF CANADA," &c., &c., &c.

FIFTH EDITION.

CHRISTMAS DAY IN THE BACKWOODS.

TORONTO, C.W.:
PRINTED AT THE OLD COUNTRYMAN OFFICE.

1855.

In her preface, Catherine Traill says she was especially concerned at the numbers of women for whom life in Canada was a disaster, stating: "Disheartened by repeated failures, unused to the expedients which the older inhabitants adopt in any case of difficulty, repining and disgust take the place of cheerful activity; troubles increase, and the power to overcome them decreases; domestic happiness disappears. The woman toils on heart-sick and pining for the home she left behind her. The husband reproaches his broken-hearted partner, and both blame the Colony for the failure of the individual." Other early pioneer women in Canada also wrote about their experiences, but Catherine Traill stands alone in her genre, according to Clara Thomas, who published a reprint of Traill's book in 1969. "With her combination of practical intelligence, strength of purpose, quiet optimism and massive common sense who undertook to supply a need" all of these courageous women felt. Catherine Traill is at all times a woman speaking with eminent practicality to other women, from her experience and from her humanity."

Right: An engraving from the tenth edition of "The Canadian Settlers' Guide"

Quoting again from Ms. Traill: "Having myself suffered from the

THE CANADIAN SETTLER'S FIRST HOME IN THE BACKWOODS.

disadvantage of acquiring all my knowledge of Canadian housekeeping by personal experience, and having heard other females similarly situated lament the want of some simple useful book to give them and insight into the customs and occupations incidental to the Canadian settler's life, I have taken upon me to endeavor to supply this want…"

Her book was first printed in 1854 in Toronto as *The Female Emigrant's Guide and Hints on Canadian Housekeeping,* but in the next year it was reprinted as *The Canadian Settlers' Guide,* and it maintained that same title, in various editions, throughout the next 150 years. It has become a classic among books of its kind throughout the world, and is still widely available. The book eventually incorporated concepts and advice from Mrs. Traill's brother, Samuel Strickland, who had published *Twenty-Seven Years' Residence in Canada West* in 1853, but whose book was far too expensive for the average pioneer to afford.

Without going into further detail about the contents of the book, it seems reasonable to assume that Jenny Kappel and her contemporaries in the Shuswap region knew about this book and were very likely to have read it and profited from its contents. The book covers such a wide-ranging panoply of useful topics that it would be almost impossible for any reader not to come away with a more practical appreciation of the art of living: from medical conditions to practical treatments, breadmaking, beekeeping, food preparation and preservation, soap and candle

making, animal husbandry, gardening, fruit and vegetable selection, growing and preserving, identifying and harvesting edible native plants…the list is lengthy and formidable. [*Ed. note – This author can highly recommend reading Mrs. Traill's impressive book, which is available for free download from the Archives of the Toronto Public Library website.*]

Left: Jenny Kappel with her sister, Catherine Elizabeth Dolan, early 1940s (from Stanley's private collection, SPC) [Ed. note – Born in 1895, "Aunt Kate" was 18 years younger than Jenny.]

As we have previously learned from Frank's memoirs, life changed dramatically for the Kappel family after they arrived in Sicamous. They built a fine house overlooking the water, the children continued their schooling, and Jenny at some point resumed her painting. With Jenny's family living in the Shuswap area, and Frank's brother and sister in the Vancouver area, there can be no doubt that the lives of every extended family member were busy and demanding. But they found time to gather and maintain meaningful contact that would have enabled both Stanley and Betty to get to know their aunts, uncles, grandparents and cousins intimately.

The few written documents I have found reveal much about Jenny Kappel's sense of taste and refinement – something she shared with her family and her community in a way that elevated everyone within her circle. Frank has already shared that the Kappel household provided a focus of social life for the citizens of Sicamous, but several more news clippings from local newspapers of the 1930s provide additional insight into the richness of the social life enjoyed by the community.

From The Vernon Herald, January 28, 1932: "SCOTTISH BARD COMMEMORATED; "Party in Sicamous Hall In Honor of Robert Burns – Varied Entertainment and Dance; Sicamous, B.C., Jan. 25 – On Saturday evening, Sicamous gave due honor to Burns, the immortal Scottish bard, with a party in the local hall.

"Mrs. J. Penzer sang Annie Laurie and other selections, George Weddup sang "Mary of Argyle", and Frank Kappel sang "Afton Water." Miss Eva Burn and "Jock" Dean recited some of Burns' poems and a few choice jokes were told by Frank Kappel."

Another article from The Vernon Herald dated February 2, 1933, read: "SICAMOUS HEARS FINE ADDRESS ON SCOTTISH POET; Burns' Night Celebrated at Sicamous Hall By Large Crowd; Sicamous, B.C., Jan. 31 – Burns' Night was celebrated at the Sicamous Hall on Wednesday evening when a large crowd assembled.

"During the program Mrs. F. Kappel gave an address on Robert Burns and his works. Scottish songs by Mrs. Thomas Penzer and Frank Westaway proved quite pleasing. F. Kappel and Miss Vera Stepp assisted at the piano. Cards, refreshments, and dancing completed an enjoyable evening of entertainment. The prizes for cards were won by Miss Elmi Herringson, Mrs. F. Kappel, E. Dodds and M. Ward."

Right: Front cover of a leading Canadian magazine dated June 1918, the Canadian Home Journal, which Jenny Thomson would almost certainly have read on a regular basis (Toronto Public Library)

These two articles provide important insight into what sort of a life Frank and Jenny Kappel eventually made for themselves. They reflect education and refinement, for one thing. The few photos we have of the Frank Kappel family also reveal Jenny to be a bit of a "fashion plate", always well dressed and draped in furs when she went out into the public arena. She set a fine table in her own home, especially on holidays. Her home was filled with her own paintings, along with the unique memorabilia she had inherited from her famous uncle, Joseph Thomson. Her living room was filled with fine furniture, floral arrangements, oriental carpets on the floor, everywhere the picture of

refinement and respectability that one might not expect in a location like Sicamous in the early 20th century. But Jenny had lived, studied, traveled, and painted in Europe, her parents were leading citizens wherever they lived, her husband was a civic leader and successful businessman in their chosen community. I think it is safe to say that Jenny and Frank Kappel were a "power couple" in every sense and would have blossomed significantly wherever they had spent their many years together.

Above left: Photo of Jenny Kappel sitting in her living room with the painting that now hangs in our home, with another view of the eclectic but elegant nature of their Sicamous home (from Stanley's private collection); Above right: Jenny sitting pensively at home, a book in her lap, already descending into the abyss of Parkinson's Disease, ca. early 1940s (from the Beesons)

Euphemia Thomson, Jenny's mother, died at the age of 84 in November 1937. Her obituary in The Vancouver Province states that "she died at the home of a daughter. Widow of the late William Thomson of Thornhill, Scotland, Mrs. Thomson was mother of seventeen. Five of her sons served in the Great War. Six sons and daughters survive. Alex Thomson of Vancouver is a son and Mrs. Frank Kappel of Sicamous, a daughter." This event was almost certainly a great loss for Janet, and it seems likely that her mother was living with her and Frank in their home in Sicamous when she passed away.

Left: Elizabeth "Betty" Kappel, Stanley's only Kappel sibling, ca. 1940 [Ed. note – Age 27] (SPC)

In a fascinating article appearing on the Toronto Public Library web site June 8, 2020, Pamela, a contributor, wrote: "For many decades, families across Ontario looked forward to getting seed catalogues in the mail so that they could start to plan their gardens. Flower and vegetable gardening were popular, and sometimes even essential over, the course of Toronto's history.

"John S. Steele, Richard Clarke Steele and Sylvester E. Briggs founded the Steele Briggs Seed company in 1873. This Toronto company paid particular attention to developing seeds suitable for the colder, Canadian climate.

"The Steele, Briggs' Garden Guide for 1928 includes a description of "The Canadian Tomato". According to the guide, it is "perfectly smooth from beginning to end of season. No variety is more uniform in shape, all the tomatoes on a cluster ripen at once and are all about the same size. Its color is a beautiful, deep glossy scarlet, and very attractive. Flesh is thick and solid with comparatively few seeds. The flavor is all that can be desired."

It seems difficult to imagine that these popular catalogs would have escaped the attention of Janet Kappel and her family.

Right: "WAMS" participants contributing to the war effort, 1940, including Betty Kappel, smiling brightly, 4th row, 4th from our right, just above and to the right of the engine carburetor (Salmon Arm Museum at R.J. Haney Heritage Village)

Meanwhile, Betty Kappel was coming into her own, in addition to teaching for 10 years in the Sicamous/Shuswap area and getting married in 1945. From the Salmon Arm Observer, Shuswap History in Pictures, August 20, 2019: "An equal opportunity class? This image certainly looks like a motor mechanics class for women. And caps are required. Photograph was taken May 6, 1940. "WAMS" participants include Frances Robinson, Mary Doyle, Lois Aitcheson, Dorothy Ruth, Thelma Hodgkin, Nora Grant, Pam Beech, Eva Ireland, Queenie Jones, Mary Fawcett, Peggy Beech, Mrs. Albert Bedford (Eileen), Rosemary Culverwell, Bessie Snyder, Betty Kappel, Gwen Scott, Mary Meek, Verna Willinston, Elsie Buchan, Mrs. Robinson, Zola Riddle, Helenita Hislop, Clara Urquhart Calvert, Muriel Williams (Mrs. Barker's niece), Mrs. Eric Bivar, Mr. R.G.A. Purkis (instructor), Mrs. Dan Robertson (Ivy Harper), Miss Grant, Miss Cathy Pressley, Helen Miller and Molly Beech."

Betty left teaching at the height of the Second World War, moved to Ottawa in January 1943, and began working for the Canadian Intelligence Service. In a letter to Dora Dunbar, his youngest Buckingham sister (Marie), written March 26th, 1943, Stanley stated: "Betty is now in Ottawa and had a Government job there in some branch of the Intelligence Service, I believe. I have only heard from her once since she left. She went down there in Jan., and I suppose is finding it rather difficult to get settled. She said she liked it very much though, and I imagine that after teaching for so long, any change would be welcome." Welcome indeed, especially if you consider the implications of being a volunteer mechanic in the "WAMS" in Salmon Arm and then becoming a spy in Ottawa. One can only marvel how liberating these experiences were for Betty, especially with a mother who had gone off to Europe for more than ten years to become an accomplished artist at a time when women were meant to become wives and mothers above all else. In addition, both Janet and Betty had accompanied Frank to England during the First World War. Even though Betty may not have remembered much from that experience due to her young age, the stories that her mother and father shared with her about that perilous time would undoubtedly have made a big impression on her.

Above: Recruitment poster encouraging Canadian women to join the military in support of the war; Posters recruited women to free up men for combat, and thousands served as clerks, mechanics, messengers and drivers. More than 21,000 women volunteered for the army, 7,100 joined the Women's Royal Canadian Naval Service and more than 17,000 were recruited for the Women's Division of the Royal Canadian Air Force. Female pilots shuttled aircraft around behind the lines, enabling 900 male pilots to join fighter and bomber crews. (Legion Magazine)

Among Jenny Kappel's most important experiences would surely have been the marriage of her children. We will read more about Stanley, including his marriage to Alice Leland, in subsequent chapters. Betty was married to Bill Ingram from nearby Kamloops in 1945. The wedding was held at the Kappel family home in Sicamous, and it appears from reports that no expense was spared.

The wedding details were widely publicized in more than 5 local and regional newspapers, including the best one from The Vernon News, June 7, 1945: INGRAM-KAPPEL:

"The flower-banked drawing room of the bride's parents, Mr. and Mrs. Frank Kappel, Sicamous, was the setting of the wedding of their only daughter, Elizabeth Beatrice, to John A. Ingram of Kamloops, on Monday, June 4th, Rev. A. B. Craig of Salmon Arm officiating.

Right: Photo taken the day of Betty Kappel's wedding to Bill Ingram, with friends of the family present (from Alice's collection, annotated by Jack Brown)

"Given in marriage by her father, the bride wore a two-piece chartreuse green crepe afternoon gown with matching accessories and a corsage of orchids. She was attended by Mrs. Betty Costain of Sicamous as matron of honor, wearing a two-piece peach crepe dress with white accessories and a corsage of spring flowers. The groom was supported by Gordon Smith of Kamloops.

Bill Ingram and Betty Kappel on their Wedding Day - 4 June 1945, Sicamous, British Columbia, Canada

Bg. L to R: Gordon Smith (best man), and Frank Englehardt Kappel (bride's father)
Fg. L to R: Mrs. B. Costain, Elizabeth (Betty) Beatrice Kappel, John (Bill) Allan Ingram, Mary Miller Low Ingram (groom's mother) and Janet Thomson Kappel (bride's mother).

Mrs. Vera Finlayson played a musical selection during the signing of the register. "The guests were received by the bride's mother, wearing a mauve suit with navy accessories, and the groom's mother in a figured silk ensemble with black accessories.

"Presiding at the urns were Mrs. C. Sacre of Kamloops and Mrs. Pat Dolan of Salmon Arm, aunt of the bride. Servitours were Mrs. W. K. Finlayson, Mrs. H. M. Paterson, Miss Eva Ireland, Mrs. W. A. Parry, and Mrs. G. Page.

"Chas. C. Barker of Salmon Arm proposed the toast to the bride, to which the groom replied. After a honeymoon at Banff and Lake Louise, the bride and groom will make their home in Kamloops.

A glowing tribute appears beneath a photo of the Frank Kappel family on the website of the Sicamous & District Museum and Historical Society, under the heading: "The People Behind Our Street Names". The name of the author of the following tribute is not attributed on the website, but it was probably Gordon Mackie, a local Sicamous historian, according to the archivist at the Sicamous & District Museum and Historical Society:

"Frank Kappel, born in Wales in 1886, was an early pioneer of the Shuswap area, arriving in Canada in 1911 and settling on a homestead in Celista. He cleared his own land, married Janet in Kamloops in 1912, worked as an accountant in Vancouver in 1913 and audited city books for Kamloops and Salmon Arm that year. He returned to the Shuswap and became a scaler. He then joined the army in 1914 and returned to the Shuswap in 1919. He joined the

R.W. Bruhn Co. in 1921 and moved to Sicamous *[Ed. note – Probably in 1922]* to manage the company from the head office on CPR Hill until it folded in 1947.

"Visiting the Kappels as a child was a treat. The house was filled with beautiful paintings and countless African artifacts. The African artifacts had come from Mrs. Kappel's brother who was an early African explorer. Mrs. Kappel was a painter of some renown, having studied in Germany until the early 1900s. Both Mr. and Mrs. Kappel spoke fluent German, French and Spanish. Their daughter Betty became a teacher and was one of my first teachers at the one-room school on CPR Hill. Stanley became a mining engineer."

Above: A photo of the Frank Kappel family taken in their home ca. 1940. [Ed. note – This may have been taken by a professional photographer, since interior photos were seldom made at the time because flash cameras weren't widely available. Notice the oriental carpet, the interesting furniture, and the paintings hanging on the walls.] (Sicamous and District Museum and Historical Society)

Another story about the Kappels appeared in a charming booklet compiled by a group of Sicamous residents in 1989 to commemorate the incorporation of Sicamous into a municipality. It is entitled: "True Stories from the Eagle Valley" and contains the following chapter that further enhances our understanding of what life must have been like, living in Sicamous, in the early 20th century. The story, attributed to Fay Mabee, says that Stanley was six and Betty was 10, and is entitled "THE KAPPELS":

"The Kappels lived in a small two-bedroom house, and none of the houses were winterized in any way. They decided to go to Salmon Arm for New Years and would be gone a night and a day.

"When they left, they left the water running into the sink, it was cold, about twenty below zero, they came home about ten thirty at night, their son was six and their daughter was ten.

"They could not get the kitchen door open, Mr. Kappel managed to get a window open, put the lights on to find ice built up four feet high up against the kitchen door and Mrs. Kappel said there was a least two feet of ice all over the floor, the water was running and freezing wherever it could get.

"Later on, the Kappels built a lovely house in Sicamous, and it was filled with things from Africa. Her uncle David Thomson *[Ed. note – This article incorrectly refers to David Thomson, when the man Fay Mabee is describing is actually Janet's uncle Joseph Thomsen.]* had been an African explorer, this was back in the eighteen hundreds, he was awarded a British Fellowship Medal for exploration by the British government. He made nineteen more trips to Africa.

"He discovered the Central African lakes, the Victoria Falls, he once met Livingston, and was very interested in collecting African things of that time: a huge shield, all kinds of spears, a lot of articles made of copper and brass, and a leopard skin.

"Anytime there was a masquerade people went to Kappels to get things: they had a great collection of brass neck rings, ivory bracelets and all those circles of ivory they wore in their lips and ears, they were as big us an ordinary saucer.

"The brass neck things were coils of brass about six to eight inches long to stretch their necks. She had nineteen sets of horns of different African animals, all these animals are extinct due to white man killing them off. They had a shield about four feet high, they were made from elephant skin and used in battle, a man could bend over behind them for protection. They had an elephant gun made from ivory and silver and it was about nine feet long, and of course made by a white man.

"We were there one evening when a man came to the door and asked to see the gun, he offered them twenty thousand dollars for it, but Mrs. Kappel told him it was not for sale. They had necklaces galore. All this stuff had been her Mother's.

"David *[sic]* Thomson died of malaria at the age of thirty-two. He wrote a lot of books and I read all of them. He led his first expedition at the age of nineteen. He went to Africa as a secretary to an explorer, but the man died after two months, and David *[sic]* took over and carried on with the project.

"After Mrs. Kappel died Mr. Kappel contacted relatives of hers, but very few wanted those things, Betty didn't as she said they were so big and took so much room.

"Mr. Kappel sent it all to a museum in Scotland and England as that is where David *[sic]* Thomson came from. There are two books, "The Blue Nile " and the "White Nile "by Moorehead and David *[sic]* Thomson is mentioned a lot. Mrs. Kappel was an artist, she had some beautiful pictures she had done, she trained in Germany. Stanley died many years ago, Betty lives in Victoria, she was a teacher and in Sicamous. Their place was an education in itself."

Jenny Kappel was nearly eight years older than Frank. Her death certificate states she had suffered from Parkinson's disease for 19 years prior to her passing at age 68. Her obituary was published in a local Shuswap area newspaper.

Mrs. F. Kappel, Shuswap Lake Pioneer, Dies, 6 April 1946:

"Attended by many friends from Salmon Arm, Sicamous and the surrounding district, the funeral of Mrs. Janet Kappel, wife of Frank Kappel, prominent Sicamous lumberman, was held on Monday afternoon from St. John's Anglican Church. Mrs. Kappel, who was a well-known pioneer of the Shuswap Lake area, died in Salmon Arm General Hospital on Saturday morning after an illness of several weeks.

"The service was conducted by Rev. A. B. Craig, vicar of St. John's Parish, and Rev. F.W. Sharman, of Enderby. Interment was in the Masonic section of Mount Ida cemetery. The large concourse of friends and numerous floral tributes testified to the high esteem in which Mrs. Kappel was held by a wide circle of friends.

"Born at Thornhill, Dumfriesshire, Scotland, Mrs. Kappel had been a resident of the district for 34 years, with the exception of two years spent in the Old Country during the First World War. The daughter of Mr. and Mrs. William Thomson, she came to B.C. in 1912 to marry Mr. Kappel, who came from the Old Country and took up a homestead at Magna Bay in 1911. The wedding took place at Kamloops.

"When Mr. Kappel enlisted for active service in 1915, Mrs. Kappel returned to the Old Country, remaining there until 1917, when she came back to Canada. In 1922 she and Mr. Kappel moved to Sicamous, where they had resided ever since.

"Keenly interested in all community activities, Mrs. Kappel was long prominent in the work of the Sicamous Women's Institute and other organizations. She was also a member of the Shuswap Chapter, Order of the Eastern Star *[Ed. note – The women's auxiliary of the Masonic Lodge]*. A kindly neighbor, with sympathetic understanding and a capacity for making friends, her home was always open and there are scores who were encouraged by her counsel or enjoyed her hospitality. She was also a talented artist, and her home was filled with many oil paintings which were the work of her brush.

"In addition to her husband, Mrs. Kappel is survived by one son, Stanley Kappel, Sheep Creek, and one daughter, Mrs. J.A. "Bill" Ingram, Kamloops, two brothers, Thomas Thomson, and Alex. H. Thomson, both of Victoria, and two sisters, Mrs. P. Dolan *[Ed. note – This was in fact Catherine Elizabeth Dolan, Janet's youngest sister.]*, Eagle Bay, and Mrs. E. MacLennan, Dundee, Scotland."

Fay Mabee may also have written the commentary (instead of Gordon Mackie) that accompanies the photograph of the four Kappels, sitting in their charming home, surrounded by such interesting memorabilia, that appears just prior to "THE KAPPELS" story. This narrative also lends weight to the concept of the cachet that the Thomson and Kappel families all derived from having been closely related to such a famous figure as Joseph Thomson.

Today, in 2022, Kappel Street runs east/west along the south side of Sicamous, all the way down to the Sicamous Narrows that connects the Shuswap Lake with Mara Lake *[Ed. note – See map below to find out where Kappel Street is)*.

Jenny was one of seventeen children, according to her mother's obituary. Raising such a large family was a truly remarkable accomplishment, and it placed a heavy burden on both of Janet's parents as well as all of the surviving siblings. To be able to support so many individuals successfully at a time before the basic necessities of life were easily acquired by an average family was an impressive achievement, as it would be for most of us in the first world of today. It is not certain how many of the Thomson children survived childhood, but we learned from the same obituary that five of Janet's brothers served in the Great War and that six siblings were still alive in 1937 at the time of her mother's death. Even though Janet died at the relatively young age of 68, her obituary suggests that only five siblings were still alive at the time of her passing.

Below: Detail map of the southern section of Sicamous today with Kappel St. visible near the bottom of the map, circled in red, running east-west past the Sicamous Bible Church between the boat launch and Dogwood Ave. (sicamous.civicweb.net)

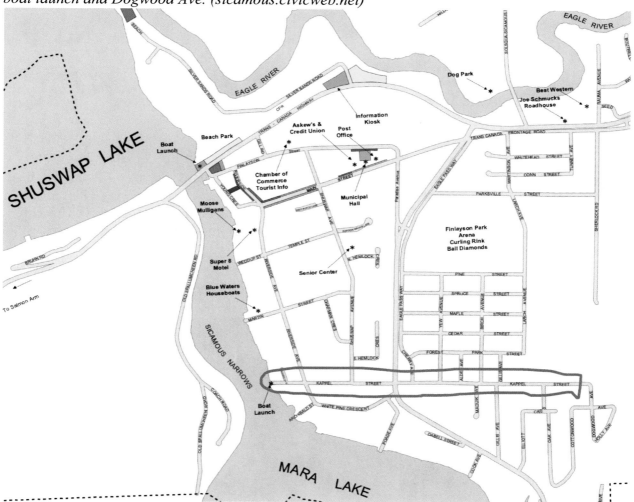

Jenny's granddaughter, Lynne (Ingram) Beeson, shared her precious memories of her grandmother, as well as her own mother: "Mum *[Ed. note – meaning Betty (Kappel) Ingram]* definitely adored her father and mother, (AND Uncle Stanley) and always said how much she missed her mother, who died before we were born. I have a few pictures on the wall of Mum in a prom dress and Mum with her mother.

"Mum, for some reason, would never discuss illness in herself or anyone else. So, when I was expecting Sean and would ask Mum what her mother died of, she would just say old age – when really her mother died very young. But Joan Crosbie, a good friend of Mum's, said once that she thought Jenny Kappel (as she was always known, despite her given name being Janet, who I am named for – my first name) died of Parkinson's. I know that her health steadily declined. So, they moved into Sicamous when Grandpa worked for Bruhn Sawmills

(there is a street named Kappel Street there – although they pronounce it with the emphasis being on the second syllable, the same way Great Uncle Stanley (grandpa's brother) pronounced it).

Left: Photo of Turner's Canadian Apples, Salmon Arm, B.C., dated 1952 (prairie-towns.com)

"Both Mum and Grandpa always told stories about the hobos who would ride the rails, and they knew that if they stopped at the Kappel house near the train tracks in Sicamous, they would be fed a meal and sent off with food. Later, Grandpa worked for the Turners' Apple Packing Plant in Salmon Arm, mainly because Jenny needed to be closer to Doctors and a hospital. Until the day Grandpa died, the Turners used to mail us two large crates of apples (one of golden delicious and one of red delicious apples) every year".

Below: Oil painting of Shuswap countryside by Janet Kappel that hangs in Kerry's home, unsigned and undated (photo provided by Kerry Dearborn)

Above: Oil painting, undated, signed "Janet Kappel", which suggests it was done in British Columbia after she was married to Frank. The two examples of Jenny's paintings in our possession are masterful examples of her remarkable and mature talent as an artist. (photo taken by the author)

CHAPTER 10 – For Home and Country ("The Ties That Bind")

One additional important detail of Jenny's life begs to be revealed. She was active throughout her many years in British Columbia with the North Shuswap Lake Women's Institute, and later, the Sicamous Women's Institute, according to her obituary.

The Canadian Encyclopedia states that the first Canadian Women's Institute was founded in Ontario in 1897, but the organization rapidly spread across the continent and became a national movement after the Great War. Its motto, "For Home and Country", reflects the organization's aims: "to promote an appreciation of rural living, to develop informed citizens through the study of national and international issues (particularly those affecting women and children) and to initiate national programs to achieve common goals".

The original impetus for the organization was Adelaide Hoodless, a Canadian woman from Ontario who had lost her own young son at the age of 14 months. Her deep trauma resulted in her beginning a crusade that involved her appearing at women's groups across the province, speaking on "the importance of women engaging in formal domestic education and organizing a unified voice to advocate in the areas of education, family health and community service to improve the lives of their families, the families in their communities, and families across Canada", according to the Women's Institute website. Her grief "gave rise to her mission to organize and educate women and mothers around the world about food safety to ensure every woman was trained in homecare and domestic science."

Right: Early pin worn by members of the FWIC

In 1919 the Federated Women's Institutes of Canada was established.

"The Federated Women's Institutes flourished alongside the growing economy and industrialization during the 1920s and 1930s. With more women entering colleges, taking up long term positions as secretaries, teachers and in shops.

"Many women started to move from the rural towns of their childhood to booming cities across Canada to raise their families. WI Canada started to focus on a more diverse range of issues affecting women of the early twentieth century.

"Early resolutions, such as an increase to the age of female consent, parental control and divorce and abandonment legislation, demonstrate the passion of WI Canada for securing women's rights in the changing social climate. Other early resolutions speak to the patriotic undertones of the WI Canada's founders and the concern members had for the improvement and marketability of agricultural activities in rural Canada.

"By the end of the 1920s, WI Canada had advocated for women's employment rights, rights to education and health care for all Canadians, and resolutions around immigration and community development. The 1930s brought much of the same until Germany declared war on Britain and its allies in 1939. Just like the Great War, all Women's Institutes, including those in Canada, focused their efforts on supporting troops, fellow Commonwealth communities and the Allied Forces in Europe. WI Canada and provincial branches organized Jam for Britain drives, sent knitwear and clothing to Europe, and raised crucial funding for the Red Cross, among other projects."

Jenny Kappel, having arrived from a life in Scotland and Europe at the age of 34, was thrust into an almost unimaginably harsh and primitive environment on a homestead on the north shore of Shuswap Lake, with few if any roads, no connecting railroad, leaving the only communication with "the outside world" by boat (or ice in the winter). There was almost no commerce in the area, leaving all the area's inhabitants to their own devices when it came to providing the basic necessities of living for themselves and their families. This was a scenario played out across the western regions of North America, but it is impossible to comprehend fully how Jenny must have felt upon arriving at Notch Hill after spending many years in the sophisticated embrace of continental Europe. To be sure, she immediately married Frank Kappel, a highly competent man, and she had key members of her own nuclear family living nearby, including her parents.

Still, for those of us living in the privileged circumstances of the modern world with so many conveniences in our homes and so many "consumer options" available to us at the stroke of a keyboard, I would invite you, dear reader, to make at least a small attempt to imagine what life must have been like for those hardy people living in that isolation with no formal health care available in the local community, with no 911 number to call should one encounter a dreadful medical emergency, with no running water in the house, no toilet in the house, and no electricity to bring light during the long winter evenings, with wood being the only option to cook the meals or heat the home. Every member of that small community was left to their own resources for the most part, but they were also dependent upon collaboration with every other member of the community to exploit whatever collective resources, talents and training each of them could offer to one another in order to survive, to raise their young children, to enable everyone to live long enough to become self-sufficient, provided that good fortune had decided to smile on you and your family. OMG!

According to Wikiwand: "The Women's Institute movement was based on the British concept of Women's Guilds, created by Rev Archibald Charteris in 1887 and originally confined to the Church of Scotland. From Canada the organisation spread back to the motherland, throughout the British Empire and Commonwealth, and thence to other countries."

In addition to having available to them the published "how-to" guides that were discussed in the previous chapter, it is very likely that Jenny Thomson, her mother, and sisters were already familiar with the Women's Guilds and were eager to become part of a similar movement once they arrived in the wilds of Canada. Whatever the case, Jenny became involved with the North Shuswap Lake Women's Institute after she arrived in British Columbia, and she continued her involvement after moving to Sicamous in 1921. And the Women's Institutes played a major role in supporting both women and the larger community. They encouraged women to learn as much as they could by providing educational opportunities that included home economics, making jam and home-preserved foods, along with food safety, healthy nutrition, childcare, and controlling family budgets. They emphasized many details of farming life that would bring extra cash into the household, such as growing vegetables and fruits, milking cows and making butter. And they held craft fairs regularly to help women sell their products. They promoted economic prosperity and independence by teaching craft skills that could be turned into cottage industries. These played a major role in raising money to build community halls in every village where citizens could gather to enjoy one another's company, discuss important issues, and dance.

From the *History of England* blog: "At the formation of the Women's Institute, its founders knew that success would 'depend on the inclusion of women of all ranks'. And the Institute played an important role in breaking down social barriers, with women from all walks of life working and learning together. All the same, in the early days, women from middle- and upper-class backgrounds often took leading roles."

In a nation such as England where rigid class distinctions have prevailed even to the present day, this concept was critical, but probably not so much in Canada where true members of the upper class were hard to come by, especially in the wilds of British Columbia.

Be that as it may, the concept of "working together" encouraged every woman to join in regardless of the circumstances of one's birth. This sense of community and commonality spilled over into the women's movements including the suffragettes of the early 20th century that have played such a pivotal role in helping women to gain a sense of their equal footing and equal importance in establishing and maintaining a healthy society.

Precious concept, indeed! Precious and vital, in fact. Jenny Thomson's life experiences that preceded her arrival in the North Shuswap Community were undoubtedly profoundly important to that community, and especially to the women who found themselves in common bond, trying to establish themselves in such a difficult and challenging environment.

The Handbook of the British Columbia Women's Institutes, published in 1948 under the authority of the Ministry of Agriculture, is a highly formalized presentation of the concept and execution of the idea of Women's Institutes in the province. It includes four important passages:

From page 1: "A nation cannot rise above the level of its homes; therefore, we women must work and study together to raise our homes to the highest level possible."

From page 2: THE INSTITUTE ODE (Tune: Auld Land Syne)

"A goodly thing it is to meet
In friendship's circle bright,
Where nothing strains the pleasure sweet,
Or dims the radiant light.
No unkind words our lips shall pass,
No envy sours the mind,
But each shall seek the common weal,
The good for all mankind."

From Page 2: COLLECT OF THE ASSOCIATED COUNTRYWOMEN OF THE WORLD (A Club Woman's Creed.)

"Keep us, O Lord, from Pettiness: let us be large in thought, in word,
Let us be done with fault-finding and leave off self-seeking.
May we put away all pretence and meet each other face to face, without

Self-pity and without prejudice.
May we never be hasty in judgment and always generous.
Teach us to put into action our better impulses, straightforward and unafraid.
Let us take time for all things: make us grow calm, serene, gentle.
Grant that we may realize that it is the little things that create differences;
That in the big things of life we are one.
And may we strive to touch and know the great human heart common to us all.
And, O Lord God, let us not forget to be kind."
   - *Mary Stewart*

From page 22:

"A lady with a lamp shall stand
In the great history of the land,
A noble type of good
Heroic womanhood."
   - *Longfellow*

Above: Modern crest pin of the FWIC

CHAPTER 11 – Canada and the Canadian Pacific Railway (Cultural and Commercial Lifeline of the Shuswap Region)

The importance of the railway to Sicamous and the entire Shuswap region throughout the latter 19th and early 20th centuries is impossible to exaggerate. All the "powers that be" of the time, many Canadian, many American, and many English, recognized how fundamental a safe, reliable, and affordable mode of transport for goods and people was to enable the full development and exploitation of the inland regions of British Columbia, and indeed, the entire northern tier of the North American continent. Prior to the advent of the railroad, the principle means of commercial transport in southern BC was by water via steamboats, barges and ferries that enabled the region to open. Most of the harvested timber was floated down rivers and streams in "logjams" in order to get it to sawmills for additional processing. All other land-based modes of transport, mostly relying on a disorganized system of roads, trails, and paths, were subject to severe limitations. Even the waterways were subject to seasonal fluctuations that included flooding and periodically insufficient water to make them navigable. In the mostly mountainous environment of southern BC, canals were simply unthinkable to make water transport more reliable, simply because building them was complicated, expensive, and would have required a series of sophisticated locks to get boats up and down the watercourses. Further to the east, the distance across the Great Plains, coupled with the need for a nearly limitless supply of water to keep water levels constant, made the construction of year-round canals realistically impossible.

This entire subject is very complex and deeply interesting, but Canadians understood very early how important it was for them to build a transcontinental railroad in order to open up the country to enable an easier flow of people, goods, and ideas. In the early 19th century, no continuous rivers or canals stretched across Canada from east to west, and any available "roads" were more likely to be dirt tracks or even simple walking paths used by Native Americans, hunters, trappers, and adventurers. The technology for building railroads carrying steam-powered locomotives originated in England in 1825 and spread to America in 1830, with Canada following suit by building its first railway in 1836. The technology of road and canal building was much older at the time, but it had at least as many limitations as railroads, especially for a continent that stretched more than 3,000 miles from coast to coast.

As an extension of "The Crown", logic would seem to dictate that the big shots in Canada should look to the big shots in England for investment capital, technological assistance, and experience in building railways. High-flying politicians, investors, and inventors provided the impetus for massive railroad building projects, but these also required enormous amounts of land to make way for construction. And since "The Crown" owned at least 90% of Canadian land in the 19th century, it is easy to understand why "The Crown" would be instrumental in granting rights-of-way and myriad other benefits to those with money and ideas who were willing to gamble on the success of such an enormous undertaking as the construction of a railway from Eastern Canada all the way to its west coast. Such massive projects almost invariably met with impending financial disaster.

According to The Canadian Encyclopedia: "The financial difficulties experienced by all early railways forced massive public expenditures in the form of cash grants, guaranteed interest, land grants, rebates, and rights-of-way. In return, the railways contributed to general economic developments, and the indirect benefits for business and employment were significant. Unlike canals, railways extended into new territories and pushed the agricultural and timber frontiers westward and northward.

Left: Chinese laborers working on the CPR Railway, British Columbia, 1884 (The Canadian Encyclopedia)

"The railways played an integral role in the process of industrialization, tying together and opening up new markets while, at the same time creating a demand for fuel, iron and steel, locomotives, and rolling stock. The pioneer wood-burning locomotives required great amounts of fuel, and "wooding-up" stations were required at regular intervals along the line.

Left: CPR crew laying tracks, Lower Fraser Valley, 1883 (Wikipedia)

"Entrepreneurs invested in the manufacture of almost everything that went into the operation of the railway, and consequently railways had a positive effect on levels of employment. Some small towns became railway service and maintenance centres, with the bulk of the population dependent on the railway shops. The railway also had a decisive impact on the physical characteristics of Canadian cities: hotels and industries were built around tracks, yards, and stations, making the railway a central feature of the urban landscape.

"On 21 October 1880, the government finally signed a contract with the Canadian Pacific Railway (CPR) Company, headed by George Stephan, and construction began in 1881. The "Last Spike" was driven on 7 November 1885 and the first passenger train left Montreal in

June 1886, arriving in Port Moody, BC, on 4 July. Completion of the railway was one of the great engineering feats of the day and was considered crucial to the nation."

Above right: Donald Smith, later known as Lord Strathcona, drives the last spike of the CPR, at Craigellachie, just a few miles northeast of Sicamous, 7 November 1885 (Wikipedia)

From Wikipedia: "The BC portion of the railway was constructed between 1881 and 1885, fulfilling a promise extended to BC when it entered the Confederation in 1871.

Middle right: The first CPR train to travel from the Atlantic to the Pacific at Port Arthur, Ontario, 30 Jun 1886 (Library and Archives Canada)

"For decades, it was the only practical means of long–distance passenger transport in Canada."

Below right: Dedicated CPR railway bridge over the Columbia River in Revelstoke, BC, Canada, ca. 1885 (Wikipedia)

The story of the construction of the Canadian Pacific Railway would require its own separate chapter, but after the last spike was driven in November 1885, Vancouver was quickly founded in 1886 at the end of the rail line, and there was no looking back. Fortunately for the heroes of our story, the railway ran right through Sicamous and eventually included a beautiful lakeside hotel and railway station on the banks of Shuswap Lake.

Almost immediately plans began for building spur lines throughout the region to exploit the nearly boundless resources that included timber, minerals, and agricultural produce. Before the spur lines could be completed, the CPR even ran a fleet of lake steamers on the major lakes throughout the region, providing early connecting links with many of the villages and towns that were beginning to spring up and flourish. It was to the great advantage of the CPR to keep its trains full while moving in both directions: mostly carrying natural resources during its eastward movements, and mostly carrying finished goods and passengers during its westward journeys.

Above: Two CPR trains, south branch and mainline, waiting to depart at the CPR Hotel at Sicamous (Sicamous Museum.ca)

In addition to railways and lake steamers, the CPR also built a series of first-class hotels in the choicest locations that were intended to attract immigrants as well as tourists to western Canada and provide additional assurance to investors that the railway would remain profitable. The scenery beyond the last stretches of the Great Plains quickly became a mountain wonderland, and tourism was rapidly becoming an important aspect of the world economy. It was logical to exploit every aspect of the environment to provide a broader base to the economic viability of the CPR. Scenery was thus added to the long list of commercial resources this beautiful part of the world had to offer anyone willing to stake their future and their own sense of courage, adventure, and entrepreneurship in this unspoiled and untapped land. These hotels also provided housing and other essential services to railway workers who were responsible for the smooth functioning of the railway network.

Most early trains were smaller and able to pull fewer cars and less tonnage, but their arrival constituted a vast improvement to commerce in western Canada. Railway beds were solid, smooth, and able to span raging rivers via bridges, pass through treacherous canyons, and penetrate otherwise impassable mountain ranges through purpose-built tunnels, all thanks to "modern engineering feats" that are impressive even by today's standards. Between 1885 and the early 1900s, the impact of the CPR on western Canada's economy was enormously important.

Prior to the arrival of the railroad, anyone wanting to take up residence in western Canada had only two means to get there: by water, via an ocean voyage to the gateway in Vancouver, then by steamboat into the interior; or by overland means from Vancouver. The overland route from Eastern Canada was also available using wagons and established "roads" that were primitive and dangerous, not to mention that any overland voyage was extremely slow and subject to the challenges posed by local weather conditions, local tribes, local predators, and local topography.

Suddenly, with the arrival of the transcontinental railroad, a trip that took months could be made in days, with far less danger and personal expense.

Right: CPR locomotive #5068 at Leanchoil, BC, ca. 1913 (Library and Archives of Canada)

Nearly every character in our story arrived in the Shuswap via the CPR. Even Ernie Buckingham, who drove a Conestoga wagon with his buddy Noble Bragg as far as Alberta, hopped a CPR freight on his way to Revelstoke, BC. Virtually every member of the greater Shuswap community in the early 20th century was deeply touched by and dependent on the railway as a vital resource.

From the *Canada's History* website: "Ties That Bind: the History of Canada's Railway System"; written by Nelle Oosterom, November 6, 2014:

"For most new immigrants who arrived in Canada prior to the 1960s, a long train ride to their eventual destination was among the most vivid of their early experiences. Their first impressions were often of days of travel through seemingly endless expanses of forest and prairie.

"At no time was immigration more brisk than it was during the first decade of the twentieth century, when Canada's population increased by one third, from 5.3 million to 7.2 million. To handle these massive numbers, CP Rail built more than a thousand colonist cars. The cars, in use from 1886 to the 1940s, offered cheap fares without the frills. *[Ed. note – In fact, Frank Kappel stated in a 1966 interview with Imbert Orchard that he took a colonist train from Ontario when he first arrived in Canada on his way to British Columbia.]*

"An immigrant interviewed by Barry Broadfoot in The Pioneer Years, 1895-1914, described travelling in the colonist car as a hellish experience: "At night was the worst. The cars were full, and babies were crying, and I can't remember any blankets. It seems nobody told anybody to bring bedding, and all our bedding was in our trunks.… I could never stand the sight of a train again. Never."

"Other newcomers didn't seem to mind. Writing in his diary in 1887, Joseph Eckersley seemed quite happy with the arrangements: "The arrangements for sleeping are contrived by sliding seats. There is a water closet & stove at each end of the car together with washing stand & bowl. The stove is useful for cooking your food as well as for heating the place."

"The Canadian National Railway and its predecessor, Canadian Northern Railway (1899–1923), also transported large numbers of immigrants. In *Canadian Northern Railway and the Men Who Made It Work* (1980), author Jack Bradford writes: "Whole families would be confined to one end of a boxcar with their livestock partitioned off with their personal effects in the rest of the car. The noise of these trains and the livestock as they passed through the town and through the necessary switching moves was terrific."

The CPR hotel in Sicamous became a cultural center for those who could afford it, but for those who couldn't, the railway provided everything from foodstuffs and dry goods to a means by which they could export their own products to "the outside world" in exchange for cash money and credit.

Above: 1924 photo of the CPR hotel in Sicamous, built in 1885; The hotel burned to the ground in 1898 but was rebuilt almost immediately, such was its importance to the CPR and the region. The hotel also housed the CPR telegraph office and waiting rooms for passengers. Passenger service was phased out in the mid-1950s, and the hotel closed in 1956. (Northern BC Archives & Special Collections)

Being the center of Sicamous culture and commerce, the CPR Hotel provided many amenities to local citizens who had grown up in a more civilized environment in Great Britain or Europe. In addition to a fine restaurant, the hotel provided a music room, reading room, and numerous other venues that could be used to celebrate and commemorate informal as well as formal occasions. Several of the negatives provided by Stanley in his extensive treasure trove reveal the Kappel family "dressed to the nines" in furs, topcoats and evening wear, suggesting they were probably on their way to a special event at the local CPR hotel.

Above: CPR Sicamous Hotel lobby and guests, ca. 1925 (Sicamous Museum.ca)

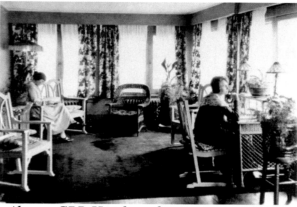

Above: CPR Hotel reading room, ca. 1925 (Sicamous Museum.ca)

Above left: Guests enjoying a meal at the famous CPR Hotel restaurant, Sicamous, ca. 1925 (Sicamous Museum.ca) Above right: Music room in the CPR Sicamous Hotel, ca. 1925 (Sicamous Museum.ca)

Left: Passengers stroll on platform, CPR Hotel, Sicamous, ca. 1925 (Sicamous Museum.ca)

The CPR also provided convenient access by residents of the Shuswap area to Vancouver and Victoria, as well as to other villages and towns in the region. Trains arrived and departed at the Sicamous Station several times daily, and although a trip from

Sicamous to Vancouver was probably a significant event in the life of anyone living in the interior, it was theoretically possible to board a train at Sicamous in the early morning, get to Vancouver before midday, shop or meet friends for lunch, and take the train back to Sicamous, arriving home that same day. Such connectivity was a bonus to residents in the interior, especially if they had family members living in "the big City". For those with the means to purchase train tickets, spending the weekend in Vancouver or Victoria was also easy to accomplish.

Left: Vancouver CPR Depot, 1911 (Library and Archives of Canada)

The most important function of a major railway system is obviously transportation. Railways supply a cheap, reliable, and relatively safe way to transport the goods one produces in their daily business, be they animal, mineral, or vegetable, to markets where they can be sold for a profit. Lumber and agricultural produce were the most important products that most members of the greater Shuswap community had to offer the world. The Kootenay region enjoyed a climate that made farming of all types a means by which an enterprising immigrant could prosper, from berries and vegetables to apples and other tree fruits. The CPR had made the middle provinces of Canada the "world's breadbasket" because the Great Plains were perfect for growing most types of grains that could be transported by rail to ports on the St. Lawrence seaway and taken by ship anywhere in the world.

The same was true for lumber products that were produced in BC, as I have previously discussed. In fact, Frank Kappel made his living from lumber products for the greater part of his working life in the Shuswap. Originally a homesteader at Magna Bay, he worked hard at many jobs requiring physical labor and/or brains in his early days: road builder, teamster, miner, carpenter, fire warden, bookkeeper, accountant, auditor, notary public, and eventually, timber scaler, a job that set the stage for the rest of his career, working for the R.W. Bruhn Lumber Company in Sicamous. In one of his memoirs, Frank revealed: "I decided I wasn't cut out for farming." For the Kappel family, the rest is history.

An informative news article was written by Deborah Chapman and appeared in the Salmon Arm Observer, dated Feb. 15, 2020. It provides fascinating insight into the importance of the railroad to the entire Shuswap region:

"Railway carried mail, circus animals and royalty to Salmon Arm:
"Imagine how excited the community was when Charles McGuire was awarded Salmon Arm's first mail contract in 1890!

"Settlers could pick up their mail at the counter in his log store during his regular retail hours, at their convenience, rather than having to meet the train's baggage man during its brief stop here on the single track.

"Charles would keep settlers' correspondence, parcels, and newspapers until they made it into town.

"The year the mail contract was awarded, the Canadian Pacific Railway opened a station on the north, or lake side of the railway tracks. The community of 200 was better connected to the outside world.

"But its location was unfortunate. In 1894, water completely submerged the tracks between the Reserve and Dan Sinclair's farm. A.J. Palmer had a hard time shipping his milk to Kamloops. He had to row his milk cans by boat to the C.P.R. slough bridge to make the train, and water was so high it periodically extinguished the fires in the trains' engines.

"A new station was constructed in 1913 nearer town, on the town side of the track and on slightly higher ground. Late passengers no longer had to crawl under a train in depot to purchase tickets from the station master's wife.

"The railway station was an important link for Salmon Arm. Strawberries, milk, apples, and other fruit were shipped to markets. Residents took the rail to Kamloops, Revelstoke and Vancouver and points between and beyond.

"The three trains a day were also a source of entertainment. Town folks strolled to the station. They were curious. Who was visiting? Who was back from away? Did anyone notice when Jimmy Day boarded the train to elope to Vancouver with Daisy Gerrard? Did the couple buy their tickets separately?

"The railway brought the Al G. Barnes' Wild Animal Circus, Rice Brothers Circus and King Brothers Circus, including their animals. It loaded thousands of boxes of apples each fall.

"At the station the community bade farewell to Salmon Arm's young men excited to enlist in two wars. The railway also brought royalty. Although her father King George VI and his Queen Elizabeth did not stop in Salmon Arm in 1939 *(it did stop in Sicamous)*, the community gathered to welcome Princess Elizabeth in 1951. The 10-minute stop was long enough for Clarice Cameron to present a bouquet of flowers to the future Queen and Mary Meek to have a private chat."

Right: The Kildonan Pipe Band greeting train at the Sicamous Hotel and CPR railway station, 1939, preparing for the Royal Visit of King George VI and Queen Elizabeth; The Royal Visit was the highlight of the year for the citizens of Sicamous. It was the first time a reigning Canadian monarch had set foot in Canada. (Sicamous Museum.ca)

From The Canadian Encyclopedia: "In 1931, the Statute of Westminster granted Canada control over its own foreign policy. The Statute changed the relationship between Canada and the monarchy, creating a distinct Canadian Crown. Canada became the political equal of the United Kingdom, sharing a common monarch. The Governor General's position transformed from representative of the British government to representative of the shared monarch alone. King George VI and Queen Elizabeth therefore toured in 1939 as King and Queen of Canada."

Above left: George VI and his royal consort, Queen Elizabeth, walking through Queen's Park, Toronto, May 1939 (Wikipedia); Middle left and below left, two images: The Royal Train at Sicamous, 1939, with King George VI and Queen Elizabeth on the observation platform of the last car, greeting onlookers at the Sicamous Hotel and CPR. railway station. (Sicamous Museum.ca)

From Wikipedia: "The 1939 royal tour of Canada by King George VI and Queen Elizabeth was undertaken in the build-up to World War II as a way to emphasise the links between Britain and the Dominion of Canada. The royal tour lasted from 17 May to 15 June, covering every Canadian province, the Dominion of Newfoundland, and a few days in the United States. This tour demonstrated and cemented Canada's allegiance to the Crown and its status as the senior dominion of the British Empire. There had been previous royal tours in Canada, but this was unprecedented in its scope. The tour was an enormous event, attracting huge crowds at each new city.

"The Royal Train was operated by the Canadian Pacific Railway on the western leg of the tour and the couple continued to be greeted by throngs of Canadians, even in the immigrant-rich but Depression-battered Prairies."

According to historian Gordon Mackie, writing in the Revelstoke Review in 2019: "Sicamous' status as a transportation nexus has afforded it many unique opportunities; perhaps none are more prestigious than as a stop on tours of Canada by the British Royals...King George VI and his wife stopped in front of the old CP Hotel and Station in 1939 and shook hands with many people from the back platform of the train; they never got off the train."

The Royal Visit would have been a major event for the citizens of Sicamous and would almost certainly have included participation by the Frank Kappel family.

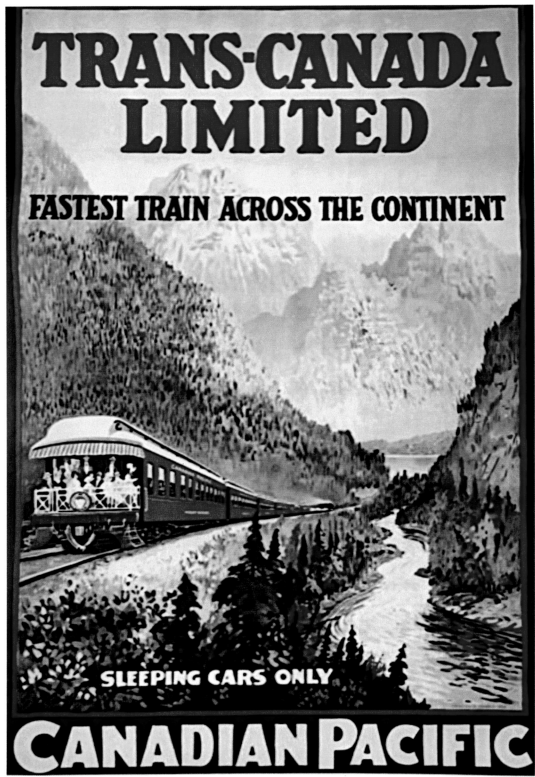

Above: 1924 CPR travel poster promoting travel to Western Canada

BOOK TWO:

A HERO'S JOURNEY

Above: Donald Angus Buckingham, ca. six months old, waving to the crowd, sitting with his older sister, Jean Ellen, at the Buckingham family homestead on Blind Bay

CHAPTER 12 – Stanley Ernest Kappel: the Journey Begins

O Canada!
Our home and native land!
True patriot love in all of us command.

With glowing hearts we see thee rise,
The True North strong and free!

From far and wide,
O Canada, we stand on guard for thee.

God keep our land glorious and free!
O Canada, we stand on guard for thee.

O Canada, we stand on guard for thee.

-   **Lyrics of the Canadian National Anthem**

Left: The Canadian flag between 1921 and 1957, as Stanley would have known it throughout most of his life

Alice once told Karen that Janet Kappel's health was always frail, and that after Betty's birth her doctor said she could not have any more natural children. This must have been devastating to both Janet and Frank, who wanted a larger family. But they found a welcome solution. The adoption of Donald Angus Buckingham took place on May 26th, 1921, four months after Stanley's birth mother died, when he was two and a half years old. Jeanie Dubberley told Kerry in an email written in November of 2019 that she had no idea until very recently that Stanley's adopted parents were Canadian, and that Stanley had remained in Canada after he was adopted in 1921. She went on to say that she didn't know if her mother knew this, either: "Mum always said that her brother was adopted by 'wealthy Americans'! To the best of my knowledge, she never saw Stanley again – certainly not after I was old enough to be aware. He never came to Victoria or Vancouver, and we never went to Spokane."

Stanley quickly grew to love his adopted family and apparently never had contact with his birth father again. It is tempting to speculate that Frank and Janet Kappel kept Stanley's adoption and whereabouts private, spinning a tale that he had been adopted by a wealthy American couple, because they wanted to avoid any attempt by Ernie or his children to contact Stanley later. They may also have wanted to spare Stanley the temptation of getting in touch with his "real" family as he was growing up.

Left: Betty and Stanley in the Kappel family garden in winter, perhaps six months after Stanley was adopted; Stanley appears to be three years old in this photo, while Betty is age eight. (from Stanley's private collection, SPC)

But that seems unlikely in the light of the nature of the greater Shuswap community at the time. Despite limitations in roads, railroads, and communications in 1921, along with a physical distance of 35 miles between Blind Bay and Sicamous, this was a small and relatively tight-knit community, with most members crossing paths in business or at community gatherings periodically. Maintaining such a pretense for long, especially when Stanley entered the public school system and began to encounter children from around the area as his interests expanded, would have been difficult.

Left: Young Stanley at age four, standing in a farmyard wielding a timberman's saw in the depths of winter, ca. 1922 (SPC)

Such an encounter between Buckingham siblings Stanley and Marie apparently occurred, according to Jeanie Dubberley, who related a charming story that her mother had told her: "They did meet once. Mum told me several times about an incident in her teens (14, I suppose, as she left Kamloops after turning 15 in December 1934). She met an extremely attractive boy at Riverside Park in Kamloops, on a lovely summer day.

Left: Photo of Stanley around age six, sitting with his mother and sister, ca. 1924 (from Lynne and Roger Beeson)

She said that there was an immediate attraction between them, and I gathered that some innocent flirting went on between them. It was, of course, Stanley, and they somehow (I don't know how) became aware that they were, in fact, brother and sister. Mum was pretty discreet, but I think that the attraction must have been profound on both sides, because she stressed that it was lucky that they found out who they were to each other 'before anything happened'. Knowing Mum, I'm sure that she meant nothing more than some kissing! She believed that the Kappels had come back to Kamloops on a summer visit – I think that she had no idea that they were in fact practically neighbours of Ernie and Jeanie and lived not far from her all those years."

Right: Stanley's formal adoption papers, dated May 26, 1921 (SPC)

We will learn more about Stanley and Marie's subsequent relationship later in the story. Suffice it to say that Stanley and Marie eventually became close friends and confidants, and they also exchanged letters and greetings for the rest of Stanley's relatively short life.

Stanley's first two years of childhood had likely been graced with two loving, capable parents as well as three older and doting sisters, which would have given him a solid emotional foundation on which to build after he became Stanley Ernest Kappel. How much of this security may have been undone during the few tumultuous months after his mother died cannot be known, but at least his birth family did not have to endure months or even years while their mother suffered from a lengthy terminal illness.

Right: Stanley, around age eight, with the family dog, ca. 1926 (from Lynne and Roger Beeson)

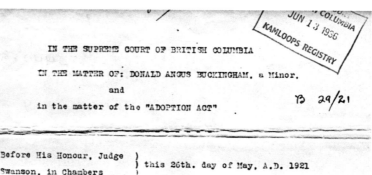

IN THE SUPREME COURT OF BRITISH COLUMBIA

IN THE MATTER OF: DONALD ANGUS BUCKINGHAM, a Minor,

and

in the matter of the "ADOPTION ACT"

Before His Honour, Judge Swanson, in Chambers) this 26th. day of May, A.D. 1921

ORDER

Upon hearing Mr. Ernest Clark, of Counsel for the petitioners herein, AND UPON reading the Petition herein, and UPON READING the Affidavit of Frank Kappel and Janet Kappel, verifying the said Petition, sworn herein the third day of May A.D.1921, and UPON READING the Consent of Ernest Buckingham, and UPON READING the Affidavit of Ernest Buckingham sworn herein the tenth day of May A.D. 1921.

IT IS ORDERED that the said Petitioners, Frank Kappel and Janet Kappel, do adopt the said infant, Donald Angus Buckingham, named in the said Petition, and that the said Donald Angus Buckingham shall from the date hereof be known as Stanley Ernest Kappel.

"John D. Swanson"

Local Judge, S.C. of B.C.

CERTIFIED TRUE COPY

Deputy District Registrar, Supreme Court.

Every description of Stanley suggests that he was well-adjusted and didn't suffer irreparable harm from the sudden loss of his mother at the tender age of two. Whatever childhood trauma he may have experienced did not take permanent hold of him or leave him seriously damaged. There is nothing to suggest that Stanley was a troubled soul; in fact, the opposite appears to be true, as we shall see.

Karen recalls her mother, Alice, many years after Stanley's death, recounting that after they were married, Stanley's birth father, Ernie, attempted to get back in touch with him. Alice said that Stanley became physically ill at the thought, but her interpretation of this reaction was that

Stanley felt immense loyalty to his adopted parents and didn't want to betray the sense of devotion he felt for Frank and Janet in any way that might damage the loving relationship he enjoyed with them. After all, Stanley was only two and a half years old when he had last seen his birth father. The only parents he had ever really known were Frank and Janet.

Left: Stanley around age eight, standing on the dock next to his grandmother, Euphemia Thomson, with Frank Kappel sitting in the boat, ca. 1926 (provided by Lynne and Roger Beeson); Below right: Stanley around age ten, sitting in his family's garden with a neighbor, ca. 1928 (SPC)

Although many adopted children eventually develop a strong interest in getting back in touch with their birth parents, such an interest had apparently not yet developed in Stanley by the time Ernie tried to reestablish contact with him. And because Stanley had the good fortune to be embraced as a full member of such a loving, supportive and successful family, it is possible that he felt no bitterness toward Ernie, in which

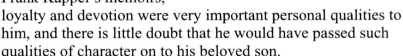

case, forgiveness would not have been required. Reading Frank Kappel's memoirs, loyalty and devotion were very important personal qualities to him, and there is little doubt that he would have passed such qualities of character on to his beloved son.

Left: Stanley around age 12, standing with his Christmas gifts, surrounded by the Kappel family back garden in Sicamous, ca. 1930 (SPC)

Stanley was an exceptionally bright and happy child, by all accounts. Frank Kappel wrote a long personal memoir to his five granddaughters in 1961 *[Ed. note – see the previous chapters on Frank for a full accounting]* and included the following passage about Stanley and his sister, Betty: "Suffice it to say that never were parents blessed with a better and finer pair of children than we. All through their childhood and after they grew up, they never gave us cause to dim the great pride we had in them, and I am ever grateful to them for the pleasure and happiness I derived from them."

Right: Stanley, around age 12, standing in the Kappel family back garden with prized Christmas gifts (SPC)

I have tried to discover details about Stanley's childhood from family documents, but there is little to be found. Consequently, my attempts to reveal the forces that played major roles in forming Stanley's personality will have to rely on research, speculation, and deduction, with significant help from Stanley's extensive collection of photographs and negatives he compiled and carefully catalogued.

Stanley was outgoing and multi-talented, with many interests that kept him busy. Growing up, Stanley played both piano and guitar, which according to Alice he learned without formal instruction. He also played hockey and skied enthusiastically, taking up ski jumping and curling as well. He possessed a fishing reel and creel when he married Alice, so he may also have been an avid fisherman. His photos show him to be trim, fit, athletic and good looking. Everyone who knew him liked him and found him to be very personable and blessed with a great sense of humor. Every photo of him suggests a confident, well-balanced, and contented young man with no evidence of bitterness or unhappiness.

The few documents I have found in BC newspapers paint a picture of an intelligent, outgoing, and enthusiastic young Stanley. An article from The Daily Province in Vancouver, dated November 29th, 1931 *(when Stanley had just turned 13)*, in a special children's section entitled "The Pow-Wow Corner", features Stanley Kappel of Sicamous: "To date there have been no snowball fights in Sicamous, according to a letter from Stanley Kappel of that city. He says, a little mournfully, that the snow is so dry it refuses to 'pack' into snowballs. However, Stan seems to have a pretty nice time skiing and sleigh riding. I guess a great many Vancouver Tillicums wish they were in his shoes (I might say his snowshoes). I'd like to hear more of what you do in Sicamous, Stan."

Right: Tillicum Pin from the 1940s that Stanley undoubtedly received and perhaps wore with pride for taking a pledge "We're All Friends Together" in the Vancouver Daily Province. The pin was free to all children willing to commit themselves to this simple pledge.

The same Sunday edition of the Vancouver Daily Province, which Stanley apparently read on a regular basis, ran to 54 pages and featured everything one might expect in a "big city newspaper". It featured an eight-page comic section that included favorites from my own childhood in the early 1950s such as Moon Mullins, Little Orphan Annie, and Winnie Winkle.

The newspaper also featured pages of Canadian and international news, business and political pages, a society page, lots of advertisements for local as well as exotic products, several pages of entertainment offerings, a Books and Authors literary page, letters to the editor, news from around the Province, and a host of other features that made it one of the leading sources of news and entertainment for Canadians living in British Columbia.

"We're All Friends Together" was the featured headline in large type that ran across the entire top of the children's page (page 36), which included the Pow-Wow Corner feature, and was entirely devoted to children and items that might interest them, including a Junior Cross-word Puzzle, stories and poetry written by children from around British Columbia. Another feature on the same page was entitled "For Girls and Boys" that included commentary by Diana Gray as well as Monty, the principal contributor to the page. In the lower right corner of page 36 was an application form that encouraged children to apply for membership in the Province Tillicum Club. Membership in the Club was free, and the only condition of membership was that the applicant must agree with the Tillicum slogan: "We're all friends together." Membership was free and included a silver Tillicum Pin. One can well imagine that Stanley was an avid member of the Club and wore his silver Tillicum Pin with pride.

The Pow-Wow Corner" dated March 7th, 1932, again features Stanley Kappel of Sicamous: "Two letters from Stanley Kappel are on my desk now, and I think it's time I answered them! With the first Stanley sent me two photographs – one of himself with his skis, and one of the view from his home. And that is no ordinary view – he lives in Sicamous, you see, and his home overlooks Shuswap Lake. In the picture it looks cold and grey, and dully beautiful – it must be nice to look from your front porch onto such a scene as this. Stanley has been turning out for baseball practice – perhaps spring is on the way after all! By the way, we'll add your name to the correspondence list next Sunday!"

The fact that The Daily Province devoted one entire page in the Sunday edition to children bears witness to another time and place, and to the importance Canadian society placed on bringing children into the community in a way that gently, but firmly, reminded them of their obligations and opportunities as full members of the Canadian experience.

Left: Newspaper advertisement for General Electric radios being featured for sale at B.C. Electric Stores appearing in the Vancouver Daily Province in 1931

In addition to reading The Daily Province, there were other opportunities for Stanley to gain exposure to the "outside world". By 1929 the Canadian National Railway (CNR) had installed a series of radio stations that stretched across the continent from Vancouver to Halifax.

According to Wikipedia: "During its nine-year existence, CNR Radio provided music, sports, information, and drama programming to Canadians. Programs were produced in English, French and occasionally in some First Nations languages, and distributed nationwide through the railway's own telegraph lines and through rented airtime on private radio stations."

Right: Front cover of first issue of "The Shadow Magazine", a Canadian/American pulp fiction offering, published twice a month, in this case, the April 7, 1931 issue, featuring stories that would have appealed to teenagers and young men (Wikipedia). [Ed. note – It was also a popular radio show that ran between 1937 and 1954. Karen remembers listening to it in the early 1950s, but Stanley may also have listened to the show in the 1930s.]

Wireless radio was the first opportunity for the Canadian government to establish a ready connection with most of its citizens. AM radio, the first frequency that was licensed for broadcasting in Canada, tended to carry long distances, especially at night, when most people were at home. Young, bright boys like Stanley may have had a small, relatively inexpensive crystal set that would have given him a window on the world through radio broadcasts, listening through headphones to whatever he could tune it. By 1929, when Stanley was 11, tube radios with speakers became available for general consumption, and the Kappel family almost certainly owned one. But broadcasts were still restricted across the hinterlands of Canada, and many Canadians relied on American radio stations broadcasting just across the border. In fact, 80% of the programs Canadians listened to in the late 1920s were from U.S. drama, comedy shows, music, and sports broadcasts. This was undoubtedly a source of bonding between Canadians and Americans that has persisted to the present day.

Right: Advertisement appearing in the Vernon News from June 3, 1926, advertising the visit of a four-ring circus on the following Saturday; Stanley was only seven that summer, but he may well have been able to attend the matinee performance with his parents and sister.

Left: Front page of Maclean's Magazine, which billed itself as Canada's National Magazine, from November 15th, 1930 (Internet Archive)

My own father, born in 1911, growing up in Spokane in the early part of the 20th century, spoke frequently of having access to radio programming from an early age. He also spoke of catching the trolley from his home area on Saturday mornings as a young boy, riding it into Spokane, and spending much of the day watching double-feature films at the Fox Theater with his friends. Although this author has been unable to discover when the first movie theater in the Shuswap area opened, the following article in the Vernon News, dated October 6, 1931, is enlightening:

TALKING PICTURES COME TO SICAMOUS; "Two Years Since Silent Films Were Last Shown – Company Re-organized; Sicamous, B.C., Oct. 6 –

"The first sound pictures in Sicamous will be heard and seen in the local hall tonight, Thursday. It is two years since the silent pictures were last shown here, as the high cost of films at that time caused the company to discontinue their operation.

"The reorganized Okanagan Cinema Company has installed a temporary machine and is showing "The Cat Creeps" as a premiere." *[Ed. note – This horror film was the "talkie" remake of the silent film "The Cat and the Canary" that was based on an old stage play of the same name and was released in November of 1930.]*

Left: Dominion Chautauqua poster for Fernie, BC, from 1921 (Fernie Museum)

This suggests that at least one local movie "theater" was available to Stanley, his sister, and their friends while they were growing up, and that they made as many pilgrimages to such an irresistible mecca as possible. We also know that other forms of entertainment were available to members of the Shuswap Community, including local musicians who played at various venues on weekends. Victrolas were generally available in the early

1900s, along with cartridges and discs of pre-recorded music that was popular throughout Canada at the time.

Tent shows have been an important part of American and Canadian history since the mid-to-late nineteenth century. From the late 19th century through the first half of the 20th century, travelling circuses were a major form of spectator entertainment in the US and Canada and attracted huge attention whenever they arrived in a town or city.

Tent theatre played a critical role in the American and Canadian entertainment industry. It first grew out of opera houses, which were to be found in almost every major city until the end of the nineteenth century. The opera houses were very poorly ventilated at the time, which did not appeal to the audiences. By contrast, the tents were outdoors and therefore had no problem with overheating or poor ventilation, because the winds would provide a nice way of cooling down the audiences. Tent theatre boomed by the 1920s, when the industry for outdoor entertainment was at its peak and declined shortly after. From the origins of tent shows to its decline and fall, tent theatre had a major influence on American and Canadian culture and left a legacy for tent shows everywhere.

From The Canadian Encyclopedia: "In 1917 the Canadian branch of Ellison-White (known from its inception as Dominion Chautauquas) booked tours in all four western provinces, playing in 40 towns during the summer and 108 towns in the autumn. In 1918 Chautauquas, which are defined as "traveling shows and local assemblies that provided education combined with popular entertainment in the form of lectures, concerts, and plays" took place in 294 Canadian towns, again all in the West. A Chautauquas offered different programs for each day of its five or six day stay at a given location. Music might be supplied by any combination of soloists, small vocal groups (such as the Adanac Quartet), choirs, instrumental ensembles, or orchestras. Song and dance acts were popular, as were ethnic music groups. Examples of the latter were the Elias Tamburitza Serenaders of Croatia, the Russian Cossack Chorus, the Serbian Tamburica Orchestra, and the Scotch(sic)-Canadian Concert Party which featured the comedian Walter Henderson singing Harry Lauder songs. Novelty acts were booked regularly for tours. These included the Carlyle Novelty Trio and Robert S. Herrick, who sang humorous songs and imitated famous female singers. Among orchestras which appeared on the tours were the Canadian Overseas Orchestra and Lieurance's Symphonic Orchestra, coached by Thurlow Lieurance, a composer and 'highest authority on Indian music'. Soloists included the Toronto baritone Ruthven H. McDonald, the Edmonton soprano Edna Reed, and the Metropolitan Opera baritone J. Horace Smithey."

Right: Dog-pulled "parade wagon" during a local Shuswap area May Day celebration, 1935; Note the appearance of Sicamous at the time. (Sicamous & District Museum and Historical Society)

The Shuswap area also hosted its share of community celebrations. In addition to the longstanding traditional holidays celebrated throughout nations with Christian roots such as Christmas and Easter, Canadians celebrated May Day on May first, along with Dominion Day, later known as Canada Day, every July 1st. In the 1930s they also celebrated King George V Day in June. This gave citizens several opportunities to get together for a parade, a party and a chance to fly the flag. As leading members of Sicamous, the Kappel family could always be expected to turn out and participate in every important community event throughout the year.

Eagle Valley School in 1928 - was also the Museum Building

Above: Local Shuswap area ceremony celebrating Dominion Day in the rear of the Sicamous Hall that includes Frank Kappel on the left, acting as one of the officials (from Stanley's private collection, SPC)
Left: The Eagle Valley School in 1928, where Stanley may have attended grammar school (Sicamous & District Museum and Historical Society)

Formal primary education was available universally in Canada, including the farthest reaches of the Canadian Provinces, in the 1920s. Stanley apparently attended grammar school in a one-room schoolhouse, a familiar community fixture in remote areas of the Far West in those days. I have not been able to gain access to written records of Stanley's early education in the Sicamous school system, but we can be certain he became educated in the basic subjects. A letter written by Betty (Kappel) Ingram, Stanley's adopted sister, describes her own early education experiences: "I started school at Magna Bay at age five to help keep the school open. This meant the lonely walk of a mile to and from school." Betty didn't say anything about how many grades she attended at the Magna Bay School, but we know that she moved with her parents to Sicamous in 1920 when Frank began his 26-year association with the Bruhn lumber company.

Upper right: Photo of the old Salmon Arm High School taken by Stanley, ca. 1935, where he completed his high school education prior to attending college; Middle right: Photo of a Salmon Arm High School classroom and classmates taken by Stanley, ca. 1935; Below right: Photo of Salmon Arm, dated 1930; This is where Stanley attended high school from 1933-1936.

The Sicamous & District Museum & Historical Society website states: "With settlers came children and the necessity of schools. Craigallachie-Malakwa 1902, Three Valley 1908, Sicamous 1910, Solsqua 1912, Taft 1914 and Eagle Valley School 1921." The local Sicamous School or the Eagle Valley School are the most likely candidates where both Stanley his primary education. It appears that Stanley next studied his middle school subjects by correspondence for two years. Frank Kappel wrote in a brief biographical sketch of Stanley: "He took two years of high school correspondence and then completed through senior matriculation at nearby Salmon Arm, B.C. high school in 1936."

A newspaper article dated July 23rd, 1932, appearing in the Vancouver Daily Province, lists Stanley as among grade school students who were promoted to high school based on their entrance exam scores. This seems to confirm that Stanley had been "home schooled" during the previous two years, and that he couldn't be recommended by his principal *[Ed. note – Since he didn't have one]* for entrance into high school. Sicamous is apparently in the Cranbrook region, Eagle Valley district, but he had to travel to nearby Salmon Arm and live apart from his family to finish his high school studies, graduating in 1936.

Right: Young Stanley, dressed in suit, white shirt and tie, ca. 1934 (SPC)

Anyone who has visited southern British Columbia has seen for themselves a corner of the world as close to paradise as one may ever encounter: pristine, bucolic, far from the cares of the urban world, with a natural bounty of resources and beauty that only the most jaded observer would fail to appreciate. Growing up on the shores of Shuswap Lake, under the loving umbrella of a successful and accomplished household, it is little wonder that Stanley flourished.

Left: A photo of Frank and Stanley from Stanley's extensive photo collection, probably taken while Stanley was a student at MSM from 1936-1941, that exhibits the relative affluence of the Frank Kappel family. (SPC)

To be loved by one's parents, to be provided all of life's necessities by adults who have achieved a solid sense of themselves and their place in the world, to have access to an established educational system, to have ample friends with whom to grow and discover the things a boy needs to know, and to be far removed from war and pestilence, disease and famine; this is the stuff that dreams are made of for most of us.

On the other hand, the relatively harsh reality of life in the Shuswap Lake region in the early 20th century cannot be denied. At one level, life was rather basic and difficult for those hardy pioneers who were settling an untamed hinterland, carving an outpost of civilization from an uncut diamond of wilderness in the farthest reaches of the North American continent, as we have already learned in previous chapters covering the lives of Stanley's forebears.

But young Stanley would have been shielded from many of the demands of this herculean task. He undoubtedly had regular chores to do around his family's home in Sicamous, and he may even have worked for others part-time while growing up. He would have had time and opportunity to experience idyllic summer days by the lake, wandering in lush meadows filled with birds and butterflies, or hiking along babbling brooks filled with trout and salamanders.

Right: Cover of the 1933-1934 Wilson's Winter Sports Catalogue, which Stanley may have used to purchase toys and hockey equipment he wanted (Toronto Public Library)

Frank Kappel wrote that Stanley was ambidextrous and could play golf with both hands. He was very athletic and seems to have tried out every sport available to him while he was growing up. He took advantage of the winter wonderland around him and became accomplished in skiing,

ski jumping, ice skating, hockey, curling, and golfing. Let's face it: life in the Shuswap in the 1920s and 30s was all about being outdoors, enjoying nature, whether on the water, on the ice, on the links, or on a trail leading to somewhere interesting. When you add living in a well-crafted home filled with his mother's art and the material accumulation of its "comfortably well off" owners that included a piano and other luxuries unavailable to most, what's not to envy?

I have previously speculated that Nature played a dominant role in Stanley's life growing up in the Shuswap. He would undoubtedly have been exposed to a magnificent diversity of flora and fauna, wherever he ventured. He would have observed many birds, mammals, fish, and reptiles, not to mention trees and shrubs during his adventures in the outdoors as a child. In addition to having a large body of water in his front yard, the area was heavily forested, giving refuge to a variety of different ecosystems and bringing delightful sounds of nature: the song of the loon's wild laughter on the lake, the hooting of an owl on a summer's evening, and so much more.

Below, four photos from Stanley's private collection: Stanley, age 15-16, was accomplished in many sports, including skiing, hockey, and golf. He also went on camping trips into the mountains with friends. (SPC)

The print media had become well established in Canada by the 1930s. The Kappel family were very likely to have subscriptions to at least one of the more popular magazines of the time that included Maclean's, Canadian Home Journal, Chatelaine, The Canadian, Argosy, or

Mayfair. Local and regional newspapers were also being published during the 1930s, including the Vernon News, The Daily Province in Vancouver, the Times Colonist, and the Vancouver Sun. Books were undoubtedly popular with Stanley and his sister: for example, *Anne of Green Gables*, written by L. M. Montgomery and considered by many critics to be the principle classic of Canadian children's literature, appeared in 1908 and continues to be read by Canadian children to this day.

Right: Stanley Kappel during high school, ca. 1935, ready for a day of prospecting, rock pick hammer in hand. [Ed. note – This photo suggests that young Stanley had been thinking about a career in mining several years prior to his graduation from high school.]

We have only a few photos of Stanley taken between his infancy, when he was photographed as the youngest member of the Ernie Buckingham family, and the photo on the right, which appears to have been taken when he was nearing his graduation, probably around age 15. This photo suggests Stanley to be an earnest and attractive young man, very duded out in nice clothing that reflects where he was and where he had spent his entire life up to this point: in a remote part of British Columbia where formal dress clothing may not have been commonly called for. But it is much more revealing in that he is holding a prospector's pickaxe. Frank Kappel's brief biographical sketch of his son states that Stanley spent the summer after he graduated from high school in 1936 working at the Sheep Creek Mine, and that this experience convinced him that he wanted to become a hard rock miner. There can be little doubt that Stanley was toying with a career in mining at least a year or two prior to his graduating from high school, and his file of negatives entitled "Sheep Creek Mine" is dated 1935 – 1941, suggests he may have started working at the mine the summer before he began his senior year of high school.

Right: Frank, Janet, Betty, and Stanley Kappel in front of their home in Sicamous, ca. 1934 (SPC)

This writer was initially puzzled as to why there were no photos of Stanley from his childhood and adolescence. The Great Depression didn't occur until Stanley was 11 years old, and Frank Kappel left no record to suggest that his family struggled to make ends meet during the depths of the depression. Most families managed to have photographic images of themselves made, even if they didn't own a camera, since some enterprising entrepreneur in nearly every community of means takes it upon him or herself to make a little extra money by taking other peoples' photographs, developing, and printing them, and then selling them to the subjects. Many of these photos ended up being taken at school and then sold to proud parents. This tradition is longstanding and so predictable that it seems unlikely that someone in the Sicamous area wasn't doing the same.

Left: Stanley (16) and Betty (21), ca. 1935. [Ed. note – By all accounts they were good friends, despite their 5-year age difference] (SPC)

I had assumed that these photos (or at least, photographic negatives) existed somewhere. Finally, in early summer of 2021, Kerry found a box that had been rescued from Alice's basement when it was being cleared out in 2008. This box contained hundreds of black and white photographic negatives that had been carefully arranged in labeled "files", apparently by Stanley. Most of the negatives were in poor-to-fair condition, but with the help of the Photoshop app I was able to turn them into photographs of highly variable quality that proved to be a treasure trove of insight into Stanley's early years in the Kappel household, growing up in the Shuswap.

Left: Photo taken by Stanley of the Frank Kappel house in Sicamous, ca. 1936. The property appears to be quite large, affording the Kappel's a modicum of privacy in a small village. (SPC)

Scouting was popular in Canada as early as 1911 when 50,000 scouts were counted as members of the International Boy Scouts, founded in England in 1908 by Lord Robert Baden-Powell. Scouts Canada probably came to BC around the same time.

Stanley was undoubtedly exposed to the Scouts and he may have become a Scout, given the nature of the organization. Frank Kappel was an avid supporter of Scouting in his later years after Janet's death, suggesting that he may have been enthusiastic for Stanley to join the Scouts as a young man. The only record I have found on the subject suggests that the first Scout troop in Sicamous was not formed until 1939, long after Stanley had left home to attend college. Even so, it would be easy to believe that Stanley was a successful member of his closest "local" Scouts organization while he was growing up.

Above left: Stanley [Ed. note – Ca. age 16 ~ 1935], boating with friends on Shuswap Lake;
Above right: Enjoying summer by the lake (from Stanley's private collection)

Right: Stanley [Ed. note - Ca. age 19 ~ 1938], enjoying a boat ride on Shuswap Lake during his summer break from his studies at the Montana School of Mines; He also worked most of each summer at the Sheep Creek Mines, so his time to enjoy summer activities would have been quite limited. (SPC)

We have no written record of Stanley's adolescence, aside from the few newspaper articles already mentioned, but we do have a plethora of photographs that were "rescued" from the box of negatives that Stanley carefully sorted and organized. These photographs paint a rich tapestry of activities and experiences that reveal Stanley's teenage years to be astonishingly "normal", by any stretch of the imagination. He had many friends and girlfriends, was frequently in their company, and appears to have been affable and affectionate with nearly everyone. The photographs show the Shuswap area in all seasons, with particular emphasis on winter and summer.

Many of the negatives are of poor quality, having suffered significant degradation over the past 90 years, but converting them to positives and manipulating them into acceptable images was a labor of love on this writer's part.

Above left: Stanley and friends enjoying the summer days at Shuswap Lake; The boat driver is Peter Brennan, Jr.; Above right: water-boarding on Lake Shuswap (Stanley is the photographer, SPC). [Ed. note – These photographs appear to have been taken ca. 1938]

Due to the shape of Shuswap Lake, two communities separated by a mile or two "as the crow flies", if they were situated across one of the lake's four major arms, may have been a few minutes apart by boat, but several hours apart by road. Some of the boat owners also used their craft as "people ferries" or "water taxis" that were on call, much like modern day Uber or Lyft taxis, to transport members of one community to a distant location across the lake where a party or other community activity was planned. This means of transport was probably more common in the first two decades of the 20th century, when both roads and cars were relatively rare, and public bus transport hadn't yet arrived in the area.

Below left and right: Stanley took many photos of the times he spent with his friends, who were clearly an important part of his life. [Ed. note – Photos of unnamed young women, ca. 1938]

Stanley's early education has been previously discussed, but the role of his older sister, Betty, in his intellectual development cannot be ignored.

An article in the Vernon News dated March 31st, 1932, states: "Miss Betty Kappel…is among the Sicamous young people at home for Easter vacation, while attending schools at various points." Another similar Vernon News article entitled "Students of Sicamous and Eagle Valley Schools Celebrate Mid-Term Holidays" on December 22nd, 1932, reported: "Miss Betty Kappel, who has been attending Normal at Victoria, returned home on Monday for Christmas vacation." Another article in the Vernon News dated January 11th, 1934, reported: "Miss Betty Kappel, after spending the vacation with her parents, returned to the Meadow Creek School District, where she has been teaching during the past term." An article in the Vernon News dated August 17th, 1939, reads: "NEW TEACHERS: At a recent meeting of the Salmon Arm School Board, Miss Betty Kappel of Sicamous…was appointed to teach at Canoe School…"

Above left: This photo was probably taken ca. 1936, when Stanley was 17, with friends Peter Brennan, Jr., and Marj Myers. Above right: an early "tailgate party" among Stanley's friends. (from Stanley's private collection, SPC))

This series of articles reveals that Betty studied at the Provincial Normal School in Victoria for two years to achieve her teacher's certificate and was required to graduate from high school before she could be accepted as a student. The school syllabus was reported to be "respectably rigorous" and was designed to train elementary and high school teachers to meet standards equal to those in other first world countries. The emphasis of the school's curriculum was the preparation of good teachers who understood the social and educational needs of students throughout British Columbia, with special attention paid to the needs of rural students attending "ungraded", or one-room, elementary schools.

Continuing Lynne Beeson's memories of her mother: "As for Mum, I know she went to boarding school at some point, as her roommate at boarding school was Jean Brechin (you may remember Stew Brechin from Eagle Bay, Karen, and Jean was his Mum. They had the cabin down the road. Thinking of which, Dolan Road, where the cabin was (named for Aunty Kate who had the next cabin for many years and whose grave is in the Blind Bay cemetery) was developed by Grandpa and Jack Brechin (Stew's Dad – Stew, by the way, was best man at our wedding). Anyways, Mum also went to "Normal School" in Victoria, which, at the time, was the teaching college (it is now Camosin College). Mum's first job was in Meadow Creek, in the hills above Celista. She and another woman shared a home near the water in Celista and in winter, she said their shoes would always freeze to the floor! I gather she went to school by horseback and her class of students was from grades 1 to 8. Mum always used to say that most of her students had never seen running water or electricity and yet several went on to great careers – like one became an astrophysicist and others became scientists etc. There was a horse drawn logger that worked above Meadow Creek and in really bad winter days he would stop at the school and pick up some of the kids – Mum would dismiss them early, so that they could get a ride close to their homes."

Stanley undoubtedly interacted regularly with Betty while she was pursuing her goal of higher education during the years between 1931 and 1933, even though she was away from home for most of both years. Betty did not marry until 1945, which suggests that she taught in rural schools in the Shuswap area for nine years after she completed her studies at the Normal School in Victoria.

Betty and Stanley's parents clearly approved of and encouraged both of their children to seek higher education, something that was perhaps less common in the 1930s than it is today. Since neither Janet Thomson nor Frank Kappel possessed degrees from institutions of higher learning, it is impressive that they made such opportunities available to their children, and even more impressive that both children were able to obtain degrees that enabled them to enjoy professional careers in their chosen fields. For less affluent families, finishing high school was frequently impossible if the income their children could generate as teenagers was needed for basic survival.

Above: Photo entitled "Students from Sicamous school on C.P.R. Hill, 1938"; This is the school where Stanley probably received his primary education. [Ed, note – The teacher in the upper left corner is Betty Kappel, Stanley's sister.] (Sicamous & District Museum and Historical Society)

Remembering Jeanie Dubberley's tale about an early encounter in Riverside Park in Kamloops between Stanley and Jeanie's mother, Marie, when they were both age 14 or 15: Donald Dunbar, Jeanie Dubberley's brother and Marie's son, recently sent copies of a collection of photos and cards his mother had kept in an album for many years. The first indication of an ongoing relationship between Marie and Stanley is a card dated Christmas 1938, that is beautifully embossed with the Montana School of Mines crest, wishing Marie and Hugh "Merry Christmas and a Happy New Year, With all best wishes in the years to come, Stan" (Marie and Hugh were married on December 1st, 1938).

The album also includes a photo of a group of teenagers lounging on the lawn of the Frank Kappel family's back garden: Marie, age 19, appears prominently in the photo, sitting next to Stanley, age 20. Additional photos, cards and letters that Stanley sent to Marie years later as he progressed on his journey through life, often with the sentiment "Love, Stan" hand-written in the lower right corner, strongly suggests that Stanley and Marie established a relationship after the "chance encounter" in Kamloops and soon became close friends and confidants. Not only did the two siblings maintain close connections during the rest of Stanley's life, but Alice also kept in touch with Marie even after Stanley died in 1952.

Above: Friends of Stanley's, mostly feminine, in the photo, identified as "Kappel's garden, August 1939", when Stanley was 20; The only other male in the photo, back row right, is identified as Peter Brennan, Jr., one of Stanley's closest friends. The young woman sitting next to Stanley at the edge of the photo is identified as Marie, age 19, who was Stanley's younger sister in the Ernie Buckingham family and was adopted out around the same time as Stanley in 1921. [Ed. note – This photo suggests that Stanley and Marie became friends sometime after they first met in Kamloops when Marie was 14. We know they stayed in touch during the rest of Stanley's life because of several letters and Christmas cards written by Stanley to Marie.]

Jeanie Dubberley wrote in a fascinating October 2021 email about her father, Hugh: "Dad's ship and two other Canadian destroyers were on a cruise along the Pacific coast when England declared war in September 1939 (just weeks after this picture was taken). When the

First World War broke out in August 1914, Canada was automatically at war at the same time.

"In 1939 there was a ten-day delay between England's declaration and Canada's. The reason is that those three destroyers had to get themselves into the Atlantic as quickly as possible, and of course the way to do that was to use the Panama Canal. It would be closed to "belligerent nations", so until the ships cleared the Canal, Canada had to remain at peace with Germany."

Above left: some of Stanley's friends enjoying themselves on the back bed of an old truck whose make, style, and vintage are unknown. Above right: one of Stanley's "unknown" girl friends in the back garden of the Kappel home. [Ed. note – This collection of converted negatives from Stanley's "stash" suggests that he and his friends spent many enjoyable hours enjoying one another's company and that Stanley had more than one girlfriend with whom he shared some degree of "intimacy".] (all SPC)

Thinking about the reality of Stanley's early life and circumstances, mixed impressions are unavoidable. On the one hand, here is a very young child, happy enough with his birth family, at age two suddenly cast into a four-month period of chaos marked by grief and loss after his mother died.

Right: Marie Dunbar, Stanley's younger sister. The inscription on the back of the photo reads: "Taken by Stanley when I was staying at Kappels (Sicamous, BC, August 1939; Writing to Hughie)." [Ed. note – Marie was married to Hughie, who was in the Canadian Royal Navy and deployed on a ship when this photo was taken.]

Below left: This photo of an unnamed "mystery woman" who was an obviously intimate friend of Stanley's, ca. 1936, when Stanley was 18, was taken from a position that suggests the two shared a degree of intimacy that had moved beyond casual or even good friends. The photo below right shows Stanley with yet a different "intimate" friend.

Below left and right: Two photos taken the same day, ca. 1934,, when Stanley was 15 and betty was 20; The photos show Betty and her boyfriend, whose name we don't know, in a close relationship, along with Stanley and Betty's beau also enjoying a very cozy pose. The three of them were obviously good friends and were enjoying one another's company on a warm summer day, but it also reveals what a warm, affectionate boy Stanley was. (SPC)

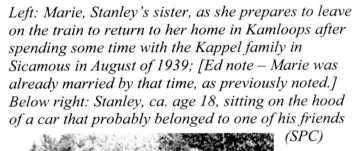

Left: Marie, Stanley's sister, as she prepares to leave on the train to return to her home in Kamloops after spending some time with the Kappel family in Sicamous in August of 1939; [Ed note – Marie was already married by that time, as previously noted.]
Below right: Stanley, ca. age 18, sitting on the hood of a car that probably belonged to one of his friends
(SPC)

Kerry remembers: "Mother (Alice) told me that Stanley went to a kind of orphanage/foster care situation for that period, and the Kappels adopted him from that facility. Mother also told me the story that Grandpa Kappel later reiterated to Kristen, that Stanley was waiting on the end of the dock for his new adoptive father to pick him up in a boat (Stanley was staying in a place across the lake from the Kappels' home). When Frank arrived, Stanley was just holding one shabby bag of his possessions, and he stepped into the boat and immediately called him "Dad." Such a moving story."

But then, suddenly, the cloud lifted for young Stanley: Frank and Janet Kappel welcomed him into their family, and life immediately improved for the young boy. Between age two and a half and 18, life must have been unexpectedly and almost unimaginably good for Stanley. Frank and Janet were both highly competent and refined parents. Frank's own autobiography reveals him to be an open and generous man, who gave of himself in service to his community throughout his entire life. It is easy to imagine how much pleasure it brought him to be granted a son like Stanley, who was bright, athletic, happy, and highly accomplished in his own right.

Kerry muses: "I also thought quite a lot about the transition for Donald Angus from his birth family, probably a rather boisterous place with lots of kids running around, and a more informal kind of home, to the formality and quiet of the Kappel home, where he was renamed Stanley Ernest. It must have been an enormous and painful transition initially. But given that Stanley was such a sensitive and "high reactive" child (per Susan Cain in Quiet), I imagine the quiet more formal and regulated life suited his personality a lot better, and in the long run unlocked a lot more of his gifts, intellect, and potential."

In all probability, Stanley's first two and a half years of life faded rapidly into the dim recesses of his memory and the tumult of that four-month period following his mother's sudden death did not dominate his consciousness during the rest of his life. The reality of his blessed membership in the Frank Kappel household was undoubtedly the dominant feature of his childhood, as it should have been. It seems safe to conclude that the many blessings Stanley received as a growing child and young adult played the most important role in shaping his personal psychology.

The mysterious nature and daunting challenge of becoming a person was an altogether different issue for Stanley as well as for every one of his peers. All of the photos in this chapter suggest a simple truth: the remoteness of the Shuswap area, coupled with the relative lack of connection to the "outside world" via immediate telecommunications, personal digital devices, social websites, or print media brought young people together and encouraged them to turn to one another for friendship and affection. Such alliances also provided desperately needed feedback regarding their own progress on their journey toward adulthood.

It is tempting to theorize that life was different for those coming of age in the early 20th century, especially for those living in the embrace of the Shuswap's splendid natural environment. One could even speculate that these young people weren't beset with the myriad complex and confusing possibilities that modern life presents us with. But that would be naïve, at least to this writer. Who am I, how do I fit in, what should I do with my life, what is the meaning of all this, what will happen when I die? These are perennial questions that have dogged mankind since we acquired the ability to think and worry. I doubt if life seemed any less complicated or more straightforward to the lovely adolescents appearing on these pages than to the youth of today.

Left: Photo taken by Stanley in the 1930s of the Rock Creek Hotel, south of the Shuswap near the US border, where a gold rush occurred in 1859, and where gold and silver were mined until 1926; The electric pole and wire stretching across the road suggests rural electrification was a reality and provided power for electric lighting, refrigeration, food preparation, and entertainment. (SPC)

Right: Photo taken by Stanley in the 1930s, probably the Kettle River near Rock Creek in Boundary County (SPC)

Left: Photo taken by Stanley during the 1930s; This local Shuswap citizen, possibly J. Rivers (or at least working for J. Rivers) and hauling a large load of split wood on an old flat-bed truck, undoubtedly influenced Stanley as he was coming of age, as did countless other colorful characters observed by the young man every day. (SPC)

CHAPTER 13 – Stanley Becomes a Mining Engineer

Anyone examining the life of Stanley Kappel would eventually wonder why he decided to become a mining engineer, a career that few young men might typically choose as their life's passion. Stanley's first major work experience probably occurred at the Sheep Creek Gold Mine, located 230 miles southeast of Sicamous and 35 miles south of Nelson, B.C., near Salmo, which lies 10 miles north of Canada's border with the United States. His father says that "he liked the mining life and decided to pursue it as a profession. He obtained a scholarship at the Montana School of Mines in Butte, and started his studies there in 1936, graduating in June of 1940." This suggests that he had been exploring mining engineering as his chosen profession prior to obtaining his first job at Sheep Creek Gold mine, and his personal collection of photographic negatives includes a file on Sheep Creek Mine dated 1935-1941. This means that his first summer working there was in 1935, a year before he finished high school, and he continued summer work at Sheep Creek until 1940. *[Editor's note – it is unlikely that he worked at Sheep Creek in 1941 because he was already in South America by that time.]*

Frank Kappel further states in his biographical sketch of his son: "Stanley was an exceptionally clever student and he graduated from Montana State University as a Mining Engineer before he was 21 years of age. Summers were spent mining in shrinkage and open-type mining operations and weekends in college contracting in Butte mines."

The history of the Shuswap is rich in mining history, particularly gold mining. No less than three gold rushes occurred in the Shuswap, starting in 1866. Shuswap's Montebello Museum Curator Deborah Chapman stated in an article appearing in the Salmon Arm Observer, July 12, 2018:

> "Miners headed for the Big Bend on the Columbia River via Shuswap Lake six years after the Cariboo Gold Rush, which began in 1860. A year later, the Columbia Gold Rush was officially a bust, she says.
>
> "Many bitter miners gave up their golden dreams, but in 1866, 80 die-hard miners wintered at Scotch Creek, having seen coarse pellets and nuggets found 10 miles from the creek's mouth.
>
> "This ignited mining fever in the Shuswap, says Chapman, noting the new Montebello exhibit, "Can You Dig it?" explores the history of placer and hard-rock mining in the Shuswap. Local historians have discovered evidence of mining operations that had taken place as late as the 1930s and '40s in the Shuswap, particularly in an area known as Scotch Gulch."

Another article appearing on July 7, 2018 in the Eagle Valley News written by Jim Cooperman, a local historian and journalist, discusses the arrival of "eccentric" prospectors and gold-seekers in the Shuswap area with dreams of striking it rich. These men established mining claims in the 1930s and 40s, although no one was more colorful than Bunny Bischoff, "the original bushman of the Shuswap."

> "Judging from the stories about Bunny, he could easily be called a local legend. When Henry and Maria Bischoff arrived in Scotch Creek from Minnesota with their five sons and three daughters in 1895, they became the first Caucasian family to settle in the North Shuswap. As the First World War began, Bunny and his brothers Pat, Matt and Cook headed

for the hills to avoid conscription. Those years of living off the land and roaming by foot across alpine plateaus to as far away as Logan Lake, likely influenced Bunny to carry on this lifestyle for most of his years.

Left: Newspaper photo of Theodore "Bunny" Bischoff, born in 1891, who was a well-known mining prospector and "local legend" in the Shuswap region when Stanley Kappel was a young man. (North Shuswap Historical Society)

"While his brothers took up homesteads above Celista, Bunny tried farming but opted instead for trapping and prospecting. He never had a regular job and perhaps he was more comfortable alone in the bush, where no one could hear his stuttering. His lease at Scotch Creek was located just east of the north fork above the falls and the 1936 Report of the Minister of Mines noted a small amount of hand work had been done 100 feet above the creek and recovery was not known.

"Bunny also had a silver and zinc mining claim on the Adams Plateau called Mosquito King and he built a nearby log cabin. In recognition of the time that Bunny spent on the Adams plateau, a chain of lakes was named after him and his brother Pat, who was also a trapper. Ralph Bischoff recalls a story told by Lester Bentley who was logging up in the plateau during the winter and saw smoke coming out of a clump of balsam. He went over to investigate and found Bunny calmly making tea in a hole in the 13-foot-deep snowpack, while taking a break from surveying lines on his claim.

"The most successful, independent miner in the Scotch Creek valley during the third gold rush was Bob Bristow, who arrived in 1931 and staked two leases on both sides of the forks. He accessed the area via a trail from Meadow Creek that was laid out by Henry Wallensteen, a Dominion forester. This trail carried on to the Adams Plateau, where Henry had a trapline and all the way to Adams Lake. In 1935, the Salmon Arm Observer reported that Bristow had found a gold nugget that weighed over half an ounce."

Young boys like Stanley Kappel, growing up in the Shuswap, would surely have heard these stories and many others recounted by their peers and elders. Is it possible that Stanley even met some of the eccentric prospectors while he was growing up? Frank Kappel, a "local legend" in his own right, was a homesteader who had found employment in a wide variety of occupations after arriving in the Shuswap area in 1911. He had worked as a logger, teamster, fire warden, chartered accountant, timber scaler, business manager, notary public, and had even ventured underground at the Brittania Mine on Howe Sound in 1914, observing in his personal memoir: "After all, swinging a shovel did not call for many brains. When a person takes a job of any kind, he must give the best he has to do the work properly, as well as he can. Heaven helps those who help themselves."

According to Britannica: "Mineral resources have formed a basis of British Columbia's economy since the arrival of Europeans. Coal and gold mining provided much of the impetus for the region's growth in the 18th century. An infusion of capital into mining, mineral processing, and mineral exploration led to renewed expansion of the sector in the early 21st century. Mines are located throughout the province and include open-pit coal mines in the southeastern and northeastern corners of the province and open-pit copper mines southwest of Kamloops."

The Wells Historical Society Museum in Wells, B.C., has a wonderful website that covers the mining industry expansion in British Columbia during the late 19th and early 20th century. Wells, which lies north of the Shuswap near the Cariboos, was a leader in gold mining during that period. Several BC newspapers covered the mining potential in British Columbia with great interest. The following commentary from the Wells Museum archives may lend significant insight into the reasons for young Stanley Kappel's deciding to become a mining engineer:

"Canada was hit hard by the Great Depression. The value of exports from Canada went from a high of $1.3 billion in 1928 to a low of $0.5 billion in 1932. By 1931, unemployment reached 28 percent in British Columbia, the highest in Canada. One in five Canadians became dependent upon government relief to survive. From 1929 to 1933, Gross National Expenditure is estimated to have declined by 42 percent while the total government debt increased by a whopping 27 percent from 1930 to 1937. The Depression affected everyone, some more painfully than others. Unemployed Chinese were expected to survive on one-third of the assistance that was provided to unemployed white males.

Right: Placer mining for gold near Wells in the Cariboo District, 1930s (Wells Historical Society)

"In the late 1930s, although the Great Depression was technically over, the country remained in a severe recession. Credit became over-extended and too much production continued while demand decreased. The countries of the world limited imports and since exports were decreasing from everyone, no one benefited. Forestry, construction, and transportation all suffered in British Columbia as demand decreased and businesses could not afford new developments.

"Within this context of world Depression, Wells was established, and it thrived. Demand for Canadian products dropped dramatically, except the demand for gold, because while the value of most products dropped the value of gold skyrocketed. People were desperate for work and willing to travel the great distance to the remote location of Wells to have stable employment. The gold mining boom in Wells offered hope and salvation in a time of great need. Since both prices and wages declined throughout the country, the standard of living increased for those with property or jobs – as was the case for those employed in Wells."

The harsh reality of the Great Depression almost surely had a noticeable impact on the Kappel family, although Frank Kappel doesn't discuss this in his memoirs. The Kappel family was well established by the time 1929 arrived, but Frank's involvement in the timber industry suggests that he had to work hard to maintain the comfortable living standard that he and his family had enjoyed during Stanley's early years in the Kappel household.

As a schoolboy, Stanley was trying on various roles while he progressed through the grades on his way to becoming an independent adult. His dreams of success during his formative years had to be colored by the reality of those economically difficult times. Young Stanley would certainly have been aware of which occupations were most likely to provide good prospects for employment. Frank and Stanley undoubtedly discussed the many possible paths Stanley might pursue on more than one occasion. In addition, Stanley's friends, along with other family members, personal heroes, teachers, and mentors would also have been "consulted" for their opinions.

We don't know if R.A. McGuire, of Salmon Arm, was a friend of Stanley's, but he was a member of the same class at the Montana School of Mines as Stanley, so it's possible the two discussed and even planned to attend MSM together. The insight provided by the Wells Museum commentary offers another possible dimension in Stanley's thought processes as he passed through his teenage years. Then there is the undeniable allure of gold that is impossible for most to ignore, even adjusting for the fact that gold mining offered an almost guaranteed path to success for a bright young man.

Life is alchemy, and the mining enterprise is essentially alchemical in nature: exploration, discovery, extraction, processing, refining. Mining has played a central role in human culture for most of our history, and gold mining is no exception. Indeed, gold has been woven into the fabric of the mythology of nearly all civilizations and eras from pre-historic times onward. Gold was used to decorate mummy cases in ancient Egypt. Gold jewelry has been recovered from many, if not most, of the graves of chieftains, pharaohs, kings, shamans, high priests, and other important officials ever since homo sapiens began to organize itself into a complex, hierarchical social order. Gold was the subject of "Jason and the Golden Fleece" in Greek mythology and was thought to be a symbol of authority and kingship. Gold thread has been used to adorn and embroider the clothing of everyone fortunate enough to occupy a high socioeconomic position. It has embellished and covered religious structures, ornaments, relics, coffins, ceilings, windows, and robes, primarily to symbolize the religious and symbolic importance of the institution.

Alchemists in the Middle Ages sought to transform ordinary material into gold. In more recent mythology, what lies at the end of the rainbow, the ultimate symbol of good fortune? A pot of gold. The sun is, after all, a golden orb that is the source of all life on earth. How could we not conclude that gold is the most important color and the most important of all precious metals in creation?

A revealing article in the Vernon News dated September 15th, 1932, when Stanley was 13, reads: "Frank Kappel and his son, Stanley, made a weekend trip to the French Creek

Development Company's placer mine on the Big Bend. Mr. Kappel said it was a nice trip. He brought back a few samples of the gold, which is presented to visitors up there."

Right: French Creek Placer Mine near Big Bend, 1936 (Wells Historical Society)

In the end, Stanley almost certainly did not stumble into his life as a mining engineer by accident. Before he graduated from high school he had already acquired a summer job in a hard rock mine far away from his beloved Shuswap friends and family. He had also acquired a catalog from the Montana School of Mines, filled out an application, and was accepted to commence his studies at an important institution of higher learning that focused solely on the mining industry and every conceivable aspect of this complex and dangerous undertaking. According to Frank Kappel, Stanley was even awarded a scholarship by the school. By the time he got to Butte in the fall of 1936, Stanley's plan to become a mining engineer was firmly established.

Four Years at the Montana School of Mines

From Wikipedia: "Underground hard rock mining refers to various underground mining techniques used to excavate *hard* minerals, usually those containing metals such as ore containing gold, silver, iron, copper, zinc, nickel, tin, and lead, but also involves using the same techniques for ores of gems such as diamonds or rubies. Soft rock mining refers to excavation of softer minerals such as salt, coal, or oil sands."

Right: Campus of the Montana School of Mines, 1900

According to the official website of Montana Technical University, the modern-day name of the academic institution that was originally the Montana State School of Mines:

"Opening in 1900 as the Montana State School of Mines, Montana Tech's funding and land came from the Enabling Act of 1889, which admitted Montana to the Union and allocated 100,000 acres of public land to establish a state school of mines.

"The School of Mines opened its doors with only one building, Main Hall, holding 21 students and offering two degrees: mining engineering and electrical engineering.

By 1919, "a bill enacted by the Legislative Assembly of Montana in 1919 created the Montana State Bureau of Mines and Metallurgy. The Bureau had two main functions: first, developing the mineral resources of the state; second, improving the safety and efficiency of mining related operations. Today, the Bureau is the principal source of earth science information for the citizens of Montana.

Left: Stanley and friends during their freshman year at MSM, standing at the entry to the new dormitory in 1936 (from Stanley's private collection, SPC)

The Thirty-Seventh Annual Catalogue of the Montana School of Mines, 1936-37, states:

"The School of Mines aims primarily to prepare students for service in mining, metallurgy, ore dressing and geology, the four main branches of the mineral industry. With this end in view, special emphasis is placed upon the teaching of mathematics, physics, chemistry, and other fundamental engineering subjects. Although a large proportion of the graduates find their life work in the mineral industry, the courses of training are designed to give a broad training in all forms of engineering.

"The cosmopolitan student body at the school of mines, consisting of around 300 students in total, lends itself to interesting discussions of national and foreign affairs. During the past few years students have been enrolled from every state in the United States, from several provinces of Canada, from Alaska, Hawaii, Australia, Barbados, Bulgaria, China, Costa Rica, Germany, India, Italy, Liberia, Mexico, Norway, Persia, Russia, and the Philippine Islands.

Left: Campus of the Montana School of Mines, 1937

"The School of Mines occupies a commanding location on the southern bench of Big Butte from which the city takes its name.

UNIVERSITY OF MONTANA BULLETIN

SCHOOL OF MINES SERIES   NUMBER 21

MONTANA
SCHOOL OF MINES

———

THIRTY-SEVENTH
ANNUAL CATALOGUE

1936-37

ANNOUNCEMENTS FOR
1937-1938

———

Butte, Montana
April, 1937

Above: the cover of the 1936-37 MSM school catalogue, much like the 1935-36 catalogue Stanley would have read as a high school senior contemplating his future. This was almost certainly the single most important document Stanley had ever held in his hands. Anyone who has attended an institution of higher learning recognizes the significance of this event and the excitement Stanley would have felt when he read it, not to mention the uncertainty and apprehension. (Butte-Silver Bow Public Archives)

"The School of Mines overlooks the city of Butte and the famous Anaconda and adjacent hills which bristle with the headframes that tap the greatest copper and zinc mines in the world. Eastward stands grizzled East Ridge, a fault scarp of 1,500 feet displacement, whose tops are snow-capped during most of the year. To the southward rise the Highlands, an imposing array of mountain peaks, and to the westward the majestic Anaconda Range.

Right: View from the MSM campus toward the Anaconda Range, 1936

"In the center of all this grandeur lies the up-to-date city of Butte, queen of all the mining camps. The city has a population of about 40,000 people, is served by 4 trans-continental railroads; has excellent hotels, theaters, and department stores; 3 fine hospitals, churches of many denominations; a half-million-dollar YMCA; city and country clubs and an excellent street railway system that runs within 2 city blocks of the School of Mines.

Right: Photo of Butte, with the MSM campus in the foreground, and the Anaconda Mountains in the distance, ca. 1937 (from Stanley's private collection, SPC)

"One hundred mine shafts pierce the hills in the vicinity of Butte and from the underground workings, 2,700 miles in length, over 15,000 tons of copper, zinc and manganese ores are shipped daily to the various reduction works in Butte, Anaconda, Great Falls and East Helena. It is in these great mines and plants that the School of Mines students receive a substantial part of their laboratory training. No other mining college can offer such a fund of first-hand information.

"The campus, consisting of 11.5 acres, is one of natural beauty, situated as it is on the high terrace at the foot of Big Butte, where the buildings can be plainly seen for miles. A cooperative plan between the School of Mines and the Rocky Mountain Garden Club for beautifying the grounds has been inaugurated, and already the campus is rapidly becoming one of the beauty spots of Butte. Numerous trees, lawns and shrubs have been planted, a new promenade walk has been built, and steps have been taken to beautify the natural amphitheater just east of the college.

Left: View of the MSM campus taken from West Park Street by Stanley in 1936 (from Stanley's private collection, SPC))

"Montana School of Mines' large athletic field, constructed in a huge natural bowl, contains a football and baseball field, running track, and two tennis courts. The school itself consists of 7 modern, fireproof structures, including Main Hall (including and extensive Library occupying one entire floor), Engineering Hall, the Metallurgy Building, the Mill Building, the Gymnasium, the Residence Hall, and President's Residence.

Left: Stanley posing with two friends in front of the MSM men's dormitory in 1937 (from Stanley's private collection)

"The cost of attending the school is $37.50 per semester for non-resident students and is free to all Montana residents. Other fees include: a one-time matriculation fee of $5.00; a registration fee of $7.50 per semester; an incidental fee of $15.00 per academic year; a student activity fee of $15.00 per year; health service fee of $2.50 per semester. In consideration of the health service fee, students are given one physical examination and necessary medical and surgical care, along with all necessary medicines and surgical supplies required for treatments.

"The cost of textbooks is about $25.00 per year. Residence fees for students living on campus are $30.00 per month for each occupant of a double room, including full board.

Each bedroom is equipped with a lavatory and clothes closet. All bathrooms have showers. Each room is furnished with study table and lamp, chairs, single beds, chiffoniers, mattresses, pillows, linens, bedding, and towels.

Right: The "new" residence hall where Stanley lived as a student at MSM, ca. 1936

"For several years hockey has been gaining interest with School of Mines students, partly because of the number of men in attendance from Canada, where this is a major sport, and partly because of the formation of independent hockey leagues in Butte.

Hockey team, 1939-40.

Above: Intercollegiate hockey team, 1939; Stanley, the team's center, is 5th from our left.

"The Holland Rink, managed by A.H. Clarke, has fostered this sport, being kept in first-class condition at all times and having made available to the Mines hockey teams at no cost to the students. Most of the competition during the past 3 years has been with local league teams, since the other Montana colleges have not adopted this sport to any degree. During 1937, however, a series was arranged with the University of Washington in Seattle.

Left: Stanley in his freshman year at MSM, 1936, age 18, ready for athletic training (from Stanley's private collection, SPC))

"In past years, when sufficient talent has been available, the Montana School of Mines has had a Glee Club and Orchestra as part of the student activities. It is recognized that such organizations are added attractions to students who are musically inclined. The Glee Clubs of 1931-32 and 1932-33 were outstanding and gave numerous programs to the student assemblies and to civic clubs in Butte, Anaconda and elsewhere.

"During the past year the Club has been active and has continued the good record of its predecessors. The School also hosts a dramatic arts club and has put on one play per year during the past 8 years. In addition, the Co-Ed Club has been maintained for the past 14 years by young women attending the School of Mines. (It should be noted that the School has a "general studies" program that allows local students seeking a college education to attend one year in that capacity; of the 47 "general studies" students listed, 19 were women. There were no women listed as students registered or enrolled in any of the technical and engineering classes of the School.)

"The subjects of instruction in the freshman and sophomore years are common to all options. They consist of mathematics (college algebra, plane trigonometry, analytic geometry, spherical trigonometry, descriptive geometry, differential calculus, integral

calculus); chemistry (general chemistry, quantitative analysis); geology (physical geology, historical geology); mineralogy; physics; industrial history; English (composition, literature); economics; drawing (topographical, technical, plane surveying); and physical education. In addition to the above, a course in mining engineering must include training in mining, geology, and metallurgy.

Left: Stanley during his sophomore year, 1937, taken in front of his dormitory (from Stanley's private collection, SPC)

Right: Stanley, age 19, varsity letterman, successful student, respected by his peers, posing with fellow freshman and hockey player, 1938 (from Stanley's private collection)

"The study of mining begins in the junior year, with discussion and study of the various steps in mining, from the earliest stages of prospecting to large commercial operations, together with the most up-to-date methods, processes and devices employed to make such operations profitable. This includes surveying, topographic drawing and map making, lectures, laboratory, field work and design. Likewise, a study of the operations required to reach the ore deposits from the surface, that is, shaft sinking, drifting, cross-cutting, raising, timbering, drilling, and blasting; stoping (the excavation of a series of steps or layers in the ground or rock) and other methods of extraction are also studied.

"In the senior year, the student is made familiar with the more intimate details of the mine plant as a whole and makes the necessary calculations for size of plant and energy required to operate it. This includes the production, transmission and use of steam, compressed air, and waterpower, and their utilization; mine haulage, rope haulage, including aerial tramways; and mine hoisting.

Right: Photo of Stanley catching a nap while studying on the lawn of the MSM men's dormitory in 1937 (from Stanley's private collection, SPC)

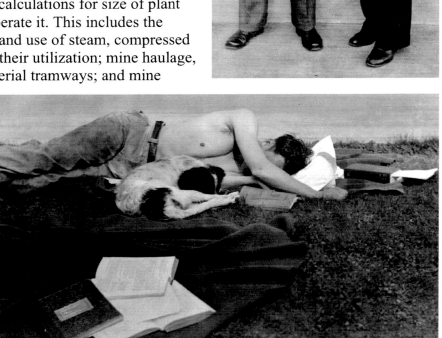

"Supplementing the lectures and field work is a course in designing and plant analysis during which the students make frequent visits to the mines and plants of the Butte district. Junior year courses include physical chemistry, engineering English, petrology, mechanics, ceramics, principles of metallurgy, mining, mining design, fire assaying, structural geology, hydraulics, graphic statistics, metallurgy of copper, mining, mining design, mines surveying and geologic field mapping. Senior year courses include economic geology, power transmissions, metallurgy of iron and steel, mining design and plant study, economics of mineral industry, mine mapping, economic geology, thermodynamics, metallurgy of lead, zinc, gold, silver, and rare metals, mine practice, mill design, and principles of mineral dressing.

"More esoteric and advanced courses are also offered, including paleontology, seismograph observatory, anthropology, archaeology of North America, prospector's short course, principles of public speaking, dramatics, contemporary reading, modern history, economic geology of metalliferous deposits, pottery manufacturing, ceramic building materials, pyrometry and calorimetry, and elementary and advanced classes in French, Spanish and German.

Above left: Photo taken by Stanley at the MSM field site near Maiden Rock showing students learning to survey terrain using a surveyor's transit during the summer preceding their sophomore year, 1937; Above right: Stanley in the field at the same site, learning to handle a surveyor's grade rod, 1937 (from Stanley's private collection, SPC))

Left: Photo taken by Stanley during his junior year in 1938; His class is beginning an extensive field trip. (SPC)

"All engineering students are also required to take the geological field work during the 3 weeks preceding the senior year. Camping equipment is furnished by the school. Detailed and reconnaissance mapping methods are practiced at several locations in western Montana. Some time is spent in the study of the stratigraphy of the Gallatin and Tobacco Root Mountains, where a geological series of pre-Cambrian to the Pleistocene is exposed. In past years the structures and stratigraphy of the Red Lodge coal field and Elk Basin oil field have been studied. Opportunity is afforded at these localities for the observation of coal mining methods and oil field drilling practice. Following the more detailed field work, a trip has been taken through the deep gorge of the Shoshone River, past the Cody dam, to the Yellowstone Park with its geysers, hot springs, and other unique phenomena. Virginia City and other early day mining camps are visited before the return trip to Butte.

Above left and right: Two photos taken by Stanley during a camping field trip, junior year, 1938

"During the second semester of the junior year, all engineering students are required to make an inspection trip to several of the mining and metallurgical plants in western Montana. The trip is supplemented by a number of shorter trips during the junior and senior years. Two weeks are spent at the end of the senior year in visiting a number of western mining districts. The geology of the districts and the mining and metallurgical methods are explained and studied. The week following the trip is spent in preparation of a detailed report of the field observations."

Stanley Ernest Kappel of Sicamous, B.C., is listed as a freshman student on page 76 of The Thirty-Seventh Annual Catalogue of the Montana School of Mines (MSM), 1936-37. Also listed are several other students from British Columbia, including sophomore Leonard McCall Dodd from Greenwood, with whom Stanley joined the newly MSM formed glee club in late 1936. Both Stanley and Leonard were also on the MSM hockey team together.

Butte, Montana, began as a mining camp in the 1860s, and went on to attract a diversity of miners from all over the world as it expanded to become one of the most productive mining areas in North America. According to *Wikipedia:*

"The mines attracted workers from Cornwall (United Kingdom), Ireland, Wales, Lebanon, Canada, Finland, Austria, Serbia, Italy, China, Syria, Croatia, Montenegro, Mexico, and all areas of the United States. The legacy of the immigrants lives on in the form of the Cornish pasty which was popularized by mine workers who needed something easy to eat in the mines, the povitica—a Slavic nut bread pastry which is a holiday favorite sold in many supermarkets and bakeries in Butte—and the boneless porkchop sandwich. These, along with huckleberry products and Scandinavian lefse have arguably become Montana's symbolic foods, known and enjoyed throughout Montana. In the ethnic neighborhoods, young men formed gangs to protect their territory and socialize into adult life, including the Irish of Dublin Gulch, the Eastern Europeans of the McQueen Addition, and the Italians of Meaderville (Butte's Irish Catholic community has been notably longstanding: As of 2017, the city has the highest percentage of Irish Americans per capita of any city in the United States).

"Among the migrants, many Chinese workers moved in, and amongst them set up businesses that led to the creation of a Chinatown in Butte. The Chinese migrations stopped in 1882 with the passage of the Chinese Exclusion Act. There was anti-Chinese sentiment in the 1870s and onwards due to racism on the part of the white settlers, exacerbated by economic depression, and in 1895, the chamber of commerce and labor unions started a boycott of Chinese owned businesses. The business owners fought back by suing the unions and winning."

"The influx of miners gave Butte a reputation as a wide-open town where any vice was obtainable. The city's famous saloon and red-light district, called the "Line" or "The Copper Block", was centered on Mercury Street, where the elegant bordellos included the famous Dumas Brothel. Behind the brothel was the equally famous Venus Alley, where women plied their trade in small cubicles called "cribs". The red-light district brought miners and other men from all over the region and was open until 1982 as one of the last such urban districts in the United States. Commercial breweries first opened in Butte in the 1870s and were a large staple of the city's early economy; they were usually run by German immigrants, including Leopold Schmidt, Henry Mueller, and Henry Muntzer. The breweries were always staffed by union workers. Most ethnic groups in Butte, from Germans and Irish to Italians and various Eastern Europeans, including children, enjoyed the locally brewed lagers, bocks, and other types of beer.

"Around the turn of the twentieth century, prosperous mining had generated considerable wealth in Butte, and at the time was the largest city between Chicago and San Francisco. Copper ore mined from the Butte mining district in 1910 alone totaled 284,000,000 pounds (129,000,000 kg), making it the largest producer of copper in North America and second only to South Africa in world production of metals. The same year, an excess of 10,000,000 ounces (280,000 kg) of silver and 37,000 ounces (1,000 kg) of gold were also discovered. The amount of ore produced in the city earned it the nickname "The Richest Hill on Earth." With its large workforce of miners performing in physically dangerous conditions, Butte was the site of active labor union movements, and came to be known as "the Gibraltar of Unionism."

By any standard, Butte, Montana, was a worldly, if not cosmopolitan, city in 1936 when young Stanley Kappel arrived to attend school at one of the most important higher institutions of mining and metallurgical engineering education in the world. The difference between the bucolic Shuswap Valley and his new home for the next four years must have been dazzling to him. How he spent his time during those eventful years remains somewhat shrouded in the mist of time, but we do have at least a few hints at what he experienced between 1936 and 1940.

Newspaper articles printed in The *Montana Standard* between 1936 and 1940 reveal details about Stanley that are available nowhere else. He was one of only 20 foreign students attending the school in 1936. He joined a newly formed glee club in November of 1936, along with

Kenneth Dodd, from Greenwood, BC, some 50 miles south of Sicamous. If Stanley didn't know Kenneth prior to that year, he undoubtedly came to know him as soon as he arrived at the school. The two had a lot in common, in addition to their love of music, and they both played on the varsity hockey team during their tenure in Butte.

Right: Photo of downtown Butte taken by Stanley in his sophomore year during a special celebration that included many marching bands, floats, and other celebratory features, 1937 (SPC)

Stanley was inducted into a national professional engineering fraternity, Theta Tau, Psi chapter, during his third year at the Montana School of Mines, and was listed as one of 26 rushees, who were entertained with a ravioli dinner, lectures by professors, and a musical quartet. To be invited to join this fraternity was clearly an honor. Kenneth Dodd, who had been a sophomore when Stanley arrived in Butte but graduated in the same class as Stanley in 1940 for unknown reasons, was also an active member of Theta Tau, and may even been instrumental in getting Stanley an invitation to join the fraternity.

Below left: Photo of marching band in Butte; Right: Photo of captive bobcat mascot paraded by MSM's opponents, the Montana State College football team, both photos taken by Stanley in autumn 1937 (SPC)

By 1939 Stanley had been elected an officer (the inner guard) of the fraternity, according to an article in *Glück Auf*, the School of Mine's student newspaper. Later that same year he was elected as the scribe of the fraternity, an even greater honor. The *Glück Auf* reported that "active pledges, alumni and faculty members are now eagerly looking forward to an enjoyable evening at our annual spring formal, to be held at Boulder Hot Springs on April 29. The occasion is the celebration of the seventh anniversary of the establishment of Psi chapter of Theta Tau on the campus." In 1937 Stanley was also chosen to serve as a member of the Copper Guards, which was the local chapter of the Intercollegiate Knights, a distinct honor for a sophomore. This group also sponsored yell activities at campus sporting events, and Stan was appointed one of the two yell leaders for the year 1937-38.

Left: MSM school pennant

In case you're interested, dear reader, here are a few charming details on the origins of the Montana School of Mines Student Newspaper: "Glück auf! is the traditional German miners' greeting. It describes the hope of the miners: *"es mögen sich Erzgänge auftun"* ("may lodes [of ore] be opened") which is short for *"Ich wünsche Dir Glück, tu einen neuen Gang auf"* ("I wish you luck, open a new lode"), because, when mining for ore, without prospecting, no-one could predict with certainty whether the miners' work would lead to a reward. The greeting also expressed the desire that miners would return safely from the mine after their shift."

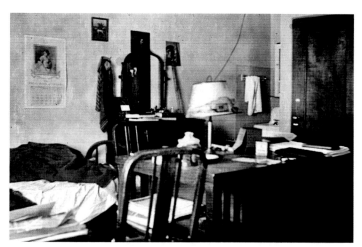

Left: Photo of Stanley's dorm room with study desk and sleeping area taken by him in 1937 (SPC)

According to a *Montana Standard* article from January 1937, members of Theta Tau fraternity had its own separate "house" in a wing of the dormitory, and members ate in the Residence Dormitory in their own private dining rooms. All out-of-town students were required to live in the Residence Dormitory, which was completed in only 1935, one year prior to Stanley's arrival. "The new residence hall is designed to be a home for students in the fullest sense of the term – a place to which students can invite their friends; a place in which mother and father are welcome to visit son; a place in which warm friendships develop and grow; a place in which students can work, play, study, sleep, eat and increase in stature – intellectually, socially and every other way. Well balanced meals, suitable for various seasons of the year, will be served. Sleeping and study quarters are well heated, well lighted, and substantially furnished."

Right: Photo of Stanley, studying in his dorm room at MSM in 1937 (from Stanley's private collection, SPC)

Please indulge this writer as I pursue this seemingly mundane topic. At a time in the evolution of education, particularly higher education, when nearly every need is met including on-site dormitory counselors, guidance counselors, staff psychologists, and a veritable army of specialists who are available to shepherd a student through the difficult process of leaving home and adjusting to life without one's parents and childhood friends, the simple provision of a place for students to live, complete with common areas, that is well lit, heated, and even includes a dining facility is the very least that one can expect from an institution of higher learning. Prior to the completion of the residence dormitory only a year before Stanley's arrival, according to the same Montana Standard article: "It is one of the finest buildings of its kind on any American campus and fills a long-met need at the college…Prior to its construction, students lived, roomed, hatched or existed wherever they could find space for human habitation. College spirit was almost nil. After-class hours found the campus deserted. When night fell and eerie winds whistled about the buildings there was no sound of human voice to proclaim: 'Here is a great college.'"

Right: Photo taken by Stanley of fellow dorm residents involved in cleaning the common room of their wing in 1937

The Montana School of Mines was deemed the "Freiberg of America" after one of Germany's and Europe's oldest and most important university towns, which included the oldest academy of mining in the world, founded in 1765. Even if this comparison suggests a bit of hometown hype, there is no doubt why Stanley had chosen to pursue his degree in mining engineer in Butte at the Montana School of Mines. Stanley, unlike most 18-year-olds who are lucky enough to pursue a higher degree, had made a focused and deliberate decision about his future. And he had succeeded in gaining acceptance at one of the world's leading technical institutions whose focus was strictly on the mining industry and its component applied sciences. In the world of international mining, MSM was and is among the best institutions of higher learning that grant fully accredited degrees in mining engineering. It is and was a technical university, rather than a technical college whose goal is to prepare its students for a specific occupation by teaching them job-specific skill sets. Even in 1936 the school had a post-graduate program and was a leading institution in the world where serious research was being conducted into understanding and improving the mining industry.

Left: A corner of Stanley's dorm room in the Theta Tau wing taken by Stanley in 1939

Much the Montana School of Mines' expansion, growing from one building when it was founded in 1900 to seven buildings by 1935, occurred because of the efforts of the Public Works Administration (PWA), a massive public works construction agency that grew out of the depths of the Great Depression. According to Wikipedia, it built works such as dams, bridges, hospitals, and schools, "to provide employment, stabilize purchasing power, and help revive the economy." The *Montana Standard* article states that the money to construct the MSM residence hall came from a PWA loan and grant.

Left: Photo of MSM students, including Stanley wielding a rake, in front of a campus building, repairing a damaged driveway, taken in 1939 (from Stanley's private collection, SPC))

Stanley played hockey for the Miners, the School's intercollegiate hockey team *[Ed. note – also known as the Orediggers])*, throughout his time at the school, starting his first year, 1936-37, and was mentioned in a *Glück Auf* article in December 1937: "Returning lettermen include the dynamic Ted Newcombe, center, who has been offered berths on stellar amateur and professional teams in Canada; Fred Scofield and Stan Kappel, who were varsity wingmen last year. Of the 17 men reporting for hockey this winter, nine are Canadians who have been skating and playing hockey ever since they could walk. The squad looked very good last year but was lacking in capable reserves and as a result lost several games which otherwise might have been won. This year, there are enough experienced men and enough promising newcomers so that the Orediggers should always put a strong team on the ice. Coach George Seager expects to whip the boys into shape for games scheduled right after Christmas. Much new equipment was ordered this year and the ice squad is now as well cared for as any other Mines team. A regulation rink has been built in Leonard bowl. The fence surrounding the rink is designed so that it may be taken down and stored away after each season."

Above left and right: Stanley, age 19, posing in respiratory protective equipment during his junior year, 1939; This was part of the introduction to MSM's mining industrial hazard management course that was require of all students. (SPC)

Below right: Orediggers new hockey field on campus at MSM, 1938

Mines Hockey Team in Action Against Missoula

An April 1938 article in *Glück Auf* reported: "Because of the expense of building a rink and buying much new equipment, the hockey team was unable to take many road trips this year, but next year they plan to play more games—possibly to go to the intercollegiate tourney at Yosemite National Park. In their last game of the year the Miners defeated the Northerners at Kalispell, 4 to 2. Built around the Canadian players, Newcombe,

Garbutt, Keesey, Christie, Scofield, Kappel, Dodd, Soul, and Lake, and reinforced by talent including Leary, Lind, Hill, Ring, Russell, Jancic and Robinson, the team has given a creditable account of itself, losing only to the Butte Copper Kings. Most of the squad returns next year, so prospects for the future are bright."

In December 1938, *Glück Auf* reported: "Opening their season against Helena Sunday, December 4, the Oredigger pucksters began what is hoped to be the most successful hockey season ever with the strongest team to represent the school on ice in its history. The squad will compete in the Montana state league race against the Copper Kings, the Butte Boosters and Helena and has scheduled games with Kalispell and Missoula. In addition, the team will travel to California early in March to play in the Intercollegiate tourney sponsored by the University of California at Berkeley. They will play two games with the powerful University of Washington club on their way to the meet after stopping in Spokane for a competition with the Gonzaga Bulldogs. Should the team develop as hoped with its veteran and new stars, then the Miners may be able to boast not only the strongest team in Montana but the strongest college sextet in the West."

THE OREDIGGERS IN ACTION

Left: Orediggers hockey game, April 1938

School documents reveal that Stanley also ran in track and field events while he was a student. Other articles from The *Montana Standard* chronicle Stanley's participation in the various field trips that all junior and senior students at the Montana School of Mines were required to take. Frank Kappel's memoirs also reveal that Stanley worked at local mines on weekends to make money to help pay for the cost of his education. The *Montana Standard* article stated: "Fifty students are given one night shift a week at the Butte mines, thus adding $5.50 weekly to their income."

Frank Kappel's memoirs also suggest that Stanley worked at the Sheep Creek mine every summer while he was a student, beginning the summer of 1935, a year before he started his studies at MSM. The fact that he continued to work summers at the mine reveals his commitment to the hard rock mining industry, and to his determination to learn about the industry from the bottom up. Stanley's file of negatives is labeled "Sheep Creek, 1935-1941, which suggests he worked in the summer of 1941. This cannot be true, since he was living and working in South America beginning in May of 1941. Regardless, Stanley learned the basic realities of the mining industry from the ground up at the Sheep Creek Mine, and would return there to work as a full-fledged mining engineer after he completed his military service in 1945.

Right: Photo of Stanley's using a surveyor's transit during an MSM class field trip in 1938 (SPC)

Alice reported to Karen long after Stanley's death how much it meant to her and Stanley that she had been working in Ione *[Ed. note – 1939-1940]* while Stanley was working at Sheep Creek. Although the two never met while Alice was nursing in Ione, which is a relatively short distance from Sheep Creek with the international border between them, she was aware that miners from Sheep Creek regularly drove across the border to visit Ione on their days off, since Ione was the closest town to the mine with supplies and temptations available to them.

Glück Auf reported in April 1940: "The annual election and installation of officers was held at the School of Mines by the Theta Tau fraternity on March 31.

"The retiring officers were: regent, Laurence Eck; secretary, Stanley Kappel; treasurer, Kenneth Dodd;

Right: MSM Hockey Team, 1936-37 season [Ed note – Stanley is in the front row.]

corresponding secretary, Edgar Barnes: inner guard, Harold Hill: outer guard, Thor Johnson, and marshal, Tommy Jancic. Plans were made for an informal house party to be held on the sixth of April 1940. The annual Spring Formal dinner-dance was held at Echo Lake Lodge on Saturday evening, April 27. A full turkey dinner was followed by dancing to Phil Thomas' orchestra. Sherman Lang was toastmaster."

In addition to playing on the varsity hockey team together, Stanley and Kenneth Dodd, both from southern BC, were fraternity brothers in Theta Tau and were also both officers at the same time. There can be little doubt they had become friends during their 4 years together at MSM, even though Stanley majored in mining engineering and Dodd majored in metallurgical engineering.

The highlight of their four years as students undoubtedly occurred late in their senior year, when many of the students participated in a grand field trip that took them on a whirlwind tour of the American West and introduced them to many different facets of the mining world to round out their education and prepare them to assume roles in the "real world" just a few months hence.

I am unable to find written documentation of this trip, but many negatives in Stanley's private collection reveal its extent, which included at least two dozen of the senior class members and must have been expensive for each of them. The group traveled principally by train, starting in Butte. Whether they traveled south or west during the first leg of their journey is unclear, but the itinerary snaked along the Pacific Coast of California and included stops in San Francisco, Los Angeles, then across the Great American Desert to Carlsbad Caverns in New Mexico, along the Rio Grande River to El Paso, Texas, up to Colorado Springs, Colorado, and back to Butte. Stanley created numerous photographic images of this once-in-a-lifetime, coming-of-age trip for these young men who were about to move into the international world of mining.

Four photos of Stanley's senior class trip, spring 1940; From top left clockwise (the black and white photos are from Stanley's collection): Stanley with classmates, standing next to the Denver Zephyr; MSM classmates sitting in the smoker car during their trip; rear and front views of the Denver Zephyr, which ran from Colorado Springs to Chicago via Denver. (SPC; color postcard)

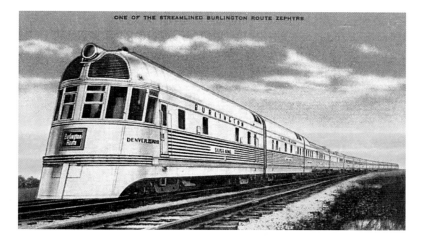

Below: Five photos taken by Stanley during his class trip around the American Southwest during his senior year at MSM, spring 1940; The locations are remote and highly informative. (SPC)

Below: Five photos taken by Stanley in San Francisco and Los Angeles in 1940 during his class trip around the American West; From top left clockwise: The Pacific Queen, a ship used in movies that was located in San Francisco Bay on Treasure Island for the Golden Gate International World's Fair in 1939; Alcatraz Island in the mist; The Hollywood Hotel in Los Angeles; Grauman's Chinese Theater on Hollywood Boulevard that includes the "Hollywood Walk of Fame", with hand and shoe prints made by Clark Gable in 1937. (SPC)

Three photos taken by Stanley in 1940 during his MSM class trip around the American West: from left clockwise: The Brown Derby Restaurant in Los Angeles; Members of the class waiting at a train station in the New Mexico heat; San Francisco Bay, with the Bay Bridge on the right and several US Navy "flying boats" sitting in the water, waiting to take off or dock on Yerba Buena Island (SPC)

Finally, after four eventful and arduous years as a student, Stanley's big day arrived. The May 25th, 1940, edition of the Salmon Arm Observer reported that Stanley's family, including his parents and sister, were traveling to Butte to attend Stanley's graduation from the Montana School of Mines. This must have been a splendid occasion for the Frank Kappel family. Their adopted son had become the first member of the extended Kappel clan to obtain a four-year college degree, something that Frank may not have expected, but which Stanley obviously had dreamed about and made happen. Stanley was now a college graduate with a professional degree in mining engineering, having accrued accolades and honors acknowledging his efforts, both athletic and academic. Now he was ready to launch into the "real world" of adults, and he seems to have been better prepared than most of his contemporaries to succeed.

Left: Stanley in formal dress at MSM, 1940, age 21 (from Stanley's private collection, SPC))

We will never know for certain why Stanley was so certain that he wanted to become a mining engineer. Many of us flounder with our life choices throughout our lives, only to flit from one pursuit to another, searching for direction, searching for meaning, searching for clues about the nature of reality. Suffice it to say: one does not select a school like the Montana School of Mines as your institution of higher learning if you think there is even the slightest chance that you may end up as a minister or a doctor or a social worker or a psychologist. Stanley was multi-faceted and multi-talented: athlete, musician, photographer. But above all else, and for the rest of his short life, he was a hard rock mining engineer, and he seems never to have wavered from that trajectory.

In May of 1940, following a simple graduation ceremony in Butte, Montana, Stanley emerged from the cocoon of youthful dependence and became a man. He also changed in one moment from a student and erstwhile hard rock miner to a fully trained mining engineer. The next phase of his life was beginning.

Below: Betty, Frank, Janet, and Stanley Kappel, at the time of Stanley's graduation from the

Montana School of Mines, May 31, 1940. The graduation festivities included, on the previous evening, the annual junior promenade at the school gymnasium, and a luncheon honoring the graduates after the ceremony at the local Butte Country Club. (SPC)

THE 1940 GRADUATING CLASS OF MONTANA SCHOOL OF MINES

Right: Stanley Kappel on graduation day, May 1940; [Ed. note – He is in the very back row, second from our right]

Fifty young men who climaxed years of intensive technical training as they received bachelor and master degrees at the Montana School of Mines commencement are pictured above with three older distinguished men of their profession, who played important roles in the impressive graduation exercises. Those in the picture, front row, left to right are: Joseph Shaw, John Bukvich, M D O'Shaughnessy, H R Spedden, Robert Raisie, all of whom were awarded master degrees; Chester H Steele, recipient of the professional degree; Senator Key Pittman, commencement speaker; Dr. Francis A Thomson, president of the college; William Brodrick, Kenneth Dodd and Stanley Huckaba. Second row: Arthur Sherman, James Sullivan, Thomas McLeod, Sam Mitchell, L T Eck, August Rombosek, Donald Cole, William O'Brien, Don Harvey, Edgar Barnes. Third row: Herman Stevens, William Tretheway, Sherman Lane, Eugene Nelson, Robert Hanley, Norman Vistes, Francis Hadnor, Robert Corbett, Warren Mahan, Thomas Jancic, Conrad Lundgren. Fourth row: Thomas Greene, James Ballard, Sidney Worthen, Murray Head, Eddie Chaides, Alan Khulman, Robert McGuire, Matthew Gooding, Edward Newcombe, William Mitchell, Lawrence Farbo. Back row: Harold Lake, Fred Hames, Arthur Hard, Thomas Barrett, Frank Archibald, John Dougherty, Wesley Moore, DeAtley Loughridge, Stanley Kappel and Francis Holderreed, who received a master's degree.

Above: Stanley and friend on graduation day, Montana School of Mines, 1940

Above: Stanley's official graduation photo from the Montana School of Mines, 1940

Five photos taken by Stanley or from Stanley's private collection (SPC) showing him in the field and enjoying life with his many friends at MSM, 1939-1940

Eight photos taken by Stanley during his time at MSM, featuring women with whom he clearly wanted to be associated

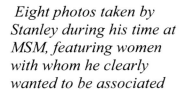

Photos taken by Stanley or found in his private collection showing scenes from his personal life during his four years at MSM from 1936-1940; It appears that Stanley had several "girlfriends" during his time at MSM, and his love of music is also apparent. (SPC)

Medley of MSM photos taken by Stanley (or his friends) between 1936 and 1940 (SPC)

We cannot know how pivotal Stanley's four years at the Montana School of Mines were in preparing him for the rest of his life, but this chapter suggests that it was profound. Nor could we sort out which of the many experiences Stanley absorbed was most influential for him, but I am certain that hockey was high on his list. An article appearing in the Helena Independent Record in the sports section on February 17, 1939, when Stanley was a junior at MSM, provides powerful and poetic insight to this writer:

"One of the last games of the current hockey season as far as league games are concerned will be played at 7:30 tonight at the Boulder avenue rink when the Helena Vigilantes meet the league leading and undefeated Montana State School of Mines Ore Diggers.

"Composed largely of men from the provinces, the Ore Diggers have one of the finest hockey aggregations ever assembled in this part of the states. They are a polished aggregation and hockey fans will want to see them in action.

"An analysis of the Mines hockey situation and success to date this year, reveals that 11 of the 16 boys on the varsity squad hail from Canada. Dr. George F. Seager is the coach of the club.

"These Canadian boys Seager has in his lineup don't flounder around the ice like amateurs. They know what they're doing when they clout the puck. They check with finesse and handle a stick with the ease of veterans and skate with the speed of the wind.

"The Vigilantes have a splendid team but they will have to call upon their entire defense power if they hope to stem the puck-chasing Miners tonight.

It is believed that the entire squad will be up and ready for battle."

The article also discusses each of the MSM team members by name, including Stanley:

Left: "Stanley Kappel, left wing and a three-year veteran, is from Sicamous, B.C."

Stanley established friendships at MSM with many Canadian and American students that undoubtedly brought him pleasure and camaraderie for the rest of his life. He encountered teachers and professors who imparted knowledge and wisdom that would have enabled and inspired him to dedicate his professional career to making a difference in his chosen field. But to this writer, who is not and never was an athlete, nor have I ever followed the details of the sporting world with any particular enthusiasm, I find myself thinking about Stanley's four years on the MSM hockey team. And I find myself filled with envy and admiration for Stanley more than ever, knowing that he was able to experience the satisfaction which comes from being an integral member of a team that was able to "check with finesse and handle a stick with the ease of veterans and skate with the speed of the wind".

Left: the front page of the Butte Montana Standard on May 31, 1940, the day that Stanley graduated from the Montana School of Mines. This is the newspaper that Frank Kappel would have read that day as he prepared to attend his son's graduation ceremony and festivities with Janet and Betty. Two themes dominate the front page, but the War in Europe is the overwhelming winner, as it occupies more than 80% of the page. The only other subject of significance is the coverage entitles "Mines School to Graduate Record Class: Fifty Students to Receive Bachelor and Master Degrees at the 38th Annual Commencement in Butte". Dignitaries attending the commencement included the Governor of Montana and a U.S. Senator from Nevada. The program included a vocal solo from the opera, "La Boehme", along with a speech by the Senator and the awarding of the degrees by the school president and faculty members. Among those listed as receiving a Bachelor of Science in Mining Engineer is Stanley Ernest Kappel of Sicamous, B.C. In addition to being the most important day of Stanley's life up to now, it is clear that the winds of war were blowing so strongly as to nearly overwhelm every other subject of the day. In addition to being a day of celebration for Stanley and his family, it was undoubtedly also a day of sober reflection and underlying anxiety over the future of the world. Stanley was about to face two daunting challenges simultaneously: becoming a member of the professional class, with its attendant demands and uncertainties; and becoming a member of the Canadian Forces in service to The Crown. Canada's decision to serve the King in its courageous efforts to stem the tide of Nazi German and the Axis Powers by declaring war on Germany on September 10th, 1939, would have significant consequences for everyone who attended the festivities in Butte on that memorable weekend in 1940.

CHAPTER 14 – Stanley Enters the Work Force, Little by Little

Right: Betty and Stanley Kappel at home in Sicamous (note one of Janet Kappel's paintings on the wall), ca.1940 (SPC)

Needless to say, 1940 was a time in history when the world was undergoing massive change. Nazi Germany had already occupied much of Europe when Stanley graduated from the Montana School of Mines. Canada had entered the war in 1939, and by 1940 young Canadians were already serving in England's valiant effort to staunch Hitler's ambitions for world domination. Stanley would have been required to register as a potential draftee in 1940, although Canada didn't initiate an official military draft until 1943. But he wouldn't have been compelled to join the fight in Europe, even though many young Canadians had already volunteered to serve in combat roles as early as 1939.

According to Wikipedia: "In June 1940, the government adopted conscription for home service in The National Resources Mobilization Act, 1940 (NRMA), which allowed the government to register men and women and move them into jobs considered necessary for wartime production. The act also allowed for conscription for the defence of Canada but did not allow conscripts to be deployed for overseas service. However, by 1941 there were enough Canadian volunteers for five overseas divisions."

One has to wonder why Stanley, after graduating from MSM in 1940, didn't join the Canadian Forces as an active-duty member until June of 1943. Stanley would certainly have invested deep thought and deliberate consultation in the matter with trusted peers and elders, including his father, before deciding to continue his mining career, rather than pursue an early career in the Canadian Forces. I have seen almost no direct discussion or documentation of this, but in a letter he wrote to his sister, Marie, in March of 1943, he sheds light on the subject: "I am going to try and get into the Royal Canadian Engineers again after that and if I can pass the physical test this time, I should have no trouble. Of course, I failed the Air Force test for a very minor ailment, which a very good surgeon from the States says is non-existent, so I hope that all may go well this time."

This would suggest that Stanley tried to get a commission in the Royal Canadian Air Force in the summer or fall of 1940, after he graduated from MSM, revealing his ambitions to become an Air Force pilot very early in the conflict with Germany. The "non-existent" minor ailment that kept him from getting his wish could have been trivial in a medical sense, since something as minor as visual acuity measuring less than 20/20 is enough to prevent entry into military flight training. The fact is that he made a deliberate attempt to enter the Canadian military in 1940, but instead pursued his career as a mining engineer during the next 3 years.

In his letter to Marie, Stanley also wrote: "If the country thinks that I'd be more use in the mines, since they are so short of mine labor, both skilled and unskilled, then I suppose that is where they will put me. However, Dad says that they are also short of young engineers in the army. Anyway, I intend to go to the Coast and find out about it…" This latter comment implies that Stanley had engaged in person with the Canadian draft board before deciding what to do next, and that he was encouraged to pursue his mining career by the appropriate military authorities. It was still early in the conflict, and no one knew exactly what to expect of Nazi Germany, or if Hitler's experiment in world domination would succeed. America didn't even enter the war until late 1941.

Stanley's box of photographic negatives contains a small file entitled "Military Training Vernon B.C. 1940" that sheds important light on his first official encounter with the Canadian Forces. Stanley spent several weeks at the training camp in the summer of 1940, but there is no evidence to suggest that he was considered a military recruit on official active duty.

Above left and below right: Photos taken by Stanley in the summer of 1940 showing the military training camp at Vernon, BC, where he spent several weeks and underwent basic introduction to military life; Below left: Stanley standing at attention, one stripe on his shoulder (the lowest rank possible), looking very serious (SPC)

Written details of the camp are unavailable, but Stanley's photos reveal it to be fairly large and consisting of several dozen primitive wooden structures that were apparently constructed to house both the trainers and trainees. The purpose of the training would have been to prepare draft-eligible young men for entry into active duty, should such a move become necessary, and to acquaint the trainees with the most basic aspects of serving under wartime conditions. It would also have given the military an opportunity to assess the desirability of each trainee for future assignments.

Right: Stanley's group of new military trainees marching with rifles in front of the camp barracks, 1940 (SPC)

The collection of negatives includes many aspects of daily life that Stanley and his cohorts would have encountered in the process of learning to become indoctrinated into military life. Since Stanley never wrote about this experience, it is impossible to know how he felt about it. But there is no doubt: he took it seriously and wanted to succeed, as he had always done during his life.

Left and below right: Interior photos of the barracks where Stanley bunked with his fellow military trainees and underwent at least one inspection by senior official (from Stanley's private collection, SPC))

As would be expected with what used to be a "universal rite of passage" for nearly all young men, the routines of military life were both rigorous and mundane. Every member of the group slept in a barracks setting that included bunk beds, which meant that personal privacy was difficult to come by. The camp military leadership included senior officers and enlisted men who were probably career military members. Their objective was to teach their young charges the fundamentals of managing one's life under these austere conditions: maintaining personal hygiene, making one's own bed, keeping clothes clean and neat, keeping shoes and boots clean and shined. Learning the fundamentals of personal discipline was first and foremost, but learning to function as a unit was equally

important in the face of what was to come for many young men who would find themselves in combat roles in foreign lands; and if not in combat, then at least in crucial combat support roles that would enable an army to function at a high level in the face of a hostile enemy. This would have included periodic inspections by senior ranking officials. Since Stanley's uniform includes only one stripe, nearly everyone else in the camp who wasn't a trainee was a "senior official".

Left: Photo taken by Stanley of a fellow trainee, taking a break from the rigors of the experience to have a smoke and provide a less serious perspective (SPC)

Based on the photographs Stanley took while he was undergoing this experience, it seems that it was limited in its scope, and probably lasted no more than two or three weeks. There was little time to socialize, but a few of the photos depict the inevitable interaction that developed between the trainees, who were from around the area, and the local women. There was also the opportunity to clown around a bit and to reveal to others that this wasn't to be taken too seriously.

All in all, Stanley's first official encounter with the Canadian Forces appears to have made a significant impression on him. He experienced directly how to handle a weapon in combat, how to march in formation, how to dig a trench, along with many other demands that can only become familiar through hands-on experience. He never had to participate directly in combat, but he was now willing to lay down his life for his country.

Left: Stanley in a trench, weapon with bayonet in hand, mimicking hand-to-hand combat; Right: Young Stanley in his uniform, enjoying a moment with a young friend (SPC)

A medley of Stanley's photos depicting life in the Vernon military training camp, including one that shows "off hours" in the company of friends, something to be treasured; These photos reveal the seriousness of young Stanley, fresh out of college, ready to take on the world, yet faced with the daunting prospect of possibly having to give up his life for Canada during a time of war. In 1940 the ferocious capability of Nazi Germany was clear yet so far away to these young men. Which of them would give up their lives for this cause could only be imagined.

The summer of 1940 must have been both memorable and momentous for Stanley Kappel. Not only had he become a fully trained mining engineer, but he had also spent several weeks training to be a soldier in the Royal Canadian Forces. And there was also time to work at the Sheep Creek Mine for at least a few weeks before he embarked on another important journey. His collection of photographic negatives includes another file from the summer of 1940 entitled "Sicamous to Sudbury 1940 (Mountains – Esterhazy)" that reveals he spent time with friends and family on Shuswap Lake, in addition to taking at least one backpacking trip with two male friends. One of these friends is an older man who appears to have been both a friend and mentor to Stanley. I have unfortunately been unable to discover this man's identity.

Another medley of photos from Stanley's private collection chronicling a backpacking trip he took with a friend during the summer of 1940. (SPC)

At some point in the late summer or early autumn of 1940, Stanley packed his bags and left the Shuswap for the last time. Even if he thought of the Kappel house in Sicamous as his home, he would never again spend long summers there as he had from the time he was very young. He must have felt profound ambivalence about his new adventure, given the fragile state of his mother's health due to Parkinson's Disease. But youth is full of itself and its own concerns, and Stanley was finally ready to enter the world of adults and become a man among men. He had been preparing for this moment for many years, thanks to his father's sterling example and encouragement.

Right: Stanley at age 21, working as a "full-fledged mining engineer" at the Sheep Creek Mine in the summer of 1940, just after graduating from MSM and just prior to starting his first major job in the mining industry at the Frood Mine in Sudbury, Ontario; He sent this photo to his sister Marie, and signed it "Love, Stan". (SPC)

Stanley left a photographic record of several last gatherings of friends and family on the shores of Shuswap Lake that I have included in this chapter.

Right: Photo taken by Stanley of Kappel friends and family, gathered to share a meal in the summer of 1940, with Shuswap Lake in the background; Betty Kappel is in the lower left, with Jenny in the upper left center, identified by the sun hat. (SPC)

These photos include touching portraits of his mother, Jenny, along with Betty, and a host of unidentified youth and adults who must all have played important roles during Stanley's journey from childhood to this point. Once again, we have no written record of this period, but the images captured by Stanley prove how precious people were in his life, and how deeply he felt about his membership in the Sicamous community. Even after an absence of four years at MSM, Stanley's photographic legacy reveals him to be basically a "local boy", with a strong sense of his roots, and a grand fondness for people of all ages, genders, and social standings. He couldn't have known what the future would bring, but he seems to have been very unafraid of his future. In fact, his images portray a young man ready to take on the world.

Medley of photos from Stanley's private collection, all taken in the summer of 1940, depicting friends and family in the Shuswap (SPC)

After a summer of long good-byes and fond farewells, Stanley traveled across Canada to Ontario, where he had been hired by the International Nickel Company of Canada (INCO). He boarded a train in Sicamous and headed east, this time across the Continental Divide of the Canadian Rockies, stopping at Banff Springs, Lake Louise, and even taking in a cattle market in Esterhazy, where family friends were living. The journey took several days. Stanley's photos of the train trip are fuzzy and unsuitable to include here.

Right: Shuswap Lake beach gathering of Stanley and his friends, summer 1940 (SPC)

Stanley had at least one male traveling companion who accompanied him as far as Lake Louise. He also made several additional stops along his journey, including Esterhazy, which is located in the southeast corner of Saskatchewan and is near one of the largest potash mines in the world. In 1940 the region was also a major center of the cattle industry in Canada. By sheer coincidence, the area was "home" to Stanley's birth father, Ernie Buckingham, in the early years of the 20th century. Whether Stanley was aware of this when he passed through Esterhazy seems unlikely.

Middle right: Photo taken by Stanley of his traveling companion on his rail journey east across Canada in the autumn of 1940; Below right: Photo taken by Stanley of the "gate" depicting the boundary between Alberta and British Columbia at the Continental Divide (SPC)

Stanley took his first job as a fully qualified mining engineer with the Frood Mine, owned by the International Nickel Company of Canada (INCO), in Sudbury, Ontario. Once again, Stanley left no written record of his time at the Frood Mine, although he left a photographic record that includes images of his

social life, but nothing to reveal how he spent his working time at the facility.

Right: Photo of an outdoor cattle market taken by Stanley near Esterhazy (SPC)
Below right: Photo of a couple taken by Stanley in Esterhazy, Saskatchewan, where he stopped for a visit with his MSM classmate and fellow hockey player, Harold Lake, on his way eastward in 1940; The couple are probably Harold's parents.

Fortunately, the internet has provided a window on the Frood Mine in 1940. The mine produced copper and nickel, and would later supply more than 40% of all the nickel used in the production of artillery shells for the entire Allied war operation during the Second World War. The mine held the title for many years as being one of the greatest nickel-copper ore bodies in the world, and it also had one of Sudbury's most colorful mining histories. Stanley apparently left no written documentation of his time at the Frood Mine, but his father suggests that his tenure in Sudbury was very limited, perhaps no more than 4-6 months. Suffice it to say that the job with the Frood mine was a perfect "first step" for Stanley.

The mining site included both major types of mining activity (surface and underground), as well as a full complement of processing facilities that converted the raw ore into refined, usable metal, ready to be employed by any industry that needed it.

A fascinating essay written in 2006 by Stan Sudol, a Toronto-based communications consultant/mining strategist and speech writer who is publisher and editor of the mining news aggregator website – *www.republicofmining.com*, provides not only a glimpse into the history of nickel mining in Canada, but also suggests important aspects of the cultural context of the day that Stanley Kappel found himself immersed in. It would surely have played a role in determining why he might have chosen to take his first post-graduate position with INCO at the Frood mine in Sudbury. From the Sudol essay, *INCO's Sudbury Nickel Mines Were Critical During World War Two,* republished on September 18, 2016:

"By anyone's estimation, the highlight of Sudbury's social calendar in 1939 was the visit of King George VI and Queen Elizabeth on June 5th, accompanied by Prime Minister Mackenzie King and a host of local dignitaries. This was the first time a reigning British

monarch had ever visited Canada, let alone Sudbury, a testimony to the growing importance of the region's vital nickel mines.

"The nickel operations in the Sudbury Basin were booming due to growing global tensions and increased spending on military budgets. Sudbury and the northeastern Ontario gold mining centres of Timmins and Kirkland Lake were among the few economic bright spots in a country devastated by the Great Depression.

Above left: Frood Mine, Sudbury, Ontario, 1928; Below left: Royal visit of King George VI and Queen Elizabeth to Sudbury and the Frood Mine, 1939 [Ed. note – The Royal Couple also visited Sicamous on their journey west.]

"In an April 15, 1938, article, Maclean's Magazine journalist Leslie McFarlane described the three mining communities as, "Northern Ontario's glittering triangle…. No communities in all of Canada are busier, none more prosperous. The same golden light shines on each. "During the royal visit, precedence was broken by allowing Queen Elizabeth to become the first female ever to go underground at the Frood Mine. Traditionally miners thought women would bring bad luck if they were permitted underground. There were probably many who thought the beginning of the Second World War on September 1, 1939, was the result of her subterranean visit.

"The German invasion of Poland was to have dramatic effects on Sudbury. Many communities across Canada, Britain and the United States played exceptional roles in producing certain commodities and munitions for the war effort. However, it would be no exaggeration to say that in North America, Sudbury was among the top few mining communities that were absolutely critical to the war effort. The International Nickel Company of Canada, as it was known back then, and its employees in Sudbury would go on to supply an astonishing 95 per cent of all Allied demands for nickel – a vital raw material and a foundation metal absolutely essential for the Allies' final victory.

Above: IMCO World War Two poster (republicofmining.com)

"Nickel's unique properties include a combination of strength, hardness, ductility, resistance to corrosion and the ability to maintain strength under high heat. It can transfer these properties to other metals making nickel a critical component for a wide variety of civilian and military products.

"World War Two was a mechanized war that utilized more technically advanced equipment than ever before. To win, the Allied armies needed guns, tanks, planes, battleships, and a host of other weaponry that could only be made from hardened nickel-steels and other nickel-alloys. For example, in the mighty flying B-29 Superfortresses, thousands of pounds of nickel alloys were used ranging from oil cooling units and fastening devices to engine parts, exhaust systems, instrumentation, and control assemblies for guns.

"The war in the Pacific was primarily an amphibious battle requiring rugged engines made from nickel alloy parts able to withstand the corrosive effects of salt water. Invasion landing craft, submarines and aircraft carriers contained various nickel steels like "Monel metal" in the hulls, propeller shafting, gas and water tanks, and vital valve and pump parts, just to name a few marine uses. Nickel hardened armor plate for tanks, nickel alloys for anti-aircraft guns and ordinance and even lightweight, tough portable bridges used in the invasion of Germany all required this essential metal.

"Given the chance, Hitler would willingly have traded the whole Silesian Basin, and thrown in Hermann Goering and Dr. Goebbels to boot, for a year's possession of the Sudbury Basin, Maclean's journalist James H. Gray aptly wrote in an October 1, 1947, article on the city. From the beginning of the war, the company's expertise and vast production and research facilities in Sudbury, Port Colborne, Huntington, New Jersey, and Britain were at the complete disposal of the Allied war effort."

The mining industry is considered a cornerstone of the world economy and would surely have been considered an essential industry during the Second World War. Another interesting facet of Stanley's time at Sudbury is that the location is not far from Ottawa, where the headquarters of the Canadian Armed Forces is located. Stanley may have traveled to Ottawa for military intelligence orientation prior to his departure for South America. Although the military draft had not been activated in 1940, he was also taking a job with an American gold mining operation in Ecuador, and it is difficult for this writer to imagine that the Canadian government would have been unaware and unconcerned about Stanley's intended activities.

When you are eligible for the draft during a time of war in which your nation has formally declared itself to be a participant (unlike the United States, which remained neutral until late 1941), it is normally required that you not only advise your government if you intend to leave the country, and that you seek formal permission in order to avoid serious personal consequences. Stanley may have been introduced to, or possibly even recruited into, the part of any government that gathers intelligence of a diplomatic, military, and industrial nature on activities of both allies and enemies that were of strategic interest to his government. There is also the history that Frank Kappel had worked in London for the Canadian Forces throughout his tenure with the military in the First World War. In Frank's interview with Imbert Orchard in 1966, he stated that he eventually worked for First Army Intelligence, decoding German messages, up until the time of the Armistice in 1918, then he was sent to Germany with an "intelligence" unit and acted as a liaison between the civilian population and the army while he was there. He also spent his last three months in the European theater in Le Havre, "because there was a lot of subversive activity going on even at that time."

More about this intriguing aspect of Stanley's story later, but suffice it to say that Stanley was an exceptional asset to the Canadian Forces for many reasons. He was highly intelligent, a fully trained mining engineer, a linguist, and an adventurous spirit. In addition, Stanley was an avid photographer prior to his arrival in South America, as evidenced by the numerous photographs he took throughout his youth. The quality of his photographs improved after he graduated from MSM, suggesting that he acquired a more expensive camera (which I have in my possession) and had access to large quantities of film and the ability to develop and print many photos. This is at a time when photographic film was in short supply for civilians, due not only to the need for film in wartime activities, but also because photographic film contains silver, another mineral vital to any modern war effort. Nevertheless, Stanley's avid interest in photography provides a window into his life in Ontario.

Judging from the photos he took during that period he enjoyed himself at the Frood Mine. It appears that he was able to keep in perspective the gravity of his passage from student status into manhood, although he undoubtedly felt stressed by what was to come. His tenure at Sudbury was brief, with no information available to explain why he left IMCO so soon.

Four photos from Stanley's private collection, showing him in various situations featuring a set of twins with whom he became happily acquainted in Sudbury (SPC)

Three more photos taken by Stanley chronicling his time in Ontario, experiencing the beauty and pleasures of life in the Canadian heartland for the first time; At least two of the young men in the photo below were fellow classmates at MSM. (SPC)

Is it possible that Stanley was asked to spend time with IMCO at the discretion of the Canadian Forces, in order to gain exposure to this war-essential component of the mining industry? This may seem a bit of a jump, that he might later be needed as a "subject matter expert" if the war

were to expand. Frank Kappel wrote in his biographical sketch of Stanley: "He later accepted a job that same year *[Ed. note – late 1940]* with the South American Development Company (SADCO), headquartered at 75 West Street, New York City, and soon sailed to Ecuador to assume the position of shift boss at their gold mining operation in Portovelo." This was surely a plum job for a new mining engineer.

Whatever the reasons for Stanley's short tenure in Ontario, he was a small fish in a very big pond at the Frood mine and was probably given very little responsibility as a newcomer just out of college. On the other hand, by taking a job with SADCO to work in a remote mining operation that was a much smaller pond, Stanley was signaling that he was ready for more responsibility in his effort to work his way up the success ladder. Everything we know points to the fact that he had been chosen by SADCO to open a new gold mine in the Portovelo district during the time he was being indoctrinated in New York City, prior to leaving for South America. After being "out in the real world" of mining for only a few months, it took real bravado to make such a huge leap into a completely unknown abyss. Would you, dear reader, have possessed such confidence and courage when you were 22 years old?

Two photos from Stanley's private collection taken as he was departing from Ontario to travel by train to New York City in late 1940. (SPC)

In late 1940 Stanley made one very important journey, perhaps the most momentous of his life. Departing from Ontario, he took a train to New York City where he spent several months at SADCO headquarters while he was introduced to the corporation. During that time he was also observed and evaluated by many members of the SADCO team in order to determine his suitability for the job he was about to be offered. He left no written or photographic record of his time in New York, but it must have been intense, intimidating, dazzling, and astonishing to him. A photo of him in a hotel room, possibly in New York City in late 1940 or early 1941, reveals a sober yet secure young Stanley, ready to take on the world.

Left: Photo of Stanley, probably taken in his hotel room in New York City in late 1940 (SPC)

It seems very likely that Stanley spent his time in New York productively. There was so much for him to learn about the business of an American company running a gold mine in a foreign country with the world already at war. His briefings would have run the gamut from the company's philosophy, the financial details of establishing profitability in the mining business, the difficulties he might encounter in a somewhat hostile foreign environment, where the local language was Spanish, the local and national politics were dicey, and the local workers were extremely poor.

Diplomatic issues, security issues, medical issues, currency issues would all have been on the table. Much would need to be learned in the field once he arrived in Portovelo, but the wisdom of introducing Stanley to the multiplicity of daunting challenges he would face as soon as he arrived in Ecuador was obvious. There can be no doubt that the time he spent at SADCO Headquarters wasn't wasted, but it is also very likely he would have preferred to spend much more time "learning the ropes" than he was given. Or maybe not. After all, he was a young man with a bright future, and he was probably very eager to reach his destination and get to work.

Right: Canadian Forces Propaganda Poster, Second World War

Below: Pan American Airways 1939 travel poster advertising the Ecuadorian Andes

CHAPTER 15 – Alice Leland: Daughter, Nurse, Wife and Mother Extraordinaire

TIME IS
- by Henry van Dyke

"Time is
Too Slow for those who Wait,
Too Swift for those who Fear,
Too Long for those who Grieve,
Too Short for those who Rejoice;
But for those who Love,
Time is not."

Enter the heroine of our story: Alice Corinne Leland was born in Spokane, Washington State, on March 16, 1918, the daughter of William and Marianne (born Dahl) Leland. She was sixth in a family of 10 children that included four girls and six boys. Her father was a Norwegian immigrant who had emigrated from the far north of Norway in his late teens and became a house painter by profession. Her mother was from North Dakota, born to Norwegian immigrants from southern Norway.

Above: The William Leland family ca. 1935, posing for a family portrait in their home on the south side of Spokane; Marianne is seated in the front row in the sofa chair. Second row, from the left: Evelyn, Margaret, Roy, Alice, William, and Ruth. Third row: Stan, Lloyd, Warren, John, and Albert. (photo provided by Susanne Setvik)

Above left: Photo of Alice ca. age 3, standing beside her older sister Margaret, with brother Albert sitting on the steps of the family home; Above right: Alice ca. age 12. Below left: The Leland family home that was built by William in 1908 where Alice and her siblings grew up (photos provided by Suzanne Setvik)

Susanne (Moline) Setvik, Karen's first cousin with whom she has always been best friends, especially throughout her early life because they lived near one another and shared many formative experiences, has written a beautiful tribute to "The Leland Family" that includes genealogic, photographic, and biographical information on that side of the family. Anyone wishing to learn more details about Alice's birth family and Norwegian ancestors would find it very worthwhile to obtain a copy of Susanne's book. Meanwhile, I am borrowing from her research and photographs in order to provide details about Alice that I have found nowhere else, and I am deeply indebted to Susanne for her contributions to Stanley's biography.

Alice grew up in a busy, rough-and-tumble household, a middle child whose basic needs were met by caring, competent and loving parents. However, she had to compete with nine other children for limited resources. As a result, many of Alice's (and her siblings') emotional needs were overlooked in the chaos of such a demanding family situation. Nevertheless, Alice thrived and grew into a beautiful young woman with hopes and dreams and ambitions.

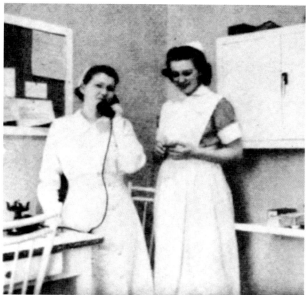

Above left: Photo of Alice at Deaconess Hospital as a nursing student, 1939; Above right: Photo of Alice when she graduated from nursing school

As a child Alice attended the Adams School in south Spokane. A news clipping from the Spokesman-Review newspaper on October 11, 1931, lists Alice as the First Vice-President of the 7th grade Adams School English Club.

Being a young woman wishing to attain personal success and independence at a time when opportunities for women were limited to professions such as teaching, secretarial activities and nursing, Alice chose to become a nurse, although she told Karen her deepest wishes had been to become a teacher and play the violin. Apparently neither goal was within her reach due to limited resources in her large, growing family.

She matriculated at the Deaconess Hospital School of Nursing six months after graduating from Lewis and Clark High School in 1936 and entered into an arduous three-year course of training and instruction. A news article appearing in the February 16, 1937 edition of the Spokesman-Review reads: "Among entrants in the class to start February 16 on a three years' training at Deaconess School of Nursing are two from Spokane: Miss Alice Leland and Miss Olive Witham." The course was extremely demanding according to Alice, and required her to work long hours, including holidays, to master the tasks required of a nurse. She told Karen many stories about the patients she cared for, including such things as suffering the embarrassment of having to bathe a male student with whom she had attended high school. But her efforts bore fruit qualifying her to become a full-fledged registered nurse upon her graduation in late 1939.

Her first job was in Ione, Washington, which had one small "hospital" that was a converted three-story home. Alice was the only nurse employed by that small hospital and she was on call continuously in case of emergencies. The room where she lived and slept was in the attic. She was paid $150 per month but was allowed a half-day off each week. Her principal recreation was hiking in the area, and she would occasionally see Canadians stopping in Ione. In her words: "Little did I know that one of the Canadians working at a gold mine 50 miles from the border would enter into my life later on and would become my husband and the father of my three girls."

BIRDSEYE VIEW OF IONE, WASH.

Left: An early photo of Ione, Washington, on the Pend Oreille River

Despite what most of us would consider almost cruel expectations on the part of Alice's employer, Alice recounted that the country doctor she worked for was a fine physician. She was granted extra time off to travel to Spokane to visit her family on an irregular basis, but she didn't own a car.

There was no regular bus service between Spokane and Ione so she had to ask others if she could ride with them when she found out they were traveling to Spokane for the day. On one occasion she remembered the middle-aged couple with whom she was riding stopped at every tavern on the way back to Ione while she waited in the car. Although the couple grew increasingly inebriated, they couldn't ask Alice to drive because she didn't yet have a driver's license. Happily she reached Ione without incident.

As an added commentary, an article written by Anna Beard appeared in "The Miner", a local Pend Oreille County newspaper, in 2002: "IONE – A nearly century-old building in North Pend Oreille County burned over the weekend, claiming the life of the 54-year-old female occupant, and destroying the home, which was originally built as a hospital around the turn of the century. The building itself was built in the early 1900s, probably around 1903, as the Ione Hospital. The hospital functioned until the mid-part of the 20th century, operating with three floors, a partial basement and one bathroom." Unfortunately, we will never be able to visit the hospital where Alice lived and worked in her very early nursing career since it was destroyed by the fire.

Alice wrote in her memoir at Karen's request around 2005: "After working in Ione for six months I accepted a job in a hospital in Salem, Oregon. One of my patients was a lovely, elderly woman who, when I told her I was eager to travel mentioned applying to the Union Pacific Railroad as a nurse on the streamlined trains. At that time, air travel wasn't great and plane crashes were frequent.

Above: A photo of Alice at the train station in Spokane with family members who had turned out to say goodbye and show her how much they loved and supported her as she faced her future boldly; Her youngest brother Roy is up on the train's observation platform beside her. Also included are (left-to-right) Hazel (Albert's wife), Margaret, George, Marianne, Lloyd, and Albert.

Right: A photo of Alice on the train departing Spokane on her way to becoming a nurse stewardess in 1940; She looks brave but uncertain. An iconic scene, similar observation platforms were used by royalty and politicians who wished to meet and address their subjects and supporters very quickly and efficiently. The Olympian [Ed. note – Seen in this photo] was the name given to a fast train operating on Union Pacific tracks by the Chicago, Milwaukee, St. Paul, and Pacific Railroad, between Chicago and the Pacific Northwest. This is not the train she would eventually be working on, but we know that she was traveling to Omaha to receive her "nurse-stewardess" training. (both from SPC)

"I was fortunate to be hired as there were many nurses after the position. I went to Omaha, Nebraska, where I lived with the Vice President of Union Pacific and his charming wife while I attended courses every day for several weeks. Part of my training was to accompany the nurse stewardess on her route from Portland to Chicago and back to Los Angeles."

This period marked the beginning of Alice's journey into the world of international travel and adventure, and revealed her to be a serious-minded and highly competent woman whose uncommonly good looks gave her great advantage. Unlike most of her contemporaries, she was apparently not yet interested in finding a husband and settling down. After completing her training in Omaha, Alice became a nurse stewardess on the Union Pacific Streamliner "City of Portland" that operated between Portland and Chicago. The train was the very first streamlined transcontinental train to operate and was the first to offer dining and sleeping services.

Left: Publicity photo of the famed "City of Portland" that operated between Portland and Chicago between 1935 and 1955 [Ed. note – Photo was taken ca. 1935, only four years before Alice would have started working on that exact train.]

Alice said she initially tried living in Chicago, but it was too expensive, so she tried her luck in Portland. "I didn't know any one there, so I asked the taxi driver to take me to an area of Portland where there were beautiful old homes. When we found a neighborhood I liked I asked the driver to wait while I checked for a room to rent. I rang the doorbell of a beautiful home, and a lovely, friendly, middle-aged woman came to the door. I asked her if she knew of any home that had rooms to rent while I was in Portland. She informed me that she had a room I could use while her sons were at college in the East. How I remember my stay there because I went three days without eating since all my money was gone. I worked for the Union Pacific for eight months."

This writer finds it truly remarkable that a relatively shy and introverted young woman with little worldly experience would venture out into the wider world as soon as her nurse's training was finished, seeking positions of daunting responsibility such as serving as the only nurse in a rural hospital in northern Washington State. She next worked at a hospital in Portland, but only for a short time, then quickly moved on to become a nurse/stewardess on a sleek, posh, exclusive streamliner train that placed her on call day and night as demanding passengers traveled from Portland to Chicago, then back to Los Angeles, passing through isolated and utterly remote locations across the western outback of the United States.

Circumstances would soon change once again for Alice. She had heard about a job opportunity for an adventurous nurse from her maternal Aunt Florence, a legendary woman in the family who was married to Mellick Tweedy, the superintendent and general manager of a gold mine at an American mining camp in South America. Florence and Mellick lived in the mining camp with their children in the late 1930s, and Florence was in regular touch with her sister, Marianne Leland. The hospital that was operated by the mining company needed a chief nurse. Alice applied for the job and was selected for the position right away. "I hurriedly went home for a short stay, then I took the train to New York City where Emily, one of the women representing the company, had made hotel reservations for my stay. She was eager for me to see New York and she and her handsome friend (a graduate of Princeton University) took me around New York and the surrounding area."

Accompanying this photo on the right, the newspaper caption from the Spokesman-Review, dated March 21, 1941, reads: "Miss Leland to Sail South: Guayaquil, Ecuador, will be the home for the next two years of Miss Alice C. Leland, daughter of Mr. and Mrs. William Leland, S4208 Crestline, who will leave Spokane for New York City. She will sail March 28 for South America where she will be with the South American Development Company. A graduate of Deaconess school of nursing, she has been working as a stewardess for the Union Pacific Railroad."

Alice remained in NYC for four days and was accompanied around the city by Emily, taking taxis everywhere. She remembers visiting all the major sights, including Greenwich Village, as well as various department stores so she could purchase clothing she would need for her time in South America. Aunt Florence had written her a letter, telling her what to buy and where to shop (Lord & Taylor). Florence had also sent her the money she would need to get everything required, including casual clothing and evening dresses, 14 formal dresses, white riding clothes, high-top riding boots, etc.

The highlight of her stay in NYC was when the Company secretary's boyfriend took both young women out to dinner at the top of the Empire State Building. On her last day Emily and her handsome friend accompanied Alice to the pier to catch her ship to South America and had a dozen roses waiting for Alice in her stateroom. She was 23 years old. This was truly the beginning of the rest of her life.

Here is an added bit of spice: the principal task for Alice's NYC hosts was to evaluate Alice's suitability to take on such an important job as helping to run one of the most important medical establishments in all of Ecuador (more on that later). It isn't preposterous to think that "the handsome friend from Princeton" may have represented the US Government's deepest and most secretive bastions of surveillance, given the critical nature of the gold mining operation at Portovelo, where Alice was going. As we shall see, Alice was entering a world of high political importance and intrigue that she would never fully comprehend during her two plus years in South America.

The trip from NYC to Guayaquil took 10 days and transited the Panama Canal. She said she had a nice cabin to herself in the best section of the ship. She also told Karen she was so seasick during the trip that she couldn't eat and lost weight. Fortunately, the ship's doctor recommended she stay out on deck as much as possible and this helped to relieve her nausea. Her seasickness even prevented her from accepting an invitation to dine at the Captain's Table. To make matters worse, she was accosted by two Spanish men while standing out on deck, but the Purser rescued her and posted a guard by her cabin.

Nearly every American who worked for SADCO in Portovelo took the same 10-day sea voyage from New York City to Guayaquil, including Stanley, who arrived several months after Alice. Only the Company's top executives and their families used commercial airlines. But that was just the beginning.

VAPOR CHILENO "ACONCAGUA" EN LAS EXCLUSAS DE MIRAFLORES, CANAL DE PANAMA.

176B. CHILEAN LINER S.S. "ACONCAGUA" IN MIRAFLORES LOCKS, PANAMA CANAL.

Left: Photo of the SS Aconcagua, the ship that Stanley (and probably Alice) took from New York City to Guayaquil, Ecuador, shown here transiting the Panama Canal in the early 20th century; Below left: Map of southern Ecuador showing Puerto Bolivar in the center (where the boat from Guayaquil took Alice), with the railroad running to Piedras (completed in 1938) that was used by Alice and Stanley; The trip from Piedras was made by station wagon, with the remainder of the trip into the mountains by mules. Portovelo, Zaruma and Minas Nuevas are located in the lower right corner of the map, circled in red.

Getting to Portovelo from Guayaquil was a major adventure that was 160 miles long and lasted three to four days. The dangerous, grueling trip involved river boats, jungle roads and waterways, a four-hour narrow-gauge railway ride, station wagons, and a painful eight-hour mule train ride that led along tortuous mule tracks through narrow gorges and over treacherous mountain passes. There was no other way to get from New York City to Portovelo in 1941, except through Quito by air.

Alice continued in her memoir: "Arriving in Guayaquil, the port was too shallow to receive large cruise ships, so we had to dock out in the sea where small boats took us into the city. It was extremely hot and humid, however I had reservations at a lovely, air-conditioned hotel (provided by the Company) where my Aunt Florence and cousin Betty were staying.

Above right: Photo of Puerto Bolivar, where the water portion of Alice's voyage ended and the overland portion by rail began; Middle right: "Auto car de-luxe", according to Stanley, the "tiny train" that transported people for four hours through jungle country to a transfer point where station wagons were waiting to take them into the mountains; Below right: Transfer point showing the station wagon that took Alice from the end of the railroad line to the mule camp, where she began the final leg of her journey through steep mountain scenery that was impassable at the time for any sort of mechanical vehicle (SPC)

"They flew back to New York the next day. After staying in Guayaquil for a few days, I was taken by a guide on a river boat. All night it rained, and the rain

dripped on me, and I was sopping wet in the early morning.

Left: Two mules carrying a heavy load in tandem on the trail from Piedras to Portovelo (SPC)

"We finally came to a dock (Puerto Bolivar) with a small building where we caught a very small train for a four-hour train trip through jungle country (to Piedras).

Left: Two photos showing Alice's stirrup being fitted to her saddle, and later on the narrow trail, riding through the mountains, looking a bit apprehensive (SPC)

"We came to a mountainous area where Company men were waiting to take me by station wagon for several hours to another mountainous area, where mules were waiting for us.

"I had never been on a horse or a mule, but off we went for eight hours on the mule's back on a mountainous trail where the mules insisted on following on the very edge of the mountain. The mules were sure-footed animals and safe to take high in the mountains.

"From time to time I would glance down below over the edge of the trail, afraid the mules would slip or fall and down we would go. We finally arrived where the station wagon was waiting. I was so crippled from being on the mule for eight hours, I was not able to walk, so two of the men made a chair with their own arms and they walked to the station wagon carrying me. Then we rode on a mountain road to Portovelo, arriving in camp late in the day.

Right: Overview of Portovelo with Alice's house at the tip of the red arrow (upper right of center), ca. 1941; Below right: Alice's house, aka "The Señoritas' House", which she shared with another American female employee, overlooking Portovelo, ca. 1941 (SPC)

"They took me to a well-built cement-stucco house. I met the secretary for the company who lived there with me during most of my stay in Portovelo. She had been Mrs. (Eleanor) Roosevelt's private secretary. There were 12-14 bachelors in camp who lived just below our house. Their house was called "The Pansy Patch", and they were very anxious to meet me because I was the only young American girl that would be living there. Marge, the secretary, was in her forties and I was 23. The young men were mining engineers, geologists, and were in their twenties and thirties.

"They aggravated me until a young mining engineer from British Columbia came on the scene. He had amoebic dysentery and was very ill. After taking the treatment the doctor ordered, he recovered quickly and we became great friends, which upset the other single men. Soon Stanley was sent to oversee a gold mine high in the mountains where it took eight hours on mule back to arrive at his future home. He was the only American there and would ride the mule back into our camp on weekends. He would also have to take a large payroll in his pack and had two loaded guns in case of a robbery during his trip back."

Below left: Alice's living room; She wrote on the back of the photo: "How do you like our curtains? I bought them in Guayaquil, when I was on my vacation, at the company's expense." Below right: Alice sitting in front of the same beautiful curtains in her living room in Portovelo at the "Casa de Senoritas", ca. 1941 (SPC)

Above left: Alice's dining room at her bungalow in Portovelo; Above right: "The Pansy Patch", where the single white men working in the mining camp lived, just below Alice's house (SPC)

But we are getting ahead of ourselves. There is a lot to be told about Stanley's experiences as a gold miner in Portovelo and Minas Nuevas before we can further explore Stanley and Alice's adventures together in South America. This is only the beginning of Alice's compelling and heroic story. Starting out as a "middle child" in a large family in Spokane, she continues through what appear to have been a series of fairly predictable passages for a young American girl with intelligence, beauty, and a sense of adventure. As we have moved through Alice's life story to date, would anyone would have predicted she would suddenly find herself in such a remote, exotic, and exciting place as an American gold mine in the Ecuadorean Andes? It seems unlikely to this observer that she accepted the job at the mining camp hospital only as an adventure. She must also have hoped to find romance, love, and marriage to a partner with whom she would decide to spend the rest of her life. Sometimes the most remarkable developments occur in the most unlikely circumstances.

I have added several maps of Ecuador below in hopes of making it a bit easier for the reader to gain an understanding of the country's place in the world, with a special emphasis on El Oro province, where Alice and Stanley would spend the next two years of their lives.

Above, left and right: Two maps of Ecuador, with Del Oro province in red, Portovelo in the lower right, and Machala (where Alice's overland journey began) in the middle.
Below right: Ecuadorian

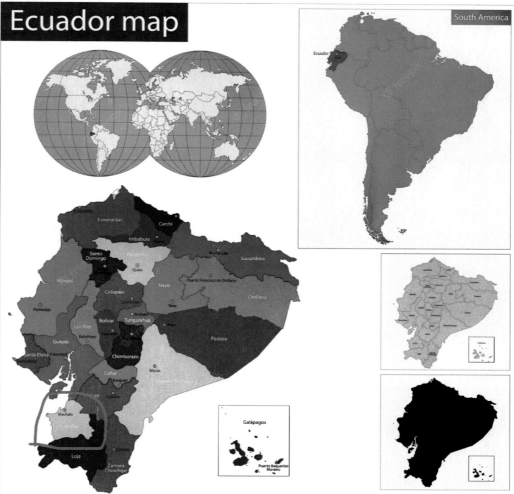

maps meant to acquaint the reader with Ecuador's location; El Oro province, where Portovelo is located, sits in the southwest corner, is circled in red. (coverstock.com)

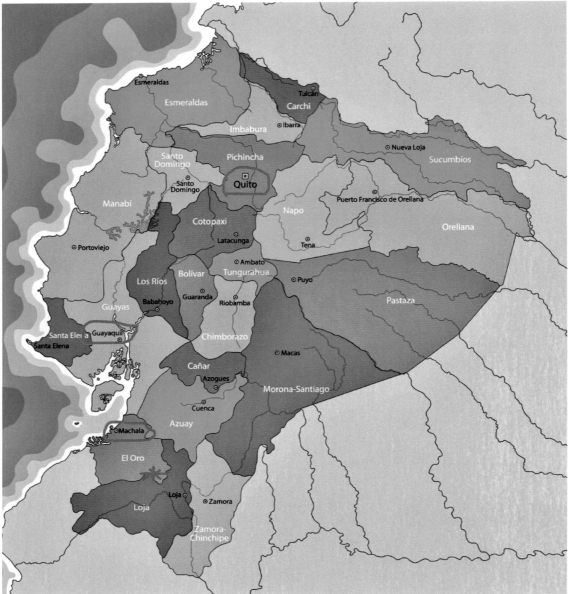

Above: Modern map of Ecuador showing the major cities and the relationship between Guayaquil, El Oro province, and Quito; Portovelo is located in the lower right corner of El Oro province at the red asterisk. (coverstock.com)

Alice told Karen that she experienced difficulty developing a strong sense of herself while she was growing up. Insensitive and possibly clueless older relatives made fun of her, her brothers picked on her, and she consequently felt insecure as a child. The church she attended in her youth emphasized sin, hell and damnation, rather than love, forgiveness and redemption. She suffered as a result, and she said she had a hard time overcoming these feelings of insecurity throughout the rest of her life. Knowing this makes the adventure she embarked upon when she accepted the position as head nurse in a remote hospital in Ecuador all the more remarkable. This writer stands in awe of Alice's undaunted courage, her unflinching sense of justice and fairness, and especially, her special empathy toward the oppressed and less fortunate members of society.

CHAPTER 16 – Stanley and Alice at the Equator: Love at First Sight

Now begins the most adventurous period of young Stanley's life. People in general tend to sort out into two basic types: those who wish to remain in the community where they were born for the remainder of their lives, and those who don't. Both Stanley and Alice fit into the latter category. Whatever loyalty and attachment they may have felt for "home" and "family", by choosing to embark on a journey as exotic and adventurous as a life in the international mining business undeniably entailed, these two kindred spirits had made a deliberate decision to cast themselves adrift and seek whatever life might offer them.

We all spend our lives running away from something, running towards something else, dreaming of how things might be, hoping that our lives will turn out to be something incredibly interesting and fulfilling, even glamorous and rewarding. Stanley and Alice were both romantics, yet they were also very serious-minded, focused, competent, and practical individuals. Both of their parents had left their families far behind when they had come of age. After Frank Kappel left Wales and arrived in Canada, he never saw his parents again. The same is true for William Leland, Alice's father, who shed his life in remote northern Norway, above the Arctic Circle, and ended up in Spokane, never again to shake his father's hand or embrace his mother. No wonder these two intrepid souls met and fell in love in the remotest place imaginable. They were endowed with the same courage and hopefulness their own parents and grandparents displayed.

Right: Stan leaving New York, May 10, 1941, aboard the S.S. Aconcagua (from Stanley's private collection, SPC)

To reorient you to the main narrative, Stanley graduated from the Montana School of Mines in June of 1940, but he didn't depart for South America until May of 1941. As we saw in a previous chapter, he spent part of the summer with his family in Sicamous, although it is also likely that he spent at least part of that summer at Sheep Creek. In due time he arrived at the Frood Mine in Sudbury, Ontario. Frank Kappel wrote that Stanley spent no more than four or five months at the Frood Mine, which takes us all the way to Christmas 1940. Perhaps he spent the holiday season with his family in British Columbia. At that point he took a job with SADCO, headquartered in New York City, and this is where his story begins to merge with Alice's story.

If Stanley didn't leave NYC until early May of 1941, that would possibly have given him four or five months in New York City. We can only imagine what he was doing during that time since we have no written journals from Stanley, but he was undoubtedly seeing the sights of The Big Apple as Alice had done. He would also have had to spend some time getting "outfitted" for his sea voyage and subsequent arrival in Portovelo as Alice had done. He may have been hosted by the same Company representative, Emily, and her handsome Princeton University friend, and he may even have had dinner at the top of the Empire State Building, as Alice had done. But remember: Alice was only in NYC for four days. If Stanley remained in NYC for at least four months, he was surely being thoroughly indoctrinated by key executives in the SADCO mining company hierarchy, not to mention US Government officials buried deep within the context of "vital US interests", all of which has been previously discussed.

Shareholders were demanding a greater share in the profits from the Portovelo gold mine, and the Ecuadorian government was expecting its share of the mine's revenues would increase, so SADCO was anxious to ensure that Stanley understood precisely what they expected of him: to expand the mine's footprint and enhance Portovelo's production of gold. It is unlikely that Stanley was intimately familiar with the challenges of mining for gold in a remote mountain wilderness, not to mention the political land mines that continued to explode on a regular basis throughout South America due to the wholesale exploitation of the continent's mineral resources by rich Americans, while at the same time the Germans, Italians, and many others were trying to do the same thing. More about that later.

Left: SS "Aconcagua"; Built for a Chilean company, the South American Steamship Company, 440 feet in length, completed in 1938, and used on the New York to Chile route via the Panama Canal, Peru, and Ecuador; The Aconcagua was taken over by the US government in 1943 and used as a troopship.

Below left and right: dining saloon and promenade deck on the ship

Dining Saloon

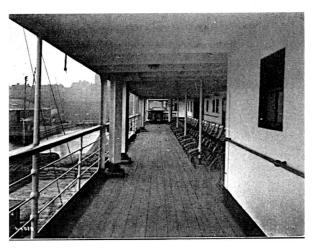

Promenade Deck

Three photos from Stanley's private collection showing scenes from his 1941 trip to South America on the SS "Aconcagua"; The photo at left, taken by Stanley, shows a burial at sea. (SPC)

Portovelo is located in the foothills of the Andes Mountains at 2,650 feet above sea level near the confluence of the Rio Amarillo and the Rio Calera. The climate is subtropical and humid, with annual temperatures ranging from 64° to 86° F. Yearly rainfall averages 53 inches, with heaviest rainfalls occurring in the months from January to June. Around the district, topography is moderately steep with elevations ranging from 3,000 to 5,400 feet above sea level (ASL). The massif of the Andes Mountain Range sits in the backdrop, readily visible from many areas in the region. According to Alice: "All these hills are colored with every hue of green imaginable.

Beautiful guitar and flute music floated on the air from the distant hills."

Left: View of the Guaya River from Guayaquil on Stanley's arrival, May 1941 (from Stanley's private collection, SPC)

Above: View of the Guaya River at sunset taken by Stanley shortly after his arrival in

Guayaquil; Left: Wharf side photo in Guayaquil taken by Stanley as he disembarked from his long sea voyage, May of 1941; Below left: Photo taken by Stanley of the "Jose Cristobal", the coastal boat Alice and Stanley both took from Guayaquil to Puerto Bolivar on the first leg of their journey to and from Portovelo (all SPC)

According to the UNESCO World Heritage website:

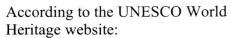

"Because Ecuador straddles the equator, parallel 0°, the seasons are caused by ocean currents: winter is the rainy period, under the influence of the warm El Niño current, whereas summer is influenced more by the cold Humboldt current and is generally the dry season. In the late 19th century and the first half of the 20th, mining reactivation and investment of French, English and US capital (1876-1959) introduced modernity and the technology prevailing at that time, with their cultural influence on tastes, fashion, uses, and customs merging with local folk traditions and knowledge.

"The gold-bearing potential of mines in their first production cycle (1575 - 1625), mines in Sexmo and Vizcaya near the town of Zaruma, made this city a center for Spanish America and the Royal Audience of Quito, driving the economy of Andean colonial society. In Spanish America, gold from Zaruma became the currency required by merchants transporting products for mining, tools, iron and sulfur, the drivers of trade between the Audience of Quito and Lima.

"During the second stage, mined ore was hauled a few kilometers downhill, for initial processing. Underground, mining continues in Zaruma and the city is still the administrative and residential center for miners, while Portovelo, along the Amarillo River, houses the industrial machines and the laborers who operate them. The importance of mining production is reflected in the name of the province where Zaruma is located: El Oro (Gold)."

Right: Cotopaxi, 23,700 feet high, is *the dominant mountain in the Andean Chain visible from the heights of Portovelo.*

According to Wimer Castro, a mining consultant who researched the area in 2008 for the Ecuadorgoldcorp S.A.:

"The hills of Zaruma and Portovelo have been mined for gold and silver for centuries. The Incas were already extracting gold and silver in the area with hydraulic mining of the oxidized parts of veins when Mercadillo, one of Pizarro´s force, followed the Amarillo River upstream and encountered the Inca mine and founded the town of Zaruma in 1549. Exploitation of the Zaruma and Portovelo districts continued during the time of Spanish colonization until 1870, when an Ecuadorian-Chilean company was established.

"In 1880, the Grant Zaruma Company, from England, bought controlling shares of the recently formed Ecuadorian-Chilean mining company. Operational rights were immediately endorsed to Southern American Development Company (SADCO), an American company, who operated the mine from 1897 to 1950 by gaining control of the district's main gold deposits in 1897.

Left: View of Portovelo Mining District, 1941; The camp hospital where Alice was chief nurse is at the tip of the upper arrow. The house where Alice lived is at the tip of the lower arrow. The mine is in the lower right corner. (SPC)

"Exploration programs of SADCO commenced in 1896 and brought the mine into production at 108t/day in 1905. The mine was subsequently deepened to 13 levels, the lowest was located at an elevation of 900 feet above sea level, 2,600 feet below the uppermost workings. In the 53 years that followed, SADCO recovered some 3.5 million ounces of gold and 12 million ounces of silver from 7.6 million tons of ore at a cut-off grade of 14.4 g/t Au and 48.9 g/t."

[Editor's note: this writer, who has no experience whatsoever in the mining industry, feels it appropriate to include a few technical details about the mining operations in the Portovelo district to honor Stanley Kappel, who was, after all, a mining engineer and would have lived and breathed this kind of detail every day that he worked in South America. More to the point: we have so few written details about Stanley's life, especially his inner life, that it seems helpful to explore details about the profession he had chosen, and the day-to-day details of what life would have been like for Stanley as a mining engineer in order to reveal something about the man.]

Left: Ecuadorian currency, 5 Sucres, 1940

Alice wrote that she arrived in Portovelo several months earlier than Stanley. During that same period Stanley, having completed his time at the Frood mine in Ontario, was busy attending orientation briefings in NYC at the SADCO Headquarters. He arrived in due time in Portovelo and, according to Alice, had contracted amoebic dysentery during his voyage, so he was very ill and needed treatment in the camp hospital by the camp's doctor and chief nurse. Alice, the chief nurse, wrote that she and Stanley quickly became "great friends, which upset the other single men in the camp." Alice wrote that "soon after his recovery from dysentery he was sent to oversee a gold mine high in the mountains (Minas Nuevas), where it took 8 hours on muleback to arrive at his future home."

Frank Kappel wrote additional details about Stanley's initial job in Ecuador: "In Portovelo, Stanley was put in charge of Calera Exploration Co. (a development operation known as Minas Nuevas) employing 50-60 men some 20 miles from Portovelo for 10 months. He returned to Portovelo, a 500-ton gold mining operation, rill and shrinkage stopes, as assistant mine foreman."

From the Wells Historical Museum website (dedicated to the process of gold mining, this museum is in Wells, BC, Canada, north of Shuswap near Prince George):

"Gold mining is the science, technology, and business of discovering gold, removing it, and selling it on the market. Gold can be found in many places. It can even be found in very small quantities in sea water. More often, though, it is found in greater quantities in veins associated with igneous rocks like quartzite, which are rocks created by heat. The gold originates deep within the earth in places called pockets. These pockets are filled with gold, heavy ore, and quartz.

Right: Portovelo mine and milling site, taken by Stanley, ca. 1941 (SPC)

"Since the costs of exploration and removal of gold from rock can be high, large companies are created in order to raise the money necessary for the development of hard rock mines. This is different from the solitary individual or small group associated with placer mining.

Right: View of Portovelo Valley with smelter and tailings at the bottom; On far side of valley are trails, mines, and open cuts in the hillside, showing evidence of mining activity in the area for many centuries, ca. 1942 (SPC)

"Before hard rock mining operations even begin, companies explore areas where gold may be found and analyse the rock. If enough gold is discovered in the ore, the technological process of hard rock mining begins."

"In the 1930s, mining was a very labour-intensive, dangerous undertaking. Miners dug tunnels into solid rock by hand. Miners often risked their health, digging with picks and shovels during long shifts in these dark, damp tunnels, building the shafts and carting out the ore.

"Most injuries underground involved falling rock, slips, and explosions, but the workers also had to inhale dust into their lungs in this era before safety regulations, safety equipment, and improved ventilation. The miners were willing to take the risks in order to provide for their families.

"The miners would cart the ore out of the mine in wheeled carts pushed on rails and take it to the mill.

"The gold milling process consisted of three general steps:
      (1) Sorting the ore by size
      (2) Crushing the rock
      (3) Extracting the gold

"The rock fragments were sorted according to size in a grizzly, which was a device consisting of a series of spaced bars, rails, or pipes, above a forward moving conveyer belt to a crusher machine.

Left: Stanley at Portovelo Camp, inspecting and sampling mine tailings as a routine part of his responsibilities as a mining engineer, ca. 1942 (SPC)

"After secondary washing, a shaker screen filtered out fragments of less than 1/2-inch diameter into a fine ore bin, or box. Larger ore fragments were pulverized or crushed in the crusher. The fine ore was fed by conveyer belt to a ball mill, which was a rotating steel cylinder filled with tumbling steel balls that further crushed the fragments to a consistency of fine sand or talcum powder. This powder was fed into a thickener with a cyanide and water solution to create a sludge (a sticky, mud-like material). The liquid sludge was diverted into holding tanks and referred to as the pregnant solution – a liquid sludge containing 70 percent of the gold.

"The sludge was drawn from holding tanks through a clarifier, a device that removed all the remaining rock or clay from a pregnant solution. In the next step, the material was taken to a de-aerator tank that removed bubbles of air and further clarified the solution."

"Zinc was added in dust form to the de-aerated solution, which was drawn under pressure through a filter press that caused the gold and zinc to precipitate onto canvas (heavy cloth) filter leaves. This zinc-gold precipitate (condensed into a solid) was then cleaned from the filters while extreme heat burned off the zinc.

"Water passing through the filters was chemically tested for gold residue before being discharged into tailings ponds. Gold-bearing water may be passed through the filtering process several times to remove all the gold and separate it from impure substances.

"Gold recovered from the ore through the milling process was poured into bricks that were shipped to be assayed and sent to the Royal Canadian Mint in Ottawa, where coins were struck (made). *[Ed. note – this applies only to gold produced in Canada, not in Portovelo.]*

"The result of the milling process produced three types of tailings rocks which cover the landscape around the mill. Hydraulic mine tailings are the resulting rocks washed down the mountainside with water monitors. Another type of tailings is taken out from the mountainside during tunneling. Both types of tailings have the appearance of pale yellow, layered mineral sands."

The above description of the gold mining process leaves out several important components that are necessary when mine tunnels are being constructed, but which have significant effects on the surrounding environment. Most underground gold mines require large quantities of timber to support the tunnels and prevent them from collapsing on the miners, a special danger when explosives are used underground to liberate the ore and help the miners avoid having to dig every ounce out of the ore veins with a pickaxe. In remote mining areas, especially before roads were built and large transport vehicles may have been practical to haul timbers from distant locations, mining engineers and mine excavators had to rely on local timber resources. The result was often significant, even total, denuding of the surrounding forests, leaving local flora and fauna exposed and completely altering the ecological balance of the area.

Placer mining, in which large hydraulic hoses are used to pump water from nearby sources at relatively high pressure to wash away all of the gravel and soil in an area, eventually collecting relatively tiny amounts of gold for the miners to harvest in sluices, was even more devastating to the environment. This was the only option in Alaska, for example, especially where forests were in short supply or simply too difficult to log, and where the gold was more readily available near the surface of the landscape. John McPhee has written an exquisite book on Alaska that describes the process of surface, or placer gold mining that devastated much of remote Alaska during the late 19th and early 20th centuries, entitled: "Coming into the Country."

Right: View of the mine tailings from the SADCO Portovelo mining smelter complex along the Amarillo River; These tailings were a source of significant pollution of the river downstream from the mining camp, where local Ecuadorians lived and worked, ca. 1942. (SPC)

From an article appearing in the Journal of Mining and Metallurgy, dated December 1925: "The mining district of Zaruma is situated in the province of El Oro, near the southwestern corner of Ecuador, about 31 miles from the coast. Here the Andes, which farther north consist of two definite parallel ranges, each crowned with volcanoes, break up into an irregular knot of mountains only 11,000 or 12,000 ft. in elevation. The western foothills of this knot extend well toward the Pacific Ocean, narrowing the coastal plain to a few miles in width. The rivers have trenched deep valleys into this foothill zone and one, Rio Tumbez, with its tributaries, excavated a great amphitheater well back toward the main range. Zaruma lies in this amphitheater, on a ridge between the two main streams – Calera and Amarillo – that go to make up the Tumbez. Portovelo, the mining camp, is in the Amarillo valley at the foot of this ridge. The river bottoms are at an elevation of 2,000 to 2,500 ft.; the ridges rise quickly to 4,000 or 5,000 ft., and a few miles eastward climb to a height of 10,000 ft. or more."

The camp at Portovelo was remote and basic by modern standards, but still sported many amenities. All drinking water had to be distilled and carried in by mules to the various living and working sites. In addition to having a clinic/hospital staffed with an American doctor and an American nurse in charge (reputed to be the best hospital in southern Ecuador at the time), the camp also included a large "whites-only" clubhouse, swimming pool, basketball and tennis courts, dining facility, and individual living quarters for the Americans, all of which were furnished by the mining company. All foreign employees were supported by local servants, who kept their homes clean, tended their gardens, cared for their horses and mules, and cooked their meals. The mining company also provided homes for the local miners and their families. Located in a mountainous mining area, the entire community was built on steep hillsides, giving everyone ample opportunity to stay in shape just getting around. Alice wrote in her photo/scrapbook:

"Mules are used for every kind of service such as delivering groceries, ice, firewood, picking up garbage, carrying distilled water, etc."

Left: Mule with distilled water tanks used for delivering fresh water to the camp, ca. 1942 (SPC)

Portovelo had a fascinating history prior to the arrival of the SADCO operation. A small mountain town dating back at least 450 years to the Inca period, with trails that were possibly even older, little had changed in that region until the arrival of the Spaniards in 1549, then the British in 1880, and finally the Americans near the turn of the 19th century. The local population were all descendants of the Incas, with a heavy Spanish flavor mixed in. Alice said that the inhabitants who were more heavily of Inca extraction were lovely people, although she was far less sympathetic to those with more Spanish blood mixed in, especially the men.

Alice wrote, in a letter dated 2005, there were also head-hunters in the district "not far from where we lived in Portovelo". While she lived there a foreign tourist disappeared during a trip into the back country. The tourist's brother arrived and mounted a search for his missing sibling. He eventually found his way to a remote village where his brother's shrunken head was on display, later reporting that his brother's features were well preserved and readily identifiable.

From the website, Ecuador.com: "Deep in the rainforest that stretches across the eastern part of Ecuador and parts of Peru lives a tribe known as the Jivaro. These fearsome warriors were among one of the very few tribal groups anywhere in the world who successfully resisted conquest and colonization by European forces. The lands of the Jivaro were known to be a source of gold, and in the late 16th century the Spanish administration established a town in Jivaro territory as a base for gold mining expeditions. The governor of the region was cruel and greedy, and he placed a crippling gold trading tax on those Jivaro who fell under his purview. This soon sparked a revolt in which up to 25,000 people who lived in the town of Logrono were killed. The governor was captured by the Jivaro, who poured molten gold into his mouth until he died (one would assume quickly). Legends say, the Jivaro taunted him by asking "Have you had your fill of gold now?"

Right: Jivaro Indian, ca. 1890-1892, artist unknow (The Smithsonian American Art Museum)

"The Jivaro, at least when provoked, were obviously not a gentle people. Their society revolved around wars with neighboring tribes and feuds within the tribe.

"These battles were not fought for land or booty; rather, the prizes were the heads of the enemy. It was believed that to take the head of one's enemy was to take his power and add it to one's own – the more heads taken; the more power would be accumulated. Where the Jivaro differed from other tribes and societies who beheaded their enemies was the way in which they treated the heads. In the case of the Jivaro, they shrunk them!"

The details of the process of head shrinking are available online, but too gruesome to show here. For those with a taste for the macabre, they could be useful whilst standing around a campfire with friends on a dark summer night.

There are so many levels of meaning in the story of the Jivaro. Let's start with the Spanish conquest of the Americas. While that led to the slaughter of countless thousands of local indigenous peoples, the majority of the deaths among the local inhabitants could be attributed to infectious diseases that were brought by the conquistadors.

The immune systems of the native culture had never been exposed to most of these virulent viruses and bacteria, so they were completely unable to resist the ravages of diseases such as smallpox and measles, the two leading killers that could decimate up to 90% of a local population. According to Jared Diamond in *Guns, Germs & Steel*: "When the Europeans arrived, carrying germs which thrived in dense, semi-urban populations, the indigenous people of the Americas were effectively doomed."

The second level of meaning deals with why the Europeans were there: to explore, to look for gold and other sources of potential wealth, and to ransack the riches of the native peoples and their land, under the protection of the Crown, for the financial benefit of everyone involved in the enterprise, and all sanctioned by the Church. Let's be clear: the primary reason that the South American Development Company was present in Ecuador in 1940 wasn't to provide jobs for the local population or to improve their lives (although Mellick Tweedy, the general manager of the entire Portovelo mining operation who remained there for nearly 30 years, was idealistic enough to think that his company's presence was promoting a better life for the local inhabitants). From the outset, stretching back to the coming of the Spaniards to the area in 1549, the removal of every available mineral of value from that region was the principal justification for the costly and dangerous enterprise that all mining operations represent.

Left: Jivaro family, photo taken ca. 1901 in the Alto Maranon River region in the upper reaches of the Amazon that abuts Ecuador (The Smithsonian Institution Bureau of American Ethnology)

The third level of meaning lies in the courage of the Jivaro, and in their ability to thwart much of what was intended by outsiders, which was the wholesale exploitation of the region and its people for the profit of "investors" who wished to enrich themselves at the expense of "others", i.e., those of lesser status in the human spectrum whose wealth was being stolen. After losing up to 90% of their number, most local native populations were unable to resist the onslaught of the Europeans. By the time the Americans arrived in the late 1800s, wishing to carry on the mining operations that had been underway for centuries, the local populace, much subdued by their religion, their fundamentally gentle nature, along with their poverty, became passive participants in what seems to be the ongoing story of mankind. But the Jivaro resisted, successfully by all accounts, and it is mostly due to their savagery that they were able to repel the Spaniards. We can easily recoil from the "uncivilized" horror of the image of a shrunken head, and so we should. But perhaps we should recoil equally from the fact that the methods of the conquering legions were no less savage, and surely no more civilized, than those of the Jivaro.

Add to this backdrop the irony that in 1941, when Stanley and Alice arrived in South America, WWII, the most ambitious attempt at military conquest the world had ever witnessed, and the most brutal example of man's inhumanity to man that reached well beyond the imaginations of the rest of the world as it unfolded, was well underway in Europe and Asia. There was also a war being fought between Ecuador and Peru at the same time (see below). Meanwhile, two supremely hopeful and naive spirits with dreams and ambitions of their own had been struck by Cupid's arrow in the backwaters of Ecuador. Two romantic, adventurous souls had unexpectedly found one another in the jungle highlands of the Andes Mountains. Love, the most powerful force in the human drama, had taken over the lives of our two young heroes. Neither the Jivaros nor the Nazis could faze them.

To be fair to them both, the story of empire is one of the oldest stories ever told. Mankind has been grabbing whatever they could get their hands on from "others" for as long as anyone can remember. It is rare to encounter a member of our race who questions this human tendency, especially prior to the 20th century. Justification is rarely even required, since the justification for greed and selfishness is usually part of the subtext of every tribe's story, hidden so deep within the dialogue that few ever question its validity. In fact, few ever question it at all. The need to protect the tribe, to enable the tribe to survive and flourish, is always the main story that is beyond reproach. Whatever embellishments the tribal big shots want to add to the basic story is where the trouble usually begins, and this part of the dialogue evolves so slowly, so subtly, that it inevitably finds its way into the subtext, well beyond the reach of most of the tribe's awareness or understanding. It is from this hidden catacomb of mythological narrative that most if not all assumptions about reality emerge.

Right: The view from the trail up to Minas Nuevas, looking down toward Portovelo, ca. 1941 (SPC)

On a more mundane level, the Montana School of Mines probably didn't offer courses in the mythological justification for greed, the ethics of empire and evangelism, or the cultural and environmental consequences of the mining industry, especially when it was being conducted in someone else's back yard. And the rest of us, who don't participate directly in the mining enterprise, are all too willing to reap the benefits in our ever more enthusiastic embrace of unbridled materialism and wholesale consumerism, the most spectacular development of the modern age. We are all in this together.

Please forgive this writer for his moment of self-indulgent reflection. Time to get back to our story. In the case of our hero and heroine, it is unlikely that they ever considered such weighty issues as empire, evangelism, and environmental destruction. All that probably mattered to either of them at their tender ages, in that magical world they were creating, was the power that was increasingly consuming them and propelling them into a future to be spent together. This is, after all, a love story, not a sensitivity training session. Actually, even if these two had been fully aware of the cruel reality of the world order, and even if they had known what fate had in store for them, there is little likelihood that they would have been discouraged in their growing passion for one another. Destiny usually finds a way of asserting itself.

Right: Visitors (including Alice) coming up to Minas Nuevas from the main camp at Portovelo for the day, ca. 1941 (SPC)

Meanwhile, life for Stanley up at Minas Nuevas was even more basic than in Portovelo. Stanley was the only American in the camp and had no real peers with whom to talk. Nor was there any obvious way to communicate directly with his bosses or his love in Portovelo since rapid telecommunications had yet to be established between the two mining camps. It is remarkable that such a young man had been given the responsibility of opening a gold mine from scratch, from design to drilling, with few modern industrial tools at his disposal.

Left: Stanley on his way from Portovelo to Minas Nuevas with miners' pay in saddle bags, 1941 (SPC)

As soon as he was well enough to travel after recovering from his initial bout of dysentery, the very thing that had brought Alice and him together, Stanley was dispatched to the highlands of the Portovelo Mining District to expand the SADCO footprint. Alice stated that Stanley was the youngest mining engineer ever assigned by SADCO to establish a gold mine. Gold and silver mining had been going on for many centuries in this area, but nothing of this scale had previously been undertaken. SADCO decided to put its trust in young Stanley to find another source of gold, hopefully easier to extract and therefore more profitable to investors. Extracting gold from the mines beneath Portovelo was becoming more dangerous and expensive as more and deeper levels were added.

This was a "make-or-break" moment for our hero, and it gave him the opportunity to learn the ropes of the mining business "on the ground" and begin to develop his talents as a mining engineer. At this point in his evolution in his chosen career, dwelling on the cultural or environmental implications of what he was doing in that location would have been counterproductive. It would most likely have resulted in his losing hope at the most critical

juncture in his transition from youth into manhood. According to Alice, Stanley thrived in his new assignment. He apparently was a good linguist, having grown up in a household where at least 3 languages were spoken (English, German, French and perhaps Welsh), and he quickly learned enough Spanish to communicate with his staff. In fact, the bosses at Portovelo said that Stanley learned Spanish faster than any other American who had come to work at the mine.

Left: Stanley at Minas Nuevas, 1941 (SPC)

Above left: Stanley, sitting on the veranda of his house, looking (and feeling) sad and lonely at Minas Nuevas (SPC)

Above right: View from Stanley's "open-air" kitchen at Minas Nuevas (SPC)

"Talks aimed at resolving the boundary issues between Peru and Ecuador dating back to 1938 had broken down, followed by repeated border skirmishes that had given ample warning of a possible outbreak of large-scale hostilities. Ecuador was unprepared to meet the July 5 Peruvian invasion, in no small degree because the Ecuadorian president's fear of being left unprotected from his opponents led him to keep the nation's best fighting forces in Quito while Peruvian troops continuously attacked the nation's southern and eastern provinces until a ceasefire went into effect on July 31. Peru's occupation ended only after January 1942, when the two nations signed the Protocol of Peace, Friendship, and Boundaries while attending the Third Conference of Foreign Ministers of the American Republics in Rio de Janeiro. Under the terms of the Rio Protocol, the informal name of the agreement, Ecuador renounced its claim to some 200,000 square kilometers of territory."

Right: Stan's desk with two photos of Alice at his quarters, Minas Nuevas, 1942 (SPC)

Portovelo was one of the principal mining towns in El Oro province in 1941. In addition to a military "on-the-ground" invasion and occupation by the Peruvian army, limited aerial bombings of the region were also carried out by the Peruvian air force! Alice mentioned to Karen that a war occurred while she and Stanley lived and worked in Ecuador, stating that all American females living in the camp had to evacuate to safer locations during the two weeks of fighting, but Alice remained behind because of her importance to the hospital. She also told Karen that the Peruvian air force wanted to bomb the camp but was somehow dissuaded, and that Ecuadorian soldiers provided protection to the camp during the brief skirmish. As the only woman remaining behind in the camp during the war, Alice was included at a dinner party thrown by Mellick Tweedy hosting Henry Luce *[Ed. note – the*

American magazine magnate who was called "the most influential private citizen in the America of his day" and "an American magazine publisher who built a publishing empire based on Time, Fortune, and Life magazines, becoming one of the most powerful figures in the history of American journalism"] and other important visitors from New York.

Stanley left no photographic or written record of the war in his scrapbooks. Alas, the two were too much in love to pay much attention to local politics.

Left: Digging the face of the Minas Nuevas mine adit (horizontal entrance) by hand, February 1942; Above right: Mules hauling 3" x 12" timber planks, completely cut by hand, for use in the new mine at Minas Nuevas (SPC)

One letter written by Stanley suggests he was madly in love with Alice and reveals him to be a very sensitive man. He wrote:

> "The whole weekend has been so perfect, and we've had such a wonderful time that, seeing you ride away today, I felt as though someone had just torn out a piece of my heart and taken it away – it feels so empty." He goes on to proclaim his devotion to Alice, and to their future together, although they had apparently quarreled while she was visiting. "Just remember that I, whatever I do and wherever I find myself, will always love you and will do what I may to keep our love above all petty things, clear and fine and endless…I hope, with my poorly expressed thoughts, that you see you have never cause to fear losing me or my love while I can still be on this earth and that my love and thoughts are ever with you. Love and a kiss, Stan."

Oh my gosh! These are the unmistakable murmurings of a love-sick fool! Anyone who has ever trodden that well-worn path knows these words by heart. And since Stanley was clearly no fool, it is obvious that he was bewitched by this beautiful woman. Fortunately, Alice was equally enchanted by this handsome man. Now there was no turning back.

In addition to the fact that Stanley was deeply smitten, his words also reveal a tender heart dwelling within him. This tenderness suggests that, despite his early challenges, he grew up in a household where love and tenderness were practiced and even encouraged.

Left: Stanley "Simon Legree" Kappel, standing at the entrance to Mina Grande at Minas Nuevas [Ed. note – Nickname given by Stanley to himself]; Above right: First attempt to "open the mine"; After the adit has been dug by hand, timbers are put in place to stabilize the entrance and allow the miners to enter the mine shaft safely. (SPC)

Below left: Landslide occurs during first attempt to open the mine adit Below right: Diamond drill brought by mule from Portovelo to Minas Nuevas to help tunnel into the solid rock and to extract gold ore from underground veins in the new mine (SPC)

Above left and right: A one Sucre nickel coin, dated 1937, and a five Centavo brass coin, dated 1942, both from Ecuador and both of which Stanley and Alice would have used while they were living in Ecuador [Ed. note – Both coins were a gift from Bruce Leibrecht, the author's favorite brother.]

Above: Photo taken by Stanley of the twin-engine, propeller-driven DC-7 aircraft he took between Guayaquil and Quito; The airline is the predecessor of Pan American Airways.
[Editor's note – The photo above suggests that Stanley didn't always use the longer railway that ran between Guayaquil and Quito, but he still had to use the water/land route to get to Guayaquil from Portovelo before flying to Quito.]

CHAPTER 17 – A Marriage Made in Heaven

Every one of us, if we think about it, would be able to identify a period in our lives that stands out as the time when we became fully aware that we were members of a greater community and began to see ourselves as more-or-less fully formed. It is the time when we leave our childhood behind and take responsibility for whatever is to come. Some of us give up our youthful affectations with great reluctance, and even resent being thrust into the realm of adulthood. And some of us are so eager to take full control of our lives that we reject too quickly the ideas and ideals of our heritage, seeking to destroy all connections with the past. Regardless, this is always a time when hormones and energies flow in torrents, when life is pregnant with possibility and opportunity; indeed, when everything seems possible. The time Alice spent in Portovelo was undoubtedly that passage for her. It defined her as a woman, as a person, and became the foundation of her personal mythology. She never escaped the spell that seduced her, even overwhelmed her, to the point that nothing ever again could match the significance and the power that brought her to the full realization of her potential. The same was almost surely true for Stanley.

Below left: Alice sunning in her garden, 1942
Right: Stanley cooling off at the pool, 1942

Alice continues: "When Stanley was in Portovelo (every two weeks), we spent most of our time swimming in a beautiful camp pool and riding horseback, exploring the countryside. On one of our trips, Stanley gave me a lovely engagement ring. About 6 months later we rode by horseback into the high-country mountains to a little town called Zaruma, where we were married quietly (so we thought) by the Justice of the Peace (November 2, 1942), because if the Company found out we would have to go out on the trail by station wagon to be married in Guayaquil by an Anglican minister from Canada." The marriage certificate lists Montana Meyland and L.G. Hebblethwaite as witnesses, suggesting at least two other members of the Portovelo mining community knew about the "secret wedding".

Left: The club pool below the Newberry Club, open only to whites, with Stanley standing in the center of the photo, ca. 1942

Stanley's second letter was written to Alice's parents on December 7th, 1942, in Guayaquil, a short time after Stanley and Alice were married in the 450-year-old town of Zaruma. He writes: "I am afraid I have been much too long in answering your very nice letter, but I think perhaps both Alice and I are getting too lazy for our own good. It is certainly not because I haven't thought of you and how much I am looking forward to meeting you both. It seems that as the time grows shorter, the more I want to get home, and home to me is both with my family and with Alice's…This is the festive season, and although it does not seem at all so here, Alice and I think of the Christmases we have had at home and feel a little more in the mood. I wish you both a very Merry Christmas and a Happy New Year and thank you for Alice who will make mine all I could ever ask, wherever we might be."

Left: Photo taken at the time of Alice and Stanley's wedding ceremony in Zaruma, November 1942 (SPC)

The purpose of this letter was to explain and justify their marriage by a Justice of the Peace in Zaruma, rather than by a Priest in a Church: "It may possibly seem to you that we were foolish to do this under the difficult circumstances that present us here, but we both wanted to feel that we belonged to each other in the way marriage calls for and…we feel within ourselves that we are one and the same and that is all we could ask for. Since this type of marriage is similar to that given by a Justice of the Peace in the States, it is all that is necessary, but we both feel that we would like to be also married in the church, or to say, in the sight of God, as I believe all marriages should be if at all possible. This we will do as soon as we arrive in Guayaquil when we leave for home…Despite the apparent irregularity of everything in general, we are tremendously happy about it and think our marriage perfect, and I think that is all that should count, after all. I know that Alice and I will be very happy, and I will always do my very best to take care of her and to love her as you have done.

"I hope you don't find Alice too much changed from having associated with me for so long. I let her think she is bossing me around once in a while just to give her something to brag about and then I do a little on my own account to put her back in her place. All in all, we have a wonderful time and I hope it is always this way."

Once again, Stanley's tender heart is revealed by his gentle words.

Kerry adds: "We have some other details of Stanley's time in Portovelo also, told to us by the son of one of the local miners who worked there, a miner like many others who died very young of lung disease. It seems that every once in a while, this miner would pocket a bit of the gold he had mined that day. Ultimately, he had enough to give to his son, to try to set him up for a better life. The son was ultimately able to buy the hotel where we stayed with Mother and Bethany, and to make a decent living for himself and his family.

"These men worked in such grueling conditions, that mules would survive it for only a very few years and then would be shot and replaced. Until I read your biographical details, I hadn't realized that Stanley also supervised this mine, in addition to his earlier work in Minas Nuevas. Perhaps he was lenient enough to turn a blind eye to the miners augmenting their meager pay with the occasional gold dust in their pocket." *[Ed. note – The highly informative film, Streams of Gold, created by John Tweedy, a cousin of the three Kappel sisters and the grandson of Mellick Tweedy (more about him later), stated emphatically that the mules who were lowered into the deep gold mines beneath Portovelo to power the elevator that enabled men and ore to be moved efficiently in and out of the mine, now nearly blind due to living in continual darkness, were sacrificed after working for only 3 months in the mines.]*

Right: Stanley cooling off with a cold-water spray in front of Alice's house, 1942 (SPC)

This brings us to more than a few interesting questions: "Why was Portovelo so important to America? Why were the Americans there at all? And why was gold so important at the time?" What occurred at Portovelo in the early 20th century was the result of local and global forces coming together in a cooperative effort to meet the needs of both parties, in this case, the Ecuadorians and the Americans. Ecuador was in a deep depression due to the collapse of the cacao industry (its major exportable commodity) in the late 1920s from which it never fully recovered.

According to Wikipedia: "World demand for cacao and other Ecuadorian export crops dropped precipitously in the wake of the Wall Street Crash of 1929: export crop value fell from US$15 million in 1928 to US$7 million in 1931 and US$5 million in 1932, causing widespread unemployment and misery."

Looking back at the late 19th century, this was also a time when the world was changing rapidly from an agrarian economy based on landowner/tenant relations toward industrialization and a wage-based economy that gave individuals more opportunities for personal fulfillment. Ecuador was a poor country that lacked the capital needed to transform itself into a modern industrial economy. America, on the other hand, was filled with opportunistic capitalists who had access to massive amounts of capital. Add to this the fact that America wished to dominate the Western Hemisphere and ensure that its hegemony would be long-lived.

Part of the American strategy was based on the Gold Standard, which was a way to stabilize the US dollar and enable it to become the standard world currency. America's own internal mineral resources could not provide the amount of gold required to support this national strategy, so it had to look outside its own borders for a reliable and sufficient source of gold. The gold veins in El Oro province of Ecuador were among the largest known reserves in the world. They were also in the Western Hemisphere, and they were not being exploited with the latest technological advances in mining and smelting, so Portovelo became a target of profound strategic interest to America in the late 19th and early 20th centuries.

Cornelius Vanderbilt apparently saw his opportunity and established SADCO, according to John Tweedy in *Streams of Gold*. Vanderbilt had access to huge amounts of capital and was willing to invest it in Portovelo. Upgrading the antiquated and dilapidated mining infrastructure at Portovelo required a nearly endless supply of money and patience. In fact, according to Carrion, SADCO's mining operation at Portovelo did not become profitable until 20 years after it was initiated, so vast was the transformation process it required. Major infrastructure upgrades included: 1) transportation to ensure access to this remote area that was without even a road that would allow movement of the processed ore to the seacoast and onto ships to take it to America; 2) community based improvements that would ensure the local workforce could live safely, in a healthy environment, with basic essentials such as clean water, sanitation, food, health care, and housing, all of this focused on establishing a reliable supply of labor to do everything that would be required to run a large-scale gold mining operation; 3) technological infrastructure that included everything from the equipment required to dig deep mine shafts, extract the ore from the hard rock that contained the veins of gold, lift it to the surface, crush the rock down to a usable grade, transport it to the smelter, and submit the ore to a sophisticated chemical process that converted it from raw ore to acceptably refined gold-bearing substance. Only after all of this had happened locally could SADCO transport the refined gold out of the country, onto waiting ships, through the Panama Canal, and eventually to the principal American repository at Fort Knox.

As was previously discussed, gold has played a central role in human culture for most of our history. In the early 20th century gold took on even greater importance to the United States and its allies. The gold standard was widely used in the 19th and early 20th centuries, having been adopted by the US in 1873. It was the British who were most firmly devoted to the gold standard during that time. If a nation went to war and needed to borrow money from another nation, the exchange required that gold bullion be transported from the reserves of the lending nation into the reserves of the borrowing nation. However difficult, dangerous and awkward this arrangement may have been, it was the basis of "trust" that was required to enable nations to conduct international trade at the time.

After the loss of their principal cash crop during the Great Depression, political instability ensued in Ecuador, leading to increasingly illiberal developments in Ecuador's government, with the Ecuadorian military taking a leading role.

According to Wikipedia: "In September 1937, President Federico Páez Chiriboga was overthrown by his minister of national defense, General Alberto Enríquez Gallo, in a military coup. Although General Enríquez ruled for less than a year, he achieved note as a social reformer by his promulgation of the Labor Code of 1938. Enríquez is also remembered for having initiated a protracted confrontation with the United States-based South American Development Company over the terms of its Ecuadorian concession and the wages it paid its Ecuadorian employees. The company refused to comply with Enríquez's entreaty that more of the profits from its mining operations stay in Ecuador, and it won the support of the United States Department of State."

To add to the drama, during the 1930s the Axis Powers were conspiring to undertake the most massive land grab the world has ever seen. Their stated goal was to literally take over the entire world. This was a step-by-step process that required an incomprehensibly complicated amount of strategic planning and industrial expansion, which in turn required a lot of money. There was much international interest in the gold reserves of South America, and this included the Nazis. Throughout the 1930s, many Germans emigrated from Germany to South America for the express purpose of establishing a network in that part of the world in preparation for what was to come.

A secure message from The Consul General at Guayaquil (McDonough) to the Secretary of State in Washington, DC, obtained by this writer online from the publicly available Archives of the US Federal Government, and listed as Item No. 616, Guayaquil, January 13, 1938, reveals much about how strategically vital the US considered the gold mining operation at Portovelo:

"The South American Development Company is the largest American interest in Ecuador and has several millions of dollars invested in this country. It is the only producer of gold in large quantities in Ecuador.

"Almost identical demands have been made of the Anglo-Ecuadorian Oilfields Ltd., a British concern which is the principal producer of petroleum in Ecuador.

"The British Consul at Guayaquil suspects that the present measures against foreign capital in Ecuador may have been inspired by Italian influence in Quito exerted through the Italian Military Mission so that Italian or German capital can get control of the mineral wealth of Ecuador. The American gold mining company and the British oil company are the only two large and important producers of mineral products in Ecuador."

Lending further credence to the strategic importance of an American-owned gold mine in Ecuador, Andrea Carrión (Ph.D. Geography, Carleton University) wrote in her brilliant Ph.D. thesis about mining in Ecuador and the mining process in the gold district of Portovelo-Zaruma, 1860-1980 *[Ed. note – I have paraphrased and selected passages from her thesis in order to adapt Ms. Carrión's highly academic 470-page masterpiece to meet the needs of my far less ambitious narrative.]*: "The political economy of resource extraction in large scale foreign-owned industrial camps creates enclosures of private rule, through a combination of physical, legal, technological, exchange, and fiscal measures that produce distancing from the domestic economy and society. In this respect, the mining enclave, although geographically isolated or situated in a relatively remote location, is central to capitalism.

"SADCO worked at a loss for the first two decades while establishing the conditions for extraction. The company constructed industrial facilities while reinforcing underground structures. The surface of the industrial complex included a sawmill, a chemical laboratory, a carpentry shop, an industrial blacksmith and automotive workshop, the foundry crushers, a cyanide plant, a compressor, the cellars, and a warehouse. The company established offices for general administration, coordination of subterranean mine works, and geological surveys. The camp also included offices for accounting, transportation, radio-communications, store

administration, and internal policing matters. Underground, the company had to rebuild works, as supporting wood was rotten, tunnels were clogged, and 'all was a pile of rubble.'

Left: Ore chutes used for transferring partially refined ore from one location to another (SPC)

"A problem common to mining was supplying the power needed to move workers, machinery, air, water, and ore. In 1912, the Portovelo Channel (1.5 km) was finished, supplying a basic water network, and by 1916, the Galvez Channel (5.27 km), with a hydroelectric installation to power the metallurgical plant and provide electricity to Portovelo and Zaruma, was up and running. Also, by 1916, a vertical tunnel 390 meters deep connected thirteen levels of underground galleries for ore extraction. The construction of the vertical shaft was a complex civil engineering project that facilitated the exploration of underground lodes and rich mineral veins. The Pique Americano (American shaft headframe) was fully lined with concrete, equipped with a steel headframe thirty meters high, and connected to a winding tower structure called El Castillo. The elevator provided the means for men and materials to enter and exit the mine, as well as allowing light and air to enter the tunnel.

Left: Entrance to the main (or American) shaft with headframe tower containing cables that operated the mine elevator, or lift, used to lower men, mules, and equipment down to the deepest levels of the mine, and to lift unprocessed ore out of the mine; The lift was powered by electricity that was locally produced by SADCO. (SPC)

Ms. Carrión continues: "The company carried out geological surveys and studied underground structures, identifying quartz mineralization. The mine was 'developing remarkably with very rich ore in unexpected tonnage.' Mining engineers developed detailed diagrams to determine the direction of steeply dipping faulted vein bodies distributed in irregular and dispersed bedded deposits, and to improve the performance of underground extraction through the filling stopes mining method. This method was somehow unique to the Zaruma mines, applicable to moderately wide deposits of solid and firm ore, allowing connections between levels by means of rises in the footwall through which waste material was introduced into the stopes. The mine subsequently reached a depth of 900 m below the uppermost workings. The method allowed for the placement of levels at a considerable distance one from another but was difficult to work on. The process caused the mixing of waste with the gold-bearing ore, and only rich material was hauled to the American shaft or the Newberry tunnel to be processed on the surface. In the latter, the company introduced locomotives to increase efficiency in transporting ore. This method is relatively unusual but similar to that applied in the gold mines of Butte, Montana, US.

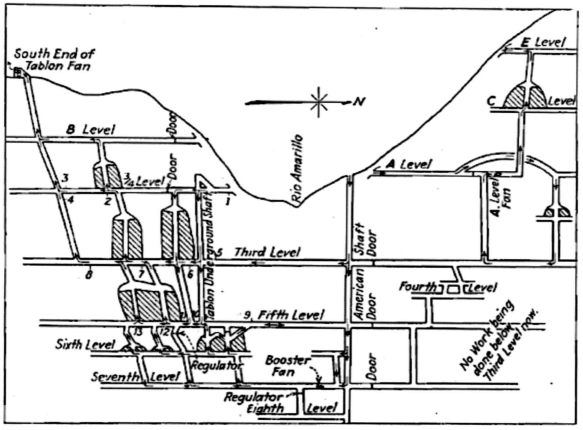

Above: Cross-section of the principal Portovelo Mine Works, 1932. (Elizabeth Tweedy Sykes Archive) [Editor's note – Access to the mines was furnished by adits (or horizontal entrances) at various elevations and by two vertical shafts. The American Shaft had two compartments, one for hoisting men, ore, and waste and the other serving as a space for a ladder and air, water, and electric lines. The vertical Tablón Shaft was a secondary winze (a steeply inclined passageway between two levels) used for servicing the mines. The lowest levels of the mine are so far below the Amarillo Riverbed that flooding regularly occurred.]

Left: SADCO smelter complex in Portovelo (SPC)

Ms. Carrión continues: "The company also operated a relatively sophisticated treatment plant to recover gold and silver. SADCO first introduced mercury amalgamation to directly recover gold and silver, and a flotation method to produce a concentrate, which was sold to smelters to retrieve the lead and copper. The company decided to change the processing method after ore volumes increased with the vertical shaft and a gold bullion robbery took place. In 1919, the company introduced a significant innovation: the cyanide agitation decanting system.

"Mining operations required tremendous quantities of lumber to line and support tunnels and as fuel for the smelting process and housing construction; this item accounted for 10 to 12% of production costs. In 1938, some 2,000 loggers provided SADCO with timber, firewood, charcoal, and mules to transport goods. The company bought timber locally, posting prices for poles of different sizes; prices increased with the distance that the lumber was transported.

Left: Side entrance to the Portovelo Mine; The sign above the entrance, according to Stanley, reads: "Above everything, safety." (SPC)

The following paragraph is a letter from A.M. Tweedy to the Ministro de lo Interior y Obras Públicas, Documentos relativos a los contratos…1923:

"The Company has established in Portovelo, which was a miserable hamlet where a few families wracked by malaria led a pitiful existence, a model mining camp where 700 workers and their families, paid well and on time, enjoy the benefits of living and working in a hygienic, prosperous, and civilized town. It has changed Zaruma from a town of infamous repute into a hardworking, orderly city, an industrial and commercial center, in which hundreds of thousands of sucres are exchanged annually.

Ms. Carrión continues: "To house the work force, the American company built a settlement south of the industrial site that represented a significant, modern sanitary project. By 1911, the "flourishing population" had a restaurant, marketplace, and butcher shop; public baths and schools for both sexes; and lovely houses for company employees and

sanitary houses for regular workers. The residential area featured American-style dwellings,
all painted green and white,
distributed in a way that
reinforced labour hierarchies
and social status within the
camp. The town had no clear
grid pattern and the church
was not the center of social
life, as in other colonial
villages.

*Right: "Goin' down"; Miners
waiting to take the elevator deep
down into the mine (SPC)*

"Portovelo was a new settlement in rugged topography composed of a migrant population who organized everyday life around the rhythms of their jobs and, as a result, professional or class identities were often more important than those associated with the land. Daily movement tended to take place around the Pique Americano, the town's most prominent building. The elevator was the entry point into the mine for men and materials. Under conditions of industrial labour, the concentration of the work force facilitated the delivery of housing and other services, the scheduling of work shifts, and policing.

"There were three main, segregated socio-residential areas: the campamento americano (American camp), houses for Ecuadorian managers and white-collar employees, and housing for mineworkers.

*Right: Overhead view
of track, which was
distributed throughout
the mining complex,
with one lone mule
pulling several ore
cars, each weighing at
least one ton (SPC)*

Ms. Carrión
continues: "The
Americans lived
with their families
in bungalows
located on the higher slopes, overlooking the industrial site, close to the general office, the church, the hospital, and the social club. This area was not open to Ecuadorians and signs prohibited trespassing. The general manager had the largest house at the top of the hill, known locally as the Casa Blanca (white house). American officials lived in single-family detached cement houses featuring basic amenities and private gardens. Unmarried foreign engineers shared a common dwelling on a nearby hill, close to the Newberry Club.

Above left: "Whites only" Newberry Club exterior; Above right: Newberry Club interior showing game room and dance floor, 1942 (SPC)

Left: Small town along the route from Guayaquil to Portovelo that Alice and Stanley would have passed through, demonstrating the circumstances of the local population (SPC)

"Ecuadorian employees had wooden single-family houses or duplexes and some workers' families lived in row houses along cobbled streets. These buildings had walls of wood planks placed horizontally rather than vertically as dictated by traditional construction methods. Americans introduced zinc roofs, a feature new to the area. Most of the male workers were unmarried and lived in a large common dormitory. After 1935, single male workers lived in multi-storey buildings in which each room opened onto a corridor and was shared by two or three workers.

Left: A "typical" country Ecuadorian house on stilts that Alice (and later, Stanley) passed during her trip from Guayaquil to Portovelo in early 1941 (all photos on this page are from Stanley's private collection, SPC)

Ms. Carrión continues: "Socio-spatial segregation was achieved in subtle ways so as to reinforce the difference between the upper classes and the populace, and to reassert the hierarchies within the mode of production. In church, the front, padded pews were reserved for foreign residents whose names were indicated on the pews. Foreigners were welcomed at the Fonda Americana, a restaurant with linen and amenities that served vegetables and fruits grown in El Jardín (the garden), a private orchard that supplied American families only. Ecuadorians had access to the Fonda Nacional, a massive soup kitchen that provided meals at a subsidized price. There were even two cemeteries, one in Barrio Machala for nationals and another in the neighbourhood El Faique where foreigners were buried.

Right: The Curipamba Hospital (where Alice was chief nurse) was the most modern in southern Ecuador and provided free services for the work force (Elizabeth Tweedy Sykes Archive)

"Sanitary measures were implemented to promote the well-being of the population, but diseases arising from mining activities undermined these efforts. Morbidity and mortality in the area was mostly due to influenza, malaria, dysentery, syphilis, tuberculosis, leprosy, chronic intoxication, anemia, sexually transmitted diseases, and mining work related accidents. Toxic gases, mineralized dust, and poor ventilation in the mines produced lung diseases. The Curipamba Hospital was said to be one of the best in southern Ecuador and provided free health services for the work force, but sick and elderly workers did not receive full wages or were fired without compensation. In other words, health concerns were focused on labour health, not the overall wellbeing of the people.

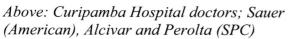

Above: Curipamba Hospital doctors; Sauer (American), Alcivar and Perolta (SPC)

Above: Alice (back row, left) with her hospital staff in Portovelo (SPC)

Left: Alice Leland, RN, the youngest chief nurse ever hired at the Curipamba Hospital in Portovelo (SPC)

Ms. Carrión continues: "The expansion of capitalism in the region included services related with the mining industry. Villages along the route connecting the mining district to the seaport developed into trading posts. For example, by 1935 the town of Piñas had 7,318 inhabitants, more than the population of Zaruma. Growth was linked to agriculture to supply the Portovelo camp, the construction of the railway system to the mining district, and the early development of banana plantations in El Oro Province.

"To 'make a bonanza out of an industrial enterprise', as stated by the newspaper The Spirit of the Age, the American mining entrepreneurs required people, supplies, machinery, and infrastructure. The extractive industry depended on external resources and markets to retain its work force, sustain the local consumer population, and ensure surplus outflows. Haring reports (note: this has to be changed) that 'transportation of materials and supplies to the mine was one of the most difficult problems which had to be faced and solved before the mine could be regarded as economic.'

"The transportation of industrial materials was a monumental undertaking. Equipment was transferred at Guayaquil to riverboats sailing to Puerto Bolívar. Machinery parts were loaded by men and transported by mules along narrow paths often following mountain ridges that topped the steep walls descending into deep ravines. On arriving at their destination, the machines were assembled by company employees. As many as 2,000 mule-loads of freight moved over the mountains per year into the area. Schraps recalls (note: this has to be changed) that in 1916 'the mule trains were always under the care of arrieros or muleteers who ran on foot ahead or behind the mules shouting at them and beating them with clubs when necessary.' For long stretches, the path was marked by a series of deep muddy depressions and the overloaded mules had to cross from one side of the trail to other in search of a point to cross. The ruta de las escaleras (stairs route), considered the most dangerous stretch, was the site of frequent accidents. The railway from Puerto Bolivar to Piedras was finished in 1938, shortening the trip from Guayaquil to Portovelo from five days to 20 hours."

Throughout Stanley and Alice's tenure at Portovelo, Mellick Tweedy was the general manager of the entire SADCO mining operation in the Zaruma District. Born Andrew Mellick Tweedy in 1884, he grew up on a 150,000-acre (mostly leased) sheep and cattle ranch in east Texas. His father, Joseph Tweedy, was from an elite east coast background that included connections to the Rockefellers and other scions of early American industry. By 1905 Mellick had graduated from Princeton University. He then studied at Columbia University's famed school of metallurgical and mining engineering and became a fully trained mining engineer by 1906. Mellick spoke fluent Spanish, partly because of the proximity of his father's ranch to Mexico. This linguistic talent undoubtedly gave him an edge in getting hired by SADCO, and he was sent to Portovelo in 1916, where he became general manager of the entire Portovelo mining operations within a year of his arrival, according to his son, John. He was married to the Kappel sisters' great aunt Florence Dahl Tweedy, a legendary figure in her family circle who was also a registered nurse and a principal reason that Alice sought employment as a nurse in Portovelo in 1940. Married in 1917, the couple reigned over the Portovelo mining camp for several decades, and all 3 of their children were born at home in the mining camp. Mellick and Florence hosted numerous diplomatic, political, industrial, and academic delegations in the camp. A previously unidentified mammal species was even named after Mellick by a visiting biologist from the US who was hosted by the couple.

Over the course of the 30 years that Mellick lived and worked in Portovelo, he became an influential member of the foreign expatriate community in Ecuador and developed close ties with the US missions in both Guayaquil and Quito. As general manager for SADCO at Portovelo, Mellick spent much of his time in Quito, Guayaquil, Washington, DC, and at SADCO HQ in New York City. His children were initially home schooled by an imported American tutor. At some point he sent his family back to the US so his children could continue their education in a more formal and appropriate setting. From then on, he spent most of his time living alone in the grand house in Portovelo, reigning over the entire community and fretting over the continual challenges that threatened the success of the SADCO mining operation.

Left and right: Stanley while staying at the Company Residence in Quito, 1942 (SPC)

By the time Stanley returned permanently to Portovelo from Minas Nuevas in 1942 to take over as assistant mine foreman for the entire operation, the Americans and Canadians were fully involved in the Second World War. Stanley and Alice's time in South America was drawing to a close, and they were eager to return home so they could do their part in the war effort. Everyone had been deeply shaken when a message came to the camp in December 1941 that Pearl Harbor had been attacked by the Japanese, and the increasing danger to the world hung over them continually after that. Alice and Stanley must have both felt the growing animosity among the mine's local workers toward their "gringo" bosses who were stealing the riches from their native land. This was a longstanding tradition that stretched back many centuries, keeping the locals in perpetual bondage and poverty while the master class reaped the spoils and lived the high life.

Left: Spanish nurses who worked for Alice at the hospital in Portovelo; Maraja, Evangelina, and Marina (SPC)

Alice continues: "I became very fond of the Spanish nurses at the hospital, whose lives were nothing but hardship. My heart ached for them and before I left, I gave them all my belongings, except for a few clothes to go home in. Many times I wanted to quit my job, but I had signed a two-year contract and I had to abide by it. My homesickness would have been unbearable if I hadn't been very busy in the hospital and worked with such kind and delightful nurses. They treated me as if I were a queen.

"Stanley still had his job in Minas Nuevas and I had my nursing job. Finally, our two-year contract was over, and we were anxious to return to the United States and Canada. Once again at 3 am we went over the trail, by station wagon, to a little rail car on tracks through the jungle country, on a river boat that always leaked from the rain, and when we were awakened, we were sopping wet.

Below left: Photo of Alice and Stanley on the boat that took them on their final leg toward Guayaquil as they prepared to leave Ecuador forever in 1943; Below right: Photo of Stanley, standing in front of the airplane he Alice and took to Mexico City from Guayaquil when they left Ecuador forever in April 1943 (Alice is the presumed photographer) (SPC)

"We hurriedly changed clothes and caught a plane to Mexico City, where we spent a week in a beautiful hotel, then we flew to the US to Butte, Montana, where we were bounced off the plane because it had to be ready for military use. We remained in Butte for a few days, then came by train to Spokane, and then to Sicamous to visit Stanley's parents, who lived on the beautiful Shuswap Lake, then on to Sheep Creek Gold Mines, where we were back in the area where Stanley and I first lived." *[Ed. note – Stanley lived in Sheep Creek while Alice lived in Ione.]*

Spending a few days in Butte must have been a walk down memory lane for Stanley, and an opportunity for Alice to gain important insight into the nature of this town where Stanley had spent four of his most formative years, studying to become a mining engineer and learning to become an adult in the process.

Alice also told Karen that Stanley apparently contracted an intestinal tapeworm while living up at Minas Nuevas due to the sloppiness of his Chinese chef. While the two of them were staying at the beautiful hotel in Mexico City during their return passage to America and home, Stanley was treated in a local hospital for the tapeworm. Karen remembers Alice saying the tapeworm was several feet long. During that same time in Mexico City Alice went to the dentist for long-overdue dental treatment that had not been available in Ecuador. However magical their "fairy-tale" existence may have been in Ecuador, it was time to get back to a more normal life and start a family.

By all accounts, Stanley Kappel performed admirably as a shift boss, foreman and mining engineer at mines owned and operated by SADCO from 1941 until 1943. According to Alice, by the time Stanley and she departed from South America in 1943 as newlyweds, Stanley had been identified as a rising star within the mining world and was destined to become a high-level corporate manager when they returned to North America to answer the call of duty as WWII was rapidly progressing. Alice said that Stanley was very eager to get back home so he could participate in the process of defeating the Axis Powers. It is unclear if Stanley's exploration efforts resulted in the discovery of enough gold to be profitably mined at Minas Nuevas. All SADCO mining operations in Portovelo ceased in 1943, the year when Mellick Tweedy suffered his heart attack and left the camp to return to America permanently. SADCO retained its rights to Portovelo until 1950, when it was turned back to the Ecuadorian government and would lie dormant for many decades.

All things considered, this was "the grand adventure" for Alice and Stanley. Both had been thrust into a culture so remote and utterly different from anything they had ever been exposed to, that it is impressive they took to it so enthusiastically and successfully. Their surroundings were exotic, the food was exotic, the music was exotic, and their circumstances would have proved extremely interesting to even the most jaded world traveler. They spent their idyll in Portovelo in a time and place far apart from the banal humdrum of American and Canadian life, and both seem to have thrived there. It is no wonder that they found one another so quickly and fell into a love that would last forever. But WWII beckoned, along with a mutual desire to return to "normal life" closer to friends and family. While at least a few young American men may have fled the war by taking jobs in Portovelo, Stanley was feeling called to serve his country in the greatest conflict of the modern era.

Stanley wrote a third letter, this one to Dora (this is Marie Buckingham, whose name was changed to Dora by her adopting mother – Dora later changed her name back to Marie) from South America in 1943:

Casilla 65,
Guayaquil, Ecuador
March 26th., 1943

"Dearest Dora,

"I got your very nice letter today, I and thank you for the congrats. I note that you wrote it on Jan. 14th, so it has taken quite a while to get here. However, the boat mail is very slow and not too secure either. You said you had sent me an enlargement at Christmas but I haven't received it as yet so it must have become lost. I hope that it has only been delayed somewhere, as so frequently happens. I got a Xmas card last week from home, dated Dec. 15th, so you see there is still a chance that it may arrive. And thank you ever so much for the swell snaps - they are really nice ones. If Jeanie grows up half as nice looking as her mother, she'll be another sweetheart with trimmings.

"As far as my getting up to see you, I think, and hope, that it may be quite possible. Alice and I are leaving here by plane on April 14th and will travel by air as far as Spokane. There we intend to stay for several weeks with her family, and then we will be up in Sicamous about May 10th or so, and stay there for two weeks. At least those are the plans as far as we have them. I am going to try and get into the Royal Canadian Engineers again after that and if I can pass the physical test this time, I should have no trouble. Of course, I failed the Air Force test for a very minor ailment, which a very good surgeon from the States says is non-existent, so I hope that all may go well this time. Alice is quite despondent about it but realizes that it is the only thing that I can do. If the country thinks that I'd be more use in the mines, since they are so short of mine labor, both skilled and unskilled, then I suppose that is where they will put me. However, Dad says that they are also short of young engineers in the army. Anyway, I intend to go to the Coast and find out about it and it will probably be on the way down that we will call in at Kamloops.

"Betty is now in Ottawa and had a Government job there in some branch of the Intelligence Service, I believe. I have only heard from her once since she left. She went down there in Jan., and I suppose is finding it rather difficult to get settled. She said she liked it very much though, and I imagine that after teaching for so long, any change would be welcome.

"You are right about the weather here being monotonous. These past two weeks we have had some nice sun though, and I suppose that after a couple of months more rain, it will clear up for the summer. The sun is really hot at this time of the year, and one has only to be in swimming for a little while to get sunburned unless you take it slow. You can't realize just how hot the sun is when it is directly overhead as it is here, even when it is cloudy you can get burned. We have movies here four days a week; that is, we have two movies which they show twice each during the week. We get some good ones, but no new ones and many of them I have seen before. There is only one projection machine and of course the operator has to stop the film after each reel to change it, and sometimes it breaks besides.

"I have been doing very little socially this last month, or since New Year's as far as that goes. Alice and I had a trip out to Guayaquil where we were married by the minister of the English Church and stayed out there for three days. It is a long trip for so short a time, but we enjoyed the change very much. Going to Guayaquil from here, you take in succession; car, mule, truck, auto-rail car, and then a night trip on the boat. You leave here at 4:30 am. on Sat. and arrive at 6:00 am. on Sun. Since I am enclosing a snap, I won't write anymore because of

the weight. Thanks again for the swell letter and we will be seeing you. I'll drop you a line from Sicamous. I am glad to hear that all goes so well with you, the baby, and Hugh, and I also hope that you two will be soon together for good. I can realize how tough it would be now that I am married myself, but I'll bet the baby, Jeanie, makes it much less lonely for you in that it keeps you busy bringing her up.
Good-bye now, and best of everything always, Love, Stan"

Look at the two portraits in the photos below. One can't help admiring them, for they are beautifully painted by an accomplished artist. I have spent years looking at those two lovely portraits almost every day without really seeing them. Who are these two people? Where are they from? What is the occasion? What is the meaning of their attire?

First, they are very likely local native Indians whose ancestors had survived the Spanish conquistadors, the British, and now the Americans who had taken their lands and extracted the mineral wealth of their homeland. The local Indian people were, according to Alice, very poor, but they were kind, gentle and dignified in their demeanor. There was no tourist industry in the area at the time, so they were dependent on agriculture and mining for their living. The man in the portrait may have worked in the local mines in Portovelo, and the woman was probably a servant who worked (but did not live in) one of the Americans' houses, clubs, or offices. Those were, after all, the principal ways to make money for these people if they hadn't inherited a patch of land and weren't able to conduct any profitable agricultural activities.

Above: Skin paintings of Ecuadorians Alice and Stanley encountered in Portovelo; the paintings were purchased by Stanley while he was in Ecuador between 1941 and 1943 and given to George and Margaret Moline as a gift; they now hang on our family room wall (photo taken by the author)

They are both quite handsome, though somber, and they are both very well dressed in these portraits, as would be expected of a sitting for an important occasion. Perhaps they were sitting for their wedding portraits to be painted by an artist who appears to be of exceptional talent and training. Perhaps the artist was hoping to sell them to tourists. The details of the portraits reveal just how good this artist was, and how well he understood light, shadow, color, and nuance. Note the careful rendering of the clothing draped over its subjects.

If these two individuals are sitting for their wedding portraits, this would have been perhaps the most important occasion to occur in their lives to date. The woman's clothing is more complex and elegant than the man's, but what they are wearing is striking for both.

Above: The two figures in these paintings are every bit as enigmatic as Stanley is to me. And just like Stanley, they have haunted me for most of my adult life.

Note the crosses embroidered along the edge of the woman's headpiece; the delicate strings of beads in her complicated necklace; the pin holding her shawl together at the left shoulder; and the knotted headband that implies she is carrying something on her back. The man's shawl is especially colorful, and his hat is nicely draped, even if it is a bit frayed along the upper edge.

Both handsome young people appear somber yet dignified, and there may even be a hint of anxiety in their eyes. Mystery, nobility, stoicism, resignation, sadness, defiance, even fierceness: all these characteristics may be revealed in these portraits. The artist leaves it up to the imagination of the viewer to draw his or her own conclusion about the portraits and their subjects, in the tradition of all good artists.

So how did Stanley happen to come into possession of these two portraits, painted on animal skins, and what meaning did they hold for him? The skill of this artist suggests formal training, and it also suggests that the paintings may have been purchased in an art gallery in a larger town or city, possibly Guayaquil, rather than locally.

Could it be that they were acquired around the time of Stanley and Alice's own wedding, and that these two portraits mirrored something that Stanley and Alice saw in themselves as newlyweds? As far as we know there was no formal portrait of Stanley and Alice taken to commemorate their wedding. Is it possible that these two precious wedding portraits are substitutes for Stanley and Alice's own wedding portraits?

Stanley came from a family of artists whose home was adorned with numerous works of art. In addition to the portraits, he and Alice collected a few pieces of silver jewelry: rings, earrings, necklaces, and bracelets, along with several small, fine silver dishes with embedded silver coins that are treasures. It is very likely that they would have collected even more, if they had not been starting out in their professional and marital careers, with very little money when they started, and now only 2 ½ years into their lives as earners.

Right: Silver bracelet, necklace, and pin, presumably Ecuadorian in origin, purchased by Stanley and Alice in 1943 (from Kristen Kappel's private collection)

Below right: Handmade Silver ashtray with four Chilean silver coins, obtained by Stanley and Alice during their time in South America; The large central coin, measuring 1 ½ inches in diameter, is from 1889, while the three smaller coins are from 1915. (from Kristen Kappel's private collection) [Editor's note – The ashtray appears to be tarnished, even though it is finely polished. This appearance is a colorful "trick of the light".]

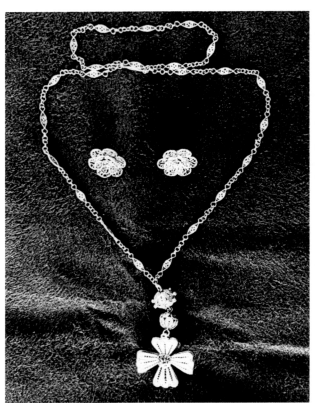

Above left and right: Handmade silver filigree necklace and earring set (from Karen's private collection); Below: Handmade silver bracelet with Inca figures (from Kerry Dearborn's private collection); [Ed. note – All pieces were purchased in Ecuador by Stanley and Alice in 1943.]

CHAPTER 18 – Lieutenant Stanley Kappel and the Royal Canadian Engineers

Love and death are the two great themes in the human drama, and war powerfully intensifies their synergism.

During the early days of their blossoming relationship, while Stanley and Alice were living in South America, the rest of the world must have seemed far away. Most of the news they received would not have arrived in real time in Portovelo, as there was no local newspaper or radio station. The harsh reality of the Second World War and nearly every other aspect of the world's troubles would have seemed distant, perhaps almost abstract, to our two newlyweds.

But that would have changed abruptly for them in April of 1943 when they left Portovelo to return home. As soon as they arrived in Guayaquil, they would have encountered the relentless bombardment of the news media's war coverage. Every major newspaper in the world carried front page stories and photos of the violence and carnage every day, and in every edition.

By the time they left Guayaquil on April 14th, the tide was turning in favor of an Allied victory in the War: British and American forces were sweeping across North Africa and had linked up in Tunisia. Winston Churchill and Franklin Roosevelt had recently met in Casablanca to discuss the inevitable invasion of mainland Europe. The Royal and US Air Forces continued their successful bombing missions on other Nazi strongholds in Germany and across the European continent. Russian troops had launched an all-out counter-attack on the Nazis at Stalingrad the previous August and achieved victory with the surrender of the German 6th Army on February 2nd. The war against the Japanese was raging in the Pacific, and the last Japanese had left Guadalcanal. Dwight Eisenhower had been selected to lead the Allied Armies in Europe in February. Equally significant, Canadians were making their mark in the war effort.

However happy Alice and Stanley were in their new life together, and however optimistic they were feeling about their future hopes and dreams, the undercurrents of the war and the threat it might impose on their blissful state would have been relentless and foreboding. Stanley shared in his letter to Marie Dunbar in March of 1943: "I am going to try and get into the Royal Canadian Engineers again. If I can pass the physical test this time, I should have no trouble. Of course, I failed the Air Force test for a very minor ailment, which a very good surgeon from the States says is non-existent, so I hope that all may go well this time. Alice is quite despondent about it but realizes that it is the only thing that I can do. If the country thinks that I'd be more use in the mines, since they are so short of mine labor, both skilled and unskilled, then I suppose that is where they will put me. However, Dad says that they are also short of young engineers in the army."

Jeanie Dubberley previously shared that her father, Hugh Dunbar, had enlisted in the Royal Canadian Navy before the war started. The Canadian government apparently postponed declaring war on Germany for ten days after the British declared war until the ship Hugh was deployed on, along with two other Canadian destroyers, could transit the Panama Canal on its way from the West Coast to begin service in the North Atlantic. The vital and dangerous role of protecting transport ships crossing the North Atlantic to help supply the British in their efforts to hold the Germans at bay on the continent fell largely to the Royal Canadian Navy.

Below: Canadian Army Recruiting Poster for the Second World War (researchgate.net)

According to Jeanie: "The Battle of the Atlantic, 1939 to 1945, was the longest continuous campaign of the entire war. Fought largely by reservists and volunteers in small ships built in Canada and operating from Canadian bases, the defence of North Atlantic trade against the submarine menace defined a naval role for Canada within a much larger alliance.

"During the 1939-1945 War the Royal Canadian Navy (RCN) grew to a strength of nearly 100,000 personnel and nearly 400 vessels. Their main duty was to act as convoy escorts across the Atlantic, in the Mediterranean and to Murmansk in the USSR. They also hunted submarines, and supported amphibious landings in Sicily, Italy, and Normandy. In all the RCN lost nearly 2,000 sailors.

"Canada entered the 1939-1945 War on 10th September 1939. Within two months the first contingents of Canadian troops arrived in the United Kingdom to supplement the British Expeditionary Forces (BEF). Forestalled by the evacuation of the British Army from Dunkirk and the Channel ports, Canada's role became one of defence of the British Isles."

"By the end of the war The Royal Canadian Navy was the third largest in the world! Volunteer enlistment was high - although my dad was already serving, he had many school friends who signed up as soon as they could. Men who didn't serve in the military generally were quick to explain that they had been working in 'essential industries', like my former father-in-law who was a foreman at a wire cable factory."

Right: Lieutenant Stanley Kappel, newly commissioned officer in the Royal Canadian Engineers, Chilliwack, BC, 1943 (SPC)

First Stop: British Columbia

Frank Kappel continues: "Stanley returned to Canada in May 1943 and enlisted in the Royal Canadian Engineers, where he attained the rank of Lieutenant. He entered active service in the Canadian Army on June 24th, 1943, according to his official military discharge letter."

The Canadian Army had decided that Stanley would best suit their needs as a military engineer, rather than leaving him to make his contribution to the war effort as a civilian mining engineer. By sheer good fortune, the Army's decision gave Stanley and Alice a chance to start the next phase of their marriage together. Most new military recruits are immediately sent to boot camp, often far away from family and friends, and immersed in an intense basic training program that changes them into another person altogether.

Alice has spoken of an idyllic period early in Stanley's military career spent at Cultus Lake near Vancouver, during the summer, when they lived in a small cottage by the lake. She recounted to Karen that she would swim across the lake to fetch the mail every day, one of her favorite memories of that period. As relative newlyweds, this was a summer of grace and enchantment for Alice, and probably for Stanley as well, in spite of the gravity of his situation as he prepared to go to war.

Top left: A view of Cultus Lake; Above left: The house on Cultus Lake where Alice and Stanley lived while he was in basic training in 1943; Above right: Stan at Camp Chilliwack, wearing his summer uniform (all SPC); Below right: King George VI cap badge issued in the Second World War to be worn by all members of the Royal Canadian Engineers, including Stanley [Editor's note – This badge can be seen on Stanley's dress cap in the photo on the previous page]

Nearby Camp Chilliwack had opened several months after the bombing of Pearl Harbor and housed several army units for territorial defense. By 1943, as the threat of Japanese invasion became more intense, Camp Chilliwack was expanded to house both the No. 112 Canadian Army Basic Training Centre and the A6 Canadian Engineering Training Centre, making it possible for Stanley to obtain dual training at one location. Stanley and Alice were apparently able to live together in the cottage on Cultus Lake while Stanley received military basic training and later military engineering training.

Stanley spent time at both Camp Chilliwack and Camp Petawawa during the necessary

training that would enable him to become a competent military engineer, starting in June of 1943. Since the world was at war, the focus was on combat engineering, whose official role "was to allow friendly troops to live, move and fight on the battlefield, and to deny that to the enemy". This was a big job, to say the least. A combat engineer's many responsibilities included the use of demolition explosives and land mines; the design, construction and maintenance of defensive works and fortifications; breaching obstacles; establishing/maintaining lines of communication; and building bridges. Engineers also provided water, power and other utilities; fire, aircraft crash and rescue services; hazardous material operations; and they were required to develop maps and other appropriate engineering intelligence, along with methods of concealment.

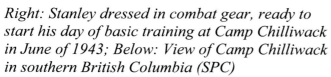

Right: Stanley dressed in combat gear, ready to start his day of basic training at Camp Chilliwack in June of 1943; Below: View of Camp Chilliwack in southern British Columbia (SPC)

Although the list might have seemed overwhelming to a new recruit, one must assume that most of the training Stanley received would have been mostly basic and introductory in nature.

His training and experience as a mining engineer would have given him a certain advantage in a military setting, since he was already something of an expert in turning trees into timbers that were used to shore up mine tunnels, not to mention the use of explosives in tunneling out mine shafts, the use of hazardous materials in mine smelting, along with the establishment and maintenance of electricity and water. Over time Stanley's talents might also eventually have qualified him to focus on a specialty area requiring advanced training.

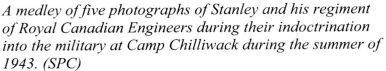

A medley of five photographs of Stanley and his regiment of Royal Canadian Engineers during their indoctrination into the military at Camp Chilliwack during the summer of 1943. (SPC)

Stanley took many photographs recording his experiences in the Army. Alice never said how Stanley felt about his time in the army, but he was careful to document as much of it as he could. Suffice it to say that Stanley was up to the task and seems to have thrived in his role as a combat engineer. Pictures usually show him relaxed and smiling.

A medley of six photographs recording, from top left clockwise: Combat arms field training; Bridge building in a rough environment using logs that have been cut down by the engineers; Stanley lying close to the ground using headphones for field communications; Stanley and a fellow soldier in the field beside their large field radio; Combat engineers building a smaller bridge across a swampy area (SPC)

Five photos showing, from top left clockwise: Alice standing on the porch of their house on Cultus Lake; Stanley "at work"; Alice with friends on the lakeshore; View of Cultus Lake (SPC)

Four photos showing Alice all smiles, from the top left clockwise: Standing on a huge, ancient tree stump (one can only guess how she got up there); Standing amid the grandeur of a Canadian forest; Walking across a bridge in summer dress; Wearing a favorite dress from her South America days, probably dressed for a special occasion that she and Stanley were attending (SPC)

Next Stop: Ontario

Meanwhile, Alice was spending one of the happiest and most carefree summers of her life. The photos Stanley took of their summer idyll together suggest a blissful state of mind.

After basic and military engineering training at Chilliwack, Stanley moved to Camp Petawawa in the Ottawa Valley of eastern Canada, sometime in the autumn of 1943. It is located 110 miles northwest of Ottawa along the western bank of the Ottawa River at its junction with the Petawawa River, near Pembroke. It is also located 180 miles east of Sudbury, where Stanley had his first job at the Frood Mine right out of college. Stanley's move marked the end of the "honeymoon" for our two heroes as Alice remained behind in Spokane, living with her parents.

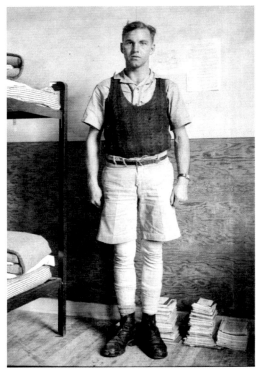

Four photos of Stanley's time at Camps Petawawa and Brockville, Ontario, where he received advanced combat engineer training in the company of other combat engineering recruits. (SPC)

During the Second World War, the camp was the site of three training centers (two artillery and one engineering), with 20,000 troops undergoing training at one time in 1943 during Stanley's time there. This next phase of Stanley's training elevated him from basic trainee status to that of a full-fledged officer in the Royal Canadian Engineers, with artillery and winter training also on the agenda at the camp. Letters would have to suffice for Stanley and Alice, for the most part. Stanley's time in Ontario was divided between Camp Petawawa and Camp Brockville, which was 140 miles from Petawawa on the St. Lawrence River, an hour south of Ottawa. From Stanley's photo collection it appears that much of this training occurred in the field, and mostly in winter.

Three photos of Stanley's residence in Pembroke while he was stationed at Camp Petawawa, including a photo recording Alice's visit at Christmas, the tree they decorated together, and Alice baking Christmas goodies in a very rustic 1940s kitchen. (SPC)

Karen recollects Alice saying that she was able to join Stanley in Pembroke for Christmas 1943, but being apart from their families out west they were lonely, in spite of being together. Stanley procured a small Christmas tree and they made Christmas as festive as possible, given their limited circumstances. At least Stanley wasn't deployed overseas to a combat zone, like so many of his contemporaries. For most of the duration of the war he and Alice were unable to be together. Loneliness and longing became part of their daily routine during those long years.

Stanley and Alice were reunited at least once in 1944, when Stanley obtained leave from the Army and they met in Sicamous for a family visit. According to an article in a Surrey newspaper, Stanley also met two of his Buckingham sisters for the first time in 24 years during his leave. Alice took the train to Sicamous from Spokane to meet him with a large bouquet of freshly cut flowers from the Frank Kappel family garden, along with other local women whose husbands were allowed to take leave to see their families.

Above left: Alice waiting at the train station in the October of 1944 for Stanley to arrive on leave from Camp Petawawa; Above right: Stanley and Alice together on Shuswap Lake in 1944 during the Stanley's summer leave from the Army that year; They stayed with Frank and Janet Kappel in Sicamous. Below left: Winter training at Camp Brockville just prior to the completion of Stanley's training (SPC)

Stanley remained in Ontario until February of 1945 and continued his training as a combat engineer. The invasion of Normandy by the Allied Forces occurred in June of 1944 and marked a major turning point in WWII. The Germans were in retreat, and it seemed only a matter of time until the war would be over. This caused a major shift in the strategy of the Allies from "enemy destroying" to "nation rebuilding", and Stanley suddenly found himself to be an asset to the Canadian Army that had nothing to do with his training and experience as an engineer. His commanders were aware of his many talents: he was bright, competent, multi-lingual, and had spent two years living in South America in challenging circumstances that involved ongoing negotiations with local politicians and labor unions, along with the growing ambitions of the Ecuadorian government to reclaim a larger share of the wealth that was being extracted by the Americans from their country's mineral resources.

Right: The US School of Military Government and Civil Affairs Training School in Virginia, where Stanley attended basic instruction in Civil Affairs starting in February 1945; All of the people on the steps of the school are wearing their respective nation's military uniform. Below right: Stanley enjoying the company of a fellow military attendee at the Civil Affairs Training School in Virginia, 1945 (both photos from SPC)

Next Stop: Virginia, then on to California

As a result, Stanley was transferred February 18th, 1945, to attend the US School of Military Government and Civil Affairs Training School, located at Charlottesville, Virginia, for a basic introduction to the principles of Civil Affairs, completing his training April 30th. After completing that phase of his training, he was transferred to Palo Alto, California, where he studied the Japanese language, culture, and government at Stanford University.

According to Wikipedia: "World War II saw the U.S. Army receive its Civil Affairs "charter." The Pentagon in

1943 activated the U.S. Army Civil Affairs Division (CAD). The major problem faced by the CAD was heavy destruction of the infrastructure of both Europe and Japan due to the Allies' efforts to stop the land and power grab undertaken by Germany, Japan, and Italy. Never before or since has U.S. Army Civil Affairs been so extensively involved in nation rebuilding for so long. The CAD was responsible for 80 million European civilians. Post-war military government proved extremely successful in our former enemies' nations.

"The CAD also returned untold millions of dollars' worth of national treasures to their countries of origin. The post-war period was the first planned use of Civil Affairs by the modern United States Army, and the greatest use of CAD assets to date."

Three photos of Stanford University, where Stanley spent several months in early 1945 studying the Japanese language and culture in anticipation of being sent to live in Japan during the post-war period to participate in the repatriation of that vanquished nation at the end of the Second World War (all from SPC)

During his time in California, Stanley had enough free time available to take several memorable trips to regional sights, including Yosemite Valley and Sequoia National Park in the Sierra Nevada Mountains. His photos also record that he took at least one ski trip, something he hadn't been able to do during the past five years since leaving his beloved Shuswap. The trip included stops high into the mountains, with one photo, presumably taken by Stanley, of the spectacular view of Upper and Lower Yosemite Falls.

Medley of photos, from top left clockwise: Stanley skiing in the Sierra Nevada Mountains; Bus trip to Yosemite Valley and Sequoia National Park with Yosemite Falls in the background; Giant sequoia with military tourists standing at its foot; Iconic photo of Upper and Lower Yosemite Falls, probably taken by Stanley (SPC)

Left: The commons at Stanford University, 1945 (SPC)

It was a feather in Stanley's cap that he was chosen by the Canadian Army to be trained to help rebuild Japan. Frank Kappel had done the same thing in Europe for several months after the end of the First World War: ferreting out intelligence on the local population regarding how well they were adjusting to their country being occupied. Stanley's training would have prepared him to do the same kind of work in Japan.

Fortunately for him and Alice, he was never called to serve in that role.

While Stanley attended civil affairs training in Virginia and California, Alice, now pregnant, remained behind with her parents in Spokane. On July 19th, 1945, Karen was born at Deaconess Hospital with Alice's sister Eve the only family member in attendance. Stanley was unable to get leave from his intense training and remained in California at the time of the delivery. In fact, he did not see his first child until several months after her birth.

This was still another difficult consequence of the war that left Alice and Stanley both lonely and disappointed since Stanley had desperately wanted to be with Alice when she delivered Karen. Things, however, changed dramatically for the young family within two months after Karen's birth. The war ended rather abruptly, and nations began their efforts to return to normal as quickly as possible.

Right: Karen's baby picture, taken in 1945

Meanwhile, Stanley's sister, Betty, returned to the Shuswap district from Ottawa as soon as the war ended while Stanley and Alice continued their own journey together. At some point Betty met Bill Ingram, who lived in Kamloops, they fell in love and were married in June of 1945, as previously documented. Since Stanley was in California during the summer of 1945 and wasn't even able to attend the birth of his first daughter in July, it seems unlikely that he was able to attend his sister's wedding in Sicamous. Such is the reality of war. It is no small matter that Stanley survived WWII intact, without having to experience the deep trauma of day-to-day combat in a hostile environment, far away from one's home and loved ones, and was able to resume a civilian life with his family soon after Karen's birth.

Right: Telegram sent from a proud grandmother (Alice's mother, Marianne) to Karen's Canadian grandparents (Karen was their first grandchild) (provided by Lynne and Roger Beeson)

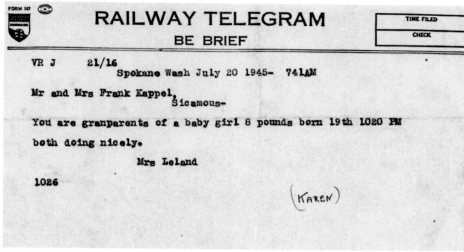

Here is a transcription of an airmail letter hand-written to Dora (Stanley's younger sister, Marie) by Stanley. It is postmarked: "Stanford University, Calif., Aug 14, 1945; addressed to Mrs. Hugh C. Dunbar, 725 Pine St. Kamloops, B.C., Canada; from S.E. Kappel Lt., Box 2681, Stanford U., Cal.; dated 13 Aug 45:

"My Dearest Dora,

"I am very bad as usual in writing letters, but I have been pretty busy, and I write Alice every day, so I don't do much else in the correspondence way."

"A lot has happened since I wrote last. I am now a proud papa of a daughter, Karen Rae who was born at Spokane on 19th of July this year & weighing 7# 14 oz. Alice had a very tough labor, from Sunday to Thursday & here I was unable to get up there. She is fine now but made a slow recovery as she had to be operated on in order to facilitate the birth. She says the baby is just fine and has her eyes & my hands and a dimple on her chin. I am sure looking forward to seeing her. I may get a leave when this course is over at the end of Sept. As a matter of fact, we expect it to be over sooner if the Japs give up very soon, so we don't know where we are at. I don't think I'll get up to Canada, though, unless I'm posted for discharge, as the travelling situation is very bad now, & especially with a baby.

"I am doing fairly well here & have obtained good grades so far. I got an A- in area study & a B+ in Japanese for the quarter. We are working in individual groups now in the afternoons and so it is more interesting taking this Mil. Gov't. work.

"We have a softball team in the Stanford league & came second in the first half. It is a lot of fun & good exercise. I am quite tanned and about as brown as I was in South America.

"Right now, I am really just marking time until that leave comes & I surely hope I am not disappointed.

"I hope you & Jeanie are keeping well and that Hugh is getting along fine in his work. I'm sure you will be a happy & grateful girl when he comes home for good. I hope the time passes quickly for you. Do you ever see Betty at all? If you do you probably know all the stuff, I've told you already, but it doesn't matter. How are May & Laura? Has Harvie been discharged yet or will he go to the Pacific? I hope I can get up to see them when I return to Canada & that we'll be able to see you far longer than just a few minutes this time.

"Well sweet, I will close for now. Write when you can. Give Jeanie a kiss for me."

"Love & kisses, Stan"

Left: Two photos of Karen and Stanley in 1945 before they moved to Sheep Creek (SPC)

Stanley very likely rejoined Alice and Karen in Spokane in September, given the letter he wrote to Marie that is dated 13 Aug 45. His homecoming was undoubtedly both joyous and challenging, since he and Alice had spent most of the past two years apart, but now there was a third member in the family. And very soon their reunion was disrupted by further business with the military. Frank Kappel's brief biography of Stanley states he was released from active duty in the Canadian Army in October 1945, although he wasn't "officially discharged" until February 1946. It appears that Stanley remained in the Army Standing Reserve until 1948 because a letter he wrote to the Army asking for advice on whether or not he should continue in reserve status is dated 1948.

Left: Photo of Alice with newborn baby Karen in her lap, sitting among members of her family in Spokane; This photo was taken by Stanley shortly after he returned from California. Other adults in the photo include Margaret (with baby Susanne), George (next to Marianne), Evelyn, and Anna Belle (SPC)

A newspaper clipping from the Surrey Leader, dated October 18, 1945, provides interesting insight into Stanley's playful side and the fact that he was able to spend time with his wife and family during this period: "Violet Goldney *[Ed. note – Stanley's niece]* celebrated her 8th birthday on Sunday with an afternoon party at which 16 small guests were present. The table was daintily decorated in pink, blue and white with a cake in the same color scheme forming the centrepiece. Highlight of the day was the unexpected arrival of "Uncle Stan", Lt. Stanley Kappel, brother of Mrs. Wm. Goldney and Mrs. H. McKibbon. This was the second time the sisters had seen their brother in 25 years, the first time being just a year ago. Stan was adopted by a family friend at the age of two, when their mother passed away."

Stanley was already busy with Karen's baby book, which he kept up diligently until he became ill in 1951. Here is one of his first entries in the book: "10-6-45: Father's 27th birthday; 10-7-45: Father left for Vancouver where he is expecting to get a discharge from the Royal Canadian Engineers."

Karen remembers Alice telling her that she was left with her grandmother, Marianne Leland, while Alice made a trip with Stanley. It seems likely that Alice may have accompanied her husband to Vancouver to attend his discharge from the army, giving them well-deserved time to become reacquainted, as well as an important opportunity to meet members of Stanley's family.

Life would never be the same for Alice and Stanley. They were able to enjoy four years together as lovers and newlyweds, and in spite of being separated for relatively long periods, those years had been kind to them, considering what could have been. But now they were a family that included baby Karen, and most of their time in the future would be focused away from their marriage and toward family life, with everything that requires.

Most newly married couples were "blessed" with a child during their first year of marriage, but Alice and Stanley did not become parents during their first 2 ½ years together. And another four years would pass before their second child was born, baby Kristen.

Right: Stanley in Spokane in the summer of 1945, sitting astride a motorcycle belonging to one of Alice's brothers, ready to take to the open road, obviously feeling the deep reality of his newly acquired freedom at the end of the Second World War (SPC)

Five photos taken by Stanley during his time at the Sheep Creek Mining Camp southeast of Salmo, BC, where he worked intermittently between 1935 and 1947 (SPC)

CHAPTER 19 – Family Life in the Sheep Creek Mining Area

Above: This is probably what Sheep Creek looked like when Alice and Karen arrived for the first time in December of 1945. (SPC)

After his release from the Army, somewhere between October 1945 and February 1946, Stanley and Alice moved to Sheep Creek, south of Nelson, British Columbia, near its border with the United States, where Stanley had started his mining career right out of high school in 1936. This time, however, he worked as a mining engineer at the gold mines both at Sheep Creek and Zincton, according to Frank Kappel. Alice once told Karen that it was thrilling to both her and Stanley, when they first met in Portovelo, that she had once worked as a nurse in Ione, Washington, only 50 miles from Sheep Creek.

Stanley was released from the Army in October 1945 and apparently went to work for the Sheep Creek Mine very soon. He spent at least a month in Sheep Creek, becoming acquainted with his new employers and the mining operations, as well as preparing the new home that he would occupy with Alice and Karen for the next 1 ½ years. Alice remembers that before she and Karen moved to Sheep Creek, Stanley drove into Nelson and came back with a beautiful porcelain China tea service and furniture to furnish their new home, a small cabin in the woods at the bottom of the steep canyon. Stanley's taste was so refined that some of the furniture he chose is still being enjoyed by his daughters in their homes.

The Kappels spent their first Christmas (1945) at Sheep Creek in their "new home". Stanley wrote in Karen's baby book regarding Karen's first Christmas: "At Sheep Creek, B.C., where she and Mother arrived Dec 8 from Spokane. There was lots of fun playing with the parcel wrappings and the many new rattles. A host of other gifts included four baby dresses, booties, slippers, exerciser, locket."

Above left: Alice's commentary on back of Stanley's photo: "Sheep Creek Gold Mine in British Columbia in white below the high mountains where we didn't see the sun for several months in the year" (SPC); Below left: Stanley and Alice's home in the Sheep Creek mining area in winter (SPC)

A telling article appeared in the Vernon News on March 14, 1946, entitled **Grindrod News Items** (Grindrod is a hamlet in southern B.C. that is located on the western banks of the Shuswap River north of Enderby): "Mrs. J. Bailey left on Wednesday for Salmon Arm where she will enter the hospital as private nurse to Mrs. Kappel, of Sicamous." Janet was eight years Frank's senior, and she passed away on April 6, 1946, at the age of 68, shortly after Stanley was discharged from the Army and he and Alice, with their new baby, had moved to Sheep Creek to restart their life together after so many years of war and separation. Janet Kappel apparently suffered from Parkinson's disease, and the devastating impact on Frank is clear. Stanley left no written record of how he felt about his adopted mother, but Janet's death must have been a source of great sadness to him, losing the only mother he had ever really known, at a time when life was really beginning to open up for him.

Left: Alice standing next to the home she shared with Stanley and Karen, Sheep Creek, winter 1946-47 (SPC)

Meanwhile, Alice remained a contented partner in the drama that was unfolding for them both at the end of Stanley's military stint: the start of their family together with their first child. Alice later told Karen that the period when they lived in Sheep Creek gold mining camp, far away from the outside world, was one of the best times in her entire life.

The small family lived in a "doll's house" of a cottage near the edge of a rushing creek in a deep canyon, with walls so steep that the sun would not shine on their home for several months during the winter. The setting was ruggedly beautiful, according to Alice.

Above: The Stanley Kappel home at Sheep Creek in summer, with Alice standing on the front steps (SPC); Left: Karen at age one during her first summer with her parents at Sheep Creek (SPC)

Winters were cold and snowy, and with no way to easily connect with the outside world by telephone, no radio or television, they could concentrate on baby Karen and the process of making a new life for themselves, together in the wilderness.

The mining camp was devoid of any retail stores, and all supplies had to be ordered by mail or messenger and brought in from the outside, with deliveries occurring only once a week. There wasn't even a post office in the camp, so all mail was carried and delivered to and from the outside world by company employees. Alice said that the only produce they received was delivered by a

Chinese grocer from Nelson every week. Around the same time Alice's brothers, Roy, and Bill, both young men curious to see what the Stanley Kappels were up to, took a load of items from Spokane up to Sheep Creek in order to help jump-start this latest adventure for the young family.

Left: Stanley and Alice with Karen in 1946; Karen is fondling Stanley's camera case. (SPC)

Stanley apparently loved working underground, and he excelled as a mining engineer. He clearly didn't shy away from taking heavy responsibilities on himself. Broadly speaking, these would have included: planning and designing the development of mine shafts and tunnels, devising the means of extracting minerals from the rock, and

selecting the methods to be used in transporting the minerals to the surface. Additional responsibilities would almost certainly have included supervising other mining operations, as well as assuming responsibility for mine safety, inspecting all areas within the mining complex for unsafe structures, equipment, and working conditions.

Above right and below left: Two photos of the Sheep Creek mine in winter (SPC)

Imagine how challenging yet important it would be to ensure that the air the miners were breathing had adequate amounts of oxygen and was free of poisonous toxins; that the roof of the mine shaft wouldn't collapse and trap the miners; that the equipment transporting miners deep into the mine wouldn't break down, or the cables and brakes wouldn't fail, causing the elevator to tumble rapidly downward into darkness and disaster.

Right: Topographical map of the Salmo District, including Sheep Creek; The area circled in red with the circled G in the center is approximately where the Sheep Creek Mining Camp was located, and where Stanley, Alice and Karen lived for more than 19 months in 1945-46. (backroadmapbooks. com)

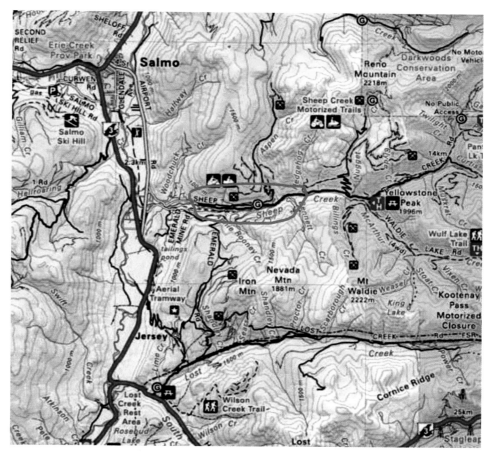

These are just a few of the threats and concerns that might confront a mining engineer every day, and it points to the fact that overseeing a mining operation is not for the timid, the faint-hearted, or the incompetent. It is clear to this writer that succeeding as a mining engineer demands a high degree of technical competence, personal courage, managerial savvy, and effective leadership skills.

Right: Karen, age two, cooling off in the summer heat with the only other child living in the Sheep Creek mining camp, the mine superintendent's son (SPC)

Alice was deeply proud of her husband and told Karen that in all the time she was with Stanley while he was in charge of mining operations, there were never any safety infractions, and no serious mining disasters occurred under his careful management.

According to an extensive geologic survey conducted around 2017 by the Mineral Deposit Research Unit (MDRU), an internationally recognized collaborative venture between the mining industry and the Department of Earth, Ocean, and Atmospheric Sciences at The University of British Columbia (UBC): "The Sheep Creek gold camp, 7 miles southeast of the town of Salmo in the Kootenay region of southern British Columbia, is part of the broader Salmo mining district. The Sheep Creek gold camp comprises numerous underground mine workings within an approximately 6 mile-long, north-trending belt of mineralized quartz veins. Mining operations were conducted from 1899 to 1951 and produced gold, silver, lead, and zinc. Mine shafts extended down to 1,600 feet below the surface. By 1951, the mines had produced a total of 46,000 pounds of gold and 23,000 pounds of silver."

Stanley's career prospered at Sheep Creek. He was "learning the ropes" of the mining business, and his reputation as a highly competent mining engineer and manager was growing by leaps and bounds. As a result, the family's tenure in that relatively small mining camp in southern British Columbia was short-lived, lasting less than two years.

Above left: Stanley holding a shotgun in the mountains around Sheep Creek; Above right: A field hunting outing with friends near Sheep Creek Mining Camp that includes a small boat which may have been used to retrieve ducks or geese (SPC)

Looking at Stanley's photographs from that period, it is apparent that he participated in local activities with colleagues and friends such as prospecting, bird hunting, deer hunting, and hiking. He and Alice were able to visit Alice's family in Spokane on a regular basis.

The Stanley Kappels spent their second Christmas at Sheep Creek, according to Stanley's entry in Karen's baby book: "At Sheep Creek, B.C. Much more interest this year & some lovely presents from Santa Claus, Grandpa Kappel & Grandpa & Grandma Leland & all her aunties & uncles. Three dolls, one of which she got from Santa at the concert – going up all by herself to get it".

According to Frank Kappel: "The family remained at Sheep Creek until July 1947, when Stanley obtained a job with the Federal Mining and Smelting Company at Wallace, Idaho, as mine and safety engineer for FM&SCO, which operated mines in the Coeur d'Alene Mountains." This was a major step up the corporate ladder for Stanley. The mining operations in the Coeur d' Alene mining district were larger than the Sheep Creek gold mining camp by several orders of magnitude. And although this meant saying farewell to Sheep Creek, it also meant a major increase in challenge and responsibility for Stanley, as well as significant improvement in both status and income. And it meant moving to an indisputably beautiful part of America that today advertises itself as "the Northwest's Playground", with Wallace even claiming to be "the center of the universe" and the "richest mining town still in existence".

Below left and right: A medley of photos taken by Stanley at Sheep Creek, including, from the top left clockwise: Young Karen playing in the snow with neighbors A fellow deer hunter in autumn; A charming photo of five children taken in Spokane when they were visiting Alice's family; Two Leland siblings, Evelyn and Roy astride motorcycles; And a fellow mining prospector on a weekend outing (SPC).

Four photos taken in the summer of 1947, when the Stanley Kappel family moved from Sheep Creek Mining Camp to the Coeur d'Alene mining district in northern Idaho to take a job with the Federal Mining & Smelting Company in Wallace; The photo in the lower left corner was taken at Liberty Lake in the Spokane Valley. The other three photos were probably taken in the garden of William and Marianne Leland. This was a major step in the life of Stanley and his family as they began living together in America for the first time and Stanley continued to make his way up the corporate mining ladder. (SPC)

CHAPTER 20 – A Portrait of Stanley Kappel

Those of us who are curious about Stanley have been looking long and hard at photographs, reading scrapbook and photo album captions, discovering precious letters written by him, and hearing stories from those who knew him personally. He died more than 70 years ago, and he has always seemed elusive to this writer. Be that as it may, I would like now to write down a few of the personal traits his story suggests in hopes of gaining a clearer understanding of what sort of person he was.

Biometrics (taken from Stanley's Canadian passport circa 1940):

- Height: 5' 11"
- Color of eyes: blue
- Color of hair: fair

Personal characteristics that are derived from what are observable in photos, from observations offered by those who knew him personally or were in some way acquainted with him, from newspaper articles, and from inference:

- Very good looking but not embarrassingly handsome
- Possessed an athletic physique but was not a pretty boy
- Competitive and competent in many different sports
- A varsity letterman in hockey while in college
- Outgoing, but in a quiet, thoughtful way
- Naturally self-confident and self-assured, but not overbearing or cocky
- Radiated a natural warmth and charm; blessed with a good sense of humor
- At ease with himself; comfortable in his own skin
- Kind, gentle, and helpful; possessed a very pleasant disposition
- A tender-hearted soul who was unafraid of expressing his tender feelings
- Didn't seek to attract attention to himself
- Affable and affectionate, always had lots of friends
- Sensitive but not overtly self-obsessed or narcissistic
- Comfortable in the world of men, including highly successful men
- Comfortable with women his age but not overly flirtatious
- Focused but not too intense
- Passionate about recording his life in photographic images
- Highly competent, a creative problem-solver
- Very bright; multi-lingual, curious and analytical
- A "man of many talents", could fix almost anything
- Ambidextrous, according to his father, and could golf with either hand
- Earnestly ambitious but not ruthless
- Easy-going and a calming presence in the company of others
- A team player, not a Machiavellian self-promoter
- Thoughtful, compassionate, and sincere
- A good husband and father; Alice said he always wanted to have a family
- A genuinely nice person whom I would want to have as my friend

Stanley's executive talents were first recognized in college: he was elected as an officer in the Theta Tau engineering fraternity the first year that he became a member (junior year) and remained an elected officer throughout his entire period of membership in that fraternity. The fact that he wasn't elected to the highest office suggests that he was not overly ambitious, and probably didn't nominate himself but was nominated by someone who knew and respected him. It is also remarkable that he was a foreigner at MSM, yet his fraternity brothers trusted him so much that they entrusted the management of the fraternity to him.

Stanley had everything it takes to become successful in the corporate world. He was outgoing, attractive, athletic, affable, warm, friendly, funny, charming, sincere, at ease with himself, intelligent, focused, competent, ambitious, compassionate, and comfortable in the world of men.

By the time Stanley arrived in the Kellogg mining district in 1947, he seems to have entered the exclusive community of men who are acknowledged by their superiors as being ready to become upper-level executives. One indicator that he had "arrived" was his resumption of golfing with his colleagues every weekend at the local golf club near Kellogg. He was also blessed with a beautiful wife and three pretty daughters, something that wouldn't have gone unnoticed or unappreciated by Stanley's superiors.

Stanley's Camera

Judging from the many photos and photographic negatives Stanley accumulated and archived over the course of his life, it is clear that he held the captured photographic image in high esteem. Many of the photos in his extensive collection include him as a subject, so other photographers were involved. These may have included family members and friends. His parents and sister were both dedicated to the arts, for example, and almost surely appreciated Stanley's enthusiasm for photography. Had it not been for Stanley's camera, coupled with his nearly obsessive desire to document many of his life's most important events, much of what we know about his relatively short life would be lost to the past. He was fond of calling his photos "snaps", short for snapshots.

Left: A photo of Stanley's camera, the Kodak Senior Six-20, that was available for the first time in 1939; It is a relatively small (3.75 x 6.75 x 2.5 inches) folding camera that would have been fairly easy to carry anywhere. This is the camera that Stanley left behind when he died, although it is uncertain how long he owned or used it. (The Henry Ford Museum of Innovation)

CHAPTER 21 – Life, Love, and Death in the Kellogg Mining District

From Frank Kappel's memoir: "In 1949 Stanley moved to the Page Mine as assistant mine superintendent and remained in that position until 1952." Stanley's new job meant another move, this time to Kellogg, just down the valley from Wallace, and Karen remembers those years and their life as a family in a charming wood-frame house with great fondness.

Above left: Bitterroot Mountain Range scenery above Mullan, Idaho (SPC)

Above right: Stanley on a hike above Mullan (SPC)

That final period would bring two new members into the family: Kristen Lee, who was born in March of 1950, and Kerry Lynne, who was born in May of 1951. It is absolutely clear that Stanley loved his wife and his three daughters, and he had made for them a prosperous life full of hope and possibility. Alice told Karen that Stanley wanted to have 5 daughters "because of his 5 sisters".

Right: Kellogg main street, ca. 1948 (SPC)

Moving from Sheep Creek to the Coeur d'Alene mining district in 1947 was an important event in the life of the three Kappels. It reflected what the future held in store for Stanley and his growing

family. In addition to being an acknowledgment of Stanley's talent, accomplishments, and potential as a future mining industry executive, it was also a further indication of the quality of education he had obtained at the Montana School of Mines.

Left: Early photo of the Page Mine, where Stanley was assistant superintendent during his first assignment with the *Federal Mining and Smelting Company at Wallace, Idaho; He was also* the *mine and safety engineer for the Company. Below right: Silver miners, Kellogg, early 20th century (SPC)*

MSM graduates and others who admired them formed a world-wide network of contacts in the mining industry who appreciated the breadth and depth of knowledge that serious students of the mining industry could be expected to procure during their time in Butte.

Stanley was stepping into the "big leagues" when they arrived in Mullan, but it was also yet another big test of his abilities as a mining engineer and executive manager. Stanley had attracted the attention of the

international mining corporate establishment, and they had high hopes for him, according to Alice.

Left: Bunker Hill & Sullivan mining smelter, Kellogg, ca. 1921 [Ed, note – This writer worked in the same smelter complex during the summer of 1964.]

Medley of photos taken by Stanley during visits to the Leland home in Spokane when the Kappels were living in northern Idaho, from top left clockwise: William, Lloyd, Stanford and Albert; Marianne; William in the garden, planting and walking (SPC)

#6 TENNIS AVE
MULLAN IDAHO, U.S.A

Above left: The first Kappel home in Mullan, Idaho, where Stanley took his first job in the US; Above right: Kitchen in Mullan home on Tennis Avenue; Both ca. 1948 (SPC)

Karen remembers the home they moved into near Wallace in the tiny town of Mullan. Their new house, located at #6 Tennis Avenue, was a white, wood-frame structure with a spacious front porch. Karen and Alice took regular walks on a pretty forest trail into Mullan to collect the mail and shop at the local general store for groceries and dry goods. On Sundays they all attended the local Emmanuel Episcopal Church in Kellogg.

Alice and Stanley kept a baby book for Karen, which we have in our possession. One entry in 1947 documented her birthday party: "Mullan, Idaho. Just moved to her new home, where Daddy will work with F.M. & S. Co. Already she has visited everyone on Tennis Ave, & has a new friend her age, Brian Williamson. She did not have a party this year and would not even eat her birthday cake Mommy made. When she is settled next year, she will have one. She got some nice presents and cards, but still does not realize what a birthday is. She says – "One, two old" in answer to "How old are you?"

Another entry by Stanley in Karen's baby book documents Karen's third Christmas: "At Mullan, Idaho. Fascinated by the Xmas tree and loved all her gifts. Daddy made her a blue table & chair, and she had her own tree on it. Santa also brought a doll buggy, a dressed magic-skin doll, a Dydee doll, 2 tea sets, a phone and 2 small dolls. We went to Spokane at Xmas Eve - Santa came to see K. & all her cousins at Grandma's & Grandpa's. Karen was scared stiff. She had seen the Santa that afternoon, too, in Penny's store & he scared her a little. She had a lot of fun, though, in Spokane with all her cousins – she especially likes Robby."

Still another note written by Stanley documents Karen's fourth birthday: "Her first birthday party at Mullan, Idaho. Guests were Karen & Sharon Nelson, Olivia & Phillip Baughman, Trudy Moldenhauer. After showing her gifts & playing some games, Mother took all the party to the park to play some more, then home to supper & to show Daddy all her new things."

Stanley also chronicled Karen's fourth Christmas, in 1948: "We all went to Spokane to Grandpa & Grandma's & sure enough Santa found out & what do you think – brought a wagon, rocking horse, truck, puzzles & many other lovely things. All the cousins (2 more by now) came up Xmas day to see the toys & play."

After they moved into their house in Kellogg in 1949, Stanley got up early on cold mornings to stoke the basement furnace with sawdust. One Christmas when Karen was five or six years old, she remembers awakening at 4:30am and going downstairs to find Stanley building and assembling a large, beautiful doll house for her.

If the Stanley Kappel family didn't spend Christmas in their own home, they usually spent it in Spokane with Alice's family. They also visited Stanley's family in BC regularly, especially in the summer. In Karen's baby book, which Stanley annotated regularly and carefully, he entered on the "First Trips" page: First zoo: Aug 1948 – Vancouver, BC, Stanley Park; first circus: 16 Jun 48 – Clyde Beatty, fed the elephants, saw tigers, lions, etc. *[Ed. note – the circus was probably in Kellogg or Wallace].*

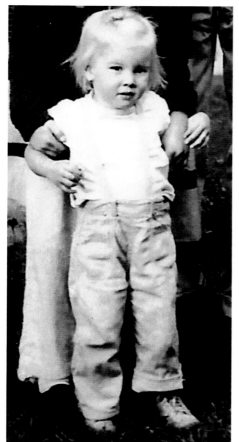

Left: Kristen at age 3; Her arrival in the Kappel household changed the family dynamics in a very positive way, but it also meant that both Stanley and Alice had less free time to annotate "baby book" details in the way they had been able to do for Karen, who was nearly 4 years old when Kristen was born. Below right: Photo taken by Stanley on the ski hill at Lookout Mountain, near Kellogg, ca. 1948 (SPC)

Kristen Lee Kappel was born in the community hospital in Wallace, Idaho, on March 11, 1949. During 1949 the family moved into a larger home in Kellogg. Kerry Lynne Kappel was born on May 3rd, 1950. Stanley annotated Karen's baby book with details of all three girls' growth and development.

Left: Photo of the Lookout Mountain ski area taken by Stanley, ca. 1949 (SPC)

Alice remembered that Stanley used to ski down Lookout Mountain with Karen on his back. She said that Stanley was very sporty and excelled as a skier, ski jumper, swimmer, and golfer. In Portovelo he had even played polo with the Americans! He would also take Karen golfing on weekends to give Alice some time to herself (and Karen's younger sisters). While he golfed with friends, Karen played happily on the swings and other playground equipment in the company of other children and mothers in attendance.

Left: Photo of Frank Kappel with his two granddaughters in 1949; Karen, standing, is four, and Dale Ingram, sitting, is two. (provided by Lynne and Roger Beeson)

Stanley played golf as a young man growing up in the Shuswap and took it up again after arriving in the Kellogg Mining District. Golf is the sport of executives: a combination of conversation, competition, performance, and athleticism that usually involves four men, preferably extroverts, spending an extended period of time together, walking, talking, connecting, networking, establishing a bond of mutual respect and confidence, comfortable enough with themselves not to allow the game to intimidate them; a sense of humor is optional but profoundly appreciated; not obsessing about each shot and whether or not the ball goes where you want it to go is supremely important; being able to laugh at yourself if your ball ends up in the trees is perhaps the most important test of a true executive. Playing golf on Saturdays was just one more indication that Stanley had fully entered the executive phase of his stellar career.

Stanley wrote a Christmas card and note in late 1949 to Marie, that demonstrates his ambitions to work his way up the corporate ladder, along with the fact that the Kappel family had recently moved to Kellogg:

Christmas Greetings

AND BEST WISHES FOR A HAPPY NEW YEAR

MR. AND MRS. S. KAPPEL
AND FAMILY

"Dearest Dora,

"Long time no write – long time no see – long time. Not because we do not think of you folks & wish we would get over to Victoria but travelling & visiting with a family are not too easy to do these days. Perhaps when they get old enough, we make it – wish you & Hugh & the kids could come see us sometime, too. We have a new address – 318 Maple St, Kellogg, Idaho. I am asst. supt. at one of the mines about 5 miles from town so we moved down here to be a little closer. I like the work much better although it is longer hours & not too much more pay. The chances for advancement are, however, vastly better. I am still with the same company however."

"Karen & Kristen are just fine & if I ever take any I shall send some snaps. I intend doing so at Xmas time."

"Have fun at Xmas and stay sober both of you – this pen that writes under water should be there."

Love, Stan"

Right: Photo taken by Stanley of Alice, sitting on the front porch of their "new" home in Kellogg, Idaho, at 318 Maple Street, where the young Kappel family moved in 1949. This was the last home they shared together as a family, and was the home where Stanley spent his last days. It is the home where life really began to blossom into the fullness of its potential for the Stanley Kappels. (SPC)

Stanley wrote a final documentation of Karen's birthdays in Karen's baby book on her fifth birthday in 1950: "Karen's first birthday party in Kellogg. Her home is now at 318 Maple St. & she has found many new friends. Those at the party were Linda Kingsbury, Alma Dickinson, Gee Lookabaugh, Rene & Leslis, Mary & Julie Whitesel. Mother had a party planned for her out on the lawn, but it rained so she had it in the house instead and everyone had a wonderful time. After the party all the boys came in to look over the presents and the cake."

Karen remembers how excited she, Stanley and Alice were when Kristen and Kerry were born. Stanley chose Scandinavian names that started with "K" for all three of his girls. He was immensely proud of each of them.

Left: Kerry Lynne at age 1 in her father's arms when the last formal Stanley Kappel family photo was taken at their home in Kellogg in 1951 (SPC)

The Stanley Kappel family was growing rapidly, and no additional entries appear in Karen's baby book after Karen's fifth birthday.

Even the most jaded cynic couldn't help admiring and even envying Stanley and his family as they came to know one another and continued to grow comfortably into their idyllic circumstances. Alice said that Stanley had decided to become an American citizen after moving to the Coeur d'Alenes. In other words, he was intent on becoming a man with two sets of parents, as well as a man with two countries. This author, having spent many months examining the life of Stanley, and becoming aware of the profound sense of sincere patriotism that most Canadians seem to feel toward their country, is doubtful that Stanley was inclined to give up his Canadian citizenship to become a full-fledged American, though it is possible that he would have taken dual citizenship.

Right: Baptism records for the 3 Kappel girls; The baptisms were performed on June 24th, 1951, probably prior to Stanley's being diagnosed with testicular cancer, at Emmanuel Episcopal Church in Kellogg, Idaho. As previously noted, Karen remembers: "On Sundays we all attended the local Emmanuel Episcopal Church in Kellogg."

Whatever the case, none
of this was meant to be, and
this family's good fortune
was not meant to endure.
Fate, instead, turned
everything upside down.

At some point during the
autumn of 1951 Stanley
began to experience
symptoms in his pelvic area,
the nature of which are
unclear. Alice encouraged him to see a urologist
in Spokane, but he demurred. Instead, he saw the
local general practitioner, Dr. Glen Whitesel, who
treated him for an infection.

But his symptoms apparently didn't improve,
at least over the long run. Stanley eventually
agreed to travel Spokane, where he was diagnosed
by a specialist with advanced testicular cancer. He
remained in Spokane for treatment for an
unknown period of time, staying with Eve and
Rudy, Alice's sister and brother-in-law. Alice
remained in Kellogg with the 3 little girls.

*Right: Stanley Kappel Family in Kellogg: Alice,
Stanley, Kerry, Karen, and Kristen, 1951 (SPC)*

Meanwhile, Stanley traveled back and forth
between Kellogg and Spokane for ongoing
treatment of his cancer, continuing to work in the
mines as long as he could manage. This period in
his and Alice's life together was surely the most
difficult challenge they had ever had to face. Alice
said that Stanley spent a lot of time reading the
Bible, looking for answers, during his last year.
But in the end, Stanley's treatment failed, and his
health continued to decline. Eventually he was
admitted to the hospital in Kellogg because his
pain was so severe that he required frequent
morphine shots. Even then, the morphine didn't
control his pain, according to Alice.

Stanley wrote a Christmas card to Marie and her family in 1951:

"I wish you would put your address on your letters D. I am sending this via the navy so don't know whether you'll get it in time or not."

"We are all fine and looking forward to Xmas. Shopping almost all done and the tree ready to go up. I suppose with Hugh home you will have a big Christmas this year. We think the kids will get a big bang out of it this year with Kerry now 1 ½ & Kristen almost 3. Karen, of course knows the ropes but still believes in Santa Claus. She is doing very well in school – her first year & likes it very much."

"Well folks, must write some more elsewhere so shall close. The best in 1952 and a Merry Xmas."

Stan

[Ed. note – Under the Christmas card greeting is written: Alice, Stan & Karen, Kristen & Kerry. See below]

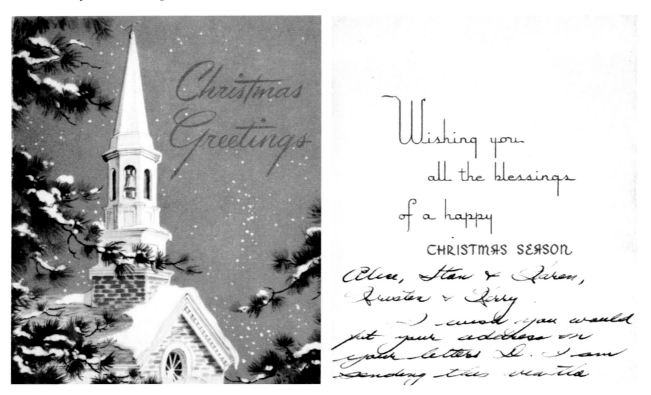

This would mark the Stanley Kappel family's last Christmas together.

After a year of struggling desperately to hold on, Stanley passed away in the hospital in Kellogg on July 4th, 1952.

Karen says she was at Dr. Whitesel's home, next door to the hospital, playing with his two daughters when Stanley died. She has always felt guilty that she wasn't there to be with him during his last minutes. Alice was with him at the end and said that she didn't want Karen to be present because he was screaming out in such pain.

Right: Alice and Stanley at home in Kellogg, 1951 (SPC)

Stanley wrote a letter to his sister, Marie, on April 30th, 1952, that reveals so much about what he was thinking and feeling at the time (only the second page of the letter survives):

"However, I was down at Spokane today for an examination again and Dr. Bracher, one of the outstanding men in the cancer field is going to have me take a series of treatments during the next 4 days. They are pretty drastic I guess, injections of nitrogen mustard into the vein, which will make me pretty sick, I guess. Apparently, this type of tumor I have is caused by the type of cancer that spreads very rapidly and it has now taken hold in my lungs where small tumors have already formed. I have been taking some pills - female sex hormone, which have arrested their growth and now this treatment I am about to take may or may not reduce the size of these and perhaps remove them. If it does not, then I will have to go to Seattle a couple of days to take activated phosphorus or iodine.

They are doing all that's humanly possible to check it and Dr. Bracher says that inasmuch as these pills have worked so well so far, he has hopes that they may be able to arrest it, at least, for a long time. So, I have about as good medical care as I could get, and the rest lies with God's will. I am most confident that I will get over this and be as well as ever again. These new treatments stop the bone marrow from making blood for a while so I will also have to get a bunch of blood transfusions in a couple of weeks. I am able to continue working......."

Stanley's letter was type-written, but the first part is not included, probably because Marie was too upset to keep it. However, Marie later hand-wrote in pencil below the letter: "I received two more letters after this one and both left me depressed for days. One was full of plans for visits back and forth between us and making sure that our children got to know each other and formed a bond that would last forever – "You and I missed so much of each other – the two youngest – we could have meant so much to each other" he wrote, and then the last letter was so different – no mention of daily treatments but rather written with the knowledge that the only meeting we would have together would be "in heaven" – "we must believe that because it <u>will</u> happen – pray for me." Thirty-three years old, <u>such</u> a waste. Alice and three wee girls whom he adored and who adored him. For five years we had been hoping for another baby – without any luck – but <u>less than 10 months later we had Donnie</u>. We gave him Stanley's real name – Donald, plus the name he was known by – Stanley. We were able to feel that the prayers we said when we prayed that Stanley wouldn't die had been answered. After all of this how could I <u>not</u> believe in God and the "wonders He performs".

Excerpts from Stanley's letter of April 30th 1952.
(died July 10th 1952)

"However, I was down at Spokane today for an examination again and Dr. Bracher, one of the outstanding men in the cancer field is going to have me take a series of treatments during the next 4 days. They are pretty drastic I guess, injections of nitrogen mustard into the vein, which will make me pretty sick I guess. Apparently this type of tumor I had is caused by the type of cancer that spreads very rapidly and it has now taken hold in my lungs where small tumors have already formed. I have been taking some pills – female sex hormone, which have arrested their growth and now this treatment I am about to take may or may not reduce the size of these and perhaps remove them. If it does not, then I will have to go to Seattle a couple of days to take activated phosphorus or iodine. They are doing all that's humanly possible to check it and Dr. Bracher says that inasmuch asthese pills have worked so well so far he has hopes that they may be able to arrest it, at least, for a long time. So, I have about as good medical care as I could get and the rest lies with God's will. I am most confident that I will get over this and be as well as ever again. These new treatments stop the bone marrow from making blood for a while so I will also have to get a bunch of blood transfusions in a couple of weeks. I am able to continue working........"

Left: One of the last letters ever written by Stanley, dated 30 April 1952, to his sister, Marie, with annotations by Marie penciled in some time after Stanley's untimely death on 3 July 1952

A bright young man at the peak of his power was reduced to a state dominated by pain, fear, uncertainty, and despair. How could he not be allowed to spend many more years seeing his wife thrive as a caring mother and partner? How could he not be present to see his three beautiful little girls grow into fine young women? Would they forget about him? Would they ever be able to get over him? Would they ever be able to forgive him for abandoning them when they were most needy? Would they ever be able to find any sense of meaning in his

untimely and needless death? How could such a
thing happen to them? How could such a
beautiful family, such a wonderful man, be torn
asunder at the very moment when everything was
going so well for them?

Alice's heart was broken beyond repair. She
never stopped loving Stanley, and she never got
over him. Despite that, she remarried two years
after Stanley's death, and spent far more years
with her second husband, Harold Peterson, than
she spent with Stanley.

Alice's life was marked by further tragedy:
Harold died from brain cancer when he was just
54. After that, she never seriously considered
remarrying. Instead, she chose to play out the rest
of her long life in the role of the grieving widow
and devoted caregiver for her elderly widowed
mother. Many years later she confided to Karen
that she wished she had remarried after Harold's
death, since she had spent nearly 40 years without
a partner.

For many years after Harold's death she
dutifully kept a photo of Harold by her bedside.
Eventually, however, Harold's photo was
replaced by Stanley's, whose picture remained by
Alice's bedside until the day she died.

Karen's cousin, Maxine Sommer, remembered
Stanley's funeral service vividly, and related a
touching story to Karen many years after the fact.
She said that Alice was very quiet during the
funeral service, and shortly after the service
ended, she disappeared into the restroom. Half an
hour later she emerged, her face dry and resolute, and she stated simply: "Now I have to find a
job and a house and take care of my daughters."

Despite everything being thrown at Alice during this terrible passage in her life, she still had
time to answer cards and letters of condolence, as evidenced by the card (left) and note she sent
to Marie Dunbar to acknowledge Marie's kindness in remembering Stanley and expressing
sympathy for Alice's suffering.

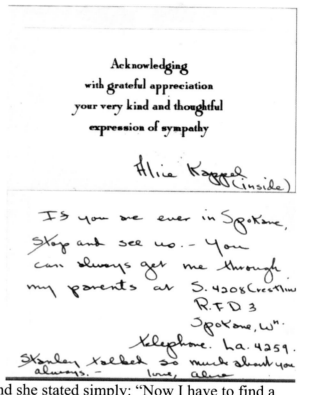

Stanley's obituary appeared in the Spokane Daily Chronicle on July 8, 1952. It read:

"Stanley E. Kappel, Kellogg, Idaho, July 8: Stanley Ernest Kappel, 34, assistant
superintendent at the Page mine, died Friday at Wardner hospital. He had been ill for 29
days. Mr. Kappel served as a first lieutenant in the Canadian army in World War II. He was a
member of the American Association of Metallurgical Engineers. Mr. Kappel belonged to the
Emmanuel Episcopal church in Kellogg.

"Survivors include his wife, Alice, and three daughters, Karen, Kristen, and Kerry, at the funeral home; his father, Frank Kappel of British Columbia and five sisters in Canada. Private services were held today from Smith & Co. parlor in Spokane. The Rev. Thomas Howarth officiated. Burial was in Riverside Park."

As a tribute to Stanley's contributions to the mining industry, several corporate mining executives from New York City flew to Spokane to attend his funeral, according to Alice. So much talent, so much grace, so much potential, and so much love of life and family, lost so tragically, lost to eternity.

The Salmon Arm Observer ran a similar obituary with a Canadian perspective: "Stanley Kappel, son of Frank Kappel, a well-known resident of the Shuswap district, died at Kellogg, Idaho, last Thursday after several months' illness. The funeral was held at Spokane, Wash.

"Stan" Kappel, who was born in Salmon Arm, was 33 years old, and had many friends in this area. After attending high school here, he graduated in mining engineering from the University of Montana in 1940. Subsequently he was granted a commission in the Royal Canadian Engineers and while serving in the Army was one of two officers chosen to take a five months' course in Japanese civil administration at Stanford University.

"After receiving his discharge, he joined the Federal Mining and Smelting Co., prominent U.S. mining firm and was engaged as a mining engineer for the company's extensive property at Wallace, Idaho.'

"Besides his father, he is survived by his wife and three children. Mr. Kappel left for the U.S. immediately after he was advised of his son's death and attended the funeral at Spokane."

DO NOT STAND AT MY GRAVE AND WEEP
- by Mary Frye, 1932

*"Do not stand at my grave and weep,
I am not there, I do not sleep.*

*I am a thousand winds that blow.
I am the diamond glint on snow.
I am the sunlight on ripened grain.
I am the gentle autumn rain.*

*When you wake in the morning hush,
I am the swift, uplifting rush
Of quiet birds in circling flight.
I am the soft starlight at night.*

*Do not stand at my grave and weep.
I am not there, I do not sleep.
(Do not stand at my grave and cry.
I am not there, I did not die!)"*

ADDENDA

EPILOGUE

Looking back on the life of Stanley Kappel, it is tempting to see his life as a series of tragedies interspersed with many blessings; it is also easy to focus on Stanley's many accomplishments during his relatively short life. For those left in the wake of his untimely death at age 33, the memories of Stanley, the specter of Stanley, and the ghost of Stanley have been dominant forces in the lives of his beloved wife and his three daughters, two of whom barely knew him. From the time I came into this family in 1962, it was almost as if Stanley were a current member of the household, his name came up so frequently, especially while Alice was still alive. What finer tribute could be paid by his family to such a wonderful man than to carry his memory with them every day of their lives?

Kerry shared with Karen her memory of Stanley, when Kerry was barely two years old, pushed away by her dying father because of his pain and despair. Kerry said she felt rejected by her father, whom she barely knew, and how sad it is to be left with this memory of Stanley as perhaps the most important detail you remember of your own father. How sad, also, to think of what plans Stanley had made in his tender heart for Kerry. One can only imagine how desperately he wanted to fulfill every one of them, had fate only given him the opportunity.

Alice once shared with Karen that a few days after Stanley died, when she was sitting in the funeral home next to Stanley's casket, while she was in the deepest depths of her own despair over losing her life mate so tragically, Stanley actually appeared to her in a vision, there in the funeral home. He told her: "Everything is OK, Alice; everything will be OK." For those of us left in the wake of Stanley's tragedy, this is surely a gift from beyond the grave. The veil between this life and the next may be thinner than we can perceive, even if it isn't entirely transparent. There is no doubt that Stanley's ghost haunted Alice throughout the remainder of her life, but there is also no doubt that, however bittersweet, it was a blessing to her to be able to remember Stanley's posthumous visit and the reassuring message he gave her.

This is such a compelling story, beginning with Ernest Silas Buckingham. An orphan who lost his mother at a young age and was cast out from his own country, he nevertheless grew into a courageous, adventurous, fun-loving man who brought great joy to the many lives he touched, only to lose his wife by a sudden twist of fate, and then struggled to keep his own family together. He was compelled to give up three of his children, two with whom he later reconnected and enjoyed through the last years of his life. He must have been doubly saddened by the death of Stanley, his only son, with whom he was never able to reconnect.

Stanley's adoption was a great blessing to both Ernie and the Frank Kappel family. It is easy to imagine that Ernie felt he had given his young son a gift that was never granted to him when he lost his own mother: the gift of being adopted by a loving family, embraced by a loving family, supported and cherished in the ways that one hopes could be the fate of every child born into this world. Frank Kappel lost his wife in 1946, long before she should have gone. Then he lost his only son in 1952 as well. Life can be so cruel.

Yet Ernie and Frank both went on to live happy, productive lives, each one living well into old age. And by all appearances they both managed to find happiness, in spite of the many challenges they had each faced over the years. I am inclined to think that Stanley would have reconnected with his birth father, given enough time and wisdom to be able to better understand what it meant to Ernie to give up three of his young children. After all, Stanley had two fathers, not one. Both of them contributed mightily to his growth and development into a fine man. Both of them grieved when they lost their son to cancer. Why shouldn't both fathers have been able to share in Stanley's success?

What legacies have all of these many characters left for those of us who remain among the living? What could we gain from their combined experiences, their shared sacrifices, their joys, their achievements, their setbacks, and their ecstasies? Each of you who has read this story will draw your own conclusion and judge the contents by your own measure, based on your own perception of reality.

And reality is merely an illusion, although a very persistent one.

The two photos below show Stanley's watch that he was apparently wearing at the time of his death in 1952. It is a gold Eterna "Curvex) watch dating from the 1930s. Eterna is a Swiss luxury watch company founded in 1856 and is still making watches. The watch has seen a lot of action, judging from the wear and tear that is evident on both the front and the back. Stanley presumably wore it while he was in South America as well as when he was down in the mines, where conditions would have been adverse for any timepiece. Engraved on the back with "S E Kappel", it may have been a very special gift he received when he graduated from high school. (both photos were taken by the author)

POSTSCRIPT

If I have learned anything from this life-changing enterprise, which began as a naïve attempt to recover and reconstruct a few salient details about the life of Stanley Ernest Kappel, and expanded into a discovery of so many remarkable characters, each with his or her own charming and inspiring story to tell, it is this message from antiquity.

Every one of us hopes to be remembered. The need to live a full, meaningful life seems buried deep within the human psyche. This need is coupled with the yearning that others will notice us and will count us among those who mattered, those who made a positive contribution, those whose lives added to the upward trajectory of the human story in some small way. If you care to listen, the voices of our ancestors cry out to us, hoping to be heard even after they have departed.

Some leave tangible evidence of what they want us to remember: Frank Kappel's touching memoir, written carefully and lovingly near the end of his life to his five granddaughters; Ernie Buckingham's remarkable audio cassette tape that chronicled his life in such charming and heartbreaking detail, dictated very close to the end of his life; and Stanley's legacy of carefully compiled albums of annotated photographs, along with hundreds of photographic negatives whose positive images somehow disappeared but were recently resurrected by this writer.

For much of my life I have awakened sometime during the night, usually around 4AM, with my mind very alert, my memory sharper than usual, and my awareness open to whatever comes. And if I pay attention, magic happens. Perhaps I've been struggling with a daunting problem and can't seem to find a solution. More likely than not, the solution appears to me out of nowhere during an early morning awakening. The only thing required of me is to listen.

Not long after I started writing this history I began to hear the voices of my subjects when I would awaken in the night. It was as if their ghosts were channeling through me, giving me ideas, giving me words, telling me what was important about their stories. It seems they were asking me to focus more on them and their stories. How uncanny that these recurring experiences inspired me to do more research or to look at one of the main characters in a different light. This often resulted in my adding one or more chapters devoted to them, rather than to my main character. To anyone who reads this book, it should be clear that their stories contributed richly to Stanley's story.

I have previously alluded to the continual surprises I experienced as Stanley's story unfolded before me. What started out to be a brief telling (since I had so little by way of documentation of Stanley's life, or at least so I thought) kept expanding, often with very little effort on my part. As my interest in these characters increased, and as my thirst for information about them enlarged, the process began to take on a life of its own. Emails we had received many years earlier (and fortunately held on to) suddenly became vital sources of discovery and insight. So much of the lovely detail contained in this story came from family members who had firsthand knowledge of long-dead subjects, and if not first-hand, they were very, very close to the stories about them. Without the help of these many kind folks, Stanley's story would have remained nothing more than the shallow retelling I had originally anticipated. Oh my…

I will take this one step further, if you will indulge me. You, dear reader, are no different from anyone else. At some level, you want your story to be known. If you have read this book, you can appreciate how remarkable the story of each character I have chosen to write about really is. And I guarantee, your story is every bit as fascinating and no less interesting. For those of us who are nearing the end of our lives, time is running out. I would gently and respectfully encourage you to tell your story before it's too late. Whether you write it down as a personal memoir, record it on tape, or put it into an album of annotated photographs, the only thing that matters is that you give yourself enough respect to capture your own essence for posterity.

Perhaps your own child or grandchild will decide to take it from there after you are gone. Time and loss, after all, tend to sharpen our curiosity about our ancestors. You never know when some old geezer who is your descendent or married to your descendent will decide to decipher the details of your story and write it down so that others can remember you and appreciate how much you really mattered.

Among my many regrets is that I didn't take more time to ask my parents about the details of their lives. Fortunately when I was much younger I did have the wherewithal to ask them to write stories about their childhoods, and the results are now among my most treasured possessions. If I could not walk a mile in their shoes, at least I could have asked them to relive and record as much of their lives as they could before they passed away. But as my story shows, it is never too late. Food for thought…

Alice shared with Karen that throughout his career as a mining engineer, there were never any safety infractions or accidents on his watch. She also shared that Stanley spoke fairly fluent Spanish with the local miners, who constituted all of the local work force and most of the mining camp staff there; apparently Stanley didn't speak Spanish before arriving in Portovelo.

I have been lamenting from the outset of this project that Stanley never kept a diary or other intimate record of himself, his inner thoughts, his hopes and dreams, his joys and sorrows. Well, it turns out I was dead wrong. Some "diarists" are predominantly verbal, and others aren't, which doesn't mean that those who aren't don't keep diaries. I suddenly realized this morning that Stanley was predominantly a visual person, as are many engineers who tend to see the world in visual rather than prosaic terms. In fact, we still have Stanley's camera and his drafting tools, strongly suggesting this was the case for him.

Stanley kept his diary in two formats: most importantly, his many photo albums; but he also kept a fairly intimate written record in the form of Karen's "baby book". We have at least five albums of Stanley's photos, carefully arranged and annotated in silver ink on black paper, an artful expression in itself. An even greater treasure trove of negatives that stretches back to Stanley's very early childhood was also discovered well into the writing of this biographical sketch that fills in many important gaps and answers many important questions about Stanley's childhood and youth. It is unclear whether Stanley had developed an interest in photography at a young age and was able to acquire a camera by the time he was 10 or 12 years old, but I would like to think this was the case. Some of the earlier negatives are of a larger size and are in better condition than the majority of the later negatives, suggesting they were taken by someone else and by a different camera, perhaps Frank Kappel, who was multi-talented and whose life interests extended into the creative arts. Or perhaps Janet, the accomplished painter, acquired an interest in photography in order to capture images of her family and her environment. The fact is, however, that we have a large number of black and white images that were taken, saved, and carefully catalogued over the course of many years while Stanley was growing up. There is little doubt that Stanley played a major role in the taking, developing, printing, and archiving of these images.

These albums reflect what Stanley was experiencing, thinking and feeling as his life unfolded. A few words accompany each of the photos so carefully selected and placed chronologically in the albums. This is very much in keeping with Stanley's basic character: he was not taciturn, but he was, in Alice's words, "very careful with the words he chose to speak, and he tended to think before he spoke." He also expressed dismay at how effusive some people could be, and he seemed to feel uncomfortable being around garrulous people, with the possible conclusion that a surfeit of words did not necessarily express sincerity.

As they say, "every picture is worth a thousand words", and I think this is clearly the case with Stanley's photo albums and negatives, especially when combined with his sparse but concise commentary. Stanley's thoughts and emotions seem to be carefully encoded in these photos. Each photo appears to be chosen to deliberately reflect the way in which Stanley perceived his life to be unfolding, and deliberately arranged and annotated to reflect the record that Stanley wished to leave to the world, especially to his own children and future generations. One might guess that he had put together photo albums from his earlier life that may have remained with Stanley's parents and have been subsequently lost to us. It doesn't take a vivid imagination to surmise why Stanley might not have wanted Alice to see some of the images in the negatives chronicling his adolescent and young adult years when he was obviously in the company of the fairer sex quite frequently.

I can't help comparing the two photos of Stanley and his adopted father, Frank. They were both taken for the same reason, to document the enlistment of both father and son in the Canadian Army for the same reason, to prepare for war with the Germans. I have commented extensively at the beginning of this story on how Stanley appears in his formal military sitting, and how atypical everything is about Stanley's appearance. Frank's photo is much more typical of a formal military photo sitting, but it seems he was always a serious man, and on this occasion his mood appears almost grave. Both father and son grew up in similar "privileged" circumstances, although Frank didn't suffer the loss of his mother at the tender age of two years.

Equally amazing is the fact that his message to future generations, however cryptic, was meant to signal the most important things that were happening in his life at the time, on an almost daily basis. In the case of Karen's baby book, all of which is the work of Stanley, his observations about her express how immensely important his first child was to him. Here is a man in the midst of many important and time-consuming demands, as a mining engineer, as a budding mining superintendent, as a husband, as a father, as a friend, and also as a son. Yet he somehow found time to carefully and thoughtfully chronicle every important detail of baby Karen's growth and development. It is touching that at the end of the baby book he also carefully pasted in two lengthy newspaper articles: one is his mother's obituary from 1946; the other reports his father's retirement nearly a year later. Why would he put such things in his daughter's baby book? One can imagine several explanations: he wanted to honor the memory of his beloved parents; he wanted to ensure that their story as very successful and highly valued members of their community would be passed down to his children; and he wanted to record the events in his "journal".

KAREN'S BABY BOOK:

Karen's baby book starts with photos of the obstetrician who delivered her, Dr. R. D. Reekie; her first nursery at Deaconess Hospital; and the room where she was born on the sixth floor. There is also a newspaper clipping announcing Karen's arrival on July 19, 1945, a note from Karen's pediatrician, Dr. Austin C. Taylor outlining appropriate care and feeding principles, and the discharge note from Deaconess Hospital after she is ready to go home for the first time. On the second page is a copy of Stanley and Alice's wedding certificate from Zaruma, a photo of The Portovelo Club, "where Mommy met Daddy, May 1941", and a photo of Zaruma, Ecuador, "Married here, 8 PM, 2 Nov. 1942, by candlelight." Next come photos of their house at Sheep Creek and Mullan, with a photo of Stanley and Alice beneath the palm trees in Portovelo. There is even a brief article entitled "If I Had a

Daughter", by Hal Boyle, carefully pasted into the baby book by Stanley, outlining a prospective father's hopes and dreams for his daughter.

This is all the work of a sweet, devoted, and above all else, sentimental husband and father. He is clearly delighted with the direction his life has taken, after many years of preparation, including 2 ½ years of turmoil at its beginning. One entry reports the stressful reality of Karen's birth: "Aunt Evelyn Patel was with 'mother' until Baby was born. Grandmother Leland and Great Uncle Ole Leland came to visit with Aunt Eve the first day. 'Father' who was in Stanford, California and could not get home because he was in the army, sent a telegram and red and yellow roses for mother and his new daughter." The telegram read: "When can I see my little girl? I'm glad Alice and the baby are alright." As for the page that reports Karen's name, which is artfully printed along with her initials, the caption "named for" is followed by "No one – father's choice". And under Karen's adorable baby picture, taken at Grandma Leland's home, the caption "Baby resembles" is followed by "Father with mother's eyes."

The rest of the book is filled with annotations about Karen's growth and development, when she took her first drink, when she first fed herself, when she first walked, when she spoke her first words, when she first caught a ball, when she repeated her first prayer, when she got her first puppy, her first friend, etc. One entry reports "10-6-45: Father's 27th birthday; 10-9-45: Father left for Vancouver to get a discharge from the Royal Canadian Engineers". There are notes on her behavioral development, and they aren't all positive. One entry, entitled "Response to necessary punishment", states: "Spankings no good if in a tantrum but effective for obedience in general cases." Another states "Is very gentle with and loves to touch babies." At age two, Stanley reports: "Usually happy and playful – has some bad tantrums". At age 2½: "Inclined to cry when way not granted", and "punishes her dolls when she has been thwarted in some desire of her own."

The book goes on to report Karen's responses to her first four Christmases and memorable birthday celebrations. Then everything ends in mid-1950, just after the arrival of baby number three. The Norwegians have an old saying about children: "One is like none; two is like ten." With the arrival of two sisters in fairly rapid succession, along with two moves as well as new and increasingly important jobs in Mullan and Kellogg, responsibilities mounted. Consequently, Stanley's time for taking delight in his growing family became more and more limited. Eventually, of course, it all grinds to a sudden halt with the diagnosis of Stanley's cancer and his subsequent struggle to survive, then his eventual submission to the inevitability of his pending death. There is no documentation of the struggles that Stanley and Alice experienced in their ongoing efforts to understand and cope with the tragedy that was about to befall them – the terror, the sadness, the depression they were both undoubtedly feeling in the context of having to carry on a routine that included the care and feeding of three growing daughters, along with Stanley's need to continue working as long as possible. But the abrupt halt in Stanley's photo albums and Karen's baby book reveals so much about what was happening to this family during Stanley's last year.

Stanley apparently left no personal verbal record of how he felt about his parents and sister. Frank Kappel and his sister both reported that he was a "good son" and a "good brother", and although he chose a career that would take him far from his parents for the rest of his life, he must have written letters that are no longer available to this writer. Both of the newspaper articles that Stanley so carefully and deliberately pasted at the back of Karen's baby book undoubtedly reflect what he felt about Frank and Janet. They reflect the lives of two loving, devoted and highly committed people who found great joy in their children, but also found great purpose in serving their communities, and there is no doubt this instilled a deep sense of pride in Stanley that he wanted to pass on to his children.

People who keep journals do it for several reasons: 1) they are sentimental and want to be able to remember their lives and look back and remember details of what they were thinking and how they were feeling at the time; 2) they hope others will someday read what they have written and appreciate the one who kept the journal. This is a way of surviving beyond one's own death, of attaining some degree of immortality.

In Stanley's case, his photo journals reflect how happy, amazed and delighted he was with the way his life was playing out. He wanted his joy to be carefully, thoughtfully and beautifully recorded – for himself, to one day be able to look back and remember – and for his children and others – whom he was lovingly displaying in their photos and comments about them. He felt things very deeply, in spite of his limited words. He was very sentimental, in spite of his cool competence. And he was a very loving man, even if he wasn't always able to express it verbally.

How do you put into words the despair you are feeling about knowing that you will soon be leaving your precious family to fend for themselves, to find their way in this world without your help and guidance? How do you express your guilt, your anger, your outrage, your incredulity at what is happening to you and to those who are most precious to you? How do you know if they will ever forgive you for abandoning them when they are most needy? How do you tell them how desperately you want to be there for them, to love them, to provide for them, to ensure that their needs will all be met by someone strong and noble and caring? How could you keep any sense of faith in the goodness of life in the face of such a terrible challenge?

A FEW COMMENTS ABOUT THE AMERICAN WHO DEVELOPED THE PORTOVELO MINES FOR SADCO

Andrew Mellick Tweedy was the son of Joseph Tweedy, a New York wool merchant who moved to Texas in the mid-1870s to develop a source of wool. He leased, purchased and homesteaded, along with three colleagues from New York who were all investors, 150,000 acres in west Texas and started a sheep ranch. The purpose was to raise sheep and send the wool back to the family wool merchants in New York. The three colleagues eventually returned to New York, but Joseph remained in Texas and his four children were born there. Mellick eventually attended Princeton University and became a mining engineer.

Mellick's father, Joseph, long since dead, had founded Knickerbocker, Texas, and this is where Mellick grew up. Joseph's four children each inherited one-fourth of the family estate, but it isn't clear what the estate entailed. However, in 1940, having acquired his own fortune as superintendent and general manager of the Portovelo mine, Mellick purchased 8,000 acres stretching for 11 miles along Dove Creek, not far from San Angelo, Texas. It is a lovely piece of land, especially given the location, with an abundance of flora and fauna, thanks to the careful management by the Tweedy family over the years. Karen and I stayed at the new ranch house two or three times in the 1980s and 90s, and were charmed by the solitude and natural beauty of the place.

Right: Two photos from Andrea Carrión's Ph.D. Thesis, with her captions: "Above left: A.M. Tweedy in riding gear, smoking a pipe in front of a group of indigenous people who observe him; The photograph was probably taken in Zaruma, in the late-1930s. At the back-left, the man wearing a suit and boots is probably a cholo who performed urban services. At the center back, there are Saraguro women wearing black ponchos and skirts, and Saraguro men in black ponchos and white trousers. To the right, the man standing with a black and white poncho with short hair is probably from the Paltas indigenous group. Racial mixture was key to transforming the social relations of production."

Below right: "The gendered division of labour reproduced internal hierarchies. As a single woman, Florence Dahl (seated), arrived in the camp to serve as a nurse at the Curipamba Hospital. In 1917 she married the mine manager Andrew Mellick Tweedy" (standing to the right). (Elizabeth Tweedy Sykes Archives)

A FINAL REFLECTION ON WRITING THIS STORY

I began writing this story with a quote about the art of writing: "Write what you know…" Now I might add another tidbit of advice for any would-be writer, having walked through a few flames to get to this point: "Write what you feel. Open your heart, and write from there. Listen to those voices that speak to you in the middle of the night, when the veil is thinnest, and the ghosts want to be heard."

APPENDIX 1: Compressed Timeline for Ernest Buckingham and his Family

Ed. note – Ernie's journey was so convoluted that I found it helpful to construct this timeline in order to keep everything straight.

Apr 28, 1852	Birth of Amanda Malvina Ley, Ernie's mother
Sept 19, 1886	Birth of Ernest Silas Buckingham, Plymouth, Devon, England
Feb 10, 1892	Ernie, age five, and his brother, Archibald, age seven, are taken from their mother and initially admitted to Barnardo's Orphanage, London
Apr 10, 1892	Ernie, age five, becomes a foster child in Broxted, northeast of London, and is placed with the Willis family, who he said in his audio cassette tape treated him well; he also said he attended school during the six years he was living with the Willis family
Apr 21, 1895	Ernie's mother, Amanda Ley, dies at age 42 from unknown causes in unknown circumstances in Plymouth, reportedly in Plymouth Workhouse, Devon, England, when Ernie was age eight
June 1898	Ernie, age 11, after more than six years in the Willis household, is taken from the Willis family by "officials" and returns briefly to Barnardo's Orphanage in London
July 14, 1898	Ernie, age 11, embarks for Quebec, Canada, departing from Liverpool on board the S.S. Labrador
July 30, 1898	Ernie, age 11, arrives in Quebec; according to official Canadian archives, "he was sent to Winnipeg after his arrival, and was placed with Mr. Gregson, who lives near Oxbow", in the southeast corner of Saskatchewan
Jan 1900	Ernie is age 13; according to Patricia Goldney Millar, information received from Barnardo's Orphanage, reported he was working for a Mr. J. Wood at Oxbow in January 1900
Early 1901	Ernie is age 14; the 1901 Canadian census lists Ernie as living with the Gregsons, and also states that he was both married and a Canadian citizen at the time (neither of these seems likely)
Feb 1, 1901	Ernie writes a letter to Barnardo's Orphanage in Toronto, stating "I am now getting on first rate" on the Gregson homestead, but the "real truth" of that letter is doubtful; Ernie later reveals in a tape he made near the end of his life that the Gregsons treated him cruelly, more like an indentured servant than the child he actually was

Nov 1901	Ernie, age 15, decides he has had enough mistreatment at the hands of his "captors", and suddenly leaves the Gregson homestead, never to return; then in 1901, Barnardo's report showed "he had had several moves during the year, and his whereabouts were unknown at that time"; however, according to Ernie's tape, Ernie fled the Gregsons and headed south toward the US border; after 5-6 miles he came to a farm, possibly owned by "Mr. J. Wood" that was reported by Barnardo's; he remains on that farm until the following summer
Dec 1902	Barnardo's Orphanage reports: It appears that some news had been received and he had been working with a gang of threshers, but no definite address was given
1902	With Ernie's services no longer required by Mr. Wood, he returns to Oxbow and immediately moves to Arcola, 20 or so miles west of Oxbow, where he is employed as an apprentice harness maker by Mr. Tommy Amos; he lives with the Amos family for the next 6 months, but when winter arrives, Mr. Amos can no longer afford to keep him
Winter 1902-3	Ernie, age 16, moves in with the Cooney family, where he was "employed" to help keep the local covered (but open on the sides) hockey/curling/skating rink in Arcola clear of snow and debris, but a heavy snowfall destroys the rink, and Ernie is once again without a job or a home
March 1903	Ernie, age 16, travels to Kisbey on the train, where he is hired by a "lame" farmer from Stoughton on Apr 1st and works on the farm through the summer
Sept 1903	Ernie, age 16, gets work with a threshing gang and finishes the threshing season with them; then he travels to Regina in search of work, but finds nothing, so he returns to Stoughton, and works on that farm until spring
Sept 1904	Ernie, age 18, "ages out" of any formal dependency on either Barnardo's orphanage sponsorship or the wardship of the Canadian government and becomes a full-fledged Canadian citizen at age 18; Ernie continues to work in the vicinity of Kisbey, Stoughton, and Arcola, until 1908 (age 18-22), but most details about his time in the region are lacking, aside from the fact that he acquired his first violin during this period
1906	Ernie turns age 20 in September; the 1906 Canadian Census lists Ernie as living as a hired man in the household of George Hall, Jr., in Kisbey, Saskatchewan; George is recorded as being 38 years old and the head of the household; four other members of the household were listed, including George's wife, Jessie, two young sons, and Ethel Regh, an immigrant from England who was listed as a "boarder"; the farm lists a total of 27 animals, including 10 horses, 4 milk cows, 4 sheep, and 9 pigs

Spring 1908	Ernie, age 22, returns to Regina in search of work; he is hired by Mr. Jenkins, a dentist from Omaha, Nebraska; Ernie remains on that farm through the winter while Mr. Jenkins and his wife return to Omaha for the "season"
Winter 1908-9	Ernie spends the winter on the Jenkins farm alone; during this time he meets Noble Bragg
1909	Ernie had worked on multiple farms throughout Saskatchewan by now, and in Regina he met Noble Bragg, who became a close friend to Ernie and may have "clued him in" regarding not just his freedom to choose his own way for the rest of his life, but also that opportunities existed for Ernie far away in other parts of Canada, where Ernie could even become both a landowner as well as his own master; Buck's parents were going to Brooks, Alberta to homestead; Ernie went along with them and drove one of their three wagons; they arrived to find their quarter section had just been crossed by a prairie fire; there was no water on the land and with no feed for their stock, the Braggs decided to return to Bassano, Alberta; instead of taking everything back with them they sold their livestock, a load of lumber, and two wagons to a man on the next homestead
Spring 1910	Undaunted, Ernie and Noble Bragg travel to British Columbia by train to start their new lives; they arrive in Revelstoke, BC, where they remain for several months, hoping to find work at a local lumber mill; while there they find their "voice" as musicians and experience great success as entertainers; when a flood devastates the mill and leaves them suddenly without any hope of finding work there, the two are hired on a surveying crew in the Shuswap region and arrive at Mobley Bay in May of 1910
1910-12	The two friends quickly become permanent fixtures in the community that extended along the north shore of Shuswap Lake; Ernie and Noble started the "Buck and Bragg Band", with Ernie playing fiddle and Noble playing banjo; Ernie is hired almost immediately as a surveyor, and works in a variety of jobs during the next two years, while traveling throughout the region to play with his friend Bragg; Ernie acquires a homestead at Blind Bay, on the southwest end of Shuswap Lake, and Noble acquires a homestead at Celista; the "Buck and Bragg Band" splits up due to the distance between the two homesteads
1912	Ernie meets a "local" Scottish girl from Celista, Jeanie Brown, who plays the mandolin; they are married December 26, 1912; Ernie is age 26 and Jean is 18; the two became performers together, with Jeanie playing the mandolin, Ernie playing the fiddle, and Tom Brown also playing the fiddle
Oct 16, 1918	Donald Angus, their fourth child, is born, along with four other siblings; the partnership of Ernie and Jeanie is flourishing, and their future together seems solid; they work very hard to support their growing family, with Ernie

spending significant amounts of time away from home working at various jobs to produce cash income for the family

Jan 27, 1921   After eight years of marriage to Ernie, Jean, having become pregnant with a sixth child, dies suddenly from complications of a ruptured ectopic pregnancy; devastated and desperate, Ernie struggles to manage this catastrophic situation, placing all five of his children with a neighbor, Mrs. Immel, for several months while he continues to travel away from home to earn money for the family's survival; Ernie eventually realizes that he cannot keep all five children with him permanently

May 26, 1921   Stanley is adopted by Frank and Janet Kappel, four months after his mother's death, when he is 2 ½ years old; the two other youngest children of Jean and Ernie, Jean Ellen and Mina Marie, are both adopted out around the same time, while Ernie's two oldest daughters, Laura Margaret and May Catherine, remain at home with Ernie

Nov 13, 1923   Ernie marries Constance Noeline Harrison, age 25, in Chase, British Columbia; they have two additional children, Elmer Ernest, born in Blind Bay; and Herbert Oliver, born in Vancouver

1927   Ernie and Connie move to Vancouver, where they remain for the rest of their marriage; Ernie works at various jobs in and around Vancouver, and continues to play his fiddle in various venues, including an old-time orchestra, "The Joy Makers", and appears regularly at dances and on the radio; everything points to the fact that the period between 1923 and 1960 was a period of stability and happiness for both Connie and Ernie

July 3, 1952   Stanley Ernest Kappel dies from cancer at age 33, never having seen his birth father again since being adopted by Frank and Janet Kappel in 1921

May 9, 1960   Connie dies of cancer, at age 61; Ernie lives another 17 years, reflecting a remarkable zest for life and a capacity for enjoying himself and his family; he visits his daughter, Laura, who lives on Shuswap Lake, frequently, entertaining the youngsters with his favorite fiddle music and poetry recitations, sharing unabashed "joie de vivre" with his family and friends

Aug 12, 1963   Ernie attends granddaughter Karen's wedding in Spokane; this marks the first time he has had any direct contact with any of his "Stanley Kappel family kin" since little Donald Angus walked out the door of his family homestead in 1921 and began a new life as Stanley Ernest Kappel

Jul 23, 1977   Ernie dies of a heart attack in Balmoral near Sorrento, BC, at age 90, shortly after recording his 90-minute autobiographical audio cassette tape

APPENDIX 2: Ernie Buckingham's Oral History

- *Recorded on a 90-minute audio cassette tape a few months before Ernie died on July 23, 1977*

With a few comments from Murl Leibrecht: This tape is a truly remarkable treasure trove, an authentic, charming, and utterly compelling story that was made by Ernie over an unknown period of time, apparently at someone else's request. He doesn't mention who asked him to make the tape. He also stopped the recording abruptly with "toodle-oo" after more than 85 minutes in order to make coffee, and apparently never got around to finishing the tape before he died, possibly within a month or two, when he was nearly 91 years old. Ernie's son Elmer adds his own important comments at the end of the tape in an effort to round out Ernie's story. But it would have been wonderful to hear Ernie tell it himself, especially how he felt when he arrived at the Shuswap. Fortunately, his words and stories have been "recorded" by his granddaughter, Patricia Goldney Millar, and his Dunbar grandchildren, so we are blessed with a fairly complete "personal" timeline of Ernie's life, starting at age five, even if many of the details have been lost to time.

Let's face it: for even the most celebrated and storied person who ever lived, someone who had countless books written about them, countless documentaries made about them, and countless newspaper and magazine articles published about them, the fact is that most of the actual details of their lives were never known by anyone but themselves and will never be known to the rest of us. In Ernie's case, it is a privilege to have as much about him available to us as we do, thanks to the efforts of a few of his closest family members who took the time to capture his remarkable story, put it into words, and share it with the rest of us.

The most important thing to be taken from this tape is Ernie's words, his thoughts and personal memories about what it was like to be him, and to behold the power of his prodigious memory, as well as his wry sense of humor, his love of life, and especially, the casual, almost offhand way in which he recounts what was a seriously challenging childhood and youth.

One final reflection: In spite of Ernie's impressive memory, he seems confused about the chronology of his life. He thinks he was 14 when he arrived in Canada, but he was actually 11; he thinks he was 17 or 18 when he left the Gregson homestead, but he was actually 14; and he continues this mistaken sense of time right up until the end of the tape. Whether he would have come to a realization of this, had he recorded his entire story and seen it transcribed, and then corrected some of the dates and ages, is anyone's guess. What we know for certain is the dates recorded by Barnardo's Orphanage, the customs officials in Canada that recorded his arrival, details from at least two Canadian census documents, along with many other resources that objectively "prove" that he arrived in Canada in 1898, when he was 11 (almost 12); where he was in 1906, at age 18 (in Saskatchewan, according to the 1906 Canadian census); when he arrived in British Columbia, at age 23 (almost 24), in 1910; and the rest is well documented by newspaper and government administrative efforts. However much Ernie may have embroidered or embellished his story in this tape, listening to it evokes a deep sense of truth and authenticity, at least in the heart of this enthusiastic admirer.

Using the timeline I constructed, I have tried to sort out the actual ages and dates that Ernie gives us, and have also attempted to reflect my efforts as I worked on Stanley Kappel's biography, in which Ernie played a brief but absolutely essential role.

From the beginning, in Ernie's own words:

"Hello, everyone. This is, to whom it may concern, possibly a long, drawn-out story of my life. I've been requested to do this on cassette tape, and I hope I can make it. I do remember most all after I was about five years old. Up to that time, I don't know what happened.

All I do know is I was an orphan. And a couple of men came along there. I was playing around the house, and they then said, do you live here? And I said, yes. My mummy is upstairs, and there was a lady there who looked after us. He says, okay, come on with us upstairs.

So, eventually, all I do know is they took me away to a great, big house. From there, I was in there about two or three days, when I was what they call... I don't know what you call it, farmed out as it were. I and another little boy above my age, too. I think he was older, a couple of years older.

And we went to a party's name with the name of Willis. Mr. and Mrs. Willis. And they had just had a little baby boy when we were there, and that's where we stayed. I thought they was our parents, really, at that time. I know now, of course, they weren't. But nevertheless, I started to school there. Five years old. And they treated us awfully nice.

I expect they got paid to keep us, I don't know, like they do in this country, you see. And we, back and forth at school. I was quite sharp at some lessons at school, and quite dull in others. But anyway, I passed through every class, as they called it there. And up until I was 14 (we know he was actually 11) years old, we stayed with them same people.

Then a lady came one day at school, and she talked to the principal a little while, and then he called me, and she says, I'm going to take you home. So, away home we goes, to Mrs. Willis's place, and, I don't know, I think some money changed hands there. This other boy, he stayed in school, I don't know, and I didn't know what was going on. So, away we went on a train, for gosh sakes.

On a train anyway. They took me on a train and landed me at this big house. Enormous place. Big playground, and lots of kids and one thing another. And I can remember quite well that the overhead railway ran right across our yard, right across the top of us. We could see it every day, dozens of them. Not too much noise either up there. It was way up high.

From what I can really remember, I was there about two weeks, and I wondered where this other little boy went to, what happened to him and all this stuff. After all, you know, we was together there at that place for ten years anyway, you see, but I never saw him after.

There were a bunch of boys, all got together, and my name was called, of course. B starts right off A, and then B, and I didn't know what we were doing there. We all had to go in and have a big bath and everything. New clothes, and we got a parcel with kind of a brown grip, with handles on it, like your airbags here now. And the first thing I knew, there was a man and a woman come and said, you're coming with us.

Now, this was all frustrating for a little fellow, you know, I didn't know where the heck to get off and what they were going to do with me or anything. And the first thing I knew, we were on a train. We went to their house. That's it. We went to their house, and we stayed there a couple of days. I expect you had to get tickets and screened and all that stuff.

Anyway, away we went on the boat. Oh, was I ever sick in that boat. I think we were ten or 11 days going across: rough sea, let me see now what time of the year it was. It would be in the summer, about June or July, I think, because I know that the little town of Oxbow, we ended up finally in Saskatchewan, the town road there was very, very dusty. It was deep in clay dust, and I used to like to play in that.

I had to wait there, until something happened, and the folks went home, and they left me in the hotel. I didn't mind it. I was in the hotel a couple of days. And then he come in with a team and a load of wood and delivered it. I got up on the seat beside him. He was quite an elderly man. Young men didn't wear whiskers those days, and he had quite a bushy, well-trimmed whisker, beard.

You might wonder how he knew where he was going, you know, but he had a cousin with a farm, a big farm there, at Oxbow, and he had been out a year before that, with a big land rush that was there, around Oxbow. The CPR were selling their land that they had got for putting the railroad through. They were selling their land at 50 cents an acre. Remember that, 50 cents an acre. Beautiful land it was, and he had come, Mr. Gregson, that was the name of the people that brought me over.

He had already got a homestead, and you could get another one there, what they called a preemption. That was a half section, two quarters. And you could buy this CPR land, and there was one quarter right next to him, angle ways with him. As level as a table. 50 cents an acre. And that's what he came out to buy that time and straighten up with his cousin for looking after his farm. He had a beautiful place there. Oats, wheat and all. You might wonder how they knew where they were coming, but that clears that up.

Nevertheless, everything went pretty smooth. That was the time of July because the wild berries had started. Blackberries and saskatoons and all that. There was abundance of them all over the place, because the Souris River run right through his place, from end to end, a mile. And there was bush… not bush, but timber, wood, elm, ash, maple, and stuff like that, on each side of the river. And the river, his land ran half a mile across there. So, the river divided him a quarter of a mile each side, you see.

And I started right in on the gardens and all, because the cousin had kept his garden up. What we call a garden here and what they called a garden was two different things. They had two gardens. One, the house garden. They had to remember this now. They had strawberries there, gooseberries, redcurrants, blackcurrants, rhubarb, all in this little house garden, and a few rows of carrots and stuff like that, beets, to pull when they were young.

Now, they had a field garden. Carrots, turnips, mangos, beets and all that kind of stuff for cattle and also for the house. And that was my job pretty well, to keep that… to thin it out. Keep the weeds out of it. And oh my God, it looked to me to be about an acre of that field garden. It must have been because they used horses and everything in it. Every once in a while, they put the horse in it, with a cultivator, and really dig her up a bit in between the rows.

That was my job anyway, all summer long. In the fall, helped take them out. I remember quite well, them gol' darn sweet *(Swede?)* turnips they called them. Them lovely turnips you buy here, about 50 cents apiece here now. And they grew in enormous size there because they had their garden in the lowland, what they call the lowland, down below the house. And in a big flood, one flood was there while I was there, that all was underwater. The Souris River overflowed and come right over the banks and down onto that. So, everything grew prolific there.

And the way we done it, I went ahead, and I had a hoe, a sharp hoe. The turnips, as you know, they grow, stand right up on the garden, right out of the ground, practically speaking.

And I went along with a hoe, and I cut these tops right off at the turnip top. Right at the turnip. Walked up the row and cut each side off, and I had them all topped like that. Then I went along with a fork and gathered all the tops up and put them in a pile.

Then the man would come along. We had a hired man, and the hired man would come along with two horses, and he would… oh, it was just a long beam. The horse, on each end of it. We called it a sweep, and you put that on… He stood on that. He got me to help him, too. I stood on it, too, as much as I could.

He had the lines to balance them and put that in there, started at the end of the row of the turnips and just started off, and that took every turnip out of the ground without injuring them. After we passed over there, they were laying on the ground, just all up and nice. Of course, we put them in what they call the big root cellars they had there, and they never froze. No. It was all well-built and all this stuff.

They had quite a number of cattle, too, you know. Not little cows, but beef animals. He would sell one every once in a while. Gregson was known for his fat stock, well looked after and well fed. So, any time of the year, a butcher could come in there and buy a couple of animals ready for the market, which stayed with me all my life. I figured that was far, far more thrifty than having a whole bunch half fed, and that's the way that worked.

Then he had the binder. He had a binder there. I remember there were three horses on this binder. Four-foot binder. I'd go around there to beat hell. No, I think the binder was five-foot. Three horses on it, not four. And then I stooked the grain. I learnt how to stook.

No, my gosh, it wasn't a binder. It was a reaper. And it cut so long, and then it swept. He would touch a thing, and it would sweep it off the canvas like a sheaf and left it on the ground. And I'd come by, and I learned how to turn it, make that twisted straw for a binder, to the twine. I got pretty fast at that. I wasn't very old yet.

And I done a lot of things that way. Helped the neighbours. He sent me over to the neighbours and all this stuff. I never was idle one minute, one waking moment. I was working at something.

[Editor's note – the next section was added later after Ernie had reviewed the previous section of his tape]:

The other things were, forgetfulness mostly on my part, like I forgot to fill the wood box in the morning, you go without sugar for a week in your porridge. That was the penalty there. Forget it again, which I did, you go without the porridge altogether for another week. That's two weeks. Oi! And there were other little things that I used to do, and that was my penalty. Go without this. Go without that. It all irritated me to beat the band, because a kid will forget, sure. You had no chance. They never did beat me for anything I did, but they had other things that they used.

Anyway, the third year I was there, I'm starting off now pretty well on my own, on this story. The third year I was there, in the fall of the year, November, the herd law was lifted for the winter. And of course, then he could let the cattle out to that big pasture he had a half section that the cattle could roam in, with that Souris River running through it. That was my job. I ended up working all day, doing something, and then go and get the cattle at night.

Now, they were free to run all over the hills there, the hills and dells, as they call them. Up and down and on. Sometimes, they wouldn't let me go early enough. The sun would be going down in the fall like that, and sometimes I couldn't find them.

They'd always be awake. They'd be in bed when I'd get home. Ten, 11 o'clock. I'd stay out like…I couldn't find them at all because they had one old cow. She wasn't a milker, but she was a leader, and she had a bell on her. But after they got fed all day long and dusk come, they'd all lay down, and that bell wouldn't move, you see. Unless it just happened to be just right when she was chewing the cud, the bell would ding-dong, ding-dong. Not very loud. Not as loud as it would be if it were feeding on the plain.

I thought I wouldn't get them. They made me get up in the morning early. Five o'clock. Go and get them, bring them home. I didn't know what they want. Of course, they wanted them home. That was it. Every night, that was the dribble.

Well, I got fed up with that kind of thing. I looked and looked and looked, and I got home that night, I know it was 11 o'clock. Of course, I didn't start until nine. It got dark then, nine o'clock, at that time of year, November. And he called out from his bedroom. Did you find the cows? I said no. Of course, they knew I didn't because they couldn't hear no bell. They were in bed. Listen, you get up in the morning now, first thing. I'll ring that bell, and you get up and go and get them. Bring them home, put them in the corral, and count them.

I didn't know what all this was about, but anyway, I said, okay. All I had to wear them days was a short, pair of short, what they call knickers, a pair of low stockings, and running shoes, and a little shirt. No coat yet.

So, I went out in the morning. There was white frost all over everything. I can remember that. It was pretty cold. I didn't know where my little jacket was. I didn't care anyway. I was fat as a pig. And away I go, up on the mountain. The sun was up then, coming up.

Of course, the cattle were up. They were about half a mile from the house. As soon as they get up on the…we were built down in the valley. Right behind the house, you'd find a little what they call a mountain, like a…that was the prairie up there. That was the flat prairie for miles. The Souris River Valley, we were in it.

Of course, I heard the bell right away. God, I was fuming inside. I said, I'm not going to put up with this kind of stuff. So, I started 'em all home, and they were all obedient like that. They all went, and they'd eat a bit, then go on home. Finally, I guess they landed home. I don't know. I never went back. I just kept walking on what they call the Boscurvis *[Ed. note – Latin for oxbow]* highway, from Oxbow to…what was the name of that place in the States? (probably Northgate) It was 12 miles to the border, the United States border. I had never been, in my three years there, across the border. So, I headed that way.

There used to be a lot of men coming *[Ed. note – to the Gregson farm]* there for loads of wood, cut wood. Just take a cord of it and take it home for the fireplaces and whatnot. Furnace. I was walking along the highway, and I was about a mile from the Boscurvis. There was a little lake there. I was hungry. Getting hungry, you know, kid. There was a house right alongside, and I saw a man there in the yard, and I went in the yard. By now, I was about 18. 17 anyway. 17 (14, in all probability). And the guy, lo and behold, he was one of the men that used to come for wood once in a while.

And he says, what the hell, he says, are you doing out here, he says, way out from your place, early in the morning? And so, I told him my story, and why and wherefores, and little, funny, pernickety things they used to do to me. They never beat me up or anything. But they had other ways of making me remember things.

Well, he says, you better come in and have some breakfast. He says, I'm batchin', and my wife is down in Ontario for the winter, and I'm going to have breakfast, tea, and stuff like that. You want to come in and have some breakfast and tell me all about it? So, I did that, and I was hungry. I ate, I guess, like a horse.

And he says, what are you going to do? I said, I don't know. I may have to go back, I guess. I don't know. I don't want to go back. I've had enough. They're just using me like a hired man.

Every moment I was awake, I had to be doing something. I couldn't just sit and relax like a boy should be able to.

So, he says, well, how would you like to stay here a while? Oh I said, I'd like that. I said, I can look after your stock, your horses and everything, which I'm used to that. I know what to feed them and everything. He says, we'll see about that. And so he says, you make up your mind. You're going to stay for a day or two, or a week. I got some grain to haul to town, and it'd be very nice to have somebody here to feed the stock in the daytime and look after the place anyway. We were about, let me see, five miles where I left, from Oxbow.

He was about... I walked about eight miles... No. I walked about six miles from there. I walked about six miles to his place. So, he says, you stick around. I'll feed you. I can't give you any money, though. I said, that's all right, I never have any money anyway.

He must have told the people, phoned them, you see, because the road didn't go by his place. The road stayed straight through from his place to Oxbow. Boscurvis highway. That was easily five miles away. But he must have saw somebody in town to tell him that I was there, you see. Every time I saw one of them redcoats (i.e., mounted policeman) riding his horse up the trail, up the road, I'd go and hide. A lot of good that did me, I know, but they never bothered me. He never sent anybody after me or anything.

And finally, the fellow came home one day, and he says, I saw Gregson, and he says, I told him you were here, and that you were happy here, and that you were feeding my stock and one thing another, and if he wanted you home, I'd take you home. No, he says, if he's happy there and not happy here, just leave him there. Just let him there and look after him. I didn't need looking after, god I was a full-grown, knowledgeable man, of all the work there was to do on the prairie. How much a bushel to put in the ground and everything.

So, he drew half a dozen loads of wheat to the elevator. I guess he wanted the money, you see. Now, he says to me one morning, I'm going to Ontario, where my wife's folks is. And he says, I'll be there all winter. I'll be back here at about the middle of March. And do you think you'd like to stay here and look after my stock?

There was a bunch of nice horses, work horses, and some cattle. There was one cow. Yes, one cow, milk cow. Do you think you can do that? Heck yes, I said, I'd like to do that. Anybody can do that. And the responsibility never entered my head at all, you know.

Away he went, and that's where I put in the longest winter I ever put in. It blew, and it snowed, and it drifted. Fortunately, the barn wasn't too far from the house, and I had some neighbours came there.

One of the neighbour men come, and he said, you want to be very careful now about going out on this here prairie. He says, in the winter, when you go from the barn to the house to the barn, you let it be so you can see the barn. Don't you go out if you can't see it, unless you have a big rope and tie it on the house, and then taking the rope and walk to the barn and tie it there securely, and then you follow that rope back and forth during the storm. Okay, I think I know now what you mean.

So, I put in the winter anyway, and he came back, him and his wife, very happy. And I saved his mail for him and sent him any letters and stuff like that. I tied them in a bundle and sent them to his address down there.

Well, when he came back, everything was so nice in the house. I kept the house clean and all. It was quite a big home, upstairs and all, but I just used down. He gave me about $50 and said he was sorry that he couldn't use me for the summer. And he said he could handle all he had there. He was just a new man there, practically speaking. In fact, it was all new up on that flat plateau.

Yes, it was all new. New people there and everything. All down the Souris River Valley, where Gregsons was, that had been settled a few years.

So, I went back into Oxbow, in the town, and I knew a lot of people there. That is, in a way, I knew them. They knew me anyway. They knew where I came from, what I'd done. Ran away from Gregson's and all.

I got to talking to the harness maker there. Amos, his name was. That's his last name, Amos. And he says, what are you going to do, kid, for the winter? He says, things are pretty tough around here in the winter. He says, there's no cattle to feed. There's no nothing. Nobody wants to have anybody around to try to earn their keep. I said, I don't know. He says, how would you like to learn harness making? I said, I don't know. Of course, harness making was the whole thing them days. There was no cars or anything. I think I might be all right, too.

He says, I got a brother, a harness maker over in Arcola. I think he could use a young fellow like you. I'll drop him a phone call and see. If so, it was only 20 miles across. I'll drive you over, because I'm going over there anyway. I want to see him, on business.

So, there he goes. The brothers talked a while. And he says, I've got a young fellow over here from Oxbow. He says, he's been over there, and he thinks he'd like to learn the harness making trade, and I know that you could maybe use him. You were talking about that once, having a young lad. Yes, he says, I can use him. That's where I got on. I could sleep in his place. Eat, board, and room in his place, you see?

Well, he was a funny little fellow, but he had a big trade there. Harness maker. Good name, all them big tugs and everything else that was connected with harness, the britching and all, all handsewn. And I learnt the hard way how to sew all that leather, join them up and sew them. And my fingers, my little fingers, both little fingers were just about cut off yanking that thread because I yanked it hard, and it was necessary, you know. And I had to learn to make that thread. Thread the needle. But it was an enjoyable time.

He wasn't making any money then. Wintertime, they'd fetched their harnesses, most of it, to be sewn up, ready for spring, all the breakages and one thing another, and we got that caught up. The extra hand like mine, I'd done all the little work, and the lads, the men that he had hired there himself, they done the heavy work. So, we got all caught up pretty well. But there was enough for the three of us.

And I used to put in my spare time around the hockey rink there, you know. The skating rink and the curling rink and all. It was one of the biggest in the territory there. It was the biggest west of Winnipeg.

And I used to go over there and talk to the fellow that was looking after that. It was just one man. He had a big deal to do there for one man, but the town paid him miserable wages, you know. And he was a married man, with one child. Lived just on the outskirts, 100 yards or so from the town, in a tar-roofed shanty. Two bedrooms in it, and a kitchen. Kitchen-sitting room. That was all. A couple of windows. Door.

And I want to tell you this now. The door, outside door opened inside. Inside. Most of them there opened outside. You pulled it open, out. It's like a barn door. And there was a reason for that.

But anyway, there come along quite a heavy snowstorm. It really snowed, and it snowed for three or four days and nights, and it banked up some snow there, not any wind, big flakes of snow. Dry, frozen snow. It banked it up there about two feet. And no farmers come in, no nothing.

So, little Tommy Amos, that was the brother that I was working for, he said, hey kid, I don't know, I can't afford to keep you any longer. He says, I hate like hell to turn you out in this kind of weather. But he says, I don't know where you'd go. But I had already, as I said, made acquaintances with Mr. Cooney, who looked after the skating rink, and I went over there, after I slept that night at Tommy Amos's place.

I went over to his place then, at the skating rink. He was working there to beat hell. And he had a lot to do because he was snowed in practically, you know, the approaches. People had to come there at night to skate, regardless.

So, I was a pretty husky lad then. I was then 18 *(more likely 15)* years old. So, without any asking or anything, I got one of the big snow shovels, and I went at it, and I dug out the walkway into the skating rink. You didn't shovel any more than you had to, I mean, out any further. You shovelled the approach from the sleigh road outside into the skating rink. Shovel the windows out, outside of the windows, because we had to open them in order to throw the ice out when we cleared the rink.

He says, why aren't you working? I said, god I got laid off. I got nothing there to do. There are no teams coming in, no harness coming in. So, I don't know what I'll do now. He says, how would you like to come over and stay with me and help me with the skating rink? He says, I don't feel very good. He says, I feel tough as hell. And he says, your hands would be very handy here, but I can't pay you one nickel. They are not paying me enough, really.

I said, I don't care. I'm not using any money anyway. My clothes was getting pretty well threadbare, though, just the same. My underwear was getting worn out. That's the main thing. I had short underwear on in that bitter cold weather, and I wanted long johns, you see. So, his wife, she…I don't know where she got 'em or anything about these things, Salvation Army. She got me two sets somewhere, free, and I felt pretty good then. Boy oh boy, I could brave most anything.

But the wind came up. The snow quit. The sky cleared just as blue as your eyes, you know, and the wind started. And Cooney, he says to me, he says, do you know the weather around? And I said, I know that we're going to get a big storm, windstorm. That means a three-day blizzard. Yes, he says, and more than that. He says, there was five stars inside the ring of the moon last night, and that's five days of storm, and he was right. There was more than five days. It blew, and it blew, and it blew. It just shifted all that soft 18 inches of snow, like salt it was.

Covered up the houses, low houses, his included. And that's the reason they had their doors opened on the inside, never outside, because they had the screen doors, the storm doors and all. The storm doors opened on the inside also. Otherwise, you'd be froze in. You couldn't get out.

So, it blew. It covered up everything. Covered up our big skating rink. We used to walk over and dig it out. Walk through that snow. Only about less than a quarter of a mile…300 yards. For some reason or other, storms didn't… I never seem to get very cold.

But anyway, one morning, I went over, no skating rink. The thing had just drifted in so full and drifted over the top. I don't know how many feet was on it when I saw it last in the daytime. And that night, nobody knows when, it collapsed. The whole thing fell in, not long after the skating rink had been plum full of people. That's all the place that the town people had to go. There were no movies, nothing like that. So, the skating rink was the place to go.

A nickel was the charge for grown-ups, and kids were free. Anybody under 14 was free. My job was to clean that before and after they left, 12 o'clock. Clean that up before it froze on. Throw it out those windows. And you would get a tonne of snow on there from the skating, you see. I had a huge scraper you run by hand.

Well, now then, what to do? Holy lightnin'! Mr. Cooney, what I was saying a while back, I just went over myself there a little bit. I told you he was feeling very tough. Well, he got the flu, and he couldn't move out of the house. I took care of the whole thing. Now, when she fell, there was no wages for Cooney. So, how was he going to keep me? He couldn't feed me.

So, I had saved this money, and I was a better saver them days than I am now. I'd saved this money that that fellow gave me, $50, because I knew I couldn't get any more until I got proper wages. And I used some of that money, and I went...Ancora...I went up to Kisbey. It was the next town, Kisbey.

Now, what time of the year that was, I don't know, but it was somewheres about March. We always got a dirty thing in March. And I met a fellow there, a farmer. He'd come in. The storm, well, away from buildings, it just drifted, went on to somebody else's place, you see, and it wasn't that bad. It was passable. People had to come to town to get groceries and stuff. There were three big stores in Kisbey, and five elevators. That's all there was. There was no population in there at all.

I met a fellow there, in the hotel. I went to the hotel. That was the place you went if you wanted to find out anything. Either that or the barber shop. I went to the hotel first. They knew I was a stranger, and they said, where did you come from? I said, Arcola. I come up on the train. I said, that's the first train that's come through. I come up on it. It didn't cost me anything either. I just got on it.

Well, then I remember I went to the store. The storekeeper, he noticed that I was a stranger in town. He said, how did you get here, after all that storm? I came up from Arcola. It snowed in. I came up on the snowplough.

He says, what are you going to do here? I said, I don't know. I'll find something, won't I? Question, if you will. Then this man come in, a farmer. He was lame. He noticed I was a stranger, and he said, you're a stranger here, aren't you? Yes, I said, I am. He says, what are you doing? Nothing. I said, I'll have to find something pretty soon.

How would you like to come out, he said, and work for me a little while? I said, that'd be fine. At least I'd have a place to sleep, wouldn't I? Yes, a good, warm house and everything. He says, I won't be able to pay you any money, though, until, well, we'll start off 1st April. Regardless, he says, 1st of April.

He says, how much do you think... I was getting to look like a man by this time, 18. I'm husky. 19 I guess I was then. Yes, I'd be 19 then. And help me around with chores and one thing another. I have a bunch of stock there to feed and snow to shovel and one thing another. You won't be working very hard, mainly because we got to clean all of the seed grain. That all got to be done. And then we got to formaldehyde it and bluestone it and everything for smut. So, I could use you quite handy, if you'd like to come out. Oh god, yes, let me out.

So, he had a cutter. A damn good team of trotters and a cutter. Two-seater, you know. We got in that, put the buffalo robe over us, pulled down our hoods over our heads, and away we went. Well, that turned out to be pretty good. I worked through all summer. And it was sand, grain and one thing another, until seeding time come, and then he started to pay me.

In the fall, I said, well, I want to go threshing. I said, I got to make more money than this for the winter. $26, $1 a day. That's all I got for working steady. Five o'clock in the morning, nine, ten o'clock at night. Well, he said...

That I could go threshing. He said, I don't know what you want to go threshing for. That's a hell of a job. No good place to sleep or anything. I said, it's good money. Threshing went up to $4 a day. Mind you, it was about 12 hours.

So, I went threshing there, and I got quite a bit of money. We got 60 days threshing there. $4 a day made quite a sum of money, and you didn't spend any. What the hell, there's nothing to…you might buy a pair of gloves or something. Sweater or something. But it was all cheap. Everything was cheap.

So, when threshing was over, I couldn't see that country anymore. So, I headed up for Regina. Well, there was nothing to do in Regina. That was a farming country, too. The wind used to sweep… Qu'Appelle was the coldest damn place around there. Regina was supposed to be, but Qu'Appelle was just down 40 miles. It was the coldest spot on that part of prairie.

So, I went back down the line. It wasn't very much. Three cents a mile on the railroad. If you could get a boxcar and jump into it, they had to stop at every station. So, I went down to what they called Stoughton. Lo and behold, Stoughton was the brother-in-law of the place I had just left. He says, darn it, he says, there are lots of little chores around town here. He says, I think I can get you on for the winter. Oh god, I said, that's fine.

He says, you can stay with me, if you wanted. I won't charge you much for board and room. And he says, you'll get paid for the work you do cleaning out the barn, and working the livery barn, and I don't know, there were a lot of different things. Hauling coal from the livery barn. Take the team and haul. Empty a car of coal and all this stuff, you see. I made out all right. I got paid a little bit for that. $1 a day.

Springtime, I headed back for Regina. I was sitting in a park there, along with a fellow by the name of Mr. Morrison. He was a retired farmer from Stoughton, and it's from where I just had come from, and that's how I'd come to talking to him. We're sitting there, talking away. Where I'd been, and what I've done, all this stuff.

A little fellow came *(Mr. Jenkins)*, stood right in front of us. This was a very, very pleasant day. Not warm, but warm as far as the prairie goes. Above zero. And he said, either one of you fellows want a job for the summer? Well, Morrison says, I really don't need any job. He says, I'm retired. But he says, this young fellow here is looking for work, and he say, I can recommend him. I've known him, known all of them for quite a while, and he says, he knows all about farming.

Well, he says, would you like to go out…to me? I said, I don't know, I don't know. What wages are you paying? What are you paying now? Starting. When do you want to start? He says, when you say you're going to go out with me, your wages start right there. No monkeying around. He was a Yankee from the States, up there for his health. Been a dentist in Omaha.

Joy he says, now, there's a chance for you, this Morrison. Well, I said, I'm taking it, too. When do we start? He says, I'm on the way home now. 17 miles we drove. It was cold. It got colder and colder. I didn't have any good clothes for riding out there, in the bare prairie, but we got out and run behind. He did, too. He got cold. The horses went anyway.

I stayed there all summer. $1 a day and board. That was high wages. This was the highest any man could get, no matter how good he was. There was no one who knew any more about that kind of farming than me. Grown up to it.

In the fall, he says, I don't think I'd like to put in the winter here, from what I've heard. He bought this place half section from a farmer. And he says, my wife and I want to go back to Omaha for the winter. He says, we'll be playing in the orchestra there again, like I left. Could you stay here for the winter?

Yes, I said, but I won't stay for nothing. No, he says, you'll get $1 a day for the winter, because I'm going to have to ask you to draw…there was no wheat there. It was all flax. I'm going to ask you to draw a carload of flax as soon as it's the time, and then another carload later on, of flax. Well I said, that's fine. I said, sure, I'll look after your stock.

Anyway, Mr. Jenkins was a great solo violinist. He was the leader, a violin leader, in a big orchestra in Omaha, and his wife was one of many good pianists that was in the country at that time. So, they had lots of music. They would get music from Omaha, in a roll. And it didn't matter if hell froze over, he would go right in the house when the mailman come, and he'd done roll that music, and if I was around, they'd holler for me to come in.

By the way, we only got our mail once a week then. Remember that? Once a week. And so, he'd get his violin out, she'd sit down, and they would play that off of there, just like they both were reading the newspaper. Never saw it before. It was wonderful the way they could play.

And in order to induce me to stay, little higher wages and all, he said he would get a good violin. I was playing the violin. I learned to play the violin. I bought it when I was working for Mr. Finn. If you remember, I mentioned Finn. He had two nice daughters. That's the one I mean.

And I went to town, and I saw a fellow there getting a violin for his kid, just before Christmas. Believe it or not, it was in a drugstore. Drugstores carried everything them days, in them little towns. But believe it or not, that violin case, bow, rosin, $5. Well, I needed a violin. I liked the violin all right.

So, I couldn't wait 'til that guy got out of the store. I watched him and marched up, and I said, I would like one of those violins. Well, being the age I was, he knew it was no good to me. So, he just simply said, he said, I wouldn't sell you one of those kinds of violins. I have a nice, little violin here, bow, rosin, some extra strings. By the way, there was no steel strings them days. All gut, every one, plain gut. And a nice case for it. Canvas case, of course.

$10. Well, that's all I had money. That's all I had with me, is $10. So, I said, that just takes away my money, my $10, and I wanted to get a couple of things here, too, for myself. What did you want? So, I told him. He went and got them, and he says, there you are. You have the violin and the two items that you wanted. $10.

My God, I couldn't wait until I got home. I had bought the old gent a couple of bottles, one bottle of gin for the missus, and a bottle of Irish whiskey for him. I learned that violin just the same.

So, I don't know. That was it. Another two or three places where you might've misunderstood me, but I might have to say this all over again. So, when I bought that there little, cheap violin, little did I know right then how much a violin would mean to me in my lifetime, and I surely have profited by buying that little violin.

Here I was, all alone in that house again. Alone in the prairie. I don't know how I ever made out, but I wasn't daunted at nothing. When I saw my way clear, I took it. And I got word. I'd been there about a month. Got word, start drawing 1,000 bushels of flax. They go by bushels there. Here, they go by tonne. 1,000 bushels of flax. The elevator can start right in as soon as you get this letter.

So, I did that, and that's where I met Bragg. He also was hauling flax off his father's place. Father had a rented place down below, about a mile straight as a string from my place. The road run right by the house.

I always started out and never thought about him. One time, I was a little slow getting started. It had drifted and drifted all night long, and the wind was coming across the big yard he had there, making drifts, and I had quite a job getting started. You always left your load ready to go. So, I hitched the four horses on it and got the big hammer, big sledge. Hit each one of the runners. There were four runners. Hit them so as to break them from freezing there, and away we went out on the road. I got in there, got out, come home.

Bragg followed in about half a mile back. I think my horses was faster than his. And we got quite a bit ahead and unloaded horses in the livery barn. I went to the restaurant to eat and started home.

A few days after that, it took about nine, from nine to ten trips to fill that elevator, then the elevator put it in a car, when there was a car ready, a railroad car. So, about the fourth or fifth trip, I seen this fellow coming again, and I said, Jesus, I'm not gonna break that goddamn trail from her to hereafter.

The road was rutted, about six or eight inches deep, and it was lovely sledding if the wind wasn't blowing. But the wind would blow crossways across that and fill those ruts full, and we had to break that trail. So, I said, hang on. When he goes by, I'll slip my four horses out of the barn, and hitch 'em up, and I'll follow him. That didn't make any difference. He hadn't gone 100 yards when the thing was full just the same, that wind just would cut the eyes right out of you, you know.

But anyway, I caught up to him. He stopped, and I caught up to him, and we talked. I think he was a couple of years younger than me. And he asked me where I was going. Well, he says, we'll start off the horses as we'll walked. So, he started his team, and we walked behind his team, and mine followed us, you see. All them horses knew what they had to do. Big, lovely, handsome horses. No Cayuses. So, I got talking to him, and he says, what do you do anyway? I said I read a lot, and I said, the farmer I'm working for…sent a bunch of apples up from somewhere.

But I could say a lot more about that kind of thing, but I don't think it'd be very attractive reading, really. So, figured all around, I guess I better start right now on what I call living. So, we'll go right on now, carry on to where Bragg's father and him and all, and I refused to work anymore for that fellow. I followed Bragg. So, we'll carry on, 'eh?

Well, away we go, on the railroad, up to Regina. We loaded all what they call settlers' effects on. We had a pig that was expecting. We had a cow, harrow, binder, mower, everything else it demanded. Four wagons and four teams. There was four of us. It was Mr. Bragg, Noble Bragg, my friend, and his brother, which I had never met before then, and myself.

So, we each to a wagon, and we loaded them all up on there. My wagon was full lumber, full to the top. About 2,000 feet of lumber. I think Braggs and them had some, too. And we found out at the Regina land office, that there was land available, homestead available, about 60 to 80 miles northwest of Bassano. That meant it was about straight north from Brooks, Alberta. This is Alberta we're talking about now.

And they couldn't do anything about allowing us what, telling us what it was or anything about it. So, they said, you go to Bassano, unload there, get the land office to give you a list of what homesteads is available, and then you go out and you find that section of land. Each one of you wants a quarter, I understand. You find that section of land, come back again and file on it, and then nobody else can get it.

In the meantime, you don't really have to live on it the first month or so. So, you can…well, we said, that's what we want. We're going out there to stay. He said, you do what I tell you and you'll be all right. So, way up there we went, on the train.

And *(the folks at the land office at)* Bassano was very sharp. They got right in there, and they told us they were looking for settlers for sure, and they told us where it was, and whereabout it was marked on the map, where this section was, that section. God, we went away happy.

Everything was loaded up and all and ready to go. Lots of grass on the prairie for the horses and the cow. We had lots of feed for the pig. By god, we had some chickens, too. They laid eggs. All this time, they were laying eggs.

We started out across the prairie. Now, anyone that's done it will tell you it's the truth. We had no idea except it was northwest of Bassano. Mr. Bragg had a bit of knowledge of…I don't know what you call it. Hunting land or something. So, he carried the map, and we went from stake to stake. We found these stakes without any trouble. He just led us right to them. We had quite a nice time. It took us about three days to get there. It was 80 miles about.

Lovely weather. Warm. And remember that. Keep that in your mind, will you? It was lovely and warm. We slept under the wagon. There were no sleeping bags them days, really, but we had lots of blankets. I had lots of blankets and tarpaulins. We slept under the wagons.

Well, up we get. The antelope was across there on the prairie. They couldn't understand these funny things on the prairie, wagons and horses and stuff. Every once in a while, a cow would give a big moo, and boy would they ever go. They can run. I guess they're the fastest thing on foot almost, in the deer line. But they'd come back again and feed and everything else.

We never shot at them. We didn't need to. We had nice, little rifles, and we had big rifles also. We used to shoot gophers, though, and one thing another. They were popping up through holes in the prairie. It was really lots of fun.

But almost to the end of, I think it was, the third day, we were told by a fellow that was coming that the prairie was burnt black in front of us, about five miles further on. He said, where do you want to go? We told him, we showed him the map. By god, he says, I believe that part is burnt also. Where I come from, it missed me.

Anyway, we had nothing else to do but to go. There we were, out there, on the lone prairie, as the fellow says, and we had this lumber. We'd put up a shack…hell, there was lots of things we overlooked, of course. So, we went on. Sure enough, five miles on then, the prairie was burnt black. It had just been burned about two days before.

That made the stakes easier to find. There was no prairie wool, as they called it, growing up to cover them. No pasture for the horses or cow. We had a bit of hay. We got to our destination anyway. One stake, and it had four numbers on it. But anyway, it had one of our numbers, so that was good enough.

We set the shack up in no time. We got there about, I should say, about half past one, in the daytime. And we just went to work, the four of us, and we put that shack up, and we had the roof on. Not shingles, but just the roof by that time, for the night. So, we all slept in our blankets and one thing another in that shack. It was 18 by 24.

Now, we had to tie the horses up there on the wagon spokes and one thing another. There wasn't a thing to eat. And a little bit of wind came up, and it blew the ashes off that grass, upon my word, everything was covered with soot. And we had to take the horses over a mile down to some river. I forget the name of that river now. Could be Bassano River or something like that.

Anyway, we took 'em down there, and we had made up a kind of stone-boat, out of the timber stuff, the two by sixes, and braced it up good. Put a barrel on that we had taken with us, with a lot of miscellaneous stuff in this barrel. We just dumped it out and put it on the stone-boat, wired the barrel on and we took it with us. And it upset twice coming up. The prairie was fairly smooth, but not that smooth.

But anyway, we got back with a barrel of water for the stock that was there that couldn't be led, like the pigs and the chickens and whatnots. We led the cow, everybody went. I'd like to have a picture of that.

But nevertheless, we talked about the whole thing, and we wondered what we should do. There was only one thing to do. Go back to Bassano and go to the land office and abandon these homesteads. Just simply tell them, we don't want them. We'll write a script. They gave us a piece of paper, and we wrote on that, and they gave us a duplicate of that, and that meant that now we didn't have a homestead. It meant a lot to me later in the year. You had to have abandonment papers, you see (in order to be able to get another homestead somewhere else, since you were only allowed one homestead).

Well, what to do now? Old Bragg says, I'm going to go back where I came from, Regina and out there, where we were, and I'll re-rent that farm if it's available. Nobody knew it was for rent anyway, so it would be available. It was only a couple of weeks, that's all, since he left it.

Well, Noble said, I'm not going to go back there, no, sir. I said, "Well I'm staying with you". Well Kerry, the other brother, said "Well, I'm going with the old man". They went east. We went west. And we dealed ourselves for Revelstoke, British Columbia, the land of the apples and all the peaches and plums. Boy oh boy, would we ever have a bunch of them. Now, we had perfect weather. The sun came out of the ground, it was flat, the sun came out of the ground and went down in the ground. No hills, no nothing.

Of course, the train came back (to Bassano) at night. It came by there about nine o'clock at night. We got on with our fiddle and our blankets and a trunk we had. We loaded that. That went on with our passage money. I had my fiddle, of course, and we went. We got to Revelstoke at midnight or thereabouts. I don't know just what it was. It was that day or the next day.

We didn't know what to do. There was two towns, they told us. Upper town, lower town. You go to lower town, all the expenses were way lower than upper town. Upper town was where the railroad station was, and all the big shots lived upper town. Lower town was not so good. It was for loggers, really, for loggers, and pole makers and everything else, river drivers.

There were three hotels there, the Lakewood, and the Oriental, and I forget the other name. Rosewood or something like that. All built on the banks of the Columbia. We were told the best place for us two, in our condition, not knowing anybody, would be the Oriental, because the man that owned it, ran it, Mr. Stone, Albert Stone his name was, he was a very good fellow with fellows that were down and out. We said, we're really not down and out, but we will be if we don't get some work.

Now, I missed the little bit of stuff there. When we got off the train, we couldn't believe our eyes. You couldn't see over the station platform for snow. That was 12-feet high. The snowplough had come along there just a day or two before and just threw that right out of there, threw it every place. We went down to lower town and believe it, this was the horseless buggy. It was a buggy with a big motor in it and a chain on the back wheel. It was the first of the horseless carriages. We went down in that. That was the taxi.

He landed us in Albert Stone's, and we got a room there, and this was the price: $5 a week, bed, board, bath, and everything that went with it, everything in a good hotel, $5 a week. So, we gave him $10 each. We thought we'd make sure we'd have it for two weeks anyway. And we said, where could we put the trunk? He said, I'll have it put up in the attic. I got a lot of them up there.

And he says, what are you going to do? We heard about the Big Eddy sawmill was going to open up soon. Oh well, he said, that won't be soon now, because we had this terrific snowstorm here. It snowed four feet, four to five feet of snow nearly overnight, one day and a night. That's why you see so much snow just lately. Well, we figured we'd be all right anyway.

We went up the bedroom. Well, we were music crazy, Bragg and I. He loved that fiddle, and I loved that banjo. So, we must have both got along pretty well together. We were in the room the next day, I said, what do ya suppose, get out and keep practicing a little? Oh, yeah. We got out and tuned up. We were just going to town there, Arkansas Traveler, Soldier's Joy and all that stuff.

I believed I could play the fiddle them days. And it wasn't long until Albert Stone came up, and he knocked at the door, and I opened it. I said, it's you. I guess we've been a nuisance. We shouldn't be playing here. Far from that, he says. Far from that, my boy. We were really boys yet, you see. He says, you come right down. Bring them instruments down to the big sitting room and play down there. You don't need to play in your bedroom. So he says, come down after lunch, after you've had your lunch.

So, we went and had dinner, what we call dinner, we called it dinner. About two o'clock, he come, he says, how about giving us a little music there now on them two instruments? So, we rattled away there for a couple of hours. A lot of people congregated, and they bought drinks. He had a wonderful, big place there, a regular lumberjacks' hotel. Lots of room, sitting room was a huge place.

And they began to dance. They came in after supper, cork shoes and half boozed up, and I quit playing, you see, and Bragg. They all stopped and looked at us. Stone was tending the bar, and he came over, and he says, what's the trouble? You want a drink or something? I said, no, I said, look at that floor. If we keep playing, there won't be any more floor left. Don't you worry about that floor, he says. You just keep playing as long as you want to play, and I'll make up with the floor.

He didn't know who he was talking to, because we could play a long, long time. And we played, and they came from the Lakewood hotel, and they came from that other hotel, and his bunch, and they all was in there.

God damn, stag dancing, mind you. No women, just men, just rarin' to beat hell, whoopin' and hollerin'. Mostly Swedish, Scandinavian. And I could play an awful lot of Scandinavian waltzes and polkas at that time. I think I can yet. They just never heard anything like that at Albert Stone. Where did you boys come from? What do you do for a living? We says, we did come here to work at the Big Eddy. That's all. So, that's the way it was.

At that time, what I should have mentioned about this whole thing was that we were absolutely strangers. We were prairie chickens, they called us. We had no idea of logging or the huge mountains that we saw when we woke up in the morning. Revelstoke is just at the foot of them all, and the raging river, Columbia River below us. The snow had started to melt up high, and holy smoke, we were really stunned, in a way.

But like I said, little did I know, when I bought that little old fiddle, how much the fiddle was going to mean to me, and it sure is paying off now. Because when the snow melted more, the Columbia raised up, and the Big Eddy was just what it was supposed to be. The mill was on the top, and the Eddy was like the thumb in your hand. The river was your hand, and the thumb was the Eddy.

You could put a couple of million feet of logs in there, and more in the cove. And they weren't toothpicks, these logs, we found out. They were anywhere from six to eight feet at the butt and 40 feet long, 20 feet long and all that stuff.

And we went down every day to see how things was, when the mill was going to start. Oh, we're just about ready, just about ready, and that was fine. We'd go back and tell Stone that, well, she's just about ready. That night, the flood really came down that river, and it went by the

Big Eddy so fast that the suction of that river drawed the logs out of that Eddy, they call them the Eddy, the Big Eddy.

It drawed them out. It started moving, and they whirled and whirled and whirled. When we went down the next morning, there was a dozen experienced dynamite men riding those big logs, boring holes in them, and putting dynamite in it to blow them up so that they would stop the whirl. They were just whirling like mad, round and round and round. I suppose there's about 20 acres of eddy there, and they were full of them big logs.

But by night, there wasn't one log left. They all went down the river. To whom we don't know. Then that ended the Big Eddy stuff. So, we went back, and of course the news had got all around that the Big Eddy had gone out.

And when we went in, I guess we didn't look very pleased, because we'd almost figured on starting the next day or so. We were running short on money. Bragg had more money than I did, because he was given more money, you see, and he didn't spend unless he had to, and I would.

Well, we're getting kind of short on money, and we don't know what to do. We don't want to stick around here until we can pay. He said, I tell you what, as long as you two boys play them two instruments here, you can stay for free.

Now, that wasn't much what they call recompense for fiddling. $5 a week was all we had to pay for board. And if we played the fiddle the way there, we'd play every night. But that was the best we could do. So, we played there, and we got no money for the playing.

But what I forgot to mention a while ago was neither Bragg or I drank whiskey or anything like that, at that time. That was pretty good for young fellows. But we smoked. And we didn't smoke cigars much, and cigarettes wasn't... I don't know. You never seen anybody smoke cigarettes (everyone rolled their own).

We were used to smoking pipes. And Noble Bragg could smoke a pipe when he was playing the banjo. I couldn't when I was playing the fiddle because the pipe went on the top of the fiddle and made a funny noise. So, I had to let off smoking until we had a kind of recess, and then I'd smoke the pipe. But we never smoked cigarettes or cigars.

So, when we didn't drink, which was to the lumberjacks' astonishment of two grown-up men not drinking whiskey, what was the matter with them? But they still made up for it. They gave us cigarettes and cigars to the tune of everything, all we wanted. So, that's how it came about, you see. We could get everything we wanted for free. Fiddle and banjo together were something worth listening to. It must have been. Anyway, I'm going to make coffee right now. So, toodle-oo."

Editor's note – this is the end of Ernie's taping session. His son, Elmer, continues with some of the rest of Ernie's story:

ELMER BUCKINGHAM: "The story was told by Ernest Silas Buckingham a few months before his death on July 24, 1977. The recording was found amongst his belongings, but unfortunately we cannot find the ending to the story. So, we can only presume that he never did get around to completing the history.

I am his son Elmer and will briefly describe the next 60 years of his life. Ernie and his buddy got the job with the survey party and worked the Shuswap Lake area for many years, and as he told you, played for many dances and parties throughout his lifetime. Some of the dates in his part of the story are out a few years. For instance, he was 12 years old when he arrived in Canada in 1898.

Ernie married Jean Brown of Celeste and had five children, Laura, May, Fern, Stanley, and Marie. All are living today, with exception of Stanley, who passed away at around 30 years of age.

Ernie's wife Jean passed away, leaving him with the five children, living in a small homestead at Blind Bay, on the Shuswap Lake. He was unable to work and care for all of them, the youngest being only two or three years of age. The three youngest were adopted out, leaving Laura and May to stay with Dad as they were older, about seven and eight, and could look after themselves with the help of the neighbours.

Ernie married Connie Harrison of Pritchard and had two sons, Elmer, and Herbert. He tried the homestead again, but the lack of water made it impossible to farm. So, he went to Chase to work in the sawmill. He also held down various and sundry other jobs until 1926, when he moved to Vancouver. He worked for BC Electric for a few years, but with the… As with others, the Depression took its toll and he was laid off.

Ernie then fell back on his carpentry trade, which he had learned during the two or three-year period between survey jobs. He went into the renovation business and worked for many years around Vancouver.

During the Second World War, he got a factory job, which he stayed with until he retired at about age 70. To augment his wages, he formed an orchestra and played for two to four dances a week for many years. This was an old-time dance band. In listening to his recorded music of late, we can only wish that recordings had been made when he was in his heyday. If there is time left on this tape, I will record a portion of his fiddle music as he played it in the last years.

There are many things that could be told about Ernie, but this tape is almost over. If other histories are located, we will augment this tape with them. Thank you for listening."

Ed. note – according to Alice, Ernie tried to contact his son, Stanley, prior to Stanley's passing in 1952, but Stanley felt so much loyalty to his adopted parents that he refused to reconnect with his birth father at the time.

APPENDIX 3: ERNIE BUCKINGHAM HISTORY

- Written by Patricia (Goldney) Millar, September 1997 *[Ed. note – this was shared with the Kappel sisters by Jack Brown in 2011]*

"Ernest Silas Buckingham, was born on September 20, 1886, in Plymouth, Devon, England, as shown on his birth certificate. He had always thought his birth date was September 26; plus further information from Barnardo's Orphanage where he was admitted February 10, 1892, shows he was born September 19. His brother, Archibald Prosper Buckingham, was also admitted to the orphanage at the same time. Their mother's name was Amanda Ley; their maternal grandfather was Nicholas Ley. Ernie's father was Joseph Buckingham; his paternal grandfather was Adam Buckingham.

Ernie and his brother spent three days at a 'receiving home' in Stepney Causeway, London E. and were then transferred to Sheppard House at Grove Road, Bow, E. 3. East London. Then April 10, 1892, they went to a foster home in Broxsted, England.

On July 7, 1898, Ernie returned to Stepney in preparation for his emigration to Canada. He sailed on July 21, 1898, on the S.S. Labrador, and arrived in Quebec July 30. After his arrival in Canada, he went to live with Mr. and Mrs. Gregson in Oxbow N.W.T. (1905, it would be known as Oxbow, Saskatchewan.) Archibald sailed on the S.S. Arawa, on September 11, 1899. The two brothers never made contact again.

Information received from Barnardo's Orphanage, reported he was working for a Mr. J. Wood at Oxbow in January 1900, then in 1901, their report showed he had had several moves during the year, and his whereabouts were unknown at that time. In December 1902, it appears that some news had been received and he had been working with a gang of threshers, but no definite address was given.

Ernie worked for farms throughout Saskatchewan, and in Regina he met Noble Bragg, whose parents were going to Brooks, Alberta to homestead. Ernie went along with them and drove one of their three wagons. They arrived to find their quarter section had just been crossed by a prairie fire. There was no water on the land and with no feed for their stock, the Braggs decided to return to Bassano, Alberta. Instead of taking everything back with then they sold their livestock, a load of lumber, and two wagons to a man on the next homestead.

Ernie and Noble decided to move on to B.C. Ernie took his fiddle, Noble took his banjo, and they hopped a freight. It was the end of March, 1910, and the snow was gone on the prairies, - but they arrived in Revelstoke to find twelve feet of snow.

Staying at the Oriental Hotel they were to have a job in two weeks at the Big Eddy Mill, but before their job started - the Columbia River flooded and the mill closed down. Word came, a survey party needed two young men in Sicamous and they left immediately. At Mobley Bay they lived in tents. The first campsite was the present site of Twin Cedars, at Anglemont. The survey party had to move camps several times to avoid high water.

At a community dance, to celebrate the opening of the new school at Celista, the survey crew found the musicians hadn't shown up. The boss 'volunteered' Ernie and Noble's services, and the 'Buck and Bragg' orchestra got their start in the Shuswap area. Ernie said, " From then on we were paid well to play anywhere we could get to." Their two-man band took them to many areas.

Noble Bragg homesteaded at Celista and quit the band. Ernie found a new musical partner in his neighbour, Ole Widmark, and together they performed at many country dances. He helped to build the Sorrento Hall, and the log church in 1912.

Ernie remembers the winter of 1912 /1913; there was no snow, and the ice on the Shuswap Lake was two feet thick. He said, "I skated from Celista to Seymour Arm.

Ernie met a Scottish girl from Celista, Jean Brown. They were married December 26, 1912, at 'Chase Ranch' by Rev. Watkins, and their wedding reception was held in the new Celista school. One of the many gifts to the young couple, was a boat from 'boat builder' Harry Fowler.

Jean played the mandolin and they entertained often in the Notch Hill settlement. Ernie was also known for his recitations such as, "Face on the bar room floor".

Jean Brown and Ernie Buckingham

Ernie and Jean pre-empted a homestead of 160 acres on a hill at Blind Bay, which later became 'Shuswap Estates' where they built a log house; one large room with an attic, and a lean-to. Ernie and Jean had a very busy life, full of work for their survival, but they also found ways to have fun with their family. They had five children; Laura Margaret, May Catherine, Jean Ellen, Donald Angus, and Mina Marie.

Ernie was always a clean-shaven pioneer, when most men had full beards; it made him look younger. Laura remembers, "he was very good-looking". This was very evident in his early photographs. Learning photography and dark-room developing was a hobby he taught himself - so there was a legacy of photographs of his early life and his family.

January 27, 1921, Jean passed away from a tubal pregnancy. Ernie found he couldn't provide care for all the children, and it was impossible to find foster homes for them. Many neighbours expressed a wish to adopt them so the three youngest were adopted out; he was able to keep the two eldest with him. He worked many places, including Chase where he worked for the mill.

Two years later October, 1923, Ernie married Constance Harrison of Pritchard. They lived in his old homestead, and several other places to accommodate Ernie's work. In 1927 they moved to the coast. They had two children; Elmer Ernest, born in Blind Bay; and Herbert Oliver, born in Vancouver.

Ernie's first job in Vancouver was working for B. C. Electric on the street-car tracks. The 1929 depression made jobs hard to get, but he always had his music. He formed an old-time orchestra, called the 'Joy Makers'; they played regularly on radio station CKMO and for dances; he also renovated houses. After the depression Ernie got a job in a furniture factory, where he learned the skills for his hobby, making doll furniture for his grandchildren, mechanical wood ferris-wheels, houses, people etc.

Ernie and Connie, and their family, continued to live and work in Vancouver. Connie worked in a gift and china shop in Vancouver; it was a job she really enjoyed. Constance died of cancer May 9, 1960.

Ernie had a zest for life; he bought a two-pant suit for his 80th Birthday party, and did the same for his 90th. He even checked with the hall committee in Burnaby to make sure the hall would be available in another ten years' time.

During the summer, Ernie was a frequent visitor at the home of his daughter, Laura and his son-in-law Bill, at Magna Bay, where he would entertain the young people with his fiddle and his recitations. He taught his great-grandchildren how to play crib.

Failing eye-sight and hearing, emphysema, and some heart trouble, didn't keep Ernie down. He would say "There's lots worse than me". He was visiting friends in Balmoral, Sorrento, playing his fiddle, when he had a fatal heart attack, July 23, 1977.

Credits for the history in this story go to:
a tape recording by Ernie Buckingham
Research by
Elmer Buckingham,
Ken Buckingham (cousin in England)
(his father Joseph James was a half-brother to Ernie)
Marie Buckingham Immel Dunbar

Credits for the memories in this story go to:
Laura Buckingham Goldney
Patricia Goldney Millar

As Ernie's oldest granddaughter, I have lots of good memories; I have the doll furniture Grampa made for me for Christmas' during the 40's, a crib, trunk, high-chair, and ironing board. I also have the china Connie gave me during the 50's, for Christmas, shower, and wedding gifts.

Ernie Buckingham writes about 1910

"About my arrival on the Shuswap Lake. I came there with Chief Doug Stewarts Survey gang May 10th 1910. As far as any accomplishments I guess I wasn't one of that kind. I fell through the ice the year I was married skating from Celista to Cliffords place when I was helping MacKay build the place. It's still there too, I saw it the last time I was up there. I got frozen in the lake in Mr. John Reedman's boat and we all walked out on the ice in a few hours, that's about the extent of my adventures. You might say I never started to live until I hit that lake."

"Coming from that hot dry Prairie it sure was a big change all I can say is that I enjoyed every day I was in the district, even with that husband of yours, getting into the root cellar, and tapping the cider barrels and pouring water on the floor below it to make the Senior Reedman think that the tap had leaked. We used to come back from the White Lake dances to get a couple more jugs of the stuff, it must have be 10 over proof, sure was strong. It seemed everyone was happy them days, all had something to keep them busy no one seemed to complain. Dancing, skating, and sleigh riding were the things we enjoyed in those days."

APPENDIX 4: THE THOMAS BROWN STORY

Ed. note – According to a biography of Thomas Brown written by his granddaughter, Laura Goldney, Ernie and Jeanie Buckingham's daughter, in 1989:

"My grandparents, Thomas and Jemima Brown, lived in Glasgow with their large family. Tom Jr. was married to Jane McGowan with 2 boys, Hugh 4 years old and James 2 years. Then there was Andrew, Joe, John, Billy, Elizabeth, Mina, Maggie and Jean who was nine years old. In 1904, when Canada was advertising for new settlers, saying that free land and golden opportunities awaited, the Browns answered the call. Some wag said that when Canada needed settlers they sent for the Browns. Hugh who was four when they landed at Halifax, has written about the trip over the Atlantic and the arrival, the train ride to their destination in Saskatchewan.

Tom (Jr.) and family got a homestead in Saskatchewan, but Grampa (Tom) and the others went to Moosejaw, Saskatchewan. Andrew stayed in Ontario and never did come west. Elizabeth married Bill Smith and moved to Vermillion, Alberta, and Mina married a distant cousin of Tom Brown. They were starting their families, so Granny already had several grandchildren.

In 1907 Joe (the 6th Brown child), who was a surveyor and civil servant, went on

Thomas Brown I circa 1900

to B.C. by C.R.P. *[Ed. note: Canadian Pacific Railway],* to Notch Hill. Notch Hill seemed to be the "jumping off" place for settlers who were bound for Eagle Bay, Blind Bay, Balmoral, Sorrento, and the north side of Shuswap Lake. There were few roads anywhere then. Joe preempted a homestead up Meadow Creek. The C.P.R. was the only link to the outside world.

Joe coaxed his father to bring the family to Shuswap as it was much nicer than the prairies, so in 1908 they all packed up and came to quite a wilderness. Joe met the train and they went by horse and buggy in Sorrento, then on a launch to what is now Celista. They must have wondered what was coming next.

There was a two-room cabin on Joe's place so that is where they all had to live until their new big house was built. Grampa filed for his homestead where Meadow Creek Estates is now. Land was cleared and the house made of logs was started. Harry Fowler, a man with many trades and talents, the first pioneer in the area, worked on the house, too, so with other help it was ready to live in by fall of 1910.

In the meantime in 1909 Tom Jr. & Jane sold their farm in Sask. and came to Celista. They were met on the beach by the whole family, & Granny was happy to see her little grandchildren. Two more had been added, Jean and young Tommy. They had to live in cabins up in the forest in the winter or on the beach in the summer in a tent, until their large house was built. Billy Jack was born in the tent in 1911 (ca.)

Granny's new house must have seemed like a palace with so many rooms and upstairs, too. They all kept busy with gardens, planting fruit trees and some lilac bushes, etc., as well as building fences. The first cow was always wandering off, and someone had to find her, which took time. Clearing land was an ongoing job to make fields for hay.

Joe worked on the Chase Ranch and met Catherine Chase daughter of Whitfield Chase. They were married in 1912 and lived on Joe's place in Meadow Creek. Billy had a homestead farther up behind Joe's and John preempted land where the church camp is now, in Magna Bay. Tom & Jane bought ten acres from Grampa as he could not get a homestead, having had one on the prairie.

They were a fun-loving family as well as hard workers, loved company, and the Scottish dances and songs made life brighter. Tom Jr. played violin, Jeanie the mandolin and they knew all the dances.

Communication was a problem. No roads yet; first trails until 1913 or 14 (when the first roads were built); no phones till 1915; and of course, no radios. Travel was by stern-wheeler or other boats. When the road went through, Harry Fowler was foreman, then the ferry started (at Scotch Creek). Horse and buggy or sleigh or walking were the only ways to get between neighbors. Building the roads meant summer jobs for most of the men. It was hard work, no bull dozers or trucks then.

In 1910 the surveyors came to Shuswap, they camped in various places on the beaches. My father, Ernie "Buck" Buckingham and friend Nobel Bragg were with them. Buck played the fiddle and Nobel the banjo or guitar, and "Buck and Bragg" became quite well known when it came to dances and parties. Buck got a homestead, 160 acres where Shuswap Estates is now, and Nobel got one in North Shuswap. In 1912, Buck married Jeanie Brown. Jeanie and Maggie loved dancing and were favorites whenever they attended the dances in Chase or Sorrento or anywhere. About this time George Chase, nephew of Whitfield Chase, married Maggie. He was 45 and she was 22 years old. His wife had died in 1907 leaving George with seven children. He had worn a black patch over one eye since childhood because of an accident. It made him a little different, also he was a very big man. They lived on the Chase Ranch until 1914, when they moved to Turtle Valley with son Lucius.

In 1913 I was born *[8 July]*, Buck and Jeanie's first child, in Chase Hospital. Also in Oct. 1913 Chasie was born to Catherine & Joe. Catherine did not live long afterward. Mina was born in 1914 to Tom & Jane, and May was born in Grampa's house in 1915 to Buck and Jeanie.

Grampa and Grannie's family was increasing! John joined the Army in 1915, went over-seas, was wounded in one leg. He married Bessie and brought her over to Celista, but she did not care for the country life so they moved to Vancouver. They had Margaret and Christopher. Chris had five children, and they did come to the lake in summer holidays.

In 1917 Grampa had a stroke, which left him in a wheelchair until his death in 1919.

By now, Buck and Jeanie had 3 more children, Jean Ellen, Donald and Marie. Aunt Maggie & George Chase had two more boys, Tom & Howard.

Tom & Jane had one more boy, Russel, but Jane died. There were seven children, Hugh the oldest at nineteen years. Aunt Maggie contracted that terrible flu that swept the country after the war, and died in 1918. My mother, Jeanie, died in January 1921, near her 26th birthday, in Kamloops Hospital.

In the fall of 1921 Granny was laid to rest, some said she died of a broken heart.

In 1922 Tom Jr., father of 7, was killed in a logging accident. The children, some of them adults, moved to the coast & found jobs and cared for the younger ones. Uncle Joe was made their guardian. Their home was sold to Mr. & Mrs. Leo Smith, who opened a store which filled a great need for the homesteaders.

From such a large family when they arrived at Shuswap Lake, there were only Uncle Billie, Uncle Joe, and son Chasey left in the area.

Uncle Joe went into partnership with Mrs. Smith in the store, and he was postmaster, then in 1939 he was made magistrate. Chasey joined the army in World War 2, then helped to run the store. They bought Sison store in Magna Bay so now there were two Brown & Smith Stores.

Billy Jack came back to Celista and lived at Uncle Joes in the big log house. He had been to technical school and learned drafting. Later he designed and helped to build the Community Hall which opened in 1934. He and Chasey and installed, for one night at least, the first cycadelic lighting system seen around here. A large circular plywood, with 3 holes carefully cut out & covered with yellow, red & blue cellophane, then attached to an old phonograph with a handle to turn by someone & with no electric lights, they used a car battery and head-lamp. It worked well except that it grew tiresome turning that handle!

Billy Jack's sister, Mina and husband Kelly Campbell came back and they ran the Magna Bay store, and had two daughters, Jean & Anne.

**Thomas Brown I, Jemima Fraser and dog Barny
in front of the old log house circa 1918**

Billy Jack married school teacher Lori Tennant, had two daughters, and they had many acres in Magna Bay. He built a lovely log house, he said it took 25 years to build, it was rather slow going for the first 15 years, then he went like H--- for the next ten.

Chasey married Pat and they had four children, 2 boys & 2 girls, and he now lives in a modern home where the old log house had been, with son Bob & family. Pat died in ??

Looking back from 1989, and seeing the changes, it would be nice if those old timers could see what they started. The cousins who were born between 1900 and 1920 do meet some times, some even live around the lake. Hugh & Jim Brown who came over on the ship from Glasgow.

APPENDIX 5: Some of The Early Pioneers of the 1890's: By Hugh Brown (1901-1990)

Ed. note – This has been transcribed unedited from Hugh Brown's original hand typed manuscript except for a few comments in brackets (by John Wm Brown – jwb); it was provided by Jack Brown, Hugh's grandson.

"My Father and Mother [Thomas Brown II and Jane Coats McGowan] decided to come out to Canada, the land of the golden opportunities, free land etc. according to the headlines in the papers over there. Conditions were very bad in Scotland at that time, so many unemployed. We boarded the ship [Allan Line SS Laurention] which was supposed to be a modern liner, but would be classified as a tramp ship under present day standards. We had to be taken out to the ship in what they called tender boats as the harbor wasn't deep enough to accommodate the ship at the docks. I think the boat was called the Sophia [SS Laurention we have the passenger manifest, jwb]. My parents didn't have much money, came over in what was called steerage which is the lowest part of the ship hull. There were only bunks in the cabins, made you feel as though you might be in a prison. It had central washrooms which you had to pay to use. Dad would tell my brothers and I a ghost story to make sure we were ready for the operation before he put the money in the slot. They also had to cook the meals in a central kitchen, which you very often had to wait your turn. There was one thing, Dad only had to use one pot as rolled oats was our chief diet three times a day, think he must have brought a whole sack full of the stuff. Mother got so seasick I don't think she ate anything after the first day at sea. (Jean recalls her mother saying she was never sick!) It took us six days to cross the Atlantic.

When we landed in Halifax we were herded in to a big warehouse on the dock like a bunch of cattle to wait our turn to get through the customs and immigration. The place was cold, had to sit on planks for seats and you were lucky if you could find a space to sit down. Couldn't get anything warm to eat or drink. After we got through the customs we were herded like a bunch of cattle again into a train that was waiting by the shed. The CPR gestapo made sure there were no empty seats. Kids that didn't have to pay was supposed to sit on their parent's laps or sit on the floor in the aisle until the conductor came along and hollered at you and made you stand. I was four years old and my brother was going on three so we were too heavy to sit on laps. Dad only paid fares to Winnipeg as he wanted to try and get a job to make some money.

We stayed in a rooming house in cramped quarters, had to cook meals in a central kitchen again. Dad was lucky, got a job the second day. He worked for three months, earned enough to buy a horse and an ox, an old wagon and a walking plow as he needed that to build a sod house if he ever found some land he liked. He also got some cheap cooking utensils and a supply of groceries and as usual a sack of rolled oats. He always said we would never starve as long as we had that stuff. By the time we got to our destination the stuff was coming out our ears.

We loaded up the wagon with what few worldly possessions we had including Mother's portable Singer sewing machine which she had carried with her all the time so far. We started out for Saskatchewan to find the free land on August 1904. We slept on the open prairie if it wasn't raining but if it was raining Dad would stretch a tarp over the wagon and we would huddle underneath it. We had been advised to follow the Qu'Appelle valley as that would be the best source of water for us, other than sloughs. It was not a very big stream but was running water which we boiled before using. The cooking was done by using the dry prairie grass and buffalo chips which didn't throw so many sparks. You had to be so careful with fires as they would get out of control in the dry grass. That's why there were so many prairie fires caused mostly with careless land seekers.

After we left the valley to go south towards Regina (the capital of the Province) we had to depend on slough water and I don't mind telling you it smelled like high heaven. You had to push the slime back and fill the containers. It had to be strained through a cloth, the boiled and strained through another cloth to make sure there were no microbes. It's a wonder we didn't get typhoid fever. Finally after being on the move for over a month Dad spotted a piece of land that he liked the looks of, 83 miles north of Regina. It had a fair sized slough on it, more stinking water until Dad could dig a well.

The first thing he had to do was build a sod house by plowing sods from the land. He also had to go 30 miles to get poles for rafters to lay the sod on. Mother did the cooking on an open fireplace made of rocks and again my brother and I had to gather buffalo chips for fuel. We slept under the tarp until the shack was built, more like a bear's den. The well was the next task, Dad would dig and Mother would haul the muck up in a bucket, pretty hard work for a woman that had never had to do anything like that in her life.

They struck a good supply of good water at 25 feet which was a God send after having to put up with that slough water. We used to have to make smudges out of buffalo chips to keep the mosquitoes off, otherwise they would eat us alive. The animals even backed their rear ends into the smoke for the same purpose. Dad was a water diviner, did a lot of it for the new settlers and very seldom ever failed to find water for them. Our nearest neighbor the first year we were there was 10 miles away, but it wasn't long before we had people on all sides of us.

The Walker brothers and wives took up land three miles west of us. They seemed to have money as they had horses and oxen. I believe they had come in from North Dakota, many more also came from the States to settle on the free land. Dad managed to buy an ox from them on time as they were going in for horses and he needed the extra animal power to do the plowing, as he wanted to get some grain planted. A person had to make so much improvement every year for five years so as to get the title to the land. You also couldn't sell the land until you had the title.

There was one Scotch couple by the name of MacIntosh that took up land next to us on the north side. She was a big fat woman, used to come to see Mother a lot as it was a place to gossip in their scotch twang. One day while they were having a spot of tea in some fine china cups, Mother had brought with her as they made the tea taste better, this lady crossed her leg like a man. After she left, I said to Mother she is man not a woman. Mother asked why I thought that? I said she crossed her legs like a man does! It took some time for me to live that down.

A bachelor who had taken up the land on our south side was from England and a very nice fellow. He and Dad worked together very well which helped both of them. Mother used to invite him over for dinner on a Sunday quite frequently. If she wanted him to come over she would tie a white cloth on a willow twig and wave it about eleven o'clock Sunday. He evidently used to watch for it as he would wave one back and it wouldn't be long before he would be heading for our place. One nice day he was almost over to our place when a bolt of lightning struck his horse on the head and killed it, but never hurt him. He would always ask to hold my nine month old brother [Thomas Brown III] while Mother was getting dinner ready. Always asked for the dishpan to set him in. He was always joking about something.

The CPR put in a branch line from Regina to Saskatoon which was a great help to the settlers in 1906. The Grand Trunk came through the same year. Dad worked on the grading of that road as many others did the same to get a little money. They were paid $1.00 a day for ten hours. Of course you could buy a dozen eggs of 10 cents and the ones that had a cow would sell their butter for 20 cents a pound.

Nokomas sprung up on the CPR three miles west of us and another place by the name of Tate was built on the Grand Trunk three miles east of us. Each of these places boasted a general store, post office and oils for the old coal oil lamps. The bachelor that lived ten miles from us opened the store at Tate as he came into money from England as his parents were business people. I could never figure out why a man with means would come out here to lead such a rough life. Never the less it was nice that he opened up his general store, so we were starting to live in God's country. The Grand Trunk ran through my Mother's brother's place and the sparks from the engines started a lot of prairie fires until the government made them equip the engines with screens to stop that trouble.

I had better give you a line up where the McGowans came into the picture. They were my mother's side of the family, three brothers [William, John, and Thomas McGowan] and the mother [Jane McMillan Russell aka Granny McGowan]. The oldest brother [William McGowan] stayed at Winnipeg as he got a job as a boilermaker in the CPR shops there. The other two and the mother came to where we were and took up land not too far from us on the south about three miles. The boys had land side by side which they were lucky to get the land. It wasn't as good land as what Dad had. Dad helped them build a sod house on the oldest brother's place. He also divined a well for them but water wasn't too good a lot of alkali in it. My oldest sister [Jean McGowan Brown] was born in their house and well I can remember that day.

Dad was making a bigger grain box for his wagon. He put Jim and I in it to keep us from coming into the house while Mother was going through the ordeal of dealing with the stork. I started monkeying around with one of his chisels and cut quite a gash in my knuckle. I was squawking and Mother was doing the same as the stork wasn't treating her too good. Gran was a mid-wife and brought in a lot of kids of the settlers and never lost a child. There were no doctors in those days unless you went to Regina and that was only possible when the CPR came through.

Mother's brother got wind of some animals for sale by a settler that was giving up farming and going back to the city. He got a nice heavy team of horses and a cow which was badly need for milk and butter. The darn cow managed to break lose and wandered off. Gran climbed up a ladder by the house and a gust of wind made her lose her balance and she fell to the ground and injured her back so bad that she was stooped over all the time for the rest of her life. That was in 1905 before the railroads came through, so she was never taken to a doctor.

In 1906 Dad and Mother's brothers got a very good crop of grain, but everybody else had the same, so that's where the elevator guys fleeced them. There was an elevator built by a man named Bradshaw at Tate and he had things pretty well his way as he was the only one that had one ready for the 1906 crop. I can remember Dad taking a load of grain to his elevator after the threshing was over. Bradshaw would sift the grain through his fingers several times and the stand and look at it, then after some hesitation he would say to Dad, "The best I can do for you is No. 3 grade at 20 cents a bushel." He knew he had Dad over a barrel as there was no competition for him and Dad needed the money to pay for the threshing. He (Bradshaw) pulled the same gag on all the settlers until there was an elevator built at Nokomas in 1907. This changed things considerably from then on, as nearly all the settlers took their grain to the one in Nokomas to such an extent that they had to build a second elevator in the following spring.

Mother's brothers were able to get lumber shipped in by the CPR from Saskatoon in the spring of 1907 and built the first lumber house in the district. They built it at the western side of the farm this time where Dad had found some good water in a new well. The brother in

Winnipeg helped them out with money, as he was making good money on the railroad. My brother Tom was born in the new house in April 1908. I understand he came into the world without too much trouble, in April 1908. That same year the crops were very poor, not enough rain. This made Dad a lot more disgruntled with prairie farming and was more anxious to move to B.C. where his folks had moved from Moose Jaw in 1907. They had taken up land on the Shuswap lake. One of their sons had gone in there two years earlier and coaxed his parents to come to B.C. which they did. They all boasted it was a much nicer place to live than on the prairie. In the of 1907, Dad took us down to Gran's to stay while Dad and Mother's oldest brother went to the foot hills 30 miles away to get some wood for the winter. It generally took a little over a week. They were on their way back when they saw a prairie fire coming towards them from the south east. They immediately started back firing to save the horses and the wagon, but luck was with them as the fire changed its course and missed them. They left the wagon there and rode the horses to the farm, but by the time they got there the fire had done its damage. The house was not damaged but the barn and the stack of winter hay was gone as well as the cow. Mother tried to get her out of the barn but she couldn't get the chain untied. A year old calf was so badly burned it died as well. Mother did manage to get our horse out on the plowed field where we were. The fire had jumped the guard.

In the summer of 1908 Mother's brother William got his fiancée [Elizabeth Alexander Forrester] out from Scotland and they got married by a gospel minister who had his farm next to Mother's brother Tom, her youngest brother. The affair took place at Gran's house. My brother Jim and I wished there were more weddings as he and I had the pleasure of scraping out the containers they (Gran and Mother) were using to make the wedding cake. We sat under the table. We liked the one they made the icing in as we never got any sweet stuff, we seldom ever saw any candy.

Dad had finally made up his mind he was going to B.C. in November 1909. He made a deal with the farmer next to us on the south to buy our place. He gave Dad a down payment of a $1,000 down and a 40% of the crop on our place for 5 years. That's what Dad built our house with on the lake. Mother's Mother [Jane McMillan Russell aka Granny McGowan] and her youngest brother Tommy came to B.C. at the same as us. The brother William and wife stayed on the farms. He improved Tom's place enough so that Tom could get title and then give the place to William.

We left Nokomas on November 23 according to brother James (I say it was December 23). We went to Saskatoon, had to stay over a day there to catch the mainline to B.C. We arrived at the Shuswap Lake November 28 1909 according to brother James, (I say it was December 28). We were held up by a train wreck at Tappen for a day as a pusher engine had ran away from Notch Hill while the crew were in the hotel café. We had a very unpleasant trip all the way, there always was delays of some sort. Smith's store boat made a special trip across the lake for us after spending a cold night on the beach at Sorrento crouched around a bond fire. When we arrived at Fowler's beach as it was called then (Celista later years), Thomas Brown Senior and all their family were there to meet us in about two feet of snow. We stayed in tents on Joe's place that winter. The rest of the story is B.C. history.

P. S. continued: I omitted to mention the first winter we put in on the land we ran out of food as Dad didn't have enough money to lay in a supply. He went to Strasbourg before freeze up and the staple foods as much as he could afford, no credit in those days. For six weeks we lived on boiled wheat and Roger's syrup and rolled oats. In the spring break-up it was impossible to go back for more groceries. In the winter of 1905-6 we went to Moose Jaw as Dad's intended brother-in-law *[Ed. note – Thomas George Brown I who will marry Jemima Brown]* said he could get some work for him which Dad needed to buy seed grain for the next year. This intended brother-in-law had a sash and door factory and built houses South Hill in Moose Jaw. He gave Dad and a couple of men the job of unloading building materials from box cars for his construction jobs. We lived in a one roomed shack and only had an old cook stove to heat the place. My oldest sister was just a baby. We went back to the farm in the spring and was able to buy seed grain from Walker. We had a very good crop for the amount of land he had under cultivation, so Dad got the threshing gang to thresh it. We stayed on the farm in the winter of 1906 and heated our shack with the straw from the grain. Dad got an air tight heater and he used to stuff that thing full of straw and then put a match to it. In no time the place would be nice and warm. Sometimes he would get up a couple of times a night to go through the routine if it was very cold.

In 1907 everybody had a good crop and that of course put the growers at the mercy of Bradshaw who owned the elevator at Tate. Dad had to sell quite a bit of his crop to pay for the threshing and Bradshaw knew it. In 1908 another elevator was built a Nokomas which gave competition to the one in Tate which made things a little better for everyone. Dad was still bound he was going to B.C. after he got rid of his 1908 crop and managed to make a deal with our neighbor farmer (Charlie Massey) who took over everything from us.

Another thing I remember which I had forgot to mention was that our little mare had a foal and when it was about 9 months old he got stuck in the mud in the slough. I ran up to the house and got Dad who managed to pull him out with a rope but the poor little fellow caught pneumonia and died a couple of days later.

Mrs. MacIntosh (mother's Scotch friend) had a boy about the same age as us, got into trouble by wading in the slough, got in over his depth. Again I ran up to the house and told the women that the boy was drowning. They managed to get a hold of the boy and pull him out. His mother held him up by the feet and Mom squeezed his belly which forced slime and water out of him. Finally he started to cough and cry. I think the slime helped to stop a lot of the water from getting into his lungs. Anyway after a few days he was alright after his close shave. Another thing I forgot to mention was that Uncle Johnnie McGowan never did anything with his land. He went back to Scotland and married his former girlfriend [Alice Beatrice Lumsden] and brought her out to Kindersley in Saskatchewan where he worked on the CNR for years. The rest from now on is BC history and I have covered that in another memoir.

APPENDIX 6: MEMOIRS OF FRANK KAPPEL

"From "Grandpa" Frank Kappel, Eagle Bay, B.C. (Shuswap Lake) in September 1961, written to his grandchildren:
DALE and LYNNE INGRAM, Victoria, B.C.
and
KAREN, KRISTEN & KERRY KAPPEL (the 3 "K.K's"), Spokane, Wash.

My dears:

First let me say how proud I am to have such a wonderful bunch of granddaughters. I wish sometimes that one or two of you could have been boys, to carry on the name, but that was not to be, and I am well pleased the way it is, for you are all lovely girls.

From time to time I have told you about incidents that happened in my young days, and you showed so much interest in them that you asked me on several occasions to sit down and write the story of my life, so that you and your children will have a better knowledge of what kind of a chap Grandpa Kappel was and what he did with his life. Unfortunately I never knew any of my grandparents – they all passed away either before I was born or I was too young to know them, so that actually I know nothing about them. But I have come to realize that grandparents are nice people to have around, to tell stories, to listen to one's little troubles, and they are usually a soft touch for a bottle of pop, a hamburger or the odd dollar for spending money. If at times I have appeared to be impatient with you, it is not because I loved you less, but because as one gets older one does not have the patience one had in one's younger days – and don't forget that you kids can be a little bit aggravating at times!

This is the summer of 1961 and I am out in my cottage at Eagle Bay on the shore of the beautiful Shuswap Lake. I am now over three quarters of a century old, so I have had good long innings, but now the shadows are lengthening, evening falls for me, the busy world is hushed, the fever of life is over and my work is done. So before the light fails I had better get busy and write this story for you.

Starting at the beginning: I was born on May 4th, 1886 at Neath in South Wales, the second of four children of Carl and Elizabeth Kappel. My father was born in London, England, of German ancestry, my mother in Neath of pure Welsh stock. My elder brother, Charlie, became a lawyer and died in 1952. I came next, then my sister Gertrude, and finally the baby of the family, Stanley. Gertrude was a teacher in the Old Country. After the First World War she came out to visit me at Magna Bay, and got married at my home there to Jim Armstrong, who had served through the war in the same outfit as Stanley. Gertrude is a clever girl - she lives now at Langford, is a widow, and spends much of her time writing stories and articles for the papers and magazines.

Uncle Stanley served through World War I in the 72nd Battalion, the Seaforth Highlanders of Canada. In the big push at Amiens in August 1918, just three months before the Armistice, he was badly wounded and his leg had to be amputated. The stump was too short for him to use an artificial leg, so he has to use crutches. He is still in Vancouver where he has lived ever since he left the hospital. He is senior partner in an old, established Real Estate and Insurance firm, but expects to retire from business at the end of this year. He has led an active life and is well-known and respected in the social and business life of British Columbia.

My father, a fine man, was in the Wine and Spirit business at Neath, and apparently was very successful, for he retired at a comparatively early age, though he later lost a lot of money in some unfortunate coal-mining ventures. He was inclined to be a somewhat strict disciplinarian – he carefully supervised our studies and while he would reprimand us for our failures at times to come up to his standard, he was most generous in rewarding us for work well done. He died in 1910.

Mother was a wonderful woman. In those days domestic help was plentiful and cheap, and we always had maids in the house so that Mother was able to devote a lot of time and care to her family. We had a lovely home at Neath and did a lot of entertaining. Both Father and Mother came of genteel families, and were away above in social and educational background. One of Mother's brothers was a celebrated lawyer, became a Member of the British House of Commons, and ended up as Senior Judge of the British Exchequer Court. He was knighted by Queen Victoria. A nephew of mine by marriage, Sir Ian MacLennan, is in the British Diplomatic Corps, and at the present time is British Ambassador to the Republic of Ireland. He was knighted a few years ago by Queen Elizabeth.

When I was four years old, my brother Charlie and I went to an "Infants School" at Neath – something like the present-day kindergartens except that we delved right into the three "R"s – Reading, Writing and Arithmetic, so that when we were old enough to enter public school, we did not have to start in the baby class. At nine years of age I started in the Neath County School, which would be the equivalent of today's high school. There again, thanks to the tutoring we received at home and during the holidays, which we spent at our Summer home at Porthcawl, we started in a higher class, and right away we had such subjects as Grammar, Algebra, Euclid, Chemistry, French, Latin and other subjects – and of course, lots of homework.

Both Charlie and I matriculated in 1901, and we were then given the choice of entering a profession or going abroad to study foreign languages. Charlie chose the law, but to me travelling abroad appeared more interesting, so I chose the latter. The next two years I spent at a large boarding school in Namur, Belgium, where I studied French. It was a Catholic school, run by the Christian Brothers, and I was one of the very few protestants there. In spite of my French studies at school, I found, when I was dumped amongst French boys who could not speak any English, that I could not express myself in French, so if I wanted to mix with them, I would just have to dig in and learn to speak French, and it was surprising how quickly I achieved this objective, and at the end of the two years I had acquired a pretty good knowledge of the French language.

The following year I went to Germany; Dad came over with me, and before he settled me down at Trier, on the Moselle River, at the home of a German schoolteacher who had been recommended to him, we took a trip down the Rhine River to Frankfurt which was most interesting. At the teacher's home in Trier there were two French boys who were there for the same purpose as myself, to learn German – we attended the teacher's classes where language was taken, and in the evenings we had private tutoring from the teacher at his home, so at the end of the year we had acquired a good knowledge of this language also, as we had all received German lessons before going to Trier.

It seemed to me then that I had been long enough at school and that I should start out on my own. So, without saying anything to Dad, I hunted me a job and got the position of foreign correspondent at a little place called Ludenscheid in a factory where they made fine copper and bronze wire, most of which was exported. Here I gained office experience and this helped me to get a much better job at Kassel in a similar capacity; I stayed there nearly a year, and Kassel was an interesting place to live, but I wanted to get to a large city, so I applied for a job with Germany's largest steamship company, the Hamburg-American Line, at Hamburg. They asked me to come up for an interview, and I got a good job there right away. I stayed with them for five years. In 1908 they sent me to Spain for eight months to get acquainted with their agencies in that country, and I spent some time at all the ports in Northern Spain and in Portugal, and when I returned to Hamburg I was given another promotion. During my stay in Spain I managed to get the odd week in Madrid and saw many Spanish bull-fights, which were gory but thrilling.

Hamburg was a very fine city. It was the custom in those days for merchants in other countries to send their sons to Hamburg to learn German business methods, so I associated there with young men my own age from all parts of the world, and we really had a gay time. Amongst other activities I was a member of a rowing club and took part in many regattas in four and eight-oared boat races. I still have some of the trophies we won at these events. One year, after the training was over, five of us took a boat and made a two-weeks trip through the rivers, canals and lakes of Northern Germany, camping out and enjoying ourselves. At the end of the trip, still having a week's holidays in hand, we went to Berlin and spent a few days there. My contacts with these chaps from practically every country in the world were most interesting, and I gained insight into the life in those countries which I could not have got from books. I mixed with all colours and creeds amongst them. They were a nice bunch of boys.

Up to about that time the British were very popular in Germany, and the natives liked to associate with them and copy their manners, their clothes, etc., and of course they loved to ventilate what knowledge they had of English. But gradually the feeling was changing. The old Kaiser had for years been building up a great and powerful military machine, and to justify the huge expenditure of the taxpayers' money he had to do something with these millions of trained soldiers who were all dressed up and had no place to go. Besides, the population was getting too large for the available room, and more "Lebensraum" – room to expand – was needed. The British Empire at that time was at its peak of power, and owned most of the world's desirable real estate – the Empire on which the sun never set. The Germans cast covetous eyes on all these overseas colonies, which they of course could only acquire by means of a successful war against Britain. So an anti-British complex was being fostered and this led eventually to World War I.

Roland and I decided we had had enough of it. So there and then we made up our minds to give up our jobs and move to pastures new. That brought the question of where to go. I had friends in the Argentine to whom I could go any time, in Mexico, in Guatemala, in the U.S.A. and in Canada. We discussed the merits and disadvantages of all these possibilities and finally decided on Canada. Two factors made us come to this decision – first, we would be among British people who spoke our language and whose way of life were the same as ours, and secondly, I was engaged to be married to a very charming Scottish lady, whom I met in Germany where she was studying art, whose family *[Ed. note - The William Thomson family, for whom Thomson Hill in Celista was named]* had moved to Canada a couple of years earlier and had settled in British Columbia. Their new home was on a beautiful lake called the Shuswap Lake, and we thought we would go there first and make that our headquarters while looking around for some place to settle and find employment. So next day we told our respective employers in Hamburg of our intention, and in spite of the glowing picture they painted to me of my future prospects with the company, they could not change my mind.

So in due course I left Hamburg and went back to Wales for a three months holiday, the first long holiday I'd had at my parents' home since I was a boy. The company asked me to let them know about when I was going to leave England, and I did this and received a reply advising me that they had booked passage for me on one of their big liners to New York, luxury accommodation etc., with the company's compliments. When I arrived at New York I was met at the boat by one of the company's officials who informed me that he had been instructed to look after me, show me the sights of New York, take me anywhere I wanted to go, all at the company's expense. This was very unexpected, and I spent a very pleasant and interesting two weeks there. Then to Montreal and after that the next step was across Canada to Notch Hill, British Columbia, where I arrived late in the evening of April 2nd, 1911.

I had been told to stay at the Royal Hotel at Notch Hill if there was no one at the station to meet me. As a matter of fact there was no one at the station to meet me, as ice conditions on the lake were such that it was not safe to walk over on the ice, but it was impossible to push a boat through the slush, so I had to wait three days before communication with the North Shore could be established. For two or three days on the train I had been looking forward to a nice hot bath on arrival at Notch Hill, but to my dismay I was informed that the "Royal" Hotel did not boast a bathroom nor any inside plumbing! Finally I saw the Shuswap Lake and it was a case of love at first sight. In all my travels I had never seen a more beautiful lake, and I decided there and then that I had no need to look any further for a place to settle down.

In those days a Homestead Law was in effect whereby a prospective settler could file on a quarter section of land, 160 acres, and when he had complied with certain regulations regarding residence and putting an area of land under cultivation, he was granted clear title. There were very few settlers around the lake at that time so one had plenty of choice. I picked out an attractive site on the lakeshore at Magna Bay, almost straight across the lake from Eagle Bay where I now am, and went to work. I soon got acquainted with a double-bitted axe, a cross-cut saw and a mattock and started cutting down trees and making a clearing. After the trees were down, they had to be burned and the stumps had to be pulled; for this latter job we had to get the help of a team of horses or of oxen – sometimes horse and ox were hitched up together, and the big stumps were blasted out with dynamite.

There was no land-clearing machinery available, and it was hard and slow work. Long, straight trees were peeled and hauled into a pile on the site where I intended to build my house. In the fall, with the assistance of neighbours, we had a "bee" and got the walls up and the roof on before Winter set in. Winter came early that year, and practically all the lumber I used in the house was hauled across the ice from Sorrento on sleighs drawn by horses. Good progress was made during the ensuing months, and by spring the house was almost ready for the finishing work inside and I had become fairly proficient as a carpenter.

Money was not the all-important factor it is today, our wants were few, we were frugal in our way of life, but still we had to eat, and many of the settlers spent three or four months of each year working out in the harvest fields or in the mines, and the proceeds of their labour would keep them in groceries for the rest of the year. In the process of clearing the land, many of the settlers would cut logs for the sawmills and cordwood for the stern-wheel boats which towed booms of logs to the mills at Chase and Kamloops. All this was hard work, and the country is indebted to the old pioneers for opening up districts which otherwise would still be uninhabited. Some people say these pioneers were crazy to try to make farms out of the bush, miles away from transportation, but it was this spirit of craziness which helped to make Canada the great country it is today, and built a railway line from the Atlantic to the Pacific. The old pioneering spirit is not much in evidence today, and the young people who remained on the farms are reaping the advantage of the work their fathers did to make these farms out of the virgin bush.

Like the other settlers, I did various jobs to earn some money to finish and furnish my house and carry on with the land clearing. I worked on the Government road as an axeman and also as a teamster. I remember one time the foreman on the road, Harry Fowler, the oldest of the old-timers, told me to go to the barn and bring out the team there to hitch on to the grader. I found two big horses in the barn and a miscellaneous collection of harness hanging up on the wall. Now, I did not know the difference between a hame-strap and a bellyband, and my efforts to get the harness on the horses were not very successful. However, a friend of mine passed by and saw I was in difficulties, so he came in and showed me how to harness the team, and I marched out behind the team, hitched it on to the grader, shouted Gee and Haw and everything was lovely. I stayed on as teamster for a couple of weeks until the regular teamster came back on the job.

Another job I tackled was carpenter on the Government Wharf which was then being built at Magna Bay. I had lots of nerve calling myself a carpenter, but managed to get away with it, and hung on to it until the job was completed. Then, in the spring of 1914 my brother and I went to the coast and got work up at the Britannia Mine on Howe Sound, working underground. This really was a new experience for us, but we learned quickly and came away with some money in our pockets. After all, swinging a shovel did not call for many brains. When a person takes a job of any kind, he must give the best he has to do the work properly, as well he can, and heaven helps those who help themselves.

When I got back to Magna Bay I found that the position of Fire Warden was about to become vacant; I applied for it and got it. Fortunately that first year there were no fires in my district, and I made good use of my time going over all my territory, learning the theory of firefighting, and making friends with the people. All my travelling was on horseback, as there were no cars and few roads and trails; I also did much of my ranging by boat, from the center of the lake where I could pretty well see the whole district. The following year there were lots of fires and I really had a busy time. The Chief Ranger at that time was Jim Evans of Salmon Arm, and he was wise enough to leave all the responsibility to the individual ranger.

One day I was really worried – the weather was hot and dry, and I had a dozen fires burning. Someone told me that old Jim had just passed in his car and as I wanted to see him badly and report on the fire situation, I just camped in the middle of the road awaiting his return. He greeted me with, "Well Frank, what's all the excitement about?" – I told him my sad story of all the fires burning, and his reply was, "Well, well. Have you got crews fighting the fires?" Yes. "Have you got a good foreman on each of them?" Yes. "Are they getting plenty of grub?" Yes. "Well, what more can you do except pray for rain. Remember that next Winter we will be having snow again, and the fires will all be out!" And he jumped in his car and left. That was a fine lesson for me, and it taught me to always keep calm and collected in an emergency – worrying and getting excited never helps.

I am getting a little ahead of my story. In the spring of 1912 my house was pretty well completed, my fiancée came out and we got married in Kamloops on June 24, 1912. *[Ed. note - The bride was Jenny Thomson.]* In due time we became your grandparents. In the fall of 1912 the weather was bad and it looked like an early winter. I thought it was just not right to expose my new wife, in her first winter in Canada, to the rigours of six months or more in the bush, with no amenities and few neighbours, so we went to Vancouver, and there I got a job right away in a Chartered Accountants office, and we rented a nice little furnished house in North Vancouver, where Betty was born the following year. During the Winter I was sent to Kamloops to audit the City books for the year 1912, and then on to Salmon Arm to do the audit of the municipality.

Now a word about your grandmother, my wife. She was a truly wonderful wife and mother, and we were happy together for 34 years. She was a great help to me in every way, as she was to all who came to her for help and advice, and they were many. She was kind, generous, a talented artist, gifted with a sharp mind, always a gracious hostess, and a real home-maker. Our home at Sicamous, as the one at Magna Bay, was the center of the social life of the community. We were blessed with two children, Betty and Stanley, and they and their friends helped to liven things up and make "Kappel's place" a wonderful place to have fun and parties. Mother's death in 1946 was a sad blow not only to the children and me but also to the whole community.

Going back to 1914. On August 4th of that year war was declared. After I got my affairs straightened out, I went to Kamloops with Uncle Tom *[Ed. note – Tommie Thomson]* and some of the other local boys and we all enlisted in the 54th *[Ed. note – Canadian Battalion]*. Many of these boys unfortunately never came back. In a short time our battalion, which was stationed at Vernon, entrained for overseas and went into camp at Bramshott in Southern England. The weather was terrible and the camp was a sea of mud, so when the sergeant major on parade one day called for men experienced in auditing, I thought here's a chance to get out of the mud, and I stepped forward. Next day I was on my way to London, where Mother and Betty were staying. I got into the Audit Office of the Canadian Corps and was quickly promoted to Staff Sergeant. But when the Spring came I wanted to get to France and applied for and obtained a transfer to the Canadian Artillery and was posted to a battery using 8" Howitzers. We took an intensive course in guns at Cooden Camp, on the South coast, and were soon in France and a few days afterwards, we were in action. It was heavy work – our shells weighed 200 pounds each – but it was interesting.

In the spring of 1918 I was called out and told to report to Canadian Corps H.Q. – there they said I was wanted up at British First Army H.Q., what for nobody seemed to know. However, when I reached there one of the first men I met was Roland Salt, who came out to Canada with me, and he told me I was being posted to Army Intelligence, thanks to my knowledge of French and German. This work was intensely interesting as we were in touch with things we knew nothing about when we were up the line. And of course, up at H.Q. we were far away from those nasty German shells.

Then came the Armistice on November 11th, 1918, and I went on two weeks leave to Blighty. I arrived in London on Armistice night and everybody was wild, and no sleep that night. On the 14th, I went to Netley Hospital, up the Thames River, to visit Stanley who had been a patient there since he was evacuated from France, but found that he had been transferred a couple of days before to a hospital in Liverpool, so I headed for Mother's home in Cardiff and spent a lovely restful holiday there. When the time came for me to return to France, the Chief of Medical Service in Cardiff, a friend of the family, hinted that it might be possible to get an extension of my leave! So he gave me a certificate to the effect that I was medically unfit to travel, and that way I was able to wangle an extra two weeks' leave. I visited Stanley in Liverpool and finally got back to the outfit in France. There I was posted in a liaison capacity to the 2nd Canadian Engineers and with them marched into Germany. My job at first was to go ahead with the quartermaster and a couple of other chaps in a nice car and arrange for billets at the Engineers' next stopping place. As soon as they arrived and were found accommodation, we stocked up our car with supplies and moved on to the next stop-over, and so we went on and finally arrived at our destination at Troisdorf, in Germany, a few miles East of Bonn. There I resumed Intelligence work and also acted as interpreter for the town commandant. Being able to speak German, my contacts with the natives were most interesting.

At the end of February I was transferred to Le Havre in France, where even at the time communistic propaganda was being spread amongst the troops, and our job was to find out the source of the trouble. We were moderately successful in this and made a number of arrests. Finally in April I was moved to England, first to Fountain Abbey in Yorkshire, then to the embarkation camp at Rhyl in North Wales. From there I took a ship at Liverpool and arrived in Halifax on May 24th, 1919. A week later I was back at Magna Bay with Mother and Betty and it was wonderful to be back here again.

Speaking of Betty, I could write pages and pages about her and Stanley. But you have heard their story from them directly – suffice it to say that never were parents blessed with a better and finer pair of children than we. All through their childhood and after they grew up they never gave us cause to dim the great pride we had in them, and I am ever grateful to them for the pleasure and happiness I derived from them. Stanley was an exceptionally clever student and he graduated from Montana University as a Mining Engineer before he was 21 years of age; he would have gone far in his profession but for his untimely death at the early age of 33. Betty is happily married and lives in Victoria.

Well, as I said, I came back home when the war was over – we came back covered with glory, and with an empty purse, as is the fate of many heroes! Fortunately I got my fire warden job back right away, and as that paid me $5.00 a day, seven days a week, which at that time was big money, we managed to keep the wolf from the door. It didn't take me long to find out that I was never meant to be a farmer. That Winter Uncle Sandy (Thomson) and I took on a logging contract at Celista – we took out a lot of logs, the hard way, but when we came to count up our take-home pay at the end of the job we were not much richer than when we started. So I was glad to get back on the fire job again, and was agreeably surprised to find that I was being promoted to be deputy fire chief for the whole district, which gave me work not only during the fire season, but also for a few weeks in Kamloops compiling statistics of the fires and mapping out the areas burned over. The following year a headquarters office was built in Sicamous, with myself in charge.

Then came fall again. At that time there was a big sawmill at Chase, the Adams River Lumber Company, and I went down there to see if I could get a job in one of their logging camps as time-keeper or store-keeper. Luckily for me there was an opening for a timber scaler at their camp up on Adams River, and I got the job. I didn't know too much about scaling, but I soon caught on, and stayed there until the contract was completed. Then I turned in a full report, made some recommendations which were well received and apparently my work was quite satisfactory. Up at the camp the wife of the contractor, Mrs. Fusee, a great horse-woman, had two racehorses that were just eating their heads off. I asked some of the old-timers what they thought my chances would be to borrow one of the horses once in a while to visit my family at Magna Bay on week-ends. They told me I was crazy to think of it, that Mrs. Fusee would not let the horses out of her sight. But one day, when I was feeling very brave, I did approach her, and to my great surprise she was delighted with the idea, said the horses needed exercise, and I could take one of them each week, turn and turnabout, so I had lots of fun galloping to Eagle Bay and back every week-end.

Then back to the fire warden job again for the Summer, this time at Sicamous, where I got better acquainted with Mr. R. Bruhn who had his headquarters there. In the fall a big logging camp was starting up at Eagle Bay, with the Adams River Company taking the logs, while Mr. Bruhn took the poles and ties. They wanted a resident scaler on the job, and this time I did not have to apply for it, they offered it to me, and of course I was glad to accept. It was not far from home and I managed to get home almost every week-end, part of the time by boat, and when the lake froze over I walked on the ice. In the Spring of the year the ice gets kind of tricky and one has to be careful, it gets mushy and wet, and someday a wind comes up and presto – overnight the ice disappears; that spring I walked across the lake on the Saturday and on Monday morning went back to camp in my motor-boat!

That year Mr. Bruhn suggested that I give up my fire warden job and come to work for him – his business was growing and he needed someone to run the office for him – I accepted and I and my family moved to Sicamous. Once we got established I built a house there, which you have all seen, and there we lived for the next 26 years. In 1924 Mr. Bruhn entered politics, got elected to the British Columbia Legislature *[Ed. note – later he also became Minister of Public Works in the B.C. Cabinet]*, necessitating more and more time away from the business, and the management fell into my hands. We had camps all over the lake and our tugboats brought in large booms of timber products which we loaded on cars and shipped via the Canadian Pacific Railway. Besides the lake business we bought poles, ties and posts at the railway sidings from Kamloops to Revelstoke and as far south as Vernon.

In the mean time I sat for my scaler examination, and in 1920 obtained my Government certificate as a Provincial Licensed Scaler. In 1925 I was appointed to be a Notary Public.

During this period I built myself a cottage at Eagle Bay, which you girls know very well, and I have spent many happy summers there.

1942 was a black year for me as far as the business was concerned. Our management consisted of four men – Mr. Bruhn, his son Ted, Mardie McKay our field man, and myself. The first three all died within a period of six months, and I was left holding the bag. Your grandmother's health was beginning to fail about that time, and this, and the business worries, began to get me down and the old stomach ulcer became active again. However, I kept on going but when Grandmother died in 1946 I had had enough, and sold out my interest in the business to Mr. Bruhn's son-in-law, Max Patterson. In 1947 I moved to Salmon Arm.

Just before I left Sicamous, the community arranged a big farewell party for me in the Community Hall. Practically all the local people came to do me honour, besides many of the notables from Salmon Arm. It was for me a very flattering event, and during the evening I was presented with a Life Membership in the Canadian Legion, a purse of money and a large carved key to the city, besides the good wishes of all. I was particularly happy that Betty was able to come up from Kamloops to take part in the evening's doings and lend me her support.

Up to the time I left Sicamous I was very fond of golf, hunting and fishing. Every fall a bunch of staid old business and professional men from Salmon Arm would form a cavalcade to Fish Lake, near Westwold – this was the so-called "Old Men's Fishing Party" and it was quite an event. It was a real pleasure to see these old gentlemen get up there in the wilds, and let themselves go in a manner which they certainly could not do in town. And actually a lot of them did fish – we had fish for breakfast, lunch and dinner. In the evenings we would build a big camp fire, shooting the breeze and singing – with the help of the stimulation which materialized from hot rum drinks! We really "had ourselves a ball". Later on when the pheasant season opened I always got my quota of birds, and when the first snow began to fall we would go after ducks and geese in the country around Nicola Lake – game was plentiful, the company good, and we had fun.

The first year I was on the Lake we formed a "Settlers' Association", of which I was secretary, to fight the powers that be for roads to connect us to the outside world, and to throw open for settlers a considerable area of timber berths which then were not open for settlement, and we met with some success and got started on a network of roads which has increased as more people came in. Ever since I have been quite active in affairs that affected the welfare of the community, especially of the young people. Canada has been good to me, and I have always tried to do my part to show my appreciation by helping to develop the district and make it a more pleasant and happy place in which to live. In politics I have always been a strong Conservative, and at different times I was secretary or president of many political bodies such as the Salmon Arm Provincial Association, the Kamloops Federal Association and the B.C. Conservative Executive. In Sicamous I was president of the "Sicamous Amusement Company" when we built the Community Hall, Charter Member and President of the Sicamous Branch of the Canadian Legion, member of the Executive and Treasurer of the Salmon Arm Branch, President of the North Okanogan Pee-Wee Hockey League, President of our Boy Scout Association and later of the Shuswap Lake District Boy Scout Association, Charter Member and President of the Salmon Arm Rotary Club where for some years I was in charge of the "Search for Talent" contests, two years one of the judges of the election contests held by the Oddfellows in connection with the United Nations, in which you, Karen, took part this year. In between there were many other activities to fill in the time! In 1954 I wrote a history of Shuswap Lake which was published in the Salmon Arm "Observer". Then for two years I was manager of the Pole and Tie Department of the Columbia Forest Products Ltd. in Salmon Arm, and almost three years as draughtsman for the Provincial Department of Highways, most of which time was spent in Kamloops.

When World War II broke out I tried to get back in the Army. They would have taken me for Home Service, which I did not want, but told me flatly that I was too old for overseas service. So I stayed in Sicamous and became Chief Air Raid Warden, President of the Red Cross, and a member of the Pacific Coast Militia Rangers.

In 1952 [Ed. note – the year Stanley died] the old stomach ulcer got me down and I had to undergo surgery first in Kamloops and afterwards in Victoria. In all I was 82 days in hospital and came out with only one third of my original stomach left. However the ultimate results were eminently satisfactory and I have enjoyed pretty good health ever since.

Now I have retired again, and this time I think it is for keeps, and I spend my time between Eagle Bay, Salmon Arm, Victoria, Spokane and Laguna Beach, California. I have lived a long life and have many happy memories to support me in my old age. What the future holds in store I do not know. In my lifetime I have seen many changes and life today is very different from what it was 75 years ago. I can well remember the horse-drawn street cars, the naked yellow gas lamps to light our homes, the penny-in-the-slot hot water heaters, the outside privies except where the new invention, the flush toilet, was being installed in the better class homes, the old wax cylinder gramophones, and so forth. Many of the conveniences which we now take for granted were unheard of. The steam automobile was just coming on the roads – these had built in steam engines, and when they got into action they shot out streams of steam which scared all the horses on the streets. Telephones and typewriters were new inventions, as was electric light. There were no radios or T.V. sets, no airplanes, refrigerators, washing machines, submarines, wonder drugs, vitamin pills, radar, motor boats, picture shows, supermarkets, luxury trains and ships, and so forth. Life was very much simpler than it is today. I do not doubt but that the next fifty years will bring forth new inventions that will make people think that we who lived in the 1960s were pretty simple and old-fashioned. You girls will live to see many of these changes, and I hope they will all be for the best and that they will make you happy.

Up to the time of the First Great War, Canada was predominantly an agricultural country, its main exports being wheat, lumber and fish. It was during that war that Canada came into manhood and started developing her industrial resources. From then on she has continued to expand in stature and in wealth until today she ranks with the old established countries as one of the great nations of the world. British Columbia has more than kept pace with the other Canadian Provinces, industrially and economically, and we who have, in our small way, helped in this development may well be proud of what has been accomplished. In 1958, the Centennial Year of this province, the Government of British Columbia presented me with an elaborate scroll, signed by the Lieutenant Governor and the Premier, commending me for my part in the prosperity and development of my community, which I felt was a great honour.

This then, is the story of my life. I certainly did not intend to make it so long, but once I got started, the thoughts and memories kept crowding in on me, and I could not stop. However, after reading this you will perhaps know more about me than you did before, and you will be able to tell your children and grandchildren what sort of a man your old grandpa was. And I hope you will think of me sometimes and remember me as one who loved you very much and who wishes you a long and happy life, and success in whatever you undertake.

God bless you.

Ed. note – These memoirs were transcribed into digital format by the author in 2022 from the original typewritten document that Frank sent to his granddaughters in the fall of 1961. The writing style clearly reflects Frank's early education in the British public school system. We were provided a copy of Frank's memoirs by Jack Brown in 2009 that are significantly abridged and grammatically altered when compared to the original copy in our possession. According to Jack, Frank Kappel's granddaughter, Lynne (Ingram) Beeson, gave his memoirs to Helen Akrigg, who gave them to the North Shuswap Historical Society (NSHS) in 1988. It is very likely that the memoir sent to us by Jack Brown was a copy of the NSHS document that was an abridged version of the original memoir. Frank Kappel passed away on March 29, 1968, in Victoria, seven years after writing his memoirs. He left a legacy of documents that chronicled his remarkable life in the form of newspaper articles, letters, and verbal communications with his family that were either written down or recalled from memory. He was even interviewed for a CBC radio broadcast by Mr. Imbert Orchard, a well-known radio journalist at the time, in 1966. Between 1959 and 1966, Orchard compiled one of the largest oral history collections in North America, including interviews with 998 pioneers of British Columbia. I purchased an mp3 copy of Orchard's interview with Frank, who was a true pioneer, in 2022, and had it professionally

transcribed. The interview is wonderfully rich and important documentation of Frank's experiences and thought processes, and hearing Frank's voice is a priceless treasure. To the best of my knowledge, no other recording of Frank's voice exists. Sadly, in spite of my best efforts, I found it too difficult to obtain permission from the CBC to use the transcribed interview in this book. However, the similarities between the Orchard interview and Frank's written memoirs suggest that Frank may have had a copy of his memoirs with him when he was interviewed by Mr. Orchard. Frank was still sharp as a tack in 1966!

APPENDIX 7: SHUSWAP HISTORY OF THE THOMAS BROWN II (JUNIOR) FAMILY
- By James (Jim) McGowan Brown

"The following is a resume of the trials, events, happiness and sorrows of the Thomas Brown family, close relatives, and good friends after arriving at Celista [BC].

The family came to Celista after five years of isolation and hardship on the prairie; poor water, mosquitoes, horseflies, blizzards in the winter, sometimes 40 below for weeks at a time, and home was a sod house. Fuel was hard to come by. British Columbia seemed so much better.

In the year 1909, Mr. & Mrs. Thomas Brown Jr. *[Ed note: Stanley Kappel's uncle]* sold their farm in Saskatchewan and moved to B. C. with their four children, Hugh, James, Jean, and Thomas. They arrived at Notch Hill on December 3, 1909, too late to get across the lake that day to Celista. W. T. Smith of Smith and Son General Store hauled them to the beach at Sorrento where they spent the night. Thomas McGowan, brother of Mrs. Brown, was with the family.

It was a bitter, cold night. The first snow of winter had already fallen and there was a cold wind blowing eastward on the lake. With some ingenuity, the men arranged some rowboats that were on the beach in a half circle, standing them on their sides and filling in the open spaces with snow. This made a fair windbreak. Collecting drift on the beach, they made a good fire in the half circle and kept it going all night. Next morning, December 4th, W. T. Smith arrived and took them to Celista in his freight launch.

They were met there by other members of the Thomas Brown Sr. family who had preceded them to Celista. They were father and mother, Thomas Sr., and Jemima; brothers John, Joseph, and William; sisters Margaret and Jean. Also, there to meet them was Harry Fowler, who truly was a friend in need. With his team and sleigh, he hauled them up to the Meadow Creek valley to the homestead of Joe Brown, where they spent the winter in a one room log cabin. It was crowded to say the least and had bed bugs which some loggers had left behind.

In the spring of 1910, Tom Brown Jr. moved the family to the lakeshore on the homestead of Thomas Brown Sr. where he had erected a lumber floor with side walls and over this a large tent. This was fairly comfortable during the summer months, but when a strong wind blew across the lake, they were never quite sure the whole thing would not blow away. The tent was situated near the lake, so there was only a short distance to carry water.

That summer, the log house of Tom Brown Sr. was being built. Harry Fowler hewed the logs and supervised the building bee. Tom Brown Sr. also purchased a cow that year. Hugh and Jim got the chore of finding the cow where she might be grazing anywhere within a radius of three miles. Hugh milked the cow morning and night, for which he received one quart of milk. If she kicked the bucket over and spilled the milk, he got nothing.

There were plenty of fish in the lake in the early days, and by keeping a flock of hens and a couple of pigs, food wasn't too much of a problem in the summer, but winter was a different story. There was no such thing as fresh vegetables, fruit, or meat except deer meat, which passed around in season or out; people had to survive.

One source of food was salmon. The government was operating a fish hatchery at Tappen and they had fish traps at the mouth of Scotch Creek. Some of the settlers raided the traps, picking out the best-looking fish, and after cleaning and cutting to size, they were stored in a barrel of salt brine and would keep over the winter.

A humorous sidelight here. The hatchery had a steamboat they used for transporting the fish eggs, etc. Tommy McGowan got the job as skipper and Billy Gray got the job as engineer. On their first day out, Billy Gray was below stoking the fire and oiling the engine and didn't notice the steam pressure building up. Suddenly, the safety valve released with a loud bang. Billy was up the ladder in a flash and jumped into the lake. He thought the boiler was blowing up. Tommy had some knowledge of such things and persuaded Billy to get back on the boat. They then decided to change jobs and things worked alright after that.

That source of fish supply ended when the C.N.R. blocked the Fraser River while blasting and only a trickle of salmon got up the river in 1913.

Pork was also stored in barrels with brine. Brown beans were the order of the day and just about everybody had a large pot simmering on the stove with beans and a slab of salt pork. The only fruits available were dried apples and prunes ("C.P.R. strawberries"). Sourdough pancakes were popular at that period, and Harry Fowler estimated that the Browns ate about seven acres of pancakes during the winter. This may have been a slight overestimate, but nobody contradicted him.

In 1910 the only roads in the settlement were rough logging roads from the back country down to the lake. The only way to get to the railroad was by boat or over the ice when the lake was frozen over. The lake froze over every winter in those days - twenty-nine inches of ice was recorded one winter.

Before travel to the outside came to a halt for the winter, people would stock up on necessities. The Thomas Brown supply would consist of four hundred pounds of flour, two hundred pounds of sugar, two hundred pounds of rolled oats, and fairly large quantities of lard, salt, butter, yeast, soap, etc.

In the late fall, Tom Brown Jr. moved the family up Meadow Creek valley to an abandoned cabin formally owned by Billy Gray, who had found a better homestead. This was a rough winter for the family. Insulation was unknown in those days, and on a clear night stars could be seen through the shake roof, although it never leaked. Water had to be carried quite a distance from the creek. One good point - wood was plentiful, not like the prairie, where it took three days to get a load of wood.

All through 1910 and on into 1911, Tom Brown had not received the money for the farm, and Mrs. Brown (who had endured five years in a sod shack on the prairie) wanted a house built of lumber. Without that money, they were unable to get a house started. In 1911 they again lived in the tent on the beach. On August 19th, William John Brown was born in the tent. Harry Fowler called him Billy Jack, and the name stayed with him.

In the late fall, the family was again moved up to the old Billy Gray cabin. The school had been built during the summer, so Hugh, Jim and Jean had to travel about three miles to get to school. During the winter there was over five feet of snow in the valley, so travel was very difficult. They got home sometimes long after dark.

That winter the money came through for the sale of the farm, and in the spring of 1912 building material was purchased from the Adams River Lumber Co. and the new house got under way with the help of all the brothers and good neighbors. Thomas McGowan drafted the plans for the house and supervised the building. The house was finished before the cold weather started; a barn was also built, a cow was bought, and things became a lot better for the Brown family.

During the preceding years, Tom Brown Jr. worked wherever he could get work. One year he worked at Sorrento clearing land, and the only way for him to get there and back was by rowboat. He would row over on Sunday night and back on Saturday after work. He also cut cord wood in the winter, which had to be hauled to the lakeshore and stacked in piles for the sternwheelers that were on the lake at that time.

A simple little device used in those days when there were no such things as flashlights was something called a "bug", for some unknown reason. It consisted of an empty jam can or lard pail on one side of which was fastened a wire bail for a handle. On the opposite side, two cuts were made like a cross. A candle was pushed through this opening and lit. This made a portable light that was easy to carry in deep snow and could withstand a strong wind. There was always one around the Brown home in those days.

Another item that could bring back memories to those who are left from that era. When the salmon were running, lights could be seen all along with lake as the Indians went out in their canoes with a pitch flare hanging over the side. One Indian sat in the stern paddling, while another stood up about the center. The fish were attracted to the light and easily speared. This way they got a winter's supply of fish.

In 1913 the provincial road building program got underway. Harry Fowler was put in charge of the work, and quite a number of the local residents found steady work for at least six months of the year, including Tom Brown, who drove team. Harry Fowler, who could do almost anything he put his mind to, surveyed by eye the route the road would take. He went ahead of the crew with an axe and blazed trees in the line the road would take, and it says a lot for his ability, as the route he laid out has hardly been changed to this day.

By the time the road was completed to the lakeshore opposite Sorrento, landing slips had been built and a free ferry began operating to Sorrento skippered by Captain Ivens. The people of the north shore could now travel by team and wagon or horse and buggy to Notch Hill. The road building program went on for a number of years east and west along the lake and up into the back country. When the road building program was finished on the north side of the lake, Harry Fowler took his crew to Chase and built the road from Chase to Turtle Valley.

As Tom Brown Jr. had homesteaded on the prairie, he could not homestead again in B. C., but he did acquire ten acres from the Thomas Brown Sr. homestead before building the house.

Harry Fowler had a large workshop on his farm on Meadow Creek and this is where dances were held until the school was built on the lakeshore. The school then became the meeting place for all social activities. The Christmas concert was one of the highlights of the year, with all the school children doing their bit. After this was over, Santa Claus would arrive, and he would hand out presents to all the children. Then the benches would be pushed to the wall, the floor swept, and the dance would begin. It wouldn't stop until four or five in the morning. Ernie Buckingham and Noble Bragg, who came in with the survey crew and stayed in the district, were popular dance musicians of that era and when they were not available, Tom Brown Jr., Hugh and Jim supplied the music for a number of years. Although the quality of their music was a far cry from the orchestras of later years, it did fill a need at the time and since it was the only music available, it was not criticized too severely.

It is of interest to note that many of the pioneers could add something to the entertainment of social gatherings of that time. Harry Fowler was very good at calling quadrilles and square dances and could get on stage and recite Robert Service poems of the north from start to finish without a note of writing. Charlie Riley was also good at calling the dances. Tommy McGowan would do the cake walk; Jean Brown would do the sword dance. Mrs. Bragg and Billy Gray would sing a duet, maybe "Danny Boy". Mrs. Bragg would get so emotional before the end of the song that tears would start, then most of the women in the audience would be in tears as well.

Joe Brown and John Brown would contribute their singing ability. Tom Brown Jr. with his fiddle and Harold Noakes with his flute would supply the background music. Then there were other contributions as well such as the odd tap dance. Nobody but nobody ever missed these social events unless they had a broken leg or something. These shindigs were the only times a lot of people got to see each other because they lived quite a distance apart and travel was difficult.

In January 1914 Mina Brown was born in the new house. Mrs. Jane McGowan (grandmother) acted as midwife. There were now six children in the Thomas Brown Jr. family.

In August the first World War broke out and some of the pioneers, including John Brown and Harry Fowler went overseas. Some didn't come back. Progress in the district took a slow pace.

In 1915 a telephone line was strung along the new road, and people could communicate with the outside.

1916 was the year the first students graduated from the North Shuswap School. In the fourth reader class were Hugh and Jim Brown.

Thomas McGowan and Beatrice Fowler were married and set up house in the Tom Jones cabin. Their children were Sidney, James, and Myra. Thomas went to the prairie in 1918 and before arriving home was stricken with the influenza that was so bad that year. It proved fatal, and Beatrice was left with three young children. She tried farming with her father, Harry Fowler, but it did not prove to be successful, and she moved to the coast, where she found work.

In 1917, Thomas Brown Sr. suffered a severe stroke and was paralyzed. In 1919 a second stroke proved fatal. Mrs. Thomas Brown Sr. passed away in 1921.

In August 1919, Russell Brown was born in the family home. It is sad to relate that Mrs. Brown died in childbirth. Beatrice McGowan took care of Russell until the elder Mrs. McGowan (grandmother) came out from the prairie and took care of him for a while until sister Jean, who was fourteen at the time, took over the duties of her mother.

In May, 1920, [Note by Jack Brown: This is wrong as the 1921 census shows the family still in Celista BC, it was probably in May of 1923 after Thomas Brown II died] Hugh and Jim left for the coast to work on the C.N. Railway. Tom Brown Jr. (father) left the Clifford farm and returned home. He later became road foreman. In 1923, he was killed in a logging accident and the family decided to move to New Westminster. The following is a synopsis of the lives of the Brown family after moving to the coast.

Hugh Brown married Freida Waters of Port Mann. They have three daughters; Margaret, Doreen, and Kathleen. Hugh worked for the B.C. Electric/B.C. Hydro for 44 years driving streetcars, interurbans, busses and finally worked as switch crew foreman in Vancouver. Hugh is retired and he and Freida now live in Surrey, B.C. Hugh was 86 on April 6, 1987.

James Brown married Harriet Shaw of Vancouver, and they have a son, Robert, and a daughter, Joyce. Jim became a steam engineer, operating steam shovels, dredges, etc. He then spent 28 years as mechanical superintendent for Anderson Bros. Lumber Co. of Vancouver. He was 85 on August 29, 1987.

Jean Brown married John R. Donald of Magna Bay. They have two daughters, Marilyn, and Elizabeth. Marilyn (Kentala) lives in Bellevue, Washington, and Betty (Wynne) lives in Coquitlam. Jack worked his way up and became successful in the insurance business. They are now retired and after living at Magna Bay for several years, moved to Coquitlam.

Thomas Brown married Jean Ruckle of Celista. They have two children, James, and Evelyn. Tom also became a steam engineer, working on tugboats and operating derricks and cranes. He operated a crane for Anderson Bros. Lumber Co. of Vancouver for 10 years until he became disenchanted with the city life and moved back to the Shuswap at Magna Bay. They bought the

Henry Wilfrus property and farmed for a while, but this didn't prove to be a paying proposition. They then went into the resort business and started the Popular Roost Motel and Campsite. Jean passed away suddenly in 1966. Tom continued on for the rest of the year then sold the business and retired. He later married Ruby Jackson of Kamloops. Tom and Ruby built a home at Anglemont and lived there until Tom died from a heart attack in 1975. Ruby sold out and now lives in Chilliwack.

William John Brown (Billy Jack) didn't like city life either and as soon as he got through technical school in New Westminster, he came back to the Shuswap and lived with Uncle Joe Brown and Cousin Chasie. He later married Louise Tennant of Salmon Arm, who taught school in the district. They had two daughters, Betty Lou, who lives in Whitehorse, and Judy, who lived in Abbotsford until her death in 1985. Bill operated a one-horse logging show for some time, then a sawmill for a number of years until he went back to logging again with modern equipment. All during this time he was farming as a sideline. Bill was also involved in real estate and bought and sold considerable amounts of land in Magna Bay and Anglemont. He was always ready to help in any community affairs. He designed the trusses for the new community hall and helped in the construction of the building. Bill passed away in 1969 after a major operation. Lou sold the farm and moved to a new home in Anglemont. Lou often spent her winters in Arizona and passed away there 1986.

Mina Brown finished school in New Westminster. She moved to Vancouver with Jack and Jean Donald and worked as a hairdresser until she married Hugh (Kelly) Campbell. They have two daughters, Jean (Marsh) and Anne (Brown), living at the coast. Mina and Kelly too became disenchanted with city life and moved to the Shuswap at Magna Bay in 1944. They later took the postmasters job and operated the Brown and Smith store at Magna Bay. After Kelly passed away from an incurable illness, Mina got a job with the Forestry Department and moved to Kamloops, where she met and married Derby Simpson, who worked for the Education Department. Mina retired in 1973 and they now reside in their new home at Magna Bay.

Russell Brown started school in New Westminster and finished school in Coquitlam, where he lived with his brother Jim. After graduating from high school, he took a four-year course at New Westminster Technical School. He also worked for Anderson Bros. Lumber Co. until World War II broke out. He then joined the Navy. He married Edith Morrison of Surrey and lived in Coquitlam. They had two daughters, Diane, and Karen, and one son, David. Diane lives in Boston; Karen lives in Coquitlam and David lives in Edmonton. Russell's wife, Edith, died suddenly in 1955 in Royal Colombian Hospital. In 1959, he married Mary O'Connell of Vancouver, and the family moved to Vancouver. After a lingering illness, Russell died in 1962. Mary lives in the family home in Vancouver. They have one son, Stephen.

Bibliography

Carrión, Andrea. The spatial restructuring of resource regulation. The gold mining enclave of Zaruma and Portovelo, Ecuador, 1860-1980. A thesis submitted to the Faculty of Graduate and Postdoctoral Affairs in partial fulfillment of the requirements for the degree of Doctor of Philosophy in Geography with Specialization in Political Economy, Carleton University, Ottawa, Ontario, 2016.

ABOUT THE AUTHOR

Murl Leibrecht was born into a humble but proud working-class family at the end of the Second World War. His parents both came from family farms, and his first memories are those of being close to the earth, to animals, both wild and tame, and to the natural world as he grew up on his parents' ten-acre farm in the semi-rural exurbs of the Spokane Valley in eastern Washington State. Times were challenging in those days, and he spent most of his childhood working. Everyone in the Leibrecht household worked hard as a matter of necessity but also as a result of their strong German heritage. There was also time for play, and the family invariably embraced the natural world in their efforts to find enjoyment and respite.

The author's favorite teacher at Vera Grade School was Mrs. Moffitt, the school librarian, who shared her passion for books and reading with everyone so enthusiastically that she left an indelible impression on the author. He became a voracious reader, finishing the entire Laura Ingalls Wilder series before he was ten. The many fine writers and poets who affected him deeply over the years included John Steinbeck, Henry David Thoreau, Robinson Jeffers, Jack London, Kurt Vonnegut, Jr., Walt Whitman, Mary Oliver, and many others.

Even though the author enjoyed reading, he came of age at a time when science was gaining a foothold in the national consciousness, and he liked science, so it wasn't surprising that he decided to pursue a more empirical pathway on the road to finding himself. He was a good student and won a scholarship to Whitman College where he majored in biology/pre-med, and eventually became a physician thanks to the training provided by University of Utah College of Medicine. Meanwhile, he married Karen Kappel, the oldest daughter of this book's main character, and they have remained devoted partners and fellow adventurers for the past 55 years.

Murl graduated from med school when the Vietnam War was winding down, and he was drafted into the Air Force because they needed doctors. Fortunately the Air Force offered him a chance to run a small clinic near Oslo, Norway where he and Karen spent more than eight years living on a grand estate beside a small lake in the verdant countryside, and where they fell in love with Europe and the European lifestyle. Murl went on to specialize in aerospace medicine, obtaining a Master of Public Health degree from Harvard, and eventually completed a career in the Air Force after running the Air Force's aerospace medicine residency and later becoming the Command Surgeon at USAF Space Command in Colorado Springs.

By then Europe had captured their hearts, so they retired from the Air Force to move back to Europe. Altogether they lived and worked abroad for 30 years, mostly in Europe. In addition to stints in London and Guam, they lived in southern Bavaria, Germany, then moved to southern Burgundy, France, into an ancient stone farmhouse that sat on five acres high on a hillside, surrounded by vineyards, not far from the village of Chardonnay. After 11 years, they decided to retire at age 70 in order to move back to the Pacific Northwest to be closer to family. They now live on a small island in the Puget Sound surrounded by tall trees and the sea, north of Seattle, close to Canada, where they are avid gardeners and lovers of wildlife.

This is the author's first attempt to write a book, and although he has emphasized the empirical sciences by choice, his love of the arts and especially literature, has remained a passion – much of this due to Karen's personal development as an avid artist and student of art history, and in particular, a lover of beauty. One thing has become increasingly clear over the decades: focusing on the positive, seeing the goodness in everyone and everything, embracing the natural world and its inspiring influence, are all vital on the path to finding peace and contentment. And connecting with a higher consciousness is central to finding happiness.